VOYAGES
IN ENGLISH
GRAMMAR AND WRITING

Patricia Healey, I.H.M.
B.A., Immaculata University
M.A., Temple University
20 years teaching; 20 years in administration

Irene Kervick, I.H.M.
B.A., Immaculata University
M.A., Villanova University
46 years teaching

Anne B. McGuire, I.H.M.
B.A., Immaculata University
M.A., Villanova University
M.A., Immaculata University
*16 years teaching; 14 years as elementary
principal; 10 years staff development*

Adrienne Saybolt, I.H.M.
B.A., Immaculata University
Pennsylvania State Board of Education,
professional certification
M.A., St. John's University
40 years teaching

LOYOLA PRESS.

Loyola Press has made every effort to locate the copyright holders for the cited works used in this publication and to make full acknowledgment for their use. In the case of any omissions, the publisher will be pleased to make suitable acknowledgments in future editions. Continued on page 543.

Cover Design: Think Book Works   Cover Artist: Pablo Bernasconi
Interior Design: Kathy Greenholdt/Loyola Press
Art Director: Judine O'Shea/Loyola Press
Editor: Catherine T. Marcic Joyce/Loyola Press

ISBN-13: 978-0-8294-2818-6
ISBN-10: 0-8294-2818-6

LOYOLA PRESS.
3441 N. Ashland Avenue
Chicago, Illinois 60657
(800) 621-1008
www.loyolapress.com

Webcrafters / Madison, WI, USA / 04-10 / 1st Printing

Contents

PART 1 Grammar

Section 1	Sentences	1
1.1	Sentences	2
1.2	Declarative and Interrogative Sentences	4
1.3	Imperative and Exclamatory Sentences	6
1.4	Complete Subjects and Predicates	8
1.5	Simple Subjects and Predicates	10
1.6	Compound Subjects	12
1.7	Compound Predicates	14
1.8	Direct Objects	16
1.9	Subject Complements	18
1.10	Compound Sentences	20
1.11	Run-on Sentences	22
	Sentence Review	**24**
	Sentence Challenge	**26**

Section 2	Nouns	27
2.1	Nouns	28
2.2	Common and Proper Nouns	30
2.3	Singular and Plural Nouns	32
2.4	Irregular Plural Nouns	34
2.5	Singular Possessive Nouns	36
2.6	Plural Possessive Nouns	38
2.7	Collective Nouns	40
2.8	Nouns as Subjects	42
2.9	Nouns as Direct Objects	44
2.10	Nouns as Subject Complements	46
2.11	Words Used as Nouns and as Verbs	48
	Noun Review	**50**
	Noun Challenge	**52**

Section 3	Pronouns	53
3.1	Personal Pronouns: Part I	54
3.2	Personal Pronouns: Part II	56
3.3	Singular and Plural Pronouns	58
3.4	Subject Pronouns	60
3.5	Pronouns in Compound Subjects	62
3.6	Object Pronouns	64
3.7	Possessive Pronouns	66
3.8	Possessive Adjectives	68
3.9	Pronouns and Antecedents	70
3.10	*I, Me, We,* and *Us*	72
3.11	Pronouns and Contractions	74
	Pronoun Review	**76**
	Pronoun Challenge	**78**

Section 4	Adjectives	79
4.1	Descriptive Adjectives	80
4.2	Proper Adjectives	82
4.3	Articles	84
4.4	Demonstrative Adjectives	86
4.5	Adjectives That Tell How Many	88
4.6	Adjectives as Subject Complements	90
4.7	Adjectives That Compare	92
4.8	Irregular Adjectives That Compare	94
4.9	*More, Most*	96
4.10	*Fewer, Fewest* and *Less, Least*	98
4.11	Position of Adjectives	100
	Adjective Review	**102**
	Adjective Challenge	**104**

Section 5	Verbs	105
5.1	Action Verbs	106
5.2	Being Verbs	108
5.3	Linking Verbs	110
5.4	Helping Verbs	112
5.5	Verb Phrases	114
5.6	Principal Parts of Verbs	116
5.7	Irregular Verbs	118
5.8	More Irregular Verbs	120
5.9	Simple Present Tense	122
5.10	Simple Past Tense	124
5.11	Future Tenses	126
5.12	Progressive Tenses	128
5.13	Present Perfect Tense	130
5.14	Past Perfect Tense	132

5.15	Future Perfect Tense	134
5.16	Subject-Verb Agreement	136
5.17	*There Is* and *There Are*	138
	Verb Review	**140**
	Verb Challenge	**142**

Section 6	Adverbs and Conjunctions	143
6.1	Adverbs of Time and Place	144
6.2	Adverbs of Manner	146
6.3	Adverbs That Compare	148
6.4	More Adverbs That Compare	150
6.5	*Good* and *Well*; Negative Words	152
6.6	Coordinating Conjunctions	154
	Adverb and Conjunction Review	**156**
	Adverb and Conjunction Challenge	**158**

Section 7	Punctuation and Capitalization	159
7.1	End Punctuation	160
7.2	Capitalization	162
7.3	Titles of Works	164
7.4	Abbreviations	166
7.5	Personal Titles	168
7.6	Commas: Part I	170
7.7	Commas: Part II	172
7.8	Apostrophes	174
7.9	Addresses	176
7.10	Direct Quotations	178
	Punctuation and Capitalization Review	**180**
	Punctuation and Capitalization Challenge	**182**

Section 8	Diagramming	183
8.1	Subjects and Verbs	184
8.2	Direct Objects	186
8.3	Possessives and Adjectives	188
8.4	Subject Complements	190
8.5	Adverbs	192
8.6	Compound Subjects and Predicates	194
8.7	Compound Direct Objects	196
8.8	Nouns as Compound Subject Complements	198
8.9	Adjectives as Compound Subject Complements	200
8.10	Compound Sentences	202
8.11	Diagramming Practice	204
	Diagramming Review	**206**
	Diagramming Challenge	**208**

PART 2 Written and Oral Communication

Chapter 1 Personal Narratives   **210**

Lesson 1   What Makes a Good Personal Narrative?   212
Lesson 2   Introduction, Body, and Conclusion   216
Lesson 3   *Study Skills:* Time Lines   220
Lesson 4   *Writing Skills:* Exact Words   224
Lesson 5   *Word Study:* Contractions with Pronouns   228
Lesson 6   *Speaking and Listening Skills:* Oral Personal Narratives   232
           Writer's Workshop: Personal Narratives   **236**

Chapter 2 Formal Letters   **248**

Lesson 1   What Makes a Good Formal Letter?   250
Lesson 2   Types of Formal Letters   254
Lesson 3   *Writing Skills:* Compound Sentences   258
Lesson 4   *Literacy Skills:* Mailing a Formal Letter   262
Lesson 5   *Word Study:* Antonyms   266
Lesson 6   *Speaking and Listening Skills:* Oral Complaints and Conflicts   270
           Writer's Workshop: Letters of Complaint   **274**

Chapter 3	**Descriptions**	**286**
Lesson 1	What Makes a Good Description?	288
Lesson 2	Sensory Language	292
Lesson 3	*Word Study:* Suffixes	296
Lesson 4	*Writing Skills:* Similes and Metaphors	300
Lesson 5	*Study Skills:* Graphic Organizers	304
Lesson 6	*Speaking and Listening Skills:* Oral Descriptions	308
	Writer's Workshop: Descriptions	**312**

Chapter 4	**How-to Articles**	**324**
Lesson 1	What Makes a Good How-to Article?	326
Lesson 2	Important Details	330
Lesson 3	*Word Study:* Prefixes	334
Lesson 4	*Study Skills:* Dictionary	338
Lesson 5	*Writing Skills:* Time Words	342
Lesson 6	*Speaking and Listening Skills:* How-to Talks	346
	Writer's Workshop: How-to Articles	**350**

Chapter 5	**Persuasive Writing**	**362**
Lesson 1	What Makes Good Persuasive Writing?	364
Lesson 2	Fact and Opinion	368
Lesson 3	*Word Study:* Synonyms	372
Lesson 4	*Study Skills:* Dictionary	376
Lesson 5	*Writing Skills:* Compound Subjects and Predicates	380
Lesson 6	*Speaking and Listening Skills:* Oral Persuasion	384
	Writer's Workshop: Persuasive Writing	**388**

Chapter 6   Creative Writing: Fables   400

Lesson 1	What Makes a Good Fable?	402
Lesson 2	Beginning, Middle, and Ending	406
Lesson 3	*Word Study:* Homophones	410
Lesson 4	*Writing Skills:* Expanding Sentences	414
Lesson 5	*Poetry:* Haiku	418
Lesson 6	*Speaking and Listening Skills:* Telling a Fable	422
	Writer's Workshop: Fables	**426**

Chapter 7   Expository Writing   438

Lesson 1	What Makes a Good Expository Article?	440
Lesson 2	Gathering Information	444
Lesson 3	*Word Study:* Negative Words	448
Lesson 4	*Writing Skills:* Rambling Sentences	452
Lesson 5	*Study Skills:* Library Catalogs	456
Lesson 6	*Speaking and Listening Skills:* News Reports	460
	Writer's Workshop: Expository Writing	**464**

Chapter 8   Research Reports   476

Lesson 1	What Makes a Good Research Report?	478
Lesson 2	Researching	482
Lesson 3	*Study Skills:* Reference Sources	486
Lesson 4	*Word Study:* Compound Words	490
Lesson 5	*Writing Skills:* Outlines	494
Lesson 6	*Speaking and Listening Skills:* Oral History Report	498
	Writer's Workshop: Research Reports	**502**

Proofreading Marks   514

Grammar and Mechanics Handbook   515

Index   536

Acknowledgments   543

Writing Traits   inside back cover

SECTION ONE

Sentences

1.1 Sentences

1.2 Declarative and Interrogative Sentences

1.3 Imperative and Exclamatory Sentences

1.4 Complete Subjects and Predicates

1.5 Simple Subjects and Predicates

1.6 Compound Subjects

1.7 Compound Predicates

1.8 Direct Objects

1.9 Subject Complements

1.10 Compound Sentences

1.11 Run-on Sentences

Sentence Review

Sentence Challenge

1.1 Sentences

A **sentence** is a group of words that expresses a complete thought. Every sentence begins with a capital letter. Most sentences end with periods.

A sentence has a subject and a predicate. The **subject** tells who or what the sentence is about. The **predicate** tells what the subject is or does. It expresses an action or a state of being.

COMPLETE SUBJECT	COMPLETE PREDICATE
Eric	played cymbals.
The cymbals	were gold and shiny.
The crowd	enjoyed the concert.
All the children	were happy.

Which of these word groups are sentences?

A **The drums are loud**

B **A brass tuba**

C **Maggie likes the trumpet**

D **Listens to the music**

You are right if you said that A and C are sentences. Each one expresses a complete thought. Each one has a subject and a predicate, and each should have a period at the end.

B and D are not sentences. They do not express complete thoughts. B doesn't have a predicate, and D doesn't have a subject.

EXERCISE 1 Match a group of words in Column A with a group of words in Column B to make a sentence. Add a period to the end of each sentence.

Column A	Column B
1. During the parade, bands	a. sounded their sirens.
2. The floats	b. played music.
3. The clowns	c. made the crowd laugh.
4. Fire engines	d. moved down the street.

EXERCISE 2 Tell which of these word groups are sentences. Tell which are not sentences.

1. The band marched in the parade
2. The band members have nice uniforms
3. Marching to the music
4. All the drumsticks
5. The drum major leads the band
6. That tuba looks heavy
7. Carrying their instruments
8. We clapped for the band
9. The music was very loud
10. A group of talented jugglers
11. Entertained the crowd
12. Dancers with colorful uniforms
13. The dancers carried red pom-poms
14. The skill of the dancers amazed the crowd

EXERCISE 3 The following groups of words are not sentences. Add a subject or a predicate to make each word group a sentence.

1. like parades very much
2. waited for the beginning of the parade
3. the floats in the parade
4. waved to the people in the crowd
5. the people along the street
6. some acrobats on the floats
7. sang popular songs from the floats
8. carried colorful flags
9. rode horses
10. at the end of the parade, the crowds

APPLY IT NOW

Write four sentences about what you did during your last school break. Circle the subjects and underline the predicates.

1.2 Declarative and Interrogative Sentences

A **declarative sentence** makes a statement. It ends with a period.

> **There are many creatures in the sea.**
> **Ocean water is salty.**

An **interrogative sentence** asks a question. It begins with a question word or with a verb. It ends with a question mark.

> **What kind of fish is it?**
> **Is that fresh water?**
> **How can I conserve water?**

Which of these sentences is declarative?

> A **How can I protect the oceans?**
> B **What happens when the oceans are polluted?**
> C **Trash can hurt sea animals.**

You are right if you said sentence C. It makes a statement and ends with a period. A and B are interrogative sentences. They ask questions and end with question marks.

EXERCISE 1 Rewrite these sentences. Add periods at the end of declarative sentences. Add question marks at the end of interrogative sentences.

1. How much of the earth's water is salty
2. Only three percent of the earth's water is fresh
3. Is lake water salty or fresh
4. Water is found in oceans, lakes, and rivers
5. Where else is water found
6. Some water is frozen as ice caps and glaciers
7. All of us can conserve water
8. Do you always turn the faucet completely off

EXERCISE 2 Make statements and questions by matching the words in Column A with the words in Column B.

Column A	Column B
1. Do people	a. often dumped into oceans?
2. Oil tankers	b. cross the oceans.
3. Sometimes oil	c. concerned about the oceans?
4. Is garbage from cities	d. spills from tankers.
5. Are you	e. care about pollution?

EXERCISE 3 Write a question for each statement. Begin with the word or words in parentheses.

EXAMPLE **Water doesn't have any calories.** (How many)

How many calories does water have?

1. A healthy person needs about eight cups of water a day. (How many)

2. About 60 percent of your body is water. (How much of your body)

3. People get water from liquids and solid foods. (How do people)

4. A person can live about a week without water. (How long can)

5. People use 80 to 100 gallons of water a day. (How many)

6. People get thirsty when they lose one percent of the water in the bodies. (When do)

7. Milk and juice are good sources of water. (What)

8. You can save water by turning off the faucet when you brush your teeth. (How can)

9. You use two gallons of water when you brush you teeth. (How many)

10. Humans cannot survive on saltwater. (Can)

APPLY IT NOW

Imagine you are a reporter. Interview a classmate. Write a question for each of these topics: recycling, saving water, and pollution. Write your classmate's answers. Example: What do you recycle? I recycle plastic.

Tech Tip Videotape your interview.

1.3 Imperative and Exclamatory Sentences

An **imperative sentence** gives a command or makes a request. It usually ends with a period. The subject of an imperative sentence is generally *you,* which is often not stated.

> **Tell me about spiders.**
>
> **Please handle the spider with care.**

An **exclamatory sentence** expresses strong or sudden emotion. It ends with an exclamation point.

> **That is one ugly spider!**
>
> **That spider web is beautiful!**

Which of these are imperative sentences?

A **That spider is gross!**

B **Stay calm.**

C **Don't harm the spider, please.**

D **Do you see the spider web?**

You are right if you said that B and C are imperative sentences. They give commands. Each ends with a period. Sentence A is an exclamatory sentence. It expresses strong or sudden emotion and ends with an exclamation point. Sentence D is an interrogative sentence. It asks a question and ends with a question mark.

EXERCISE 1 Match a group of words in Column A with a group of words in Column B to make an imperative sentence or an exclamatory sentence.

Column A	Column B
1. Read this article	a. very scary!
2. Some spiders	b. about amazing spider facts.
3. That is	c. can be poisonous.
4. Do not	d. more about spiders.
5. Tell me	e. touch spiders unless you know they are harmless.

EXERCISE 2 Rewrite these sentences. Add periods at the end of imperative sentences. Add exclamation points at the end of exclamatory sentences.

1. Oh, that's a big spider
2. Look at its web
3. Gross, that spider has eight eyes
4. Hold out your hand
5. Please be gentle with the baby spider
6. Watch it closely
7. Oh, it's tickling my hand
8. Oh, no, it's running away
9. Don't step on it
10. Pick up the spider carefully
11. How lovely that spider web is
12. Look at the drops of rain in the web
13. Don't touch that spider web
14. How interesting spiders are

EXERCISE 3 Rewrite the sentences. Add a period, a question mark, or an exclamation point at the end of each sentence.

1. Stella, John, and Matthew went to the beach one hot Saturday morning
2. Wow, it sure was hot
3. John dropped the towel and sand toys he was carrying
4. Did you bring the new toy Mom bought for us
5. John nodded and began to unpack the toys from the bag
6. Bring the towels closer to the tree for shade
7. Where is the sunscreen

APPLY IT NOW

Think of a hobby or game you enjoy. Describe it by writing four or five imperative sentences and ending with one exclamatory sentence. Example: Be sure to keep stirring the pudding. Enjoy your dessert!

1.4 Complete Subjects and Predicates

Every sentence must have a **subject** and a **predicate.** The subject names the person, place, or thing talked about in a sentence. A **complete subject** includes the specific person, place, or thing and all the words that go with it. A **complete predicate** is the verb and the words relating to it. It describes the action or state of being of the subject.

Zeus shown on an ancient coin

COMPLETE SUBJECT	COMPLETE PREDICATE
The class	studies geography.
All the students	like to learn new things.
Jamie and Marie	are excited about the class.

What is the complete subject of the following sentence? What is its complete predicate?

The teacher listed the Seven Wonders of the Ancient World.

If you said the complete subject is *The teacher,* you are right. *The teacher* names the person the sentence is about. The complete predicate is *listed the Seven Wonders of the Ancient World.* It tells what the teacher did.

EXERCISE 1 Find the complete subject in each sentence.

1. Our class learned about the Seven Wonders of the Ancient World.
2. An ancient Greek writer created the list.
3. An Egyptian pyramid is on the list.
4. The list contains a temple, statues, tombs, a lighthouse, and a garden.
5. All the structures were built thousands of years ago.
6. Engineers of the ancient world designed the amazing structures.
7. My partner and I are researching on the Colossus of Rhodes.
8. The pyramid and a lighthouse were built in Egypt.

Egyptian pyramid

EXERCISE 2 **Find the complete predicate in each sentence.**

1. Now the students know the names of all the Seven Wonders.
2. The Egyptians built the Great Pyramid at Giza for a pharaoh's tomb.
3. A 40-foot statue of Zeus stood in a temple in Greece.
4. Only images on coins depict that statue.
5. An ancient statue on the island of Rhodes dominated the harbor.
6. The Statue of Liberty looks a little like that statue.
7. The Pharos of Alexandria guided sailors.
8. The word *pharos* was the Greek word for "lighthouse."
9. The Hanging Gardens of Babylon grew on terraces.
10. Drawings show archaeologists' ideas about the gardens.

EXERCISE 3 **Find the complete subject and the complete predicate in each sentence.**

1. The Lighthouse of Alexandria was on a Greek island.
2. Ships used it as a guide to the harbor entrance for nearly 1,500 years.
3. An earthquake toppled the lighthouse in 14 AD.
4. Archaeologists do not know any details about the lighthouse.

EXERCISE 4 **Finish each sentence with a complete subject or a complete predicate from the list.**

The Great Pyramid	are triangles
The Maya people	is 449 feet high
The Egyptians	

1. _____ is the only ancient wonder that still stands.
2. The Great Pyramid _____.
3. _____ used two million blocks of stone to build it.
4. _____ also built pyramids.
5. The sides of the pyramids _____.

Tech Tip With an adult, research the country online.

1.5 Simple Subjects and Predicates

The subject names the person, place, or thing talked about. The most important word in the subject is usually a noun. The noun is the **simple subject.** Asking *who* or *what* before the predicate reveals the subject.

The predicate describes what the subject is or does and contains a verb. The verb is called the **simple predicate.**

	SIMPLE SUBJECT	SIMPLE PREDICATE	
The	flag	waved	in the wind.

	SIMPLE SUBJECT	SIMPLE PREDICATE	
The	principal	raised	the flag.

What are the simple subject and the simple predicate in this sentence?

Every new country needs a flag.

If you named *country* as the simple subject, you are correct. *Country* is the noun. It is the most important part of the subject. If you named *needs* as the simple predicate, you are correct. *Needs* is the verb. It is the most important part of the predicate.

EXERCISE 1 Find the simple subject in each sentence.

1. Students say the Pledge of Allegiance every day at school.
2. The pledge honors the American flag.
3. A writer wrote the pledge in 1892.
4. Francis Bellamy intended the pledge for schools.
5. People said the pledge during flag-raising ceremonies.
6. Its words have changed slightly over the years.
7. Today classes say the pledge at the start of a school day.
8. Two ideas in the pledge are liberty and justice.

EXERCISE 2 Find the simple predicate in each sentence.

1. People call the U.S. flag by several names.
2. The name "Star-Spangled Banner" comes from the national anthem.
3. Francis Scott Key used the phrase in a poem in 1814.
4. The poem honored a flag in Baltimore Harbor.
5. According to legend, a ship's captain coined the name Old Glory.
6. Someone gave the captain a large 24-star flag for his ship.
7. He saw the flag flying at the start of a voyage in 1831.
8. He excitedly said "Old Glory."

Betsy Ross and a friend sew the first American flag.

EXERCISE 3 Find the simple subject and the simple predicate in each sentence.

1. The original U.S. colonies used many different flags.
2. Some flags resembled the British flag.
3. The country's leaders wanted a different flag.
4. Betsy Ross tailored clothes for George Washington.
5. Washington recognized Betsy's remarkable sewing skills.
6. This talented tailor produced the first American flag.
7. The 13 stars on Betsy's flag were in a circle.
8. The nation added stars for new states.

EXERCISE 4 Complete each sentence with a simple subject or a simple predicate from the list.

calls   citizens   stands   stars   says

1. Many _____ decorate the U.S. flag.
2. U.S. _____ respect the American flag.
3. The American flag _____ in the room.
4. My grandfather _____ the flag *Old Glory*.
5. The class _____ the Pledge of Allegiance.

APPLY IT NOW

Write four sentences containing facts about the state in which you live. Underline each simple subject once. Underline each simple predicate twice.
Example: The largest state is Alaska.

1.6 Compound Subjects

Every sentence has a subject. The subject is who or what the sentence is about. Usually, the simple subject is a noun. A **compound subject** has two or more simple subjects connected by *and* or *or.*

SIMPLE SUBJECT

Cats   are curious.

COMPOUND SUBJECT

Cats and kittens   are curious.
Cats or kittens   make good pets.

Notice that the compound subjects include two simple subjects: *cats* and *kittens.*

Which of these sentences have compound subjects?

A **Katie helps at an animal shelter.**
B **Max and Mandy do volunteer work there too.**
C **The animals are happy in their new homes.**
D **Veterinarians or volunteers play with the animals every day.**

You are right if you said that sentences B and D have compound subjects. *Max* and *Mandy* are two simple subjects joined by the word *and. Veterinarians* and *volunteers* are two simple subjects joined by the word *or.*

EXERCISE 1 Find the compound subjects in these sentences. Then find the simple subjects.

1. Dogs and cats are in the animal shelter.
2. Volunteers and visitors play with the animals.
3. My mom and I sometimes volunteer at a shelter.
4. A black cat and a calico cat were playing together.
5. Both a lively collie and a friendly boxer were available for adoption.
6. A worker or a volunteer will show you the animals.

EXERCISE 2 Tell whether each sentence has a simple or a compound subject. Name the subject.

1. Many animals need a good home.
2. Amy and Ryan wanted a dog.
3. Riley and Bogie are two Labradors.
4. A car hit Riley.
5. Riley's leg was broken.
6. A cast and medicine helped Riley.
7. The children's family adopted him.
8. Bones or rawhide treats would make Riley very happy.

EXERCISE 3 Rewrite the sentences. Use a compound subject to complete each sentence. Remember to use *and* or *or*.

1. _____ are small dogs.
2. _____ are bigger dogs.
3. _____ make strange pets.
4. _____ are good names for pets.
5. _____ are not good pets.
6. _____ are my favorite breeds.
7. _____ are popular breeds.

EXERCISE 4 Combine each pair of sentences into one sentence with a compound subject.

1. My brother has a dog. I have a dog.
2. Jason feeds Belford every day. I feed Belford every day.
3. Because we both have homework, Jason takes Belford for a walk after school. Because we both have homework, I take Belford for a walk after school.
4. Holly is a friend of Belford's. Mac is a friend of Belford's.

APPLY IT NOW

Write four sentences about pets that you have or a friend has. Use a compound subject in at least two sentences. Example: A dog and two cats live in my grandmother's house.

1.7 Compound Predicates

Every sentence has a predicate. The simple predicate is the verb that tells what the subject is or does. A **compound predicate** has two or more simple predicates connected with *and, but,* or *or.*

SIMPLE PREDICATE

Tourists	visit	different cities.

COMPOUND PREDICATE

Tourists	sightsee and shop.
Tourists	get tired but feel happy.

Sightsee and *shop* are simple predicates joined by *and* to make a compound predicate. *Get* and *feel* are simple predicates joined by *but* to make a compound predicate.

Which of these sentences have compound predicates?

A Janine walks to the museum.

B Candace drives a red car.

C Jeff takes the bus or rides the subway.

D Tito visits the aquarium and watches the fish.

You are right if you said sentences C and D have compound predicates. *Takes* and *rides* are two simple predicates joined by the word *or. Visits* and *watches* are two simple predicates joined by the word *and.*

EXERCISE 1 Tell whether each sentence has a simple or a compound predicate. Name the verbs in the predicates.

1. My family hiked last weekend.

2. We climbed and scrambled up the steep mountain.

3. The weather started nice but turned bad.

4. The hikers shivered and shook in the rain.

5. I found my rain poncho and put it around me.

6. The rain stopped suddenly.

7. The afternoon was bright and sunny.

8. I removed my poncho and folded it.

9. We hiked to the top of the mountain and stopped for a while.

10. The sun turned orange and set behind the mountain.

EXERCISE 2 Combine each pair of sentences into one sentence with a compound predicate.

EXAMPLE **Tourists buy souvenirs. They take photos.**
Tourists buy souvenirs and take photos.

1. Jerome and his family went to Boston. They saw the sights.

2. They could not decide if they should take the subway. They could not decide if they should take the bus.

3. The guide led them along the Freedom Trail. He told them about the history of the places.

4. People at the Boston Common sat on benches. People ate lunch.

5. The family visited a market. They did not eat there.

6. The family went to a park. They saw a baseball game.

7. Jerome talked to a baseball player. He got an autograph.

8. Jerome brought a camera. He took a lot of photos.

EXERCISE 3 Tell whether each sentence has a compound subject or a compound predicate.

1. My sister and I went to the museum.

2. We waited in line and bought tickets.

3. Some people walked around the dinosaur skeleton and took pictures of it.

4. Visitors either explored the exhibit on their own or took a tour.

5. The guides and the guards at the museum were helpful.

6. I know a lot about dinosaurs but learned more at the museum.

APPLY IT NOW

Write four sentences about something you have done with your family or friends. Use a compound predicate in at least two sentences. Example: My family swam and water-skied.

1.8 Direct Objects

The **direct object** is the noun or pronoun that receives the action of the verb. Many sentences need a direct object to complete their meaning.

To find the direct object of a sentence, ask *whom* or *what* after the verb.

DIRECT OBJECT

The Mississippi River divides the   country.

The Mississippi River divides *what? Country* is the direct object. It tells what the Mississippi River divides.

DIRECT OBJECT

The river provides a   route   for transportation.

The river provides *what? Route* is the direct object. It tells what the river provides.

What is the direct object in this sentence?

The Ojibwa Indians named the river.

The direct object in this sentence is *river.* The Ojibwa Indians named *what?* The answer is *river.*

This sentence has a compound direct object.

A shipping channel moves *goods and people* up and down the river.

The compound direct object in the sentence is *goods and people. Goods* and *people* are two simple direct objects joined by the word *and.*

EXERCISE 1 Find the direct object or compound direct objects in each sentence. Read carefully.

1. The ice age changed the earth.
2. Melting water from glaciers formed valleys.
3. The flowing water carved the Mississippi River and the Grand Canyon.

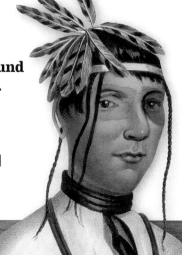

4. Europeans like Louis Joliet led voyages of exploration.

5. Henry Schoolcraft discovered the river's source.

6. Barges on the river still carry many products.

7. The Mississippi River divides the United States into east and west.

8. This mighty river carries water from many other rivers.

9. The long Missouri River joins the Mississippi at St. Louis.

10. The Mississippi meets the Ohio River at Cairo, Illinois.

11. In the 1660s Europeans explored the Mississippi.

12. Mark Twain wrote books about life on the Mississippi in the 1800s.

13. Boats on the Mississippi provide transportation and entertainment.

14. Some boats ship wheat and soybeans.

15. Many boats end their journeys near ports like New Orleans.

16. The Mississippi provides water to people near the river.

17. More than 260 kinds of fish inhabit the river's waters.

EXERCISE 2 Complete each sentence with a direct object from the list.

boundaries   color   **Gulf of Mexico**
soil   water

1. The Mississippi River carries _____ from the area between the Rocky Mountains and the Appalachians.

2. The Mississippi forms the _____ of several states.

3. The southern part of the river has a muddy _____.

4. There the Mississippi leaves _____ along its banks.

5. The river enters the _____ in small channels.

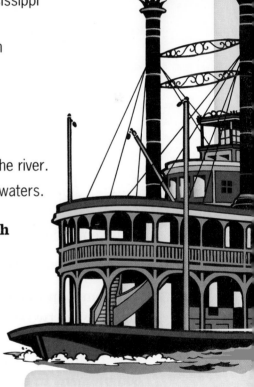

APPLY IT NOW

Using another textbook, find four sentences that contain direct objects. Write the sentences and circle the direct objects. Be sure to include the name of the textbook you used.

Grammar in Action. Find the third direct object used in the excerpt on page 226.

Sentences • 17

1.9 Subject Complements

A **subject complement** follows a linking verb. It is usually a noun or an adjective that tells more about the subject. The most common linking verb is *be* and its various forms *(am, are, is, was, were).*

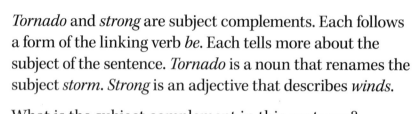

SUBJECT	LINKING VERB	SUBJECT COMPLEMENT
The storm	was	a tornado.
The winds	are	strong.

Tornado and *strong* are subject complements. Each follows a form of the linking verb *be*. Each tells more about the subject of the sentence. *Tornado* is a noun that renames the subject *storm*. *Strong* is an adjective that describes *winds*.

What is the subject complement in this sentence?

The storm was fierce.

The subject complement is *fierce*. It is an adjective that follows the linking verb *was*. It tells more about the subject *storm*.

This sentence has a compound subject complement.

Many people were safe but homeless after the hurricane.

The compound subject complement is *safe but homeless. Safe* and *homeless* are two simple subject complements joined by the word *but*.

EXERCISE 1 Find the simple or compound subject complement in each sentence.

1. Powerful storms in the Pacific are typhoons and cyclones.
2. Similar storms in the Atlantic are hurricanes.
3. Some hurricanes are strong and destructive.

4. Flooding from hurricanes is also the cause of damage.

5. Hurricane Katrina in 2005 was a disaster.

6. Its damage was severe.

7. New Orleans was a city in its path.

EXERCISE 2 Complete each sentence with a subject complement from the list.

common	Florida	month
straight	fearful	

1. Hurricanes in the Atlantic are most _____ in the fall.

2. September is the usual _____ for these storms.

3. A state with many hurricanes is _____.

4. The path of a hurricane is not _____.

5. Many people on the Atlantic coast and Gulf Coast are _____ of hurricanes.

EXERCISE 3 Tell whether each underlined subject complement is a noun or an adjective.

1. The hurricane season is late <u>summer</u> and <u>fall</u>.

2. The path of a hurricane is <u>changeable</u>.

3. The center, or eye, of a hurricane is <u>calm</u>.

4. The causes of a hurricane's damage are its <u>wind</u> and <u>rain</u>.

5. A result of a hurricane can be <u>flooding</u>.

6. Another result of a hurricane is <u>destruction</u> of houses.

7. The tracking of a hurricane's path is the <u>job</u> of meteorologists.

8. Satellites are <u>tools</u> for the tracking of hurricanes.

9. Hurricanes are <u>common</u> in Florida.

APPLY IT NOW

Write four sentences describing your family members or friends. Use a noun or an adjective as a subject complement in each sentence. Underline each subject complement. Example: My grandmother is a <u>librarian</u>.

Grammar in Action

What is the subject complement in the last sentence in the excerpt on page 210?

1.10 Compound Sentences

When two short sentences are related to each other, they can be combined into a **compound sentence.** To combine two short sentences into one longer sentence, add a comma followed by *and, but,* or *or.* The first word in the second part of the compound does not start with a capital letter unless it is *I* or the name of a person or place.

Two sentences that are related:

> **Lightning flashed. Thunder boomed.**

Compound sentence:

> **Lightning flashed, and thunder boomed.**

Two sentences that are related:

> **The lights flickered. They did not go out.**

Compound sentence:

> **The lights flickered, but they did not go out.**

Two sentences that are related:

> **We will play a game. We will watch TV.**

Compound sentence:

> **We will play a game, or we will watch TV.**

What two sentences were combined to make this compound sentence?

> **The sun came out, and it was warm.**

You were right if you said: The sun came out. It was warm.

EXERCISE 1 Match each sentence in Column A with a related sentence in Column B to make a compound sentence.

Column A	Column B
1. The snow fell all night, but	a. I put a hat on him.
2. Mom made breakfast, and	b. we can build a snow fort.
3. We can go sledding, or	c. it had stopped by morning.
4. Mom made a snowman, and	d. we went back in the house.
5. We were tired and cold, and	e. we ate in a hurry.

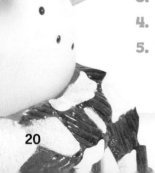

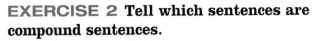

EXERCISE 2 Tell which sentences are compound sentences.

1. Sledding and ice-skating are popular winter sports.
2. My friends and I go sledding in the park.
3. We go ice-skating outdoors at the park, or we go ice-skating indoors at the rink.
4. We spin and twirl on our ice skates.
5. Ice hockey is a team sport, and it requires ice-skating ability.
6. I am not a very good ice-skater, but I can ski well.
7. My sister likes ice hockey and skating as well.
8. My brother plays ice-hockey and lacrosse.
9. I wear heavy boots and gloves in the winter.
10. Winter sports are fun, but I like summer sports better.

EXERCISE 3 Combine each pair of short sentences into a compound sentence. Use a comma and *and*, *but*, or *or*.

1. Winter in Wisconsin is cold. It snows a lot.
2. Ice fishing is popular. Jean doesn't like to sit out in the cold.
3. Danny likes to ski. He doesn't know how to ice-skate.
4. He wants to learn. His brother will give him lessons.
5. We went to the rink. We watched his brother do tricks.
6. Danny put on his skates. He wobbled onto the ice.
7. He tried to stay on his feet. He kept falling down.
8. He'll keep trying. I know he will succeed.
9. Cross-country skiing is on flat land. Alpine skiing is on mountains.
10. Rachel goes cross-country skiing. She doesn't go Alpine skiing.

APPLY IT NOW

Write at least five compound sentences about sports that you and your friends like to do. Each sentence should have a comma and *and*, *but*, or *or*.

1.11 Run-on Sentences

A **run-on sentence** results when two sentences are combined but not connected properly. A run-on sentence occurs when two sentences are separated by only a comma or by no connectors at all.

A run-on sentence is easily fixed by making a compound sentence with a comma and the word *and* or *but*. Another way to fix a run-on sentence, particularly a long run-on, is to divide it into two or more separate sentences.

Run-on sentence: I went to the store, I bought milk.

Correction: I went to the store, and I bought milk.

Run-on sentence: I needed milk the store did not have any.

Correction: I needed milk, but the store did not have any.

Which of these sentences is a run-on?

    A Sam drank the milk. It tasted good.

    B My friend lives on a farm, and I went to visit her.

    C Cows produce milk, many people drink it.

You are right if you said C. It has two sentences run together with only a comma—without the word *and*.

A is correct because there are two separate sentences that have proper punctuation at the end of each. B is a correctly combined sentence. It links two sentences with a comma and the word *and*.

EXERCISE 1 Tell whether each sentence is a run-on sentence or a correct compound sentence.

1. Jeff likes cows, he wants to live on a farm.
2. Frank owns a farm, and he has many cows.
3. Jeff visits the farm, he helps Frank.
4. Frank knows about cows, and he teaches Jeff.
5. Holsteins have black spots, the spot pattern on each cow is different.

6. Holsteins are good dairy cows, they can each produce about 21,000 pounds of milk a year.

7. Jersey cows produce less milk, but it is richer.

8. Cows have one stomach, it has four compartments.

9. They eat for 8 hours a day, and they lie down for 13 hours.

10. Cows need a lot of water, they drink a bathtub full every day.

11. They turn grass into energy, and their special stomach does the task.

EXERCISE 2 Correct the run-on sentences. Add *and* or *but*.

1. I drink a glass of milk every day, I put some on my cereal.

2. I like milk, my brother doesn't it like very much.

3. My brother likes chocolate milk, he drinks hot chocolate.

4. My uncle has cows on his farm, he also has pigs.

5. I tried to milk a cow, it was hard.

6. I like to visit a farm, I don't want to live on one.

Holstein

EXERCISE 3 Rewrite these run-on sentences as compound sentences.

1. A cow can give about 8 gallons of milk each day, it drinks 16 gallons of water.

2. A heifer is a cow that is only one year old, it weighs between 450 and 500 pounds.

3. Cows produce milk every day farmers need to milk them every day.

4. Calcium is found in milk people need calcium to be healthy.

5. Calcium can also be found in broccoli, I don't like broccoli.

APPLY IT NOW

What is your favorite animal? Is there an endangered species that interests you? Write information about this animal, using four compound sentences. Be sure to use correct punctuation.

Tech Tip With an adult, research your animal online.

Sentence Review

1.1 Tell which of these word groups are sentences. Tell which are not sentences.

1. The granola bar tastes good
2. Crumbs on the table
3. Picking the fruit and nuts out of the granola bar
4. Granola bars and milk go well together

1.2 Complete each sentence with a period or a question mark.

5. Indian food is delicious
6. Have you tried it
7. Is it spicy food
8. Some dishes are mildly seasoned
9. Samosas are made with potatoes and chickpeas

1.3 Complete each sentence with a period or an exclamation mark.

10. My goodness, what a tall building this is
11. Please follow the guide to the observation deck
12. Wow, it's a magnificent view
13. Step away from the window
14. Yikes, looking down makes me dizzy

1.4 Find the complete subject and the complete predicate in each sentence.

15. Jack and Rory found a time capsule.
16. Schoolchildren buried it in 1973.
17. Each student added something special.
18. The two boys read a newspaper from the capsule.

1.5 Find the simple subject and the simple predicate in each sentence.

19. People wash clothes at the laundromat.
20. Clothes spin in both washing machines and dryers.
21. The detergent smells nice and fresh.
22. Sometimes socks disappear in the dryer.

1.6 Tell whether each sentence has a simple or a compound subject.

23. Cashews and pecans are nuts.
24. Walnuts or almonds are sometimes sprinkled on salads.
25. Muffins and breads sometimes have walnuts as an ingredient.

26. The bowl of nuts was almost empty.

1.7 **Tell whether each sentence has a simple or a compound predicate.**

27. The paint on the walls cracked and peeled.

28. The painter scraped the walls.

29. Then she mixed and applied the paint.

30. She examined the walls and fixed some spots.

1.8 **Find the simple or compound direct objects in each sentence.**

31. The girl made a decorative mosaic.

32. She collected old plates.

33. She found old tiles at garage sales.

34. Later she broke the plates and a few tiles with a hammer.

35. Then she arranged the pieces attractively.

36. She created a colorful pattern.

1.9 **Find the simple or compound subject complement in each sentence.**

37. Amusement parks are my favorite places.

38. The roller-coaster ride was exciting and fun.

39. The drop was scary.

40. All the horses on the carousel were colorful.

41. My favorite ride is the carousel.

1.10 **Tell which sentences are compound sentences.**

42. In science class we studied cockroaches and beetles.

43. Beetles can be many different colors, but ants are usually black.

44. Butterfly wings are thin and fragile.

45. Bees pollinate flowers, and worms enrich the soil.

46. Insects can be helpful, or they can be harmful.

1.11 **Tell whether each sentence is a run-on sentence or a correct compound sentence. Rewrite the run-on sentences as compound sentences with *and* or *but*.**

47. The children went bowling, and they had fun.

48. Tom rolled the ball, he knocked down four pins.

49. Lucy tried for a strike, the ball went in the gutter.

50. Sonia is a good bowler, and she teaches her friends.

Tech Tip

Go to www.voyagesinenglish.com for more activities.

Sentence Challenge

EXERCISE 1 Read the paragraph and answer the questions.

1. Do you like pandas? 2. Pandas are endangered. 3. That means there aren't many of them left. 4. That's a shame! 5. Giant pandas are fussy eaters. 6. Pandas eat only bamboo. 7. There is not enough bamboo anymore. 8. People cleared land and eliminated bamboo plants. 9. China has created refuges for pandas. 10. Scientists and other people help pandas stay alive.

1. What kind of sentence is sentence 1?
2. In sentence 1 what word is the direct object?
3. In sentence 2 what is the complete predicate?
4. Is sentence 4 a declarative sentence or an exclamatory sentence?
5. In sentence 5 what is the complete subject?
6. In sentence 5 what is the subject complement?
7. In sentence 6 what is the simple subject?
8. In sentence 6 what is the simple predicate?
9. In sentence 9 how is *refuges* used?
10. In sentence 10 what is the complete subject? What is the complete predicate?
11. Which sentence has a compound predicate?
12. Which sentence has a compound subject?

EXERCISE 2 Read the paragraph and answer the questions.

1. Pandas are in danger, koalas are in danger too. 2. Pandas live in China, but koalas live in Australia. 3. Pandas eat only bamboo, and koalas eat only eucalyptus leaves. 4. Eucalyptus trees are disappearing, koalas don't have enough food anymore. 5. Koalas are called bears, but they are marsupials, like kangaroos.

1. Identify the correct compound sentences.
2. Which sentences are run-on sentences?
3. Rewrite the run-on sentences.

Nouns

2.1 Nouns

2.2 Common and Proper Nouns

2.3 Singular and Plural Nouns

2.4 Irregular Plural Nouns

2.5 Singular Possessive Nouns

2.6 Plural Possessive Nouns

2.7 Collective Nouns

2.8 Nouns as Subjects

2.9 Nouns as Direct Objects

2.10 Nouns as Subject Complements

2.11 Words Used as Nouns and as Verbs

Noun Review

Noun Challenge

2.1 Nouns

A **noun** names a person, a place, or a thing.

If you are in a city, you can see many different people, places, and things.

PEOPLE	PLACES	THINGS
cab driver	restaurant	bicycle
Mayor Collins	gas station	ticket
shopper	museum	pigeon
pedestrian	bank	traffic light
firefighter	Jake's Pizzeria	Madison City Ballet

Which noun names a person in this sentence?

A police officer stood near an intersection and blew a whistle.

A police officer

B whistle

C intersection

You are right if you said A. A *police officer* is a person who protects other people.

A *whistle* is a thing that makes noise. An *intersection* is the place where two streets meet.

Can you name other people, places, and things in a city? The words you name are probably nouns.

EXERCISE 1 Tell whether each underlined noun in the sentences below names a person, a place, or a thing.

1. Washington, D.C., is an important city.
2. Leaders govern the country from there.
3. There are many monuments, statues, and offices.
4. Museums have artworks and historical objects.
5. Residents and visitors can get around on underground trains.
6. Lovely flowers bloom on cherry trees in the spring.

Washington, D.C., was named to honor President George Washington.

EXERCISE 2 **Find the nouns in each sentence. The number of nouns in each sentence is in parentheses.**

1. Capitals are special cities. (2)

2. The governor works in the capital of a state. (3)

3. The president of the United States lives in Washington. (3)

4. That city is the capital of the country. (3)

5. The lawmakers work in a building called the Capitol. (3)

6. Capitols are often large buildings with domes. (3)

7. The area beneath the dome is called the rotunda. (3)

8. Millions of people have visited the Capitol. (3)

White House and a cherry tree blossom

EXERCISE 3 **Complete the chart. Write people, places, and things in your city or town.**

PEOPLE	PLACES	THINGS

EXERCISE 4 **Complete each sentence with a noun or nouns.**

1. The _____ visited Washington, D.C.

2. They made a list of _____ to see.

3. _____ asked to see the Lincoln Memorial.

4. The _____ suggested the Air and Space Museum.

5. The family saw the _____ on the trip.

6. Everyone's _____ hurt at the end of the day.

APPLY IT NOW

Write five sentences about a trip you took. Where did you go? Who went with you? What did you see? Underline all the nouns.

Grammar in Action

Find the first noun in the body of the letter on page 252.

2.2 Common and Proper Nouns

A **proper noun** begins with a capital letter and names a particular person, place, or thing. A **common noun** names any one member of a group of people, places, or things.

PROPER NOUNS	COMMON NOUNS
Person	
Javier Mendez	teacher
Abraham Lincoln	president
Place	
San Francisco	city
Delaware	state
Thing	
Atlantic Ocean	ocean
Sirius	star

Which of the following is a proper noun?

A **street**

B **road**

C **Madison Avenue**

You are right if you said C. *Madison Avenue* is a proper noun. It names a specific street. Both parts of the noun begin with a capital letter.

EXERCISE 1 Match each proper nouns in Column A with the common noun in Column B.

Column A	Column B
1. *James and the Giant Peach*	a. state
2. New Orleans	b. planet
3. Maine	c. book
4. Jupiter	d. writer
5. Fifth Avenue	e. city
6. Roald Dahl	f. street

EXERCISE 2 Tell whether each noun is a proper noun or a common noun. Write a common noun for each proper noun and a proper noun for each common noun.

1. athlete
2. Sweden
3. holiday
4. *The Incredibles*
5. lake
6. TV show
7. Vermont
8. song
9. Thomas Edison
10. poet

Poet Emma Lazarus

EXERCISE 3 Find the nouns in each sentence. The number of nouns is shown in parentheses. Tell whether each is a proper or a common noun.

1. Emma Lazarus was a poet. (2)
2. Emma lived in New York City. (2)
3. The young girl studied languages and wrote poetry. (3)
4. The young poet started to help people. (2)
5. These people had come to the United States from Europe. (3)
6. These new Americans needed jobs and homes. (3)
7. Emma taught skills needed for jobs. (3)
8. France presented the United States with a statue. (3)
9. This artwork symbolized liberty. (2)
10. Its location was to be New York Harbor. (2)
11. Americans needed to raise money for the monument. (3)
12. Emma wrote a poem as a donation. (3)
13. The poem told about Europeans who came to America for a new life. (4)
14. The poem was eventually put on the base of the Statue of Liberty. (3)
15. Visitors to the statue can read the words of this talented American. (4)

APPLY IT NOW

Answer each of the following in complete sentences. Underline all the proper nouns.
1. What is your name?
2. Tell one interesting fact about yourself.
3. Tell something interesting about your city or town.

2.3 Singular and Plural Nouns

A **singular noun** names one person, place, or thing. A **plural noun** names more than one person, place, or thing.

The plural of most nouns is formed by adding -*s* to the singular.

SINGULAR	PLURAL
map	maps
house	houses

The plural of a noun ending in *s, x, z, ch,* or *sh* is formed by adding -*es* to the singular.

SINGULAR	PLURAL
guess	guesses
fox	foxes
fuzz	fuzzes
beach	beaches
dish	dishes

The plural of a noun ending in *y* after a consonant is formed by changing the *y* to *i* and adding -*es*.

SINGULAR	PLURAL
city	cities
baby	babies
berry	berries

If a noun ends in *y* after a vowel, simply add -*s*.

SINGULAR	PLURAL
day	days
key	keys
monkey	monkeys

EXERCISE 1 Find the nouns in each sentence. The number of nouns in each sentence is in parentheses. Tell whether each noun is singular or plural.

1. Rebecca attended two parties recently. (2)
2. One celebration was for her own birthday. (2)
3. Many wrapped boxes were on the table. (2)
4. The guests ate all the snacks. (2)
5. The girl made a wish and blew out the candles. (3)
6. Two puppies were sitting in a box outside the door. (3)
7. Then the guests played games and watched videos. (3)
8. The only problem was that the party seemed too short. (2)

EXERCISE 2 Write the plural for each singular noun.

1. inch
2. cup
3. country
4. play
5. glass
6. hobby
7. ax
8. mitten
9. dash
10. star
11. rose
12. wagon
13. story
14. fox
15. patch

EXERCISE 3 Complete each sentence with the plural form of the noun or nouns in parentheses.

1. For my birthday this year, all my _____ (friend) and I went to a circus.
2. _____ (Circus) are really fun.
3. The _____ (performer) are amazing.
4. Some _____ (juggler) were twirling _____ (dish) on sticks.
5. Bareback _____ (rider) were standing on _____ (horse).
6. There are many _____ (activity) going on at once in the three _____ (ring).

APPLY IT NOW

Choose a paragraph from a magazine or newspaper. Make two lists: one for singular nouns and one for plural nouns. Write all the nouns in that paragraph in the correct list.

Grammar in Action.

Find the second plural noun in the body of the letter on page 252.

2.4 Irregular Plural Nouns

The plurals of some nouns are not formed by adding *-s* or *-es* to the singular. These are called **irregular plurals.**

You need to learn these irregular plurals. If you forget how to spell an irregular plural, you can look it up in a dictionary.

SINGULAR	PLURAL
ox	oxen
child	children
tooth	teeth
foot	feet
mouse	mice
woman	women
goose	geese
wolf	wolves
knife	knives

Some nouns have the same form in the plural as in the singular.

SINGULAR	PLURAL
sheep	sheep
deer	deer
moose	moose
series	series

EXERCISE 1 Write the plural of each irregular noun.

1. goose
2. foot
3. child
4. man
5. deer

6. ox
7. woman
8. tooth
9. person
10. leaf

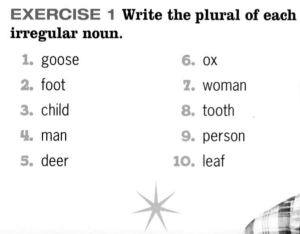

EXERCISE 2 Complete each sentence with the plural form of each noun in parentheses.

1. When young _____ (child) lose their baby _____ (tooth), they put them under their _____ (pillow).

2. The young _____ (boy) and _____ (girl) get _____ (treat) for their teeth.

3. In some _____ (place) people say that tooth _____ (fairy) come and make the exchange.

4. But not all _____ (country) have tooth _____ (fairy).

5. Some _____ (culture) have tooth _____ (mouse)!

6. In Scotland, fairy _____ (rat) buy the _____ (tooth) with _____ (coin).

EXERCISE 3 Complete each sentence. Use the correct form of the irregular noun in parentheses. Tell whether it is singular or plural.

1. A _____ with a toothache went to the dentist. (man)

2. Three _____ ran through the waiting room. (mouse)

3. Two _____ in the waiting room dropped their toys. (child)

4. A _____ told them to remain calm. (woman)

5. The dentist told the man that three of his _____ had to be pulled. (tooth)

6. A team of _____ couldn't have budged one of them. (ox)

7. Two _____, who were dental assistants, helped the dentist. (woman)

8. The dentist gave the man some medicine, and the man counted _____ as he fell asleep in the dentist's chair. (sheep)

APPLY IT NOW

Choose two singular nouns and two plural nouns from the charts on page 34. Write four sentences, using one of the words in each sentence.

2.5 Singular Possessive Nouns

A **possessive noun** shows possession or ownership. A **singular possessive** shows that one person or thing owns something.

> Catherine's shopping bag is filled with food.
>
> The market's food is fancy.

Catherine's shopping bag means that the shopping bag belongs to Catherine. *Market's food* means the food that the market has for sale.

To form the singular possessive, add an apostrophe and the letter *s* (*-'s*) to a singular noun.

SINGULAR	SINGULAR POSSESSIVE	POSSESSIVE PHRASE
Richard	Richard's	Richard's chore
cow	cow's	cow's milk

What is the correct way to show that each of the following belongs to Bruce?

car   **bicycle**   **wagon**

You are right if you said *Bruce's car, Bruce's bicycle,* and *Bruce's wagon.* By adding *-'s* to *Bruce,* you show that the car, the bicycle, and the wagon belong to him.

What if you wanted to say that the items belonged to *the boy*? You are right if you said *the boy's car, the boy's bicycle,* and *the boy's wagon.*

EXERCISE 1 Complete each sentence with the possessive form of the singular noun in parentheses.

1. The _____ job is to run the city. (mayor)

2. _____ office is in City Hall. (Mr. Conlon)

3. The _____ job is to deliver mail. (mail carrier)

4. Our _____ mail carrier is Mrs. Alvarez. (neighborhood)

5. The _____ job is to help us cross the street. (patrol officer)

6. A _____ job is to remove garbage. (garbage collector)

7. My _____ garbage is placed outside for pickup on Tuesday mornings. (family)

8. _____ job is to stop fires. (Mr. Ward)

9. A _____ job is dangerous. (firefighter)

10. My _____ job can be challenging. (teacher)

EXERCISE 2 Rewrite each sentence as a singular possessive phrase.

EXAMPLE **The judge has a gavel.**

the judge's gavel

1. A police officer has a badge.

2. Macie has neighbors.

3. The principal has an assistant.

4. Elio lives in a house.

5. The street cleaner has a broom.

6. My sister owns a DVD player.

7. The nurse has a uniform.

8. The doctor wears a white coat.

9. My neighbor has a cat.

10. The cat sleeps in a bed.

11. The delivery person drives a truck.

12. The hiker has a backpack.

APPLY IT NOW

Think about things that the people in your neighborhood own and the jobs they do. Write four sentences that show possession.
Example: Our librarian's name is Ms. Jones.

2.6 Plural Possessive Nouns

A **plural possessive** shows that more than one person or thing owns something.

|boys' games|babies' toes|wolves' teeth|

To form the plural possessive of regular nouns, add an apostrophe (') after the *s* of the plural form. Remember to form the plural of a regular noun before adding the apostrophe.

SINGULAR	PLURAL	PLURAL POSSESSIVE
boy	boys	boys'
baby	babies	babies'

To form the plural possessive of irregular nouns, add -'s.

SINGULAR	PLURAL	PLURAL POSSESSIVE
man	men	men's
ox	oxen	oxen's

What is the plural possessive for this sentence?

The _____ apples are red.

A lady

B lady's

C ladies'

You are right if you said that C is the plural possessive. When an apostrophe is added to the word *ladies,* it means the apples belong to more than one lady.

EXERCISE 1 Find each plural possessive form in the sentences. Not all the sentences have plural possessives.

1. Farmers' lives were often difficult on the prairies.
2. The oxen's job was to plow the fields.
3. A farmer's house could be made of sod.
4. Children's chores were often hard.
5. A pioneer's farm had only simple machinery.

EXERCISE 2 Complete this chart with the plural form and the plural possessive form of each noun.

Singular	Plural	Plural Possessive
1. rabbit	_____	_____ ears
2. child	_____	_____ chores
3. settler	_____	_____ homes
4. Spaniard	_____	_____ horses
5. family	_____	_____ homes

EXERCISE 3 Write the possessive form of the plural noun in italics.

1. The Plains *Indians* home was in central North America.

2. These Native *Americans* source of food was the buffalo.

3. *Men* tasks included hunting the buffalo.

4. Their *horses* speed allowed them to chase buffalo.

5. Buffalo were important, and the *animals* skins were used for clothing, bedding, and tepees.

6. *Women* tasks were to cook, make cloth, and farm.

7. *Warriors* deeds were praised.

8. The end of the buffalo herds changed some Indian *nations* lifestyles.

EXERCISE 4 Rewrite each sentence as a singular or plural possessive phrase.

EXAMPLE: **The pioneers had homes.**
the pioneers' homes

1. The settlers had oxen.

2. Horses have manes.

3. Iowa has farms.

4. An ox has strength.

5. The child had chores.

APPLY IT NOW

Think about a group of people in your community, such as teachers, police officers, doctors, taxi drivers, or bakers. Write four sentences about their way of life. Use plural possessives.

 With an adult, research occupations online.

2.7 Collective Nouns

Nouns that name a group of things or people are called **collective nouns.**

The *orchestra* plays at many all-school meetings.

The collective noun *orchestra* names a group of musicians considered together as a unit.

COLLECTIVE NOUNS

army	company	herd	pair
audience	crew	litter	police
band	family	majority	swarm
class	flock	minority	team
club	group	pack	tribe

A singular collective noun usually uses a singular verb. Note that singular verbs in the present tense end in *s*.

The quartet plays.

The duo dances.

Which sentences include collective nouns?

    A **A ballerina twirls.**

    B **The singer hums.**

    C **The crowd applauds.**

You are right if you said that only C includes a collective noun. *Crowd* names a group. *Ballerina* and *singer* each name one person.

EXERCISE 1 Match each collective noun in Column A with a plural noun in Column B.

Column A	Column B
1. crew	a. wolves
2. pack	b. students
3. club	c. sailors
4. army	d. cattle
5. company	e. soldiers
6. herd	f. employees

EXERCISE 2 Find the collective noun in each sentence.

1. The class wanted to help clean up the old park.
2. The children wrote to the city council.
3. A committee considered the issue.
4. A team of city workers cleaned the park.
5. Now families go to the park to play and relax.
6. Flocks of geese stop at the park's newly cleaned pond during the spring and fall.

EXERCISE 3 Complete each sentence with a collective noun. Use words from the list on page 40.

1. My family chose a puppy from the _____.
2. Our _____ decided to do a recycling project.
3. My friend plays the tuba in the _____.
4. We saw a _____ of bees near the hive.
5. The _____ cheered at the end of the concert.
6. The _____ arrived at the scene of the accident.

EXERCISE 4 Complete each sentence with a singular verb in the present tense.

1. Our class _____ (participate) in a beach cleanup every year.
2. A crowd _____ (gather) on the beach in the morning.
3. Each family _____ (take) a large bag.
4. Every group _____ (clean) a different area of the beach.
5. A flock of seabirds _____ (pass) overhead.
6. The group _____ (be) tired but proud of its work at the end.

APPLY IT NOW

Choose three collective nouns and write a sentence for each.
Example: The audience applauded my speech.

2.8 Nouns as Subjects

A noun may be used as the **simple subject** of a sentence. The subject tells what the sentence is about. It tells who or what is or does something.

> *Boats* **sail.**
>
> **The** *sea* **can be rough.**

Boats is a noun that tells what sails. *Sea* is a noun that tells what can be rough.

To find a subject, ask *who* or *what* before the predicate.

The *sails* **on old ships look magnificent.**

To find the subject, ask *what* looks magnificent. The answer is the subject, *sails.*

Which noun is the subject in this sentence?

Joanne learned about a sailing expedition.

You are right if you said *Joanne. Joanne,* the subject, tells who learned about the sailing expedition. *Expedition* is also a noun, but it is not the subject. It did not learn anything.

England once had the most powerful navy in the world.

Ask *who* had the most powerful navy in the world? The answer, *England,* is the subject of the sentence. *Navy* and *world* are also nouns, but they are not the subject of the sentence.

EXERCISE 1 Complete each sentence with a subject noun from the list.

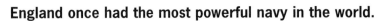

| Antarctica | sleds | explorer | Poles | travel |

1. _____ is a land of cold and ice.

2. _____ in Antarctica is very dangerous.

3. _____ with dogs are the means of transportation.

4. The _____ were areas for exploration.

5. The first _____ at the South Pole was Roald Amundsen in 1911.

EXERCISE 2 **Find the simple subject in each sentence. To find the simple subject, ask *who or what is* or *does something*.**

A member of the *Endurance* crew with new friends

1. Ernest Shackleton was a British explorer.

2. His goal was to cross Antarctica.

3. His expedition started out in 1914.

4. *Endurance* was the name of his ship.

5. The ship became trapped in pack ice.

6. The crew was stranded there for many months.

7. Their camp was actually on a large area of ice for a time.

8. The party crossed the wild seas in a small boat.

9. The group finally arrived on an inhabited island.

10. Shackleton had to walk across the entire island for help.

11. Help arrived in time to rescue the crew.

12. This story is told in Shackleton's book *South*.

EXERCISE 3 **Complete each sentence with a subject noun.**

1. _____ sail on the seas.

2. The _____ tossed the ship.

3. The _____ blew.

4. _____ felt seasick.

5. The _____ calmed.

6. The _____ eventually returned to the harbor.

APPLY IT NOW

Think about a current event, either locally or internationally. Write four sentences describing it. Underline the simple subject in each sentence.

Tech Tip With an adult, research your current event online.

2.9 Nouns as Direct Objects

A noun may be used as the **direct object** of a sentence. The direct object tells who or what receives the action of the verb.

The Egyptians built *pyramids*.

The Egyptians built *what?* The noun *pyramids* is the direct object of the sentence. It tells what the Egyptians built.

To find the direct object in a sentence, ask *who* or *what* after the verb.

Pyramids contain *tombs* **of the pharaohs.**

Pyramids contain *what?* The answer is *tombs*. It is the direct object.

What is the direct object in this sentence?

Workers carried stones.

If you said the direct object in this sentence is the noun *stones,* you are correct. *Stones* tells what the workers carried.

Which noun is the direct object in this sentence?

Pyramids have four sides.

Sides is the direct object. It tells what the pyramids have.

EXERCISE 1 Complete each sentence with a direct object from the list.

belief   government   tombs   Egyptians   power

1. We studied the ancient _____.
2. The Egyptians established a strong central _____.
3. The pharaoh had considerable _____.
4. The Egyptians had a strong _____ in the afterlife.
5. Archaeologists still find _____ of ancient Egyptians.

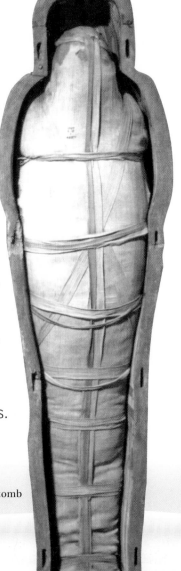

Mummy from an Egyptian tomb

EXERCISE 2 **Find the noun used as a direct object in each sentence. The verb in each sentence is in italics.**

1. Pharaohs *ruled* ancient Egypt.
2. The word *pharaoh means* "king."
3. Nefertiti *married* a pharaoh.
4. Nefertiti and her husband, Akhenaten, *ruled* the country.
5. Sculptors *carved* her portrait in stone.
6. For a time, history *forgot* the queen.
7. Scientists now *may have found* her actual mummy.
8. The woman in the sculpture *has* a long, curved neck.
9. The woman *wears* a crown.
10. Some scientists *dispute* this idea.
11. Maybe someday archaeologists *will find* the answer.

EXERCISE 3 **Find the noun used as a direct object in each sentence. Then find the verb.**

1. Let's explore the Nile River.
2. Egyptians celebrated the river.
3. The Nile brought wealth.
4. Its water helped farmers.
5. Every year the waters flooded the river's banks.
6. It left rich, black soil for the farmers.
7. The farmers raised food for the pharaoh.
8. Farmers raised crops in the rich soil.
9. Egyptian farmers grew wheat.
10. The Nile River had a big role in Egyptian life.
11. The river provided drinking water.
12. It also supplied water for crops.
13. Today the river crosses nine African countries.
14. Tourists take cruises along the river.

Queen
Nefertiti

APPLY IT NOW

Write three sentences about a leader that you have heard of or have read about. The person may be a pharaoh, a president, or a coach. Use a noun as a direct object in each sentence. Underline each direct object.
Example: Many people liked President Kennedy.

Grammar in Action

Find the first direct object in the excerpt on page 248.

2.10 Nouns as Subject Complements

A **subject complement** gives information about the subject. A subject complement follows a linking verb, such as the verb *be* and its various forms (*am, is, are, was, were*).

A noun can be a subject complement. A noun used as a subject complement renames the subject.

> **Natalie Nelson is a young** *girl*.
>
> **Despereaux is a** *mouse*.

Girl and *mouse* are nouns used as subject complements. Each noun follows a linking verb and renames the subject of the sentence.

> **Natalie Nelson = girl**
>
> **Despereaux = mouse**

What noun is the subject complement in this sentence?

> **Keiko was a whale.**

The subject complement is *whale*. It is a noun that follows the linking verb *was*. It renames the subject, *Keiko*.

Find the subject complement in this sentence.

> **Andrew Clements is an author.**

The subject complement is *author*. It renames the subject, *Andrew Clements,* and it follows the linking verb *is*.

EXERCISE 1 The subject complement in each sentence is italicized. Tell the noun it renames.

1. J. K. Rowling is the *creator* of the character Harry Potter.
2. Her novels are popular *books* with young people and adults.
3. Harry Potter is a *student*.
4. His best friend is *Ron*.
5. Hermione is another *child* at Harry's school.
6. Quidditch is a *sport* played with brooms.

EXERCISE 2 Tell what the subject complement is in each sentence.

1. *The Secret Garden* is a work of fiction.
2. The account of Achilles is a myth.
3. The contents of *Where the Sidewalk Ends* are poems.
4. The story of Rip Van Winkle is a legend.
5. *Charlotte's Web* is a story about a spider and a pig.
6. *Chasing Vermeer* is a mystery.

EXERCISE 3 Complete each sentence with a subject complement.

1. Abraham Lincoln was a _____.
2. Pretzels are a _____.
3. Soccer is a _____.
4. Australia is a _____.
5. Math is a _____.
6. Eagles are _____.

EXERCISE 4 Tell how the underlined noun is used in each sentence: as a subject, a direct object, or a subject complement.

1. <u>Peter Warren Hatcher</u> is a character in a series of funny books.
2. Judy Blume wrote the <u>series</u>.
3. Peter is a young <u>student</u>.
4. Peter has a younger <u>brother</u>.
5. His brother's nickname is <u>Fudge</u>.
6. Fudge causes <u>trouble</u> for Peter.
7. Sheila Tubman is Peter's <u>classmate</u>.
8. *Tales of a Fourth Grade Nothing* is one <u>book</u> in the series.

APPLY IT NOW

Write four sentences that tell about family members. Use a noun as a subject complement in each sentence.
Example: Margot is the baby.

Grammar in Action. Find the first noun used as a subject complement in the excerpt on page 248.

2.11 Words Used as Nouns and as Verbs

Many words can be used both as nouns and as verbs. The word *camp,* for example, can be used as a noun or as a verb.

> **We camp in the woods on our family vacation.**
>
> **I went to a camp by a lake last summer.**

In the first sentence, *camp* is used as a verb. It shows action. In the second sentence, *camp* is used as a noun. It names a place.

Tell how the word *plan* is used in these sentences. In which sentence is it a verb? In which sentence is it a noun?

> **My plan for the summer is to go to camp.**
>
> **I plan to go to camp this summer.**

You are right if you said *plan* is used as a noun in the first sentence and as a verb in the second sentence. In the first sentence, *plan* is a thing. In the second sentence, *plan* is an action.

The word *sails* also can be used as a noun or as a verb. Can you tell how *sails* is used below?

> **The wind fills the sails of the boat.**
>
> **The family sails on the lake.**

You are right if you said *sails* is used as a noun in the first sentence and as a verb in the second sentence.

The word *photograph* can be a noun and a verb. *Photograph* can fit in the blank in both sentences.

> **The _____ shows me at camp.**
>
> **I will _____ my friends at camp.**

Put the word *photograph* in the first sentence. How is it used? It is a noun. Notice that the word *The* comes before it. The words *the* and *a* often come before nouns. Put the word *photograph* in the second sentence. How it is used? It is a verb. It is an action word.

EXERCISE 1 Tell whether the italicized word is used as a noun or as a verb.

1. Many people *visit* the Grand Canyon.
2. My family is planning a *visit* there next summer.
3. People can *drive* along the South Rim of the canyon.
4. It is a *drive* with magnificent views.
5. Some people *hike* across the canyon.
6. The *hike* takes most people more than a day.
7. This *walk* takes people down one side of the canyon.
8. Then they *walk* up the opposite side.
9. Other people *ride* mules in the canyon.
10. The *ride* seems a bit scary to me.

EXERCISE 2 Complete each sentence with one of the words below. Tell whether the word is used as a noun or as a verb.

| dance | place | shop | drop | practice | water |

1. There is a pet _____ in my neighborhood.
2. I _____ for clothes at the mall.
3. My sisters have soccer _____ on Saturday.
4. They also _____ after school on Tuesday.
5. Don't _____ the can of paint.
6. There's a _____ of paint on your T-shirt.
7. I can _____ the macarena.
8. Do you know the _____?
9. I _____ the plants regularly.
10. Be careful not to give them too much _____.
11. You should _____ your boots in the closet.
12. I know the _____ where the treasure is hidden.

APPLY IT NOW

Write sentences using each word as a noun and as a verb. Tell how you used each word.
1. rain
2. watch
3. play
4. dream

Noun Review

2.1 Find the nouns in each sentence.

1. Walruses are clumsy on land.

2. In the water, these animals are fast swimmers.

3. Their tusks are used to keep enemies away.

4. This animal lives in the area of the Arctic Ocean.

2.2 Find the nouns in each sentence. Tell whether each is a common or proper noun.

5. George Washington Carver was born a slave.

6. The former slave went to school and earned two degrees.

7. Carver created many new products from peanuts.

8. These items included cosmetics, paints, and dyes.

2.3 Find the nouns in each sentence. Tell whether each is singular or plural.

9. All living things depend on each member of a chain for food.

10. Animals that eat plants are called herbivores.

11. Carnivores are animals that eat other animals.

12. A person is considered an omnivore because humans eat plants and animals.

2.4 Complete each sentence with the plural form of the noun in parentheses.

13. The librarian read nursery rhymes and folktales to the _____. (child)

14. Tell us the story of the three blind _____. (mouse)

15. Little Bo Peep lost many of her _____. (sheep)

16. Jack had nimble _____. (foot)

2.5 Complete each sentence with the singular possessive form of the noun in parentheses.

17. _____ favorite animal is the sea turtle. (Eva)

18. A _____ nest is built by digging a hole in the sand. (female)

19. The _____ eggs are the size of table tennis balls. (turtle)

20. Predators threaten a _____ survival. (hatchling)

21. A _____ instinct is to head toward the moonlight and the sea. (baby)

2.6 Complete each sentence with the plural possessive form of the noun in parentheses.

22. John Sutter tried to keep quiet the _____ discovery of gold. (workers)

23. _____ thoughts turned to gold. (Americans)

24. Many _____ choice was to travel by train. (men)

25. Most _____ dreams did not come true. (miners)

2.7 Find the collective noun in each sentence.

26. The herd of cattle grazes on the grass.

27. A flock of seagulls flew over the boat.

28. Out of the woods ran a pack of wild dogs.

29. A litter of kittens was playing.

30. Around the lemonade flew a swarm of bees.

2.8 Find the simple subject in each sentence.

31. Abe Lincoln lived in a log cabin.

32. Log cabins were practical in the 1800s.

33. Pioneers built them from available materials.

34. Timber was plentiful in those days.

35. Some homes are still built from logs.

2.9 Find the direct object in each sentence.

36. Clouds cover Venus.

37. The planets reflect sunlight.

38. Jupiter has several moons.

39. Rings of ice and rock orbit Saturn.

40. Astronauts gathered information about space.

2.10 Find the subject complement in each sentence.

41. Orlando is a city in Florida.

42. Florida is a southern state.

43. The first stop on our trip was Miami.

44. Disney World was another destination.

45. The Everglades is a home for alligators.

2.11 Tell if each italicized word is a noun or a verb.

46. My sister *plants* seed in pots.

47. My sister and I *water* the plants.

48. This plant *blossoms* in the spring.

49. This plant has white *blossoms*.

Tech Tip — Go to www.voyagesinenglish.com for more activities.

Noun Challenge

Read the paragraph and answer the questions.

1. Newfoundlands are dogs that are famous for rescuing people in distress. 2. They can swim and reach people in trouble in the water. 3. One dog named Star carried a rope out to a boat in trouble. 4. A crowd on shore then pulled the craft to safety. 5. The passengers' lives were saved. 6. More recently a dog named Boo jumped into a rushing river to save a drowning man. 7. The man was not able to shout for help, but the dog sensed the man was in trouble. 8. The dog hadn't been trained for rescue work, so the story is even more amazing. 9. A Newfoundland is a special breed. 10. The dog's webbed feet make it a good swimmer. 11. Its strong body is a powerhouse. 12. It swims the breaststroke rather than the dog paddle. 13. These dogs will dive into really deep water and can swim through high waves. 14. Clubs exist for Newfoundland owners.

1. Which noun is the subject of sentence 1?
2. Find the common nouns and the proper nouns in sentence 3.
3. Find a collective noun in sentence 4.
4. In sentence 4 what noun is the direct object?
5. In sentence 5 what is the singular possessive of *passengers' lives*?
6. In sentence 8 how is *dog* used?
7. In sentence 9 what noun is the subject complement?
8. What kind of noun is *dog's* in sentence 10?
9. In sentence 10 what is the singular form of *feet*?
10. How is *powerhouse* used in sentence 11?
11. What noun is the subject of sentence 13?
12. In sentence 13 is *water* used as a noun or as a verb?
13. How is *clubs* used in sentence 14?
14. In sentence 14 what kind of noun is *clubs*?

Pronouns

3.1 Personal Pronouns: Part I

3.2 Personal Pronouns: Part II

3.3 Singular and Plural Pronouns

3.4 Subject Pronouns

3.5 Pronouns in Compound Subjects

3.6 Object Pronouns

3.7 Possessive Pronouns

3.8 Possessive Adjectives

3.9 Pronouns and Antecedents

3.10 *I*, *Me*, *We*, and *Us*

3.11 Pronouns and Contractions

Pronoun Review

Pronoun Challenge

3.1 Personal Pronouns: Part I

A **personal pronoun** is a word that takes the place of a noun. Here is a list of personal pronouns.

I	she	he	we	it	you	they
me	her	him	us	its	yours	them
mine	hers	his	ours			

In the second sentence below, *they* takes the place of *peasants; him* takes the place of *king.*

> **The** *peasants* **cheered for the** *king.*
> *They* **cheered for** *him.*

Pronouns help avoid repeating nouns, and they make your writing sound smoother. Read this paragraph.

> **The Middle Ages occurred between AD 500 and 1500. During that time nobles lived in castles. Nobles were powerful. Nobles were under a king's rule. Nobles promised to serve their king and country.**

Now read the paragraph with pronouns. What are they?

> **The Middle Ages occurred between AD 500 and 1500. During that time nobles lived in castles. They were powerful. Nobles were under a king's rule. They promised to serve their king and country.**

You are right if you said *They.* In the third and fifth sentences, *They* takes the place of the noun *nobles.* Notice how using pronouns makes the writing sound smoother.

Read this pair of sentences. What pronoun goes in the blank?

> **Marisa reported on castles. _____ told us that castles in Middle Ages usually had thick stone walls and towers.**

You are right if you said *She. She* can take the place of the noun *Marisa.*

EXERCISE 1 Find all the personal pronouns in these sentences.

1. You can see objects from the Middle Ages at a museum.
2. They include things such as swords, armor, and tapestries.
3. The guide told me about life in the Middle Ages.
4. She said it was difficult.
5. We asked how a man became a knight.
6. He had to have enough money to buy armor and a horse.
7. I saw armor for a horse when I went to the museum.
8. For a class project, we made a model of it.

EXERCISE 2 Complete the chart. Write the pronouns that can replace each noun. Use the list on page 54 for help.

Noun	Pronoun	Pronoun
1. king	he	_____
2. queen	_____	her
3. castles	_____	them
4. horses	they	_____
5. shield	_____	

EXERCISE 3 Tell what personal pronoun can take the place of each word or group of words in italics.

1. *A lord* might have several manors.
2. *A manor* usually included a castle, a village, and a church.
3. *Peasants* lived in the village.
4. The peasants gave *the lord* part of their crops.
5. The wool was spun by *the woman*.
6. *A man* might be in the field planting crops.
7. *A common house* was made of mud.

APPLY IT NOW

Write four sentences about a period of history that interests you. Rewrite each sentence, using a pronoun to replace the noun.
Example: Castles were made from stone.
They were made from stone.

Tech Tip With an adult, research the historical period online.

3.2 Personal Pronouns: Part II

Personal pronouns refer to the person speaking; the person spoken to; or the person, place, or thing spoken about. They are **first person, second person, or third person.**

	SINGULAR	PLURAL
FIRST PERSON	I, me, mine	we, us, ours
SECOND PERSON	you, yours	you, yours
THIRD PERSON	he, him, his she, her, hers it, its	they, them, theirs

- First person pronouns refer to the person speaking.

    _I_ like to paint.   _We_ like to paint.

- Second person pronouns refer to the person spoken to.

    You should paint a picture.

- Third person pronouns refer to the person, place, or thing spoken about.

    Elsa painted _her_.

Which sentence has a pronoun in the third person?

   A **I wore a smock.**
   B **You paint well.**
   C **They painted portraits.**

You are right if you said sentence C. _They_ names the people spoken about. _They_ is a third person pronoun. Sentence A has a pronoun in the first person—_I,_ and sentence B has a pronoun in the second person—_You._

EXERCISE 1 Tell whether each pronoun in italics is in the first, second, or third person.

1. Painting is fun for *us*.
2. Andrea asked *him* for the yellow paint.
3. *He* painted a golden retriever.
4. Why did *you* paint a dog?
5. *I* painted a picture of my favorite cat.
6. *We* display our works in the school halls.

EXERCISE 2 In each sentence, find the pronoun and tell whether it is in the first, second, or third person.

1. We use a variety of art materials.
2. She used sunflowers seeds in a mosaic.
3. The colorful paper weaving is his.
4. Was the chalk drawing on black paper made by her?
5. We made animal sculptures out of clay.
6. What art materials do you like to use?
7. They use very strong, bright colors for theirs.
8. Can you pass the acrylic paint to us?

EXERCISE 3 Complete each sentence with a pronoun according to the directions in parentheses.

1. _____ used a lot of blue paint. (second person)
2. _____ painted landscapes. (third person)
3. _____ entered the collages in the art contest. (first person)
4. _____ made papier-mâché masks. (first person)
5. _____ won first prize. (third person)
6. The judges congratulated _____. (first person)
7. _____ (first person) displayed _____ in the trophy case. (third person)

APPLY IT NOW

Write three sentences about your art class. Use first, second, and third person pronouns in your sentences.
Example: We made ceramic vases last year.

Grammar in Action

Identify the third personal pronoun in the excerpt on page 286.

Pronouns • 57

3.3 Singular and Plural Pronouns

A **singular personal pronoun** refers to one person, place, or thing. A **plural personal pronoun** refers to more than one person, place, or thing.

SINGULAR	PLURAL
I, me, mine	we, us, ours
you, yours	you, yours
he, him, his	they, them, theirs
she, her, hers	
it, its	

SINGULAR

Angela recycles paper.
She recycles paper.

PLURAL

Conserving water and paper is important to Mom and Dad.
Conserving water and paper is important to *them*.

The pronoun *She* is singular. It refers to one person. The pronoun *them* is plural. It refers to more than one person.

Which sentence has a plural personal pronoun?

A It is a gigantic tomato.

B She doesn't use pesticides.

C They grow vegetables.

You are right if you said sentence C. *They* is a plural pronoun.

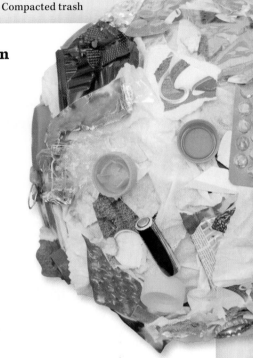

EXERCISE 1 Tell whether each pronoun in italics is singular or plural.

1. *I* set up a recycling program.
2. He asked me, "How can I help *you*?"
3. *He* told other students about the program.
4. *They* brought many things to recycle.
5. I put *ours* in the bin.
6. Molly had a bag with 20 plastic bottles in *it*.
7. She gave me *hers*.
8. *She* said the bag wasn't heavy.
9. *We* collected newspapers, cans, and bottles.
10. The teachers took *them* to the recycle center.

EXERCISE 2 Find the pronoun in each sentence. Tell whether it is singular or plural.

1. The teacher told us some tips for recycling.
2. She gave some simple rules.
3. Look for items with recycled materials even though they cost more.
4. In a store say "I don't need a bag."
5. Get a reusable canvas bag and use it for shopping.
6. Buy quality products, and use them for a longer time.

EXERCISE 3 Replace the word or words in italics with the correct personal pronoun. Tell whether that pronoun is singular or plural.

1. *The students* worked to help save the environment.
2. *Shana* walks to school.
3. *Jacques* turns off the lights in empty rooms.
4. *Marie, Michelle, and David* planted trees.
5. Mr. Li told *Kay and me* about *energy-saving lightbulbs*.
6. Nisha taught *Jane* about *endangered animals*.

APPLY IT NOW

Write five sentences about how you or someone you know protects the environment. Use a pronoun in each sentence. Tell whether each pronoun is singular or plural.
Example: She recycles glass. singular

3.4 Subject Pronouns

A personal pronoun may be used as the subject of a sentence. The subject tells what the sentence is about. It tells who or what does something. **Subject pronouns** are used as subjects.

SINGULAR	PLURAL
I	we
you	you
he, she, it	they

I shiver.   *She* shivers.   *We* shiver.

I, She, and *We* are subject pronouns. They answer the question *Who shivers?*

To find the subject of a sentence, ask *who* or *what* before the predicate. Can you find the subjects in these sentences? Which subjects are pronouns?

A **We like cold weather.**

B **The Ice Age happened long ago.**

C **It had extremely cold weather.**

Sentence A has a pronoun for a subject. Ask, *Who likes cold weather?* The answer is *We.* For sentence B ask, *What happened a long time ago?* The answer is the noun *Ice Age.* For sentence C ask, *What had extremely cold weather?* The answer is *It,* a pronoun.

Read these sentences. What subject pronoun goes in the blank?

Kevin found a book on mastodons in the library.
_____ checked it out and read it.

You are right if you said *He. He* can take the place of the noun *Kevin. He* is the subject pronoun.

Mastodon

Saber-toothed tiger

EXERCISE 1 Find the pronoun used as a subject in each sentence.

1. Do you know about the most recent Ice Age?
2. It started about 70,000 years ago.
3. We learned about it from our teacher.
4. She told us many things about ice ages and glaciers.
5. Did you know that ice covered a third of the earth?
6. We learned that there was an ice age more than three million years ago.
7. It led to a series of warm and cold cycles when glaciers grew bigger or smaller.
8. We don't know the specific reasons for the beginnings and the endings of ice ages.

EXERCISE 2 Use a subject pronoun to take the place of the word or words in italics.

1. *Steve* asked about ice-age animals.
2. *Mrs. Alvarez* told the class about the saber-toothed tiger.
3. *The saber-toothed tiger* had teeth up to seven inches long.
4. *Simon and I* asked about mastodons.
5. *Mastodons* had curved tusks and long, furry coats.
6. *Human hunters* may have caused the mastodons' extinction.

EXERCISE 3 Rewrite each sentence with a pronoun used as the subject.

1. Rachel hates cold weather.
2. She and her friends like hot weather.
3. Mason likes cold weather.
4. Jake and I like to build a fort out of snow.
5. Winter is my favorite season.

APPLY IT NOW

Imagine it is winter. Does it snow where you live, or does it stay warm? Write four sentences about what you do during the winter. Use a subject pronoun in each sentence.
Example: We sled on the hill in the park.

3.5 Pronouns in Compound Subjects

Two or more nouns or subject pronouns can be used together as a **compound subject.** They are connected by *and* or *or.* The subject pronouns are *I, you, we, he, she, it,* and *they.* Study these compound subjects.

> *Angela* **and** *Hector* **went to the city.** (two nouns)
>
> *Angela* **and** *he* **went to the city.** (a noun and a pronoun)
>
> *She* **and** *Hector* **went to the city.** (a pronoun and a noun)
>
> *She* **and** *he* **went to the city.** (two pronouns)

Which sentence has a compound subject with two pronouns?

A **You and I went to New York.**

B **I rode on the subway.**

C **Carrie and Stella visit him in the city.**

You are right if you said sentence A. *You and I* is a compound subject with two pronouns—*You* and *I.* Sentence C is a compound subject, but it has two nouns—*Carrie* and *Stella.*

Which pronoun correctly completes the sentence?

> **Stella and (I me) flew in an airplane.**

You are correct if you said *I.* The pronoun *I* is a subject pronoun. It is part of the compound subject.

In speaking and writing, it is polite to put *I* after other subject words that refer to people.

> **Stella and *I* can talk about the trip.**
>
> **She and *I* can talk about the trip.**

EXERCISE 1 Find the compound subject in each sentence. Name all the subject pronouns.

1. My mother and I talked with the travel agent.

2. She and he arranged for plane tickets.

3. My family and I took a taxi from the airport.

4. Tom and he ran through Central Park.

5. He and she planned to meet on Fifth Avenue.

6. My dad and she bought hot dogs from a street vendor.

7. My sisters and I visited the Museum of Modern Art.

8. We and many other people enjoyed the exhibits.

EXERCISE 2 Choose the pronoun or pronouns that correctly complete each sentence.

1. My family and (me I) took a boat ride.

2. (We Us) and the other tourists saw the Statue of Liberty.

3. My sisters and (them they) took a lot of photos.

4. (He Him) and (she her) told us about the statue's history.

5. My sisters and (he him) listened attentively.

6. The other tourists and (me I) learned about the immigrants.

EXERCISE 3 Rewrite each sentence, using a compound subject. Use a subject pronoun from the list to complete each sentence.

I   he   she   we   they

1. Lauren and _____ saw the Empire State Building.

2. _____ and _____ walked through Central Park.

3. Patrick and _____ fed the ducks.

4. _____ and _____ rode the subway.

5. Molly and _____ saw a Broadway play.

6. Ben and _____ went to a museum.

7. Mia and _____ plan to put their photos on the Web.

APPLY IT NOW

Tell about a place that you and your family have visited. Write five sentences. Use compound subjects with pronouns. Example: My family and I went to Washington, D.C.

3.6 Object Pronouns

A personal pronoun may be used as the direct object of a sentence. Ask *whom* or *what* after the verb to find the direct object. **Object pronouns** are used as direct objects.

SINGULAR	PLURAL
me	us
you	you
him, her, it	them

The reporter questioned *Roberto*.

The reporter questioned *him*.

Roberto is the answer to the question *The reporter questioned whom? Roberto* is a proper noun used as the direct object of the sentence. The noun can be replaced by the object pronoun *him,* as shown in the second sentence. *Him* acts as the direct object.

Which sentence uses a pronoun as a direct object?

A **The politician gave a speech.**

B **He used note cards.**

C **He dropped them.**

You are right if you said sentence C. The word *them* comes after the verb and is the direct object. It answers *He dropped what?*

Pronouns can be part of compound direct objects. Read this pair of sentences. What object pronoun goes in the blank?

The governor congratulated Senator Leder and her husband. He congratulated _____.

You are right if you said *them. Them* can take the place of the nouns *Senator Leder* and *husband. Them* is the direct object of the verb *congratulated.*

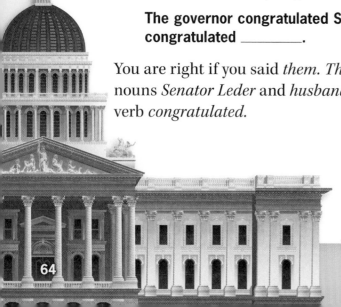

EXERCISE 1 Find the pronoun or pronouns used as direct objects in each sentence.

1. Mrs. Pringles teaches us about state government.
2. The governor heads it.
3. Voters elected him and the state representatives.
4. We saw them when we visited the state capital.
5. The representative called her with the exciting news.
6. He invited us over for dinner.
7. We visited him and them in the state capital.
8. He questioned Kate and me about our studies.

EXERCISE 2 Use an object pronoun to take the place of the word or words in italics.

1. Matt told *Sarah* about the voting age.
2. The candidate gave *many speeches*.
3. The politician thanked *the voters*.
4. The politician won *the election*.
5. Sheila asked *her dad* about the election.
6. Mom helped *Sheila and me* with our civics assignment.
7. The losing candidate congratulated *his opponent*.
8. Reporters questioned *the senator* about the proposed law.

EXERCISE 3 Rewrite each sentence with a pronoun used as the direct object.

1. I told Jason about the election.
2. He had asked my sister about it.
3. Civics interests my sister and me.
4. Voters elect their representatives.
5. The representatives pass laws.
6. Citizens must obey the law.

APPLY IT NOW

Write four sentences about the state in which you live. Use object pronouns as direct objects in each of your sentences. Underline the object pronouns.

With an adult, research your state online.

3.7 Possessive Pronouns

A **possessive pronoun** shows ownership or possession. Possessive pronouns stand alone.

The snake is *Natasha's.* (possessive noun)

The snake is *hers.* (possessive pronoun)

	SINGULAR	PLURAL
FIRST PERSON	**mine**	**ours**
SECOND PERSON	**yours**	**yours**
THIRD PERSON	**his, hers, its**	**theirs**

A possessive pronoun can take the place of the person and the object owned.

NOUN PHRASE	POSSESSIVE PRONOUN
My pet **is gray.**	*Mine* **is gray.**
Your pet **is gray.**	*Yours* **is gray.**
Ching Mae's pet **is gray.**	*Hers* **is gray.**
Liam's and Tom's pets **are gray.**	*Theirs* **are gray.**

Which sentence uses a possessive pronoun?

A **I fed your dog.**

B **Nick fed biscuits to the dog.**

C **Olivia fed hers.**

You are right if you said sentence C. *Hers* is a possessive pronoun that tells about something that belongs to Olivia.

EXERCISE 1 Find the possessive pronoun or pronouns in each sentence.

1. Hers has white paws.

2. What special features does yours have?

3. Mine is black all over.

4. Theirs is a Persian cat, while ours is a Siamese cat.

5. I think hers is a calico cat.

6. Is the cute white cat his?

7. I think its owner is Joe.

8. Eleanor's cat's name is Coco, and hers is Sugar.

EXERCISE 2 Match the object owned in Column A with the possessive pronoun that can replace it in Column B.

Column A	Column B
1. my parrot	a. hers
2. her canary	b. his
3. their gerbils	c. yours
4. Antonio's cat	d. mine
5. your poodle	e. ours
6. our spaniel	f. theirs

EXERCISE 3 Change each sentence so that it has a possessive pronoun. Remember that a possessive pronoun stands alone.

EXAMPLE *Tanita's cat* is black.

Hers is black.

1. *My dog* likes to play with a Frisbee.

2. The Chihuahua is *Grace and John's*.

3. Did you feed *your canary*?

4. *Gus's guinea pig* is friendly.

5. We built a special house for *our beagle*.

6. *Angela's parrot* has a huge cage.

7. *My gerbils* have a cage with a wheel.

8. Will you describe *Sofia's and Jacob's pets*, please?

APPLY IT NOW

Describe several pets of neighbors, relatives, or friends. Write five sentences that use possessive pronouns. Be sure the pronouns stand alone.
Example: His has spots. Theirs wears a collar.

3.8 Possessive Adjectives

A **possessive adjective** shows who owns something. A possessive adjective goes before a noun. It does not stand alone.

Here is a list of possessive adjectives.

	SINGULAR	PLURAL
FIRST PERSON	my	our
SECOND PERSON	your	your
THIRD PERSON	his, her, its	their

My bicycle **is fast.**
Her bicycle **is black.**
Their bicycle **has two seats.**

The words *My, Her,* and *Their* are adjectives. They are used before the noun *bicycle* to show who owns each bicycle.

Which sentence uses an adjective to show ownership?

A **I like bicycles.**

B **Tim's bicycle has bent handlebars.**

C **His bicycle has wide tires.**

D **The bicycle with narrow tires is hers.**

You are right if you said sentence C. The word *His* describes the noun *bicycle.* Notice that sentence D has a possessive (*hers*), but *hers* is a pronoun. Sentence B also has a possessive (*Tim's*), but *Tim's* is a possessive noun.

EXERCISE 1 Find the possessive adjective in each sentence.

1. What is your choice of a favorite outdoor activity?

2. Her favorite sport is skating in the park.

3. Hiking in the mountains is their choice.

4. My idea of fun is a long bike ride.

5. Our choices are all different.

EXERCISE 2 In each sentence, find the possessive adjective. Tell the noun that it describes.

1. I rode my bicycle to a friend's house.

2. His bicycle was in the garage.

3. He pumped air into its tire.

4. We pedaled our bicycles down the path.

5. The bicycle had a holder for his water bottle.

6. Their bike ride was fun.

7. His mom made lemonade for us.

8. Did you always wear your helmet?

EXERCISE 3 Complete each sentence with a possessive adjective.

1. Moira packed _____ gear.

2. Thomas brought _____ compass.

3. Did you put a map in _____ bag?

4. We made _____ lunches.

5. Did you bring _____ canteen?

EXERCISE 4 Find the possessive in each sentence. Tell whether it is a possessive pronoun or a possessive adjective.

1. Did you bring your in-line skates or hers?

2. The red helmet is hers.

3. What is our route going to be?

4. Our park has rules for skating, and we follow its rules.

5. The idea for a group skate was theirs.

APPLY IT NOW

Imagine you are going for a bike ride or a hike with friends. Write four sentences about the things that you and your friends will need. Use a possessive adjective in each sentence. Remember that a possessive adjective goes before a noun.

3.9 Pronouns and Antecedents

Personal pronouns have antecedents. An **antecedent** is the word that the pronoun replaces. The pronouns *he, him,* and *his* refer to male antecedents. *She, her,* and *hers* refer to females. *It* and *its* refer to animals and things.

> **Marco Polo lived in the 1200s. Marco Polo was a famous explorer.**
>
> **Marco Polo lived in the 1200s. He was a famous explorer.**

In the second set of sentences, the personal pronoun *He* is used instead of the noun *Marco Polo. He* takes the place of the noun *Marco Polo* and avoids repeating that term. *Marco Polo* is the antecedent of *he.*

A pronoun and its antecedent must agree in person and number. In the example above, the pronoun *He* is third person singular. Its antecedent, *Marco Polo,* is third person singular. *He* is used because Marco Polo was a man.

What is the antecedent of the pronoun *them* in this sentence?

> **The DVD on explorers helped us learn about them.**

You are right if you said *explorers.* The pronoun *them* is third person plural. The antecedent *explorers* is third person plural.

EXERCISE 1 Find the antecedent in each sentence for the italicized pronoun.

1. Hundreds of years ago, people did not have good transportation, so *they* could not travel easily.
2. The Silk Road connected Asia to China, and *it* was made up of several important trade routes.
3. A journey along the Silk Road was difficult, and *it* could be very dangerous.

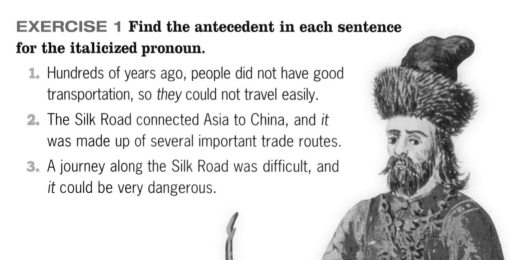

Marco Polo

4. Some European merchants bought valuable goods from Asia and carried *them* back to Europe.

5. Silk was a valuable material, and the Chinese knew the secret of making *it*.

6. Spices from the East were also valuable; *they* included pepper, cinnamon, and cloves.

EXERCISE 2 Choose the correct pronoun to complete each sentence. Make sure that the pronoun agrees with the antecedent in italics.

1. The *students* were studying Marco Polo, and (they he) did projects on people, places, and events of his times.

2. Chinese *inventions* interest me, so I chose (it them) for my project.

3. Sue had a *book* on China, and she lent (it them) to me.

4. Our *teacher* gave a slide presentation on China, and (he they) showed pictures of the country's historic places.

EXERCISE 3 Find the pronoun and its antecedent in each sentence.

1. Marco Polo lived in Venice, but he is most famous for a trip elsewhere.

2. Venice's merchants were adventurous, and they traded with many different countries.

3. Ships carried spices from the East, bringing them to Venice.

4. Marco, his father, and an uncle planned the trip they would take.

5. The Polos' destination was China; the men knew it had many inventions that did not exist in Europe at the time.

6. Marco Polo traveled the Silk Road; he made the trip to China.

APPLY IT NOW

Tell about something interesting that you have learned in school. Write four compound sentences like those in Exercise 1. Circle the pronouns and underline their antecedents.

Grammar in Action.

Find the first pronoun and its antecedent used in the excerpt on page 293.

3.10 *I, Me, We, and Us*

First person pronouns refer to the speaker.

- Use the words *I* and *me* to talk about yourself. Use *I* as the subject of a sentence. Use *me* after the verb as a direct object.
- Use *we* and *us* to talk about yourself and at least one other person. Use *we* as the subject of a sentence. Use *us* after the verb as a direct object.

SUBJECT		OBJECT	
I	play sports.	Sports interest	me.
We	like sports.	Sports thrill	us.

These pronouns may be part of compound subjects and compound objects. Be sure to check how the compound is used.

> *Jake and I* like sports. (compound subject)
>
> Sports thrill *Jake and me*. (compound direct object)

Which sentences are correct in their use of the pronouns?

    A I play soccer.

    B Karen and me play soccer.

    C Karen's dad invited me to the game.

    D Karen's dad took her and I to the game.

You are right if you said sentences A and C. In sentence A, *I* is used correctly as the subject, and in sentence C, *me* is used correctly as the direct object. *Me* is used incorrectly as part of a compound subject in sentence B, and in sentence D, *I* is used incorrectly as part of a compound direct object.

EXERCISE 1 Use *I* or *me* to complete each sentence.

1. My friend and _____ are forwards on the soccer team.
2. My friend accidentally tripped _____ in practice.
3. The coach taught my friend and _____ about kicking.

4. _____ thanked him for his help.

5. _____ scored the winning goal in the last game.

6. My teammates joined _____ on the field in celebration.

7. Marguerite and Hans applauded _____.

8. _____ can't wait for the next game.

EXERCISE 2 Use *we* or *us* to complete each sentence.

1. _____ played volleyball.

2. The other team beat _____ before.

3. The coach told _____ about trying hard.

4. He inspired _____, and _____ were ready to play.

5. _____ scored many points.

6. Finally, _____ won the game.

7. _____ celebrated our win as fans applauded _____.

EXERCISE 3 Choose the pronoun that correctly completes each sentence.

1. (I Me) really like basketball.

2. My brother and (I me) often shoot baskets in our yard.

3. My dad sometimes joins (we us).

4. Our dad helps him and (I me) with our game.

5. (We Us) also play basketball at school.

6. (I Me) play on the school basketball team.

7. (We Us) played 14 games this year.

8. Our opponents have not beaten (us we) yet!

9. My dad took my friend and (I me) out for smoothies after the game.

10. He said that (we us) deserved it, and he told (we us) that he was proud.

APPLY IT NOW

Think about your favorite sports. Write four sentences. Use *I*, *me*, *we*, and *us*. Choose from these sports or any others you are familiar with.

gymnastics   ice-skating
swimming   hockey
soccer   football

3.11 Pronouns and Contractions

Personal pronouns can be joined with some verbs to form contractions. An apostrophe (') replaces the missing letter or letters in a contraction.

Here is a list of common contractions with pronouns:

I'm = I am	I've = I have
you're = you are	you've = you have
he's = he is *or* he has	she's = she is *or* she has
it's = it is *or* it has	we're = we are
we've = we have	they're = they are
they've = they have	

I've read about the heart. = *I have* read about the heart.

It's a muscular pump. = *It is* a muscular pump.

Possessive adjectives are often confused with contractions. Possessive adjectives express possession and do not contain apostrophes.

PRONOUN + VERB	POSSESSIVE ADJECTIVE
You're = *You are* breathing.	*Your* heart is important.
It's = *It is* beating.	*Its* role is important.
They're = *They are* organs.	*Their* role is important.

Which choice correctly completes the sentence?

(Your You're) able to see a large model of a heart at the museum.

You are correct if you chose *You're*. The sentence means *You are able to see a large model of a heart at the museum.*

Blood cells

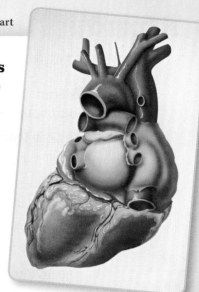

EXERCISE 1 Tell whether each word in italics is a possessive adjective or a contraction. Name the two words that make up each contraction.

1. An important part of *your* body is the circulatory system.
2. *It's* essential because it carries food to the body.
3. *Its* job is to carry blood to cells.
4. *They're* the smallest parts of our bodies.
5. *You've* got a heart, veins, and arteries.
6. *Their* roles in the circulatory system are different.

EXERCISE 2 Choose the possessive adjective or contraction that correctly completes each sentence.

1. (You're Your) veins are part of the circulatory system.
2. (They're Their) vessels that carry blood back to the heart.
3. After the food and oxygen have been removed from the blood, (it's its) color in the veins is dark red.
4. The heart is an important part of your body; (it's its) the key part of the circulatory system.
5. (It's Its) always pumping blood into the arteries.
6. (You're Your) heart may beat more than 100,000 times a day.

EXERCISE 3 Rewrite the sentences that have mistakes in the use of possessive adjectives or contractions. Not all sentences have mistakes.

1. We're studying the circulatory system.
2. Its a complex system, and it includes the lungs.
3. What are some facts youve learned about lungs?
4. Their the place where blood gets oxygen.
5. You're blood goes from you're lungs back to you're heart.

APPLY IT NOW

Write six sentences on any topic. Show the correct use of these words: *your, you're, they're, their, its, it's.*

Pronoun Review

3.1 Find the personal pronoun in each sentence.

1. You can learn to speak foreign languages.
2. He is fluent in German and Russian.
3. They speak Chinese and English at home.
4. The school offered us Japanese lessons.

3.2 Tell whether each underlined pronoun is in the first, second, or third person.

5. We enjoy sledding in the winter.
6. Ask them to wait.
7. Mom told us to wear heavy clothing.
8. Do you have a new sled?
9. I walked back up the hill.

3.3 Tell whether each underlined pronoun is singular or plural.

10. We pitched a tent in the woods.
11. He built a campfire in the clearing.
12. The group cooked hot dogs over it.
13. They sang songs around the campfire.

14. Tanya asked me to suggest the next song.

3.4 Find the pronoun used as a subject in each sentence.

15. What do you know about how caves are formed?
16. They are often carved out of limestone rock.
17. She told us that water slowly wears away rock.
18. It grows bigger over time.
19. On our last vacation, we explored a cave.

3.5 Find the compound subject in each sentence. Name all the subject pronouns.

20. Do you and Mandy want to play checkers?
21. My brother and he played dominoes on Saturday.
22. She and he have an ongoing game of chess.
23. She and I learned how to play solitaire from our grandmother.

3.6 Find the pronoun used as a direct object in each sentence.

24. Cameron and I invited her to attend the basketball game.
25. The game entertained us.
26. Their team won it.

27. The result disappointed them.

28. They took me home.

3.7 **Find the possessive pronoun in each sentence.**

29. Hers is green with window boxes.

30. What does yours look like?

31. Ours has a balcony.

32. I think theirs is the one on the corner.

33. Mine is a one-story house with a red door.

3.8 **Find the possessive adjective in each sentence.**

34. I set up my fish tank in the living room.

35. His betta fish is alone in her glass bowl.

36. Her tetra is brightly colored.

37. Their colors are amazing.

38. Our job is to clean the tank.

3.9 **Find the antecedent for the underlined pronoun in each sentence.**

39. My friend said that conserving energy is important to her.

40. Her mom bought a new car, and it runs on electricity.

41. We collected cans and put them in a red bin.

42. Tom likes to recycle, and he even does it at school.

43. My parents conserve, so they air-dry clothes.

3.10 **Choose the pronoun that correctly completes each sentence.**

44. (We Us) played badminton during gym class.

45. Another pair played Matt and (I me) in a match.

46. (I Me) returned the serve to the other side.

47. The teacher complimented (I me) on my swing.

48. Our friends congratulated (we us) on our win.

3.11 **Tell whether each underlined word is a possessive adjective or a contraction. Name the two words that make up each contraction.**

49. In talking about bats, Mr. Dodd said they're not blind.

50. He's told us some myths about these creatures.

51. Their hearing is so good that they can fly at night.

52. Your report on bats was interesting.

53. She's no longer afraid of bats.

Go to www.voyagesinenglish.com for more activities.

Pronoun Challenge

Read the paragraph and answer the questions.

1. Bicycles have really changed since they were invented in the 1790s. 2. You walked the first bicycles along because they had no pedals. 3. They were more like scooters, but with big wheels. 4. Today mine has pedals, brakes, gears, and large wheels. 5. Even though certain types of racing bikes have neither brakes nor multiple gears, I want them on my bike. 6. Dad, Mom, and I bike often. 7. Our town has a bike path through the forest preserve. 8. It's used a lot in nice weather, and my family and I use it too. 9. Dad and Mom used to race bikes. 10. He and she tell me all about their favorite courses.

1. In sentence 1 what is the antecedent of the pronoun *they?*
2. In sentence 2 what pronoun is in the second person?
3. In sentence 4 what kind of pronoun is *mine?*
4. In sentence 5 what word is an object pronoun?
5. In sentence 5 what pronoun is in the first person?
6. In sentence 6 what word is a subject pronoun?
7. In sentence 7 what word shows ownership? Is it a pronoun or an adjective?
8. Is the first word of sentence 8 a contraction or a possessive pronoun?
9. In sentence 8 what is the compound subject? What is the pronoun in the compound subject?
10. In sentence 10 what word is the possessive adjective?
11. What is the subject of sentence 10?
12. What are the antecedents of *He* and *she* in sentence 10?

Adjectives

4.1 Descriptive Adjectives

4.2 Proper Adjectives

4.3 Articles

4.4 Demonstrative Adjectives

4.5 Adjectives That Tell How Many

4.6 Adjectives as Subject Complements

4.7 Adjectives That Compare

4.8 Irregular Adjectives That Compare

4.9 *More, Most*

4.10 *Fewer, Fewest* and *Less, Least*

4.11 Position of Adjectives

Adjective Review

Adjective Challenge

4.1 Descriptive Adjectives

Adjectives describe or tell about nouns. A **descriptive adjective gives more information about a noun.** It can tell how a thing looks, tastes, sounds, feels, or smells. It can tell about size, number, color, shape, or weight.

Here are some descriptive adjectives.

green   itchy   delicious   fragrant   loud

Here are those adjectives used to describe nouns.

green **hat**   *delicious* **soup**   *loud* **noise**

itchy **socks**   *fragrant* **roses**

Descriptive adjectives often come before the nouns they describe.

The *blue* <u>waves</u> reach the *sandy* <u>shore</u>.

Blue and *sandy* are descriptive adjectives. They give more information about the nouns *waves* and *shore*.

What are the descriptive adjectives in this sentence? What nouns do they describe?

The noisy children are making huge castles in the sand.

You are right if you said *noisy* and *huge. Noisy* tells how the children sound. *Huge* describes the size of the castles.

EXERCISE 1 Find the descriptive adjective in each sentence. Tell the noun the adjective describes.

1. Reefs are warm habitats in the ocean.
2. They occur in shallow water.
3. The massive structure of a reef often contains coral.
4. Coral is formed from tiny animals.
5. When they die, their skeletons add to the stony structure.

6. Reefs provide safe homes for animals.

7. Colorful sea urchins live there.

8. Tropical fish swim around the reef.

EXERCISE 2 Find the descriptive adjectives in each sentence. Tell the noun each adjective describes.

1. Coral thrives in clear, shallow water, but it can also live in muddy water.

2. Hard coral and soft coral are types of coral.

3. Hard coral makes up the solid core of tropical reefs.

4. Soft coral has the shape of ordinary vegetables, such as broccoli or asparagus.

5. This beautiful coral has brilliant colors.

6. This red or orange coral grows on the top of reefs.

7. Soft coral has tiny rods throughout its tissue.

8. It does not have a hard external skeleton.

9. The lovely coral feels like soft, bendable leather.

10. The amazing reefs are a remarkable environment.

EXERCISE 3 Add a descriptive adjective before each noun.

1. _____ flamingo
2. _____ orchid
3. _____ parrot
4. _____ fish
5. _____ tree
6. _____ island

EXERCISE 4 Add a noun that could be described by each pair of adjectives.

1. big, friendly
2. large, noisy
3. fresh, crunchy
4. dark, gloomy
5. delicate, graceful
6. old, creaky

APPLY IT NOW

Write five sentences about a beautiful place that you have visited, such as a park or a lake. Use a descriptive adjective in each sentence.
Example: The orange sun set over the cliff.

4.2 Proper Adjectives

A common noun names any one member of a group of people, places, or things. A proper noun names a particular person, place, or thing. An adjective formed from a proper noun is called a **proper adjective.** A proper adjective begins with a capital letter.

> Proper noun: *Ireland* is famous for its wool.
> Proper adjective: *Irish* sheep have soft wool.

Here are some proper nouns and the adjectives formed from them.

PROPER NOUN	PROPER ADJECTIVE
Africa	African
Canada	Canadian
Egypt	Egyptian
Germany	German
Poland	Polish
Spain	Spanish
Vietnam	Vietnamese

Which sentence includes a proper adjective?

A I eat linguine.

B Pasta is good.

C I like Italian food.

You are right if you said sentence C. *Italian* is a proper adjective. It is formed from the proper noun *Italy*.

EXERCISE 1 In each sentence find the proper adjective. Tell the noun it describes.

1. We tasted Viennese pastries in Austria.
2. I drank Chinese tea.
3. Mexican cocoa is usually made with cinnamon.
4. The Korean national dish is kimchee, pickled cabbage.
5. Yams are popular in Nigerian cooking.

EXERCISE 2 Write the proper adjective for each proper noun. Correctly place the proper adjective in the chart.

Brazil	England	Japan
Britain	Europe	Portugal
Colombia	Greece	Venezuela

-ese	-n	-an	-ian	-ish	Other
_____	_____	_____	_____	_____	_____
_____	_____			_____	

EXERCISE 3 Rewrite each sentence, adding a proper adjective formed from the proper noun in parentheses. Check a dictionary for the correct spellings.

1. The _____ bouzouki looks like a guitar. (Greece)

2. The sitar is the best-known _____ instrument. (India)

3. The _____ didgeridoo looks like a bassoon. (Australia)

4. _____ bagpipes are difficult to play. (Scotland)

5. Some _____ music uses steel drums. (Jamaica)

6. Many _____ musicians play the flute. (Peru)

7. A _____ stringed instrument is the balalaika. (Russia)

8. A _____ storytelling drum is made of hide decorated with designs. (Morocco)

9. Traditional _____ horns can be made of seashells. (Hawaii)

10. Fiddles accompany the polka, a traditional _____ dance. (Poland)

APPLY IT NOW

Imagine that you are planning a trip around the world. Write three or four sentences about the places you'll visit. Use proper adjectives in some of your sentences.
Example: I will go to Ireland and eat some Irish soda bread.

Tech Tip With an adult, research different places online.

4.3 Articles

The articles are *a, an,* and *the.* Articles point out nouns.

- *A* and *an* are **indefinite articles.** They point out any one of a class of people, places, or things.

   a **dollar**   *a* **president**   *an* **engraving**

- Use *a* before a word that begins with a consonant sound. Use *an* before a word that begins with a vowel sound.

   a **quarter**   *a* **uniform**   *an* **hour**   *an* **ancient coin**

- *The* is the **definite article.** It points out a specific person, place, or thing.

   the **plumber**   *the* **San Francisco Mint**   *the* **coffee mug**

Can you find the articles in this sentence? What noun does each point out?

The San Francisco Mint survived an earthquake.

The definite article *the* points out the noun *mint.* The indefinite article *an* points out the noun *earthquake.*

Which one of these sentences uses the definite article?

A **The money we collected is missing.**

B **We put coins in a quart jar.**

C **I have an ancient penny.**

You are right if you said sentence A. *The* is the definite article.

EXERCISE 1 Add the indefinite article *a* or *an* before each noun.

1. _____ nickel
2. _____ eagle
3. _____ dime
4. _____ olive branch
5. _____ eye

6. _____ quarter
7. _____ portrait
8. _____ coin
9. _____ bill
10. _____ invention

EXERCISE 2 Find all the articles in each sentence. Tell the noun each article points out.

1. The first mint in the United States was created in 1792.

2. A man named David Rittenhouse was the director of the mint.

3. The mint's coins were made of gold, silver, or copper.

4. Until 1873 the mint was an independent agency.

5. A mint is now located in each of four cities: Denver, San Francisco, Philadelphia, and Washington, D.C.

6. The mints produce billions of coins a year.

7. A mark on each coin identifies the city where the coin was made.

8. Each coin has an initial on it.

9. The first Lincoln penny was coined in 1909.

10. He was the first president to have his portrait on a coin.

David Rittenhouse

EXERCISE 3 Complete the paragraphs with articles. More than one article may be correct in some sentences.

Look at (1) _____ quarter. What do you see on it? Do you see (2) _____ name of (3) _____ state? In 1999 (4) _____ U.S. Mint started to issue (5) _____ series of quarters with states on them. (6) _____ coins were issued for states in (7) _____ order in which they entered (8) _____ United States.

Many of (9) _____ state coins have (10) _____ following on them: (11) _____ state symbol, (12) _____ famous person from (13) _____ state, or (14) _____ event in (15) _____ history of (16) _____ state.

Grammar in Action What is the third article on page 324? Is it definite or indefinite?

APPLY IT NOW

Think about coins or other things you carry in your pocket or backpack. Write four sentences about these objects. Underline each article you use. Examples: I see a shiny penny. The penny has Lincoln's picture on one side.

4.4 Demonstrative Adjectives

A **demonstrative adjective** points out a specific item or items. The demonstrative adjectives are *this, that, these,* and *those.* They come before nouns.

- *This* and *that* point out one person, place, or thing.
- *These* and *those* point out more than one person, place, or thing.
- *This* and *these* point out items that are near.
- *That* and *those* point out items that are farther away.

Near:	*This* **turkey is big.** (singular)
	These **turkeys are small.** (plural)
Far away:	*That* **turkey seems too big for us.** (singular)
	Those **turkeys seem to be the right size.** (plural)

Which sentence has a demonstrative adjective?

A **The turkey is done.**

B **These mashed potatoes are delicious.**

C **Put some gravy on the turkey.**

You are right if you said sentence B. *These* points to mashed potatoes that are near and plural in form.

EXERCISE 1 Find the demonstrative adjective in each sentence.

1. This letter from Edward Winslow is a record of the first Thanksgiving.
2. These drawings show the colonists at Plymouth.
3. Those colonists shared the first Thanksgiving feast with the Wampanoag Indians.
4. The holiday is somewhat different these days.
5. That tradition of celebration has continued.
6. People ate venison at that first dinner.
7. Nowadays we generally eat turkey for this holiday.
8. Please pass me those sweet potatoes.

EXERCISE 2 Use the correct demonstrative adjective before each noun. Use the word in parentheses to help you choose.

1. _____ tour of Plymouth colony was interesting. (far)

2. Do you want to look at _____ pictures? (near)

3. We learned a lot from _____ guides. (far)

4. _____ ship is a copy of the *Mayflower*. (near)

5. We could walk through _____ tiny compartments. (near)

6. _____ compartments held passengers on the long voyage. (far)

7. _____ village is a copy of the colonists' farmhouses. (far)

8. _____ people are acting the roles of colonists. (near)

9. They are posing with _____ tourists. (far)

10. _____ woman is showing how colonists cooked fish. (far)

11. Native Americans lived in places like _____ large house. (near)

EXERCISE 3 Find the demonstrative adjectives in the sentences. Tell whether each adjective points out something that is singular or plural and the noun the adjective points out.

1. I'll set this table.

2. Let's use that tablecloth.

3. These cranberries are tart.

4. Put some of those vegetables on your plate.

5. May I have a slice of that pumpkin pie?

6. Is there any more of that stuffing?

7. Put those flowers on this table.

8. You should use this vase for those flowers.

APPLY IT NOW

Imagine you have invited a friend over to your home for a snack. Write four sentences that tell about the snack. In each sentence, use a demonstrative adjective and circle it.
Example: These corn muffins are Mom's specialty.

4.5 Adjectives That Tell How Many

Some adjectives tell exactly how many or about how many. They come before nouns.

Exactly how many: *Three* **polar bears were in the den.**

About how many: *Several* **polar bears were in the den.**

Numbers can be used as adjectives to tell exactly how many.

one **iceberg** *three* **zookeepers**

These words can be used as adjectives to tell about how many: *few, many, most, several, some.*

many **zoos** *some* **animals**

Which sentence has an adjective that tells about how many?

A **Polar bears live in the Arctic.**

B **Some polar bears live in zoos.**

C **Polar bears are white.**

You are right if you said sentence B. The adjective *some* tells about how many polar bears. *Some* is not an exact amount.

EXERCISE 1 Add an adjective that tells exactly how many or about how many to each noun. Tell whether the adjective tells exactly how many or about how many.

1. _____ animals
2. _____ bears
3. _____ icebergs
4. _____ trees
5. _____ homes
6. _____ zoos
7. _____ scientists
8. _____ seals

EXERCISE 2 In each sentence find the adjective that tells how many. Does it tell exactly how many or about how many?

1. I have seen many TV programs on polar bears.
2. Polar bear cubs weigh an average of one pound at birth.
3. A mother polar bear usually has two cubs.
4. When the cubs leave the den, each generally weighs 30 pounds.
5. The mother shows the cubs some ways to hunt seals.
6. A polar bear can smell a seal 20 miles away.
7. It takes the cubs a few years to learn how to hunt well.
8. A polar bear may have several sets of cubs in a lifetime.
9. Cubs may live with their mothers for 28 months.
10. Scientists say there are 20,000 polar bears in the world.
11. Most polar bears make their dens on mountains or hills.
12. Some polar bears make their dens in snow on sea ice.

EXERCISE 3 Complete each sentence with an adjective that tells how many. Use the directions in parentheses to help you choose.

1. We saw _____ polar bears at the zoo. (about how many)
2. _____ polar bears were eating. (exactly how many)
3. A polar bear ate _____ fish. (exactly how many)
4. Polar bears are quite an attraction at our zoo, and _____ people visit them daily. (about how many)
5. Polar bears' big paws are like _____ huge paddles. (exactly how many)
6. _____ different kinds of animals are food for polar bears, including seals, fish, and ducks. (about how many)
7. A polar bear's nose lets it smell prey _____ miles away. (about how many)

APPLY IT NOW

Write five sentences about an animal you like. Use adjectives that tell how many in each sentence and underline them.

 With an adult, research your animal online.

4.6 Adjectives as Subject Complements

An adjective that comes after a linking verb acts as a **subject complement.** A subject complement describes the noun or pronoun that is the subject of the sentence.

The most common linking verb is *be* and its various forms: *is, am, are, was,* and *were.*

> **E. B. White *is* famous.**
>
> **His books for children *are* popular.**

Famous and *popular* are adjectives used as subject complements. *Famous* follows the linking verb *is* and describes the subject, *E. B. White. Popular* is an adjective that follows the linking verb *are* and describes the subject, *books.*

Which sentence has an adjective used as a subject complement? What does it tell about?

> A **E. B. White created the character Stuart Little.**
>
> B **Stuart Little was a mouse.**
>
> C **White's characters are likable.**

You are right if you said sentence C. *Likable* is an adjective used as a subject complement that describes *characters. Likable* follows the linking verb *are.* In sentence B the linking verb, *was,* is followed by a noun, *mouse.* The subject complement is a noun.

EXERCISE 1 Find the adjective used as a subject complement in each sentence. Tell the noun the adjective describes.

1. The story is famous.
2. The pig was afraid.
3. Wilbur was small.
4. The spider was friendly.
5. Charlotte was clever.
6. Her webs were delicate.

7. The words in the web were wonderful.

8. People were curious about the words.

9. Wilbur was safe.

10. *Charlotte's Web* is great!

EXERCISE 2 In the sentences find the words used as subject complements. Tell if each is a noun or an adjective.

1. *From the Mixed-Up Files of Mrs. Basil E. Frankweiler* is a novel for young readers.

2. The main character, Claudia, is upset.

3. To Claudia, her parents are not appreciative of her.

4. Claudia and her brother are runaways.

5. The runaways' new home is a museum.

6. At night the museum is empty and quiet.

7. A statue in the museum is beautiful.

8. The story behind the statue is a mystery.

9. Both children are curious about the statue.

10. The plot of the novel is fascinating and complex.

E. B. White at work with his dog in 1955

EXERCISE 3 Complete each sentence with a noun or an adjective used as a subject complement. You may add more than one word to complete the sentence.

1. Computer games can be _____.

2. A grilled cheese sandwich is _____.

3. Amusement parks are _____.

4. My hero is _____.

5. The insect is a _____.

6. Our team was _____.

APPLY IT NOW

Write five sentences about a book you have read and the characters in it. In each sentence use an adjective as a subject complement. Underline the adjective. Include the name of the book.

Tech Tip With an adult, read a review of your book online.

4.7 Adjectives That Compare

Adjectives can be used to make comparisons. To compare two people, places, or things, *-er* may be added to an adjective. To compare three or more people, places, or things, *-est* may be added to an adjective.

Adjective:	November is *cold*.
Compare two things:	December is *colder* than November.
Compare three or more things:	January is the *coldest* month of all.

Find the sentence with an adjective that compares.

A **Ponce de León was an explorer.**

B **Columbus was braver than Ponce de León.**

C **Columbus was an explorer and sailor.**

In sentence B *braver* compares two explorers.

Here are some spelling rules for adding *-er* and *-est*.

- If the adjective ends in *e,* drop the *e* and add the ending.

  safe   safer   safest

- If the adjective ends in *y* following a consonant, change the *y* to *i* and add the ending.

  sunny   sunnier   sunniest

- If the adjective ends in a single consonant following a single vowel, double the consonant and add the ending.

  big   bigger   biggest

Ponce de León

EXERCISE 1 Complete the chart.

Adjective	Compare Two Things	Compare Three or More Things
1. tall	_____	_____
2. scary	_____	_____
3. wide	_____	_____
4. great	_____	_____
5. cute	_____	_____
6. hot	_____	_____
7. dusty	_____	_____
8. fat	_____	_____

EXERCISE 2 Find the adjective that compares in each sentence.

1. Exploration is one of the oldest human activities.
2. Early explorers of the North and South Poles may have been the bravest explorers of all.
3. Their voyages were harder than those of other explorers.
4. The weather is harsher at the poles than in other places.
5. Robert Peary was one of the earliest explorers of the poles.
6. Roald Amundsen was luckier than Robert Scott because he reached the South Pole first.

EXERCISE 3 Choose the correct adjective that compares in each sentence.

1. Antarctica is (larger largest) than Australia.
2. Its area is (smaller smallest) than that of the United States.
3. It is the (windy windiest) of all continents.
4. Antarctica is (colder coldest) than North America.
5. It is also (drier driest) than Africa.

APPLY IT NOW

Find two or three advertisements on TV or in a magazine that use adjectives that compare. Write the sentences in which the adjectives appear. Underline the adjectives.

4.8 Irregular Adjectives That Compare

Some adjectives that compare are not formed by adding -er or -est. They are **irregular adjectives.** Two common irregular adjectives are *good* and *bad*.

ADJECTIVE	COMPARE TWO THINGS	COMPARE THREE OR MORE THINGS
good	better	best
bad	worse	worst

I make *good* muffins.

My dad's muffins are *better* than my muffins.

My big brother makes the *best* muffins of all.

Which sentence uses an irregular comparative adjective?

A **The bakery sells bagels.**

B **This is the best bakery in town.**

C **All the muffins have fruit in them.**

You are right if you said sentence B. *Best* is a form of *good*, and it is used in comparing all the bakeries in the town.

Which choice correctly completes the sentence?

The garlic bagel tastes (worse   worst) than the tomato bagel.

The correct answer is *worse*. It is used to compare two sets of items. Note that *better* and *worse* are often used with *than*.

Which choice correctly completes the sentence?

The apple tarts are the (better best) items in the bakery.

The correct answer is *best*. It compares all the items in the bakery.

EXERCISE 1 Choose the correct adjective to complete each sentence. Use *good, better,* or *best*.

1. I have a _____ idea.

2. Let's see who bakes the _____ banana bread.

3. Jane made _____ banana bread.

4. Mark baked _____ bread than Jane did.

5. These are _____ cranberry scones.

6. I think cranberry scones are _____ than banana bread.

7. We've had a _____ time eating these.

8. Moira's pumpkin muffins are the _____ muffins of all.

EXERCISE 2 Choose the correct adjective to complete each sentence. Use *bad, worse,* or *worst*.

1. My first cooking experience was _____.

2. It was even _____ than my attempt to bake a pie.

3. My cooking left a _____ smell in the kitchen.

4. Mom said it was the _____ odor ever in her kitchen.

5. I think my cooking is _____ than that of my little brother.

6. The results of my cooking are the _____ eating experience a person can have.

EXERCISE 3 Choose the correct adjective that compares in each sentence.

1. My friend's oatmeal raisin cookies were the (best better worse) I ever tasted.

2. She gave me this (good worse better) recipe for them.

3. My brother said that my second batch of cookies was (worse good worst) than my first batch.

4. My grandmother thought that both batches of cookies were very (good best worst).

5. I think that the cookies were even (good better best) than mom's cookies.

Yum!

APPLY IT NOW

Think of your favorite and least favorite foods. Write six sentences about those foods. Use *good, better, best, bad, worse,* and *worst.*
Example: I think peas taste better than beans.

Grammar in Action. What is the first adjective used to compare on page 324? What two objects are being compared?

4.9 *More, Most*

Some adjectives that compare use *more* and *most*. Usually, these adjectives are longer than the adjectives that use *-er* and *-est*. *More* is used in comparing two things. *Most* is used in comparing three or more things.

ADJECTIVE	COMPARE TWO THINGS	COMPARE THREE OR MORE THINGS
dishonest	more dishonest	most dishonest
intelligent	more intelligent	most intelligent

- Use *more* or *most* with adjectives of three or more syllables.

  This is a *popular* exhibit.

  Snakes are usually *more popular* than birds.

  The bat house is our *most popular* exhibit this year.

- Use *more* or *most* with some two-syllable adjectives.

  It's quite *humid* today.

  Today is *more humid* than yesterday.

  August is the *most humid* month of the year.

Check a dictionary if you are unsure of how the comparative forms of an adjective are formed—by adding *-er* and *-est* or by using *more* and *most*.

Which choice correctly completes the sentence?

I think that a rain forest is (more beneficial most beneficial) than a coral reef.

You are correct if you chose *more beneficial.* The word *beneficial* has more than two syllables, two items are being compared, and *than* is used in the comparison.

EXERCISE 1 Find the adjectives that compare in each sentence.

1. The most extensive rain forests are in South America.
2. The plants and animals of the tropical rain forests are more diverse than those of any other ecosystem.
3. Evergreen trees are more common than any other trees.
4. Insects are the most numerous species.
5. I think that the animals and plants of the rain forest are more beautiful than those in other ecosystems.
6. Parrots and butterflies are among the most colorful animals.
7. Some of the most important rain-forest products are chocolate and spices.
8. A rain-forest plant, the periwinkle, produces one of the most powerful drugs for cancer.

EXERCISE 2 Choose the correct adjective that compares to complete each sentence.

1. Preserving the rain forest has become (more critical   most critical) than ever before.
2. This is one of our (more serious   most serious) problems.
3. Rain forests are (more important   most important) than people may think: they produce much of our oxygen.
4. Rain-forest plants are among the (more useful   most useful) plants because of their medicinal value.
5. The (more common   most common) animals in the rain forest are insects.
6. We should be (more careful   most careful) with the earth's resources than we have been.
7. The temperature in a rain forest is (more stable   most stable) than in other ecosystems.
8. Some scientists think that rain forests are the (more ancient   most ancient) ecosystems.
9. Saving the rain forest may be humans' (most urgent   more urgent) task.

APPLY IT NOW

Write three sentences using these adjectives: *interesting, beautiful, important*. Add *more* or *most* to each.

4.10 *Fewer, Fewest and Less, Least*

Fewer, fewest, less, and *least* are used in comparing things. Use *fewer* and *fewest* with plural nouns that you can see, touch, and count: *players, games, children.*

Use *less* and *least* with plural nouns that generally cannot be seen, touched, and counted: *health, teamwork, patience.*

In these sentences *fewer* and *fewest* are used with the plural noun *sports.*

> **That park offers *fewer* sports than the one nearby.**
> **This park offers the *fewest* sports of all the city parks.**

In these sentences *less* and *least* are used with the noun *progress.*

> **We made *less* progress than the other team.**
> **We made the *least* progress of any team.**

Which choice correctly completes the sentence?

> **(Fewer Less) students tried out for the team this year.**

You are right if you said *fewer. Students* is a plural noun that you can see, touch, and count, and so *fewer* is the correct choice.

EXERCISE 1 Decide if each noun can be seen, touched, and counted.

1. baseball	6. pride
2. health	7. uniform
3. ballpark	8. responsibility
4. league	9. score
5. pitcher	10. children

EXERCISE 2 Decide if each noun can be seen, touched, and counted. Then write phrases to show whether you should use *fewer, fewest, less,* or *least* with each noun.

EXAMPLE: **locker**   yes   **fewer lockers, fewest lockers**

Noun	Can you see, touch, and count it?	Fewer, Fewest or Less, Least?
1. excitement	_____	_____
2. cloud	_____	_____
3. bat	_____	_____
4. humidity	_____	_____
5. ticket	_____	_____
6. energy	_____	_____
7. coach	_____	_____
8. knowledge	_____	_____

EXERCISE 3 Choose the correct word to complete each sentence.

1. Our team has won (fewer less) games this year than last year.

2. However, the team across town still had the (fewest least) support in our league.

3. We have (fewer less) good hitters this year than last.

4. We have had (fewer less) time for practice this year.

5. There was (fewer less) rain last year than this year.

6. We've scored (fewer less) runs this year.

7. In fact, we've scored the (fewest least) runs of all the teams in the league.

8. Our best pitcher, Sophia, has allowed the (fewest least) hits of all the pitchers in the league.

APPLY IT NOW

Imagine that you are at a sporting event. Using that as your topic, write four sentences using *fewer, fewest, less,* and *least.*

4.11 Position of Adjectives

Many adjectives come before nouns. Adjectives used as subject complements, however, come after the nouns they describe. These adjectives come after linking verbs, such as the verb *be* and its various forms.

The *tiny* **puppy trembled.** (before noun)

The puppy was *tiny*. (after linking verb)

In the first sentence, the adjective *tiny* comes before the noun *puppy*. In the second sentence, the adjective *tiny* comes after the linking verb *was*. *Tiny* describes the subject *puppy*. *Tiny* is a subject complement.

In which sentence does the adjective come after the noun it describes?

A **Animals can have unusual defenses.**

B **Some jellyfish are poisonous.**

C **Snakes in the rain forest use their green skin as camouflage to hide among the trees.**

You are correct if you chose sentence B. The adjective *poisonous* follows the linking verb *are*. *Poisonous* describes the subject, *jellyfish*.

In sentence A the adjective *unusual* comes before the noun *defenses*. In sentence C the adjective *green* comes before the noun *skin*.

EXERCISE 1 Tell the position of each italicized adjective—before a noun or as a subject complement.

1. Many animals have *effective* defenses.

2. Some defenses are rather *common*.

3. Some animals have or produce *bad* smells.

4. A skunk's smell, for example, can be *unpleasant* to enemies.

5. Some kinds of animals graze in *large* numbers.

EXERCISE 2 Find the descriptive adjectives in the sentences. Tell whether the adjective comes before a noun or whether it is a subject complement.

1. The frightened octopus is defending itself.
2. Its long tentacles spread out.
3. A scared turtle hides in its hard shell.
4. Its shell is protective.
5. The amazing porcupinefish is spiny.
6. Its spines make it an unattractive meal.
7. Stingrays have sharp barbs on their tails.
8. They flick their long tails to scare away enemies.
9. A defense of some geckos is special.
10. Their tails are helpful because they can drop off to distract a nearby enemy.

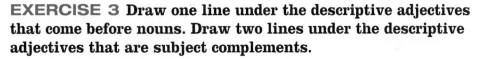

EXERCISE 3 Draw one line under the descriptive adjectives that come before nouns. Draw two lines under the descriptive adjectives that are subject complements.

Snakes are reptiles. Reptiles include turtles, alligators, crocodiles, and lizards. Snakes are legless. A snake has scaly skin. Its shiny skin is actually dry. Several times a year, snakes shed their skin by rubbing it against a rough surface. Its body is flexible and can roll into a ball. It has a narrow, forked tongue. The eggs of snakes are soft and fragile. Most snakes are harmless, though a few are poisonous.

Snakes have defenses besides poison. The color of snakes' skins helps them hide. For example, snakes that live on the ground are brown or gray, while snakes that live in trees are green. Some poisonous snakes are bright to warn away enemies. Only hungry or frightened snakes actually go on the attack.

APPLY IT NOW

Write four sentences to tell about animals that live in your neighborhood. Use adjectives that come before nouns and adjectives that are used as subject complements. Then underline the adjectives.
Example: The dog's sharp teeth showed as it snarled. The dog's bark was loud.

Adjective Review

4.1 Find the descriptive adjective in each sentence. Tell the noun the adjective describes.

1. Many hyenas have dark stripes on their fur.
2. Hyenas are intelligent animals.
3. They use clever methods in hunting.

4.2 Find the proper adjective in each sentence. Tell the noun the proper adjective describes.

4. The Canadian skier won a gold metal.
5. The Olympic pool was the site of exciting swimming races.
6. The Chinese diver performed difficult dives.

4.3 Find the article in each sentence. Name the noun the article points out.

7. In 1906 an earthquake destroyed San Francisco.
8. Many of the city's buildings were destroyed.
9. A fire broke out because of damaged electric lines and broken gas mains.
10. About two-thirds of the population was left homeless.

4.4 Find the demonstrative adjective in each sentence. Tell whether the noun the adjective points out is near or far.

11. Can you bring those groceries into the house?
12. These bags of groceries are heavy.
13. That gallon of milk needs to be refrigerated.

4.5 Find the adjective that tells how many in each sentence. Does the adjective tell about how many or exactly how many?

14. We noticed five whales swimming next to our boat.
15. The pod, or group, followed us for many hours.
16. Killer whales can live for several decades.
17. Some species of whales are endangered.

4.6 Find the adjective used as a subject complement in each sentence. Tell the noun the adjective describes.

18. The dog is friendly.
19. His behavior is good.
20. After visiting the groomer, the dog's coat is shiny.
21. The owner is proud of her dog's appearance.

4.7 Complete each sentence with an adjective that compares. Use the adjective in parentheses.

22. Mexico is _____ than Ireland. (sunny)

23. A town in Libya hit the _____ temperature ever in 1922. (high)

24. The _____ place in the world is Mawsynram, India. (wet)

25. The Sudan is much _____ than Seattle. (dry)

4.8 Choose the correct adjective to complete each sentence.

26. Alma is a (good best) artist.

27. She draws (good better) pictures than I do.

28. Zachary told me he was the (bad worst) painter in class.

29. I think I paint (worst worse) than he does.

4.9 Choose the correct adjective that compares to complete each sentence.

30. The (more delicious most delicious) dessert on the menu is pumpkin bread pudding.

31. It is (more delicious most delicious) than the fruit tart.

32. The mixed berries are a (more popular most popular) choice than the carrot cake.

4.10 Choose the correct word to complete each sentence.

33. Ms. Parker's class has (fewer less) students than Ms. Berkley's.

34. Mr. Patel's class has the (fewest least) pupils.

35. Because the students had read the directions, there was (fewer less) confusion with the assignment.

36. The purple group made the (fewest least) progress on the project today.

4.11 Find the descriptive adjective in each sentence. Tell if it comes before a noun or if it is a subject complement.

37. The pigs were fearful of the wolf.

38. The big wolf frightened the pigs.

39. The wolf blew the weak houses down.

40. Even the powerful wolf could not destroy the house of brick.

Go to www.voyagesinenglish.com for more activities.

Adjective Challenge

Read the paragraphs and answer the questions.

1. A beaver is a furry animal that has a wide, flat tail. 2. North American beavers use their strong teeth to cut down and eat trees. 3. Are they the busiest of all animals? 4. Many observers think so.

5. The beaver's tail is one of its most interesting features. 6. Its tail is quite big. 7. It can be 12 inches long, six inches wide, and about one inch thick. 8. A beaver's tail has scaly skin. 9. Beavers use their tails to steer when they swim, to send a warning message when they are frightened, and to prop themselves up when they eat.

10. These animals are not welcome in some places. 11. Beaver dams can sometimes block the flow of streams. 12. Some farmers say that they cause flooding and wish that there were fewer beavers.

1. In sentence 1 name all the adjectives.

2. In sentence 2 find a proper adjective.

3. In sentence 3 what is the adjective that compares?

4. In sentence 4 does *many* tell exactly how many or about how many?

5. In sentence 5 what is the adjective that compares?

6. In sentence 6 what is the descriptive adjective? Does it come before a noun, or is it a subject complement?

7. In sentence 8 what is the article? Is it definite or indefinite?

8. In sentence 8 what is the descriptive adjective? Does it come before a noun, or is it a subject complement?

9. In sentence 10 find a demonstrative adjective.

10. In sentence 11 find the noun used as an adjective.

11. In sentence 12 find the adjective that tells how many. Does it tell about or exactly how many?

12. In sentence 12 find the adjective that compares.

Verbs

5.1 Action Verbs

5.2 Being Verbs

5.3 Linking Verbs

5.4 Helping Verbs

5.5 Verb Phrases

5.6 Principal Parts of Verbs

5.7 Irregular Verbs

5.8 More Irregular Verbs

5.9 Simple Present Tense

5.10 Simple Past Tense

5.11 Future Tenses

5.12 Progressive Tenses

5.13 Present Perfect Tense

5.14 Past Perfect Tense

5.15 Future Perfect Tense

5.16 Subject-Verb Agreement

5.17 *There Is* and *There Are*

Verb Review

Verb Challenge

5.1 Action Verbs

Many verbs express action. **An action verb tells what someone or something does.**

> **Aesop *wrote* many fables.**
>
> **His fables *teach* lessons.**

Wrote and *teach* are action verbs. *Wrote* tells what Aesop did. *Teach* tells what the fables do.

Here are some more action verbs.

bring	eat	talk
brush	give	throw
copy	laugh	touch
draw	sing	watch
drive	stir	write

Which sentences have action verbs?

A **The students read books of folktales.**

B **The students are in the library.**

C **The students talk about the books.**

You are right if you said sentences A and C. *Read* and *talk* are both action verbs that tell what the students do.

EXERCISE 1 Find the action verb in each sentence.

1. In one fable by Aesop, a fox fell into a deep well.
2. The fox shouted for help.
3. A goat walked by.
4. It heard the fox's shout.
5. The fox told the goat about the cool water in the well.
6. The goat jumped into the well for water.

7. The fox climbed onto the goat's back.

8. The fox then scrambled out of the well.

9. The goat stayed in the well.

10. In this way the fox tricked the goat.

EXERCISE 2 Complete the sentences with action verbs from the list.

invited	left	prevented	put	tried
served	tricked	returned	visited	went

1. A stork _____ a new town.

2. A fox _____ the stork to dinner.

3. The fox _____ the stork a dish of soup on a flat plate.

4. The stork's long beak _____ it from eating the soup.

5. The stork _____ away hungry.

6. One day the stork _____ the fox's invitation.

7. The stork _____ the food in a container with a long neck.

8. The fox _____ to get at the food, but it was unsuccessful.

9. The fox _____ the stork's house hungry.

10. So the stork _____ the fox in the same way.

EXERCISE 3 Complete each sentence, using an action verb.

1. A slimy worm _____ up my arm.

2. Who _____ the salad?

3. The herons _____ on the beach.

4. Jerome _____ the paper dragon.

5. Terrance _____ the cellar door.

APPLY IT NOW

Write a sentence for each noun below, using an action verb.

Example: trucks
Trucks rumble down the highway.

1. pilot   4. worm
2. wind   5. artist
3. waves   6. dog

Grammar in Action.

What is the first action verb on page 363?

5.2 Being Verbs

Not all verbs show action. **A being verb shows what someone or something is.**

ACTION VERBS

The sun *shines*.
The earth *revolves* around the sun.

BEING VERBS

The sun's rays *are* warm.
Too much sun *is* dangerous.

The action verbs *shines* and *revolves* tell what the sun and the earth do. *Are* and *is* are being verbs. They do not express action; they simply tell something about what the rays and the sun are.

Here is a list of some being verbs.

am	was	had been
is	were	have been
are	has been	will be

Which sentence has a being verb?

A The sun sets at 8:00 p.m.
B The sunset is beautiful.
C The sun rises in the east.

You are right if you said sentence B. The verb *is* is a being verb.

EXERCISE 1 Find the being verb in each sentence.

1. Sunset is a lovely time of day.
2. The colors of the sunset are reds, oranges, and yellows.
3. Last night at sunset we were on a high balcony.
4. The sunsets have been colorful this week.
5. Tomorrow the sunset will be at 8:15 p.m.

EXERCISE 2 Find the verb in each sentence. Tell whether the verb is an action verb or a being verb.

1. Our teacher told us many things about astronomy.
2. The information was extremely interesting.
3. Hot stars send off a blue glow.
4. Red is the color of cooler stars.
5. Yellow stars are in between blue and red.
6. A smaller star is a dwarf.
7. Our sun is a yellow dwarf.
8. Scientists study the sun to learn more about the stars.
9. The sun is our major source of light and energy.
10. Hot gases form the sun.
11. The sun is huge compared to the earth.
12. The temperature of the sun is 10 million degrees at its core.
13. My science report gives many details about the sun.
14. I am interested in facts about the sun.

EXERCISE 3 Complete each sentence, using a being verb from the list on page 108.

1. The sun _____ hot today.
2. I _____ in the sun too long.
3. My skin _____ reddish.
4. I _____ uncomfortable.
5. I _____ more careful in the future about staying in the sun.
6. Sunscreen _____ a good protection from the sun.
7. The ultraviolet rays of the sun _____ harmful.
8. A tan _____ a sign of damage to your skin.

APPLY IT NOW

Write about the place you are in now or a place where you have been or will be. Describe it in four sentences, using being verbs.
Examples: I have been to the library today. The library was very quiet.

5.3 Linking Verbs

A being verb can be a linking verb. A **linking verb** joins the subject of a sentence to a subject complement. The subject complement renames or describes the subject of the sentence. The subject complement can be a noun, a pronoun, or an adjective.

SUBJECT	LINKING VERB	SUBJECT COMPLEMENT
The pretzels	*are*	**a snack.** (noun)
The person who brought pretzels	*was*	**she.** (pronoun)
A pretzel	*is*	**salty.** (adjective)

In the first sentence, the linking verb *are* joins the subject *pretzels* with the noun *snack*. In the second sentence, the subject *person* and the pronoun *she* are joined by the linking verb *was*. In the third sentence, the linking verb *is* joins the subject *pretzel* with the adjective *salty*. *Snack, she,* and *salty* are subject complements.

Which sentences have linking verbs?

A **The pretzel was delicious.**

B **The person who ate the last pretzel was he.**

C **Charlie ate the pretzel.**

You are correct if you said sentences A and B. Both sentences have the linking verb *was*. In sentence A *was* is followed by an adjective. In sentence B *was* is followed by a pronoun.

Mmmm . . . tasty!

EXERCISE 1 Find the linking verb and the subject complement in each sentence.

1. Pretzels are popular.

2. Pretzels are soft or hard.

3. Some hard pretzels are sticks.

4. These pretzels are straight.

5. A covering on some pretzels is yogurt.

6. Chocolate is a covering for other pretzels.

7. The pretzel is a breakfast food in parts of Germany.

8. The center for pretzel making in the United States was Pennsylvania.

EXERCISE 2 The linking verb in each sentence is in italics. Find the subject complement or subject complements that are linked to the subject. Tell whether the subject complement is a noun, a pronoun, or an adjective.

1. Pretzels *are* a traditional snack.

2. A monk *was* the inventor of the pretzel.

3. The first pretzel *was* leftover bread dough.

4. Its shape, like arms folded, *was* special.

5. Germany *was* the first home of the pretzel.

6. The first pretzels *were* soft.

7. Hard pretzels *were* originally a mistake by a baker.

8. The person who cooked the pretzels too long *was* he.

9. People, however, *were* delighted.

10. The new pretzels *were* tasty and crunchy.

EXERCISE 3 Complete each sentence with a linking verb that makes sense. Choose from the list of being verbs on page 108.

1. Pretzel baking _____ an art.

2. The first pretzels _____ handmade.

3. In 1879 two men _____ the first people to make a machine to twist pretzels.

4. I _____ a pretzel fan.

5. The bag _____ now empty!

6. Pretzels _____ popular for a long time to come.

APPLY IT NOW

Choose a food listed below. Write three sentences about it. Use a linking verb in each sentence.

waffles   tacos
sandwiches   fruit salad

Example: Sandwiches are my favorite meal.

5.4 Helping Verbs

A verb can have two parts—a **helping verb** and a main verb. A helping verb always comes before another verb.

Here are some helping verbs.

am	was	do	has	will	could
is	were	did	have	would	should
are	had	can	must		

Study how helping verbs are used in these sentences.

WITHOUT A HELPING VERB

The children *play* jacks.

WITH A HELPING VERB

The children *can* play jacks.

The children *should* learn the rules of jacks.

The children *are* learning the game of jacks.

I *have* played jacks with Mom.

Which of these sentences does not have a helping verb?

  A I will teach you the game.

  B Jessie should bounce the ball.

  C She grabbed two jacks.

You are right if you said sentence C. In sentence A *will* is a helping verb that goes with the verb *teach*. In sentence B *should* is a helping verb that goes with the verb *bounce*.

EXERCISE 1 Find the helping verb in each sentence.

1. Mom and Dad had played jacks as children.

2. We can try several games.

3. Mom was explaining how to play onesies.

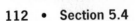

4. The jacks are scattered on the floor.

5. A ball is tossed in the air.

6. The ball may bounce once.

7. The player must grab a jack.

8. A player should catch the ball in the same hand.

EXERCISE 2 Tell whether the verb in italics in each sentence is a helping verb or a linking verb.

1. Jacks *are* fun.

2. Amanda's jacks *were* colorful.

3. We *are* making our own rules.

4. I *will* bounce the ball high in the air.

5. She *has* missed one jack.

6. The last jack *is* purple.

7. Cal *should* grab that jack.

8. We *can* play again.

EXERCISE 3 Underline the main verb in each sentence. Then complete the sentences with a helping verb. More than one helping verb may be correct.

1. I _____ play marbles well.

2. I _____ know how to play jacks.

3. You _____ have 10 jacks and a ball for the game.

4. I _____ win at jacks with more practice.

5. My friends _____ practicing jacks together.

6. You _____ find a flat surface for the game.

7. In the past, stones _____ be the jacks.

APPLY IT NOW

Write four sentences about what you like to do on the weekends. Use a helping verb in each sentence.
Example: I have played soccer.

Grammar in Action
What is the first helping verb in the excerpt on page 369?

5.5 Verb Phrases

A **verb phrase** is made up of one or more helping verbs and a main verb.

Helping verbs: I *should have* given you the funny cartoon.

Main verb: I should have *given* you the funny cartoon.

Verb phrase: I *should have given* you the funny cartoon.

What is the verb phrase in this sentence?

The cartoonist can draw funny characters.

A **can**

B **can draw**

C **draw**

You are right if you said B. *Can draw* is the verb phrase. It is made up of the helping verb *can* and the main verb *draw.* A has only the helping verb *can,* and C has only the main verb *draw.*

Can you find the verb phrase in this sentence?

The newspaper will be delivered before 7:00 a.m.

You are correct if you said *will be delivered. Will* and *be* are helping verbs, and *delivered* is the main verb. *Be, been,* and *being* can be helping verbs that follow other helping verbs in verb phrases.

EXERCISE 1 Find the helping verb or verbs and the main verb in each sentence.

1. I am reading a book of *Peanuts* cartoons.
2. Charles Schulz's cartoons have become world famous.
3. Schulz's family had been given a dog.
4. That dog would inspire Schulz's most famous character.
5. The cartoon dog would be given the name Snoopy.
6. An early sketch by the young Schulz was printed in a local paper.
7. Schulz was paid little money for his first efforts.
8. Since then his comic strip has appeared in some 2,600 newspapers.
9. Charlie Brown was called the hero of losers.
10. But people have found Charlie very sympathetic.
11. Linus would carry a blanket with him everywhere.
12. Schulz had put his own experiences into his strip.
13. Schulz's last Peanuts strip was drawn in 2000.
14. You can find many of his cartoons in books.

EXERCISE 2 Add a helping verb to complete the verb phrase in each sentence. Identify the complete verb phrase you form.

1. I _____ bought a book with cartoons this morning.
2. You _____ read it when I finish.
3. Marie _____ share her book with me.
4. We _____ laughing about this cartoon.
5. The dog in the cartoon _____ writing a novel.
6. Riley _____ show us a funny cartoon.
7. You _____ go to the library to find books of cartoons.
8. I _____ drawing my own cartoons.

Charles Schulz

APPLY IT NOW

Think of a book series you enjoy reading. Write four sentences about the series. Use a verb phrase in each sentence.
Example: I have read the Mary Pope Osborne books.

5.6 Principal Parts of Verbs

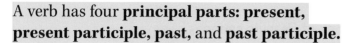

A verb has four **principal parts: present, present participle, past,** and **past participle.**

PRESENT	PRESENT PARTICIPLE	PAST	PAST PARTICIPLE
play	playing	played	played
learn	learning	learned	learned
bake	baking	baked	baked

- The present participle is formed by adding *-ing* to the present. The present participle is often used with a form of the helping verb *be* (*am, is, are, was,* and *were*).

   Some artists *paint* **outdoors.** (present)
   The artist is *painting* **flowers.** (present participle)

- The past and the past participle are formed by adding *-d* or *-ed* to the present. The past participle is often used with the helping verb *has, have,* or *had.*

   The artist *painted* **flowers.** (past)
   The artist has *painted* **flowers.** (past participle)

- To form the present participle of verbs ending in *e*, drop the final *e* and add *-ing: use + ing = using.*
- To form the present or past participle of a verb ending in a consonant following a vowel, double the consonant before adding *-ing* or *-ed: plug + ing = plugging, tag + ed = tagged.*

EXERCISE 1 Tell whether the verb in italics is the present, present participle, past, or past participle part of the verb. Look for forms of the verb *be* before present participles and *has, have,* or *had* before past participles.

1. The painter *sketched* the man's wrinkled face.
2. Veronica had *posed* for a portrait.
3. A sculptor *molds* clay.
4. Some artists *work* with metal.

5. That student is *painting* with watercolors.

6. Jason had *used* pastels in the drawing of the lily.

7. She is *using* charcoal for her sketch of the park.

8. Lucy *prepared* the canvas.

EXERCISE 2 Complete the chart with the correct parts of the verbs.

PRESENT	PRESENT PARTICIPLE	PAST	PAST PARTICIPLE
			enjoyed
	practicing		
clap			
		hummed	

EXERCISE 3 Complete each sentence with the form of the verb in parentheses.

1. We always _____ the local art fair. (visit—present)

2. Artists are _____ their works. (show—present participle)

3. Li is _____ an artist paint. (watch—present participle)

4. Li _____ a lot by watching the painter. (learn—past)

5. That artist has _____ an original style. (develop—past participle)

6. The judges _____ him first prize. (award—past)

APPLY IT NOW

Choose a verb from Exercises 2 or 3. Use the verb in four sentences. In each sentence use a different principal part of the verb: present, present participle, past, or past participle. Tell which part is used in the sentences.

5.7 Irregular Verbs

The past and the past participle of a regular verb end in *d* or *ed*. The past and the past participle of an **irregular verb** are not formed this way.

Begin, bring, do, and *know* are irregular verbs. The chart shows the principal parts of these irregular verbs. Remember that the present participle and the past participle are often used with a helping verb.

PRESENT	PRESENT PARTICIPLE	PAST	PAST PARTICIPLE
begin	beginning	began	begun
bring	bringing	brought	brought
do	doing	did	done
know	knowing	knew	known

We *begin* class at 8:30. (present)

We *are beginning* now. (present participle—with the helping verb *are*)

We *began* class at 9:30 yesterday. (past)

We *have begun* class at 8:30 today. (past participle—with the helping verb *have*)

Which word correctly completes the sentence?

Justin (begin   begins) class at 8:00.

You are right if you said *begins.* For the present with a singular noun subject or the pronouns *he, she,* and *it,* use the present form ending in *s.* Note that *does* is the present form of *do* used with singular subjects and the pronouns *he, she,* and *it.*

EXERCISE 1 Complete each sentence with the correct part of *begin.*

1. The class _____ the lesson on gravity last week.
2. The teacher _____ class as soon as the bell rings.
3. We are _____ to understand the concepts.
4. I have _____ my experiment on gravity already.

EXERCISE 2 Complete each sentence with the correct part of *bring.*

1. I have _____ feathers for our experiment.
2. We always _____ a clipboard with paper to the science area.
3. I am _____ my record sheet with me to record the results.
4. Ariane always _____ her science notebook with her.

Galileo

EXERCISE 3 Complete each sentence with the correct part of *do.*

1. The class is _____ an experiment on gravity.
2. We _____ the steps very carefully yesterday.
3. We have _____ the same things today.
4. We always _____ our experiments thoroughly and follow the steps exactly.

EXERCISE 4 Complete each sentence with the correct part of *know.*

1. Martina had _____ a lot about gravity before studying it in class.
2. We plan to work together on a project, and she _____ about a gravity experiment with a ramp.
3. My brother _____ about Galileo's experiment on gravity before he studied it in sixth grade.
4. I now _____ something about gravity too.

APPLY IT NOW

Choose one of the words *begin, bring, do,* or *know.* Write four sentences. Use a different part of the verb in each sentence.

5.8 More Irregular Verbs

Choose, buy, break, and *teach* are **irregular verbs.** The chart shows the principal parts of these verbs.

PRESENT	PRESENT PARTICIPLE	PAST	PAST PARTICIPLE
choose	choosing	chose	chosen
buy	buying	bought	bought
break	breaking	broke	broken
teach	teaching	taught	taught

We generally *choose* seats in the front. (present)

We *are choosing* our seats. (present participle— with the helping verb *are*)

We *chose* our seats. (past)

We have *chosen* our seats. (past participle— with the helping verb *have*)

Which form of the verb correctly completes the sentence?

Have you ever (broke   broken   break) a dish?

You are right if you chose *broken.* The past participle form is needed with the helping verb *have.*

EXERCISE 1 Complete each sentence with the correct part of *choose*.

1. Chloe _____ pink socks to match her shirt.
2. The coaches are _____ players.
3. I have _____ a new book from the library.
4. I never _____ to do dishes if I can do another chore.
5. Last night I _____ to vacuum the rug.

EXERCISE 2 Complete each sentence with the correct part of *buy*.

1. I am _____ Diana a gift for her birthday.
2. My mom has _____ decorations for the party.
3. Mom usually _____ balloons for our parties.
4. She _____ the ingredients for a cake yesterday.

EXERCISE 3 Complete each sentence with the correct part of *break*.

1. Tyrone _____ his arm last week.
2. He had _____ his toe last year.
3. He is _____ lots of things because he can use only one arm.
4. He said he has _____ a vase at home.

EXERCISE 4 Complete each sentence with the correct part of *teach*.

1. My mother is _____ me chess.
2. At first she _____ me the names of the pieces.
3. She already has _____ me the basic rules.
4. She and my father are also _____ me backgammon.
5. My aunt _____ chess at the local park.

Ugh! Dishes again?

APPLY IT NOW

Choose one of the words *break, buy, choose,* or *teach*. Write four sentences. Use a different part of the verb in each sentence.

5.9 Simple Present Tense

The tense of a verb shows when an action or a state of being takes place. A verb in the **simple present tense** tells about something that is always true or about an action that happens again and again.

> **Whales** *swim* **in the ocean.**
> **Whales** *eat* **fish.**
> **A whale** *leaps* **from the water.**

The verbs *swim, eat,* and *leaps* are in the simple present tense. These verbs tell things that are true about whales. The verbs tell about actions a whale does again and again.

A verb in the simple present tense ends in *s* when the subject is a singular noun or the pronoun *he, she,* or *it.* A verb in the simple present tense does not end in *s* when the subject is plural. Which sentence is in the simple present tense?

> A **Amy always watches for whales at the aquarium.**
> B **I saw a whale at the aquarium.**

You are right if you said sentence A. *Watches* is in the simple present tense. Sentence B tells about something that took place in the past.

EXERCISE 1 Identify the subject in each sentence and tell if it is singular or plural. Then complete the sentence with the correct verb in parentheses.

1. Dolphins (perform performs) in a show at the aquarium.
2. The auditorium quickly (fill fills) up with people.
3. Spectators (watch watches) the dolphins leaping.
4. Visitors in the first rows often (get gets) wet.
5. Trainers (teach teaches) the dolphins tricks.

EXERCISE 2 Complete each sentence with the correct verb in parentheses.

1. Bottlenose dolphins (live lives) in groups called pods.
2. A calf (stay stays) with its mother for three to six years.
3. Dolphins (jump jumps) up to 16 feet in the air.
4. A bottlenose dolphin ordinarily (swim swims) at speeds of 3 to 7 miles per hour.
5. Every so often its usual speed (increase increases).
6. Scientists (record records) dolphin speed at up to 22 miles per hour.
7. Adults (range ranges) in length from 7 to 11 feet.
8. An adult (weigh weighs) between 600 and 850 pounds.
9. The Hawaiian Islands (provide provides) a home to many dolphins.
10. Their playfulness (make makes) bottlenose dolphins popular in aquarium shows.

EXERCISE 3 Complete each sentence with the verb in parentheses. Use the simple present tense.

1. Dolphins _____ through the water. (slide)
2. A powerful tail fin _____ a dolphin. (propel)
3. This fin _____ up and down. (move)
4. A dolphin _____ through a blowhole. (breathe)
5. It _____ its breath while under water. (hold)
6. A dolphin's dive _____ up to 10 minutes. (last)
7. Pollution _____ dolphins. (harm)
8. Oceans _____ a home for most dolphins. (provide)

APPLY IT NOW

Write five sentences about a dolphin or another animal you are interested in. Use the simple present tense in your sentences.

Tech Tip With an adult, research the animal online.

5.10 Simple Past Tense

A verb in the **simple past tense** tells about something that happened in the past.

> **Dinosaurs *lived* thousands of years ago.**
> **Last year we *studied* about dinosaurs.**
> **The teacher *showed* a video about *T. rex*.**

The verbs *lived, studied,* and *showed* are in the simple past.

Most past tense verbs end in *ed*. Remember that irregular verbs in the past do not end in *ed*.

> **We *discussed* dinosaurs in class.** (regular verb)
> **I *read* a book on dinosaurs last year.** (irregular verb)

Here are some spelling rules for *ed* endings.

- If a verb ends in *e*, just add *-d: name + d = named.*
- If a verb ends in *y* following a consonant, change the *y* to *i* and add *-ed: try + ed = tried.*
- If a verb ends in a consonant following a vowel, double the consonant and add the ending: *wrap + ed = wrapped.*

Which sentence shows the simple past tense?

> A **The class is learning about fossils.**
> B **We learn about fossils in science.**
> C **We learned about dinosaur fossils.**

You are right if you said sentence C. The *ed* ending on *learned* indicates a past action.

T. rex

EXERCISE 1 Find the verb in the simple past tense in each sentence.

1. Titanosaurs lived at the end of the age of dinosaurs.
2. Some grew to a large size.
3. Hard plates covered the backs of the Titanosaurs.
4. These big animals probably ate several tons of food a day.
5. Few fossils of Titanosaurs survived through time.

Alamosaurus, a type of Titanosaur

EXERCISE 2 Write the simple past tense of each verb. Some verbs are irregular. Check a dictionary if you need help.

1. sing
2. chew
3. stomp
4. serve
5. growl

6. smell
7. grab
8. dry
9. blow
10. walk

EXERCISE 3 Complete each sentence with the verb in parentheses. Use the simple past tense.

1. Dinosaurs _____ out about 65 million years ago. (die)
2. Paleontologists recently _____ a Titanosaur skull and skeleton together. (find)
3. Most skulls _____ over millions of years. (disappear)
4. The scientists _____ carefully to remove this rare fossil from the ground. (work)
5. Titanosaurs _____ plants. (eat)
6. They _____ to the group of dinosaurs called sauropods. (belong)
7. They _____ long necks. (have)
8. Scientists also _____ Titanosaur eggs. (discover)

APPLY IT NOW

Write five sentences about what you did yesterday. Use the simple past tense in each sentence.

5.11 Future Tenses

The word *will* and the phrase *going to* are ways to express something that will take place in the future. Both forms are used to talk about predictions and to express the **future tense.**

> **Many families *will donate* food to the food pantry.**
>
> **The supermarket *is going to be* busy tomorrow.**

The helping verb *will* is used with the present to form a future tense; for example, *will + help = will help.* The helping verb *will* is often used when someone agrees to do something soon.

> **I *will go* to the supermarket with my parents.**

When the future is expressed with *going to,* the verb *am, is,* or *are* precedes *going to,* which is followed by the present form of the verb; for example, *is + going to + make = is going to make.* The form *going to* is often used when someone wishes to express an action that has already been planned.

> **He *is going to buy* canned goods.**

Which sentence expresses the future?

> A **Sam's family helps out at the food pantry.**
>
> B **Sam bought cereal at the supermarket.**
>
> C **Sam will donate boxes of cereal.**

You are right if you said sentence C shows the future. *Will donate* is in the future tense and indicates something that will happen in the future.

EXERCISE 1 Identify the verb or verb phrase in each sentence. Tell the tense of each verb.

1. We will make a shopping list.
2. We are going to walk to the store.
3. Sonny found a cart.
4. I am going to put apples in it.
5. Pilar wants doughnuts.
6. Mom is going to say no.
7. We will buy rice and beans.
8. Sophie chose some canned goods.
9. We are going to take the cans to the food pantry.
10. We are on our way home now.

EXERCISE 2 Rewrite each sentence in the future tense, using *will*.

1. I volunteer at Wheaton's food pantry.
2. My family shops for groceries.
3. We buy food on sale.
4. My mom looks for food in large packages.
5. We donate the food.
6. Dad put the food into bags.

EXERCISE 3 Rewrite each sentence in the future tense, using *going to*.

1. Who brings the groceries to the food pantry?
2. Dad delivers the food.
3. I ride with him.
4. We bring food twice a month.
5. I help with the bags.
6. We give the bags to the volunteers.
7. People come to the food pantry for food.

APPLY IT NOW

Write five sentences about things you could do to help people in need. Use the future tense with *will* or *going to*.
Example: I will donate several pieces of clothing.

 Post your helpful ideas on a class wiki or blog.

5.12 Progressive Tenses

A verb in the **present progressive tense** tells about an action that is happening now. The present progressive tense is formed with *am, is,* or *are* and the present participle.

A verb in the **past progressive tense** tells what was happening over a period of time in the past. The past progressive tense is formed with *was* or *were* and the present participle.

> **Lucy** *is brushing* **her teeth.** (present progressive)
>
> **Lucy** *was brushing* **her teeth when her dad shouted, "Hurry up!"**
> (past progressive)

Which sentences are in a progressive tense?

A **Marcus brushes his teeth after dinner.**

B **He is plugging in his electric toothbrush.**

C **Marcus was searching for his cinnamon-flavored toothpaste this morning.**

You are right if you said sentences B and C. *Is plugging* is in the present progressive tense. *Was searching* is in the past progressive tense.

EXERCISE 1 Find the verb phrase in each sentence. Tell whether the verb phrase is in the present progressive tense or the past progressive tense.

1. Felicity was flossing her teeth.
2. The dentist was examining my teeth.
3. The hygienists were cleaning teeth.
4. He is polishing Jake's teeth.
5. She was taking X-rays.
6. Dr. Palazzo is telling me about tooth care.
7. She was showing me how to brush.
8. Are you taking good care of your teeth?

EXERCISE 2 Write the present progressive tense and the past progressive tense of each verb. Use the pronoun in parentheses as the subject of the verb phrase.

EXAMPLE **sleep (I)**   **I am sleeping**   **I was sleeping**

1. rinse (you)
2. wash (we)
3. scrub (he)
4. chew (they)
5. comb (she)
6. floss (they)
7. change (we)
8. bathe (I)

EXERCISE 3 Complete each sentence with the tense of the verb in parentheses.

1. My tooth _____ me. (hurt—past progressive)
2. My mom _____ an appointment with the dentist. (make—present progressive)
3. We _____ in the dentist's office. (wait—past progressive)
4. The assistant _____ me about the problem. (ask—past progressive)
5. The dentist _____ at my teeth. (look—past progressive)
6. I _____ a little scared. (feel—past progressive)
7. Now I _____ several minutes brushing my teeth three times a day. (spend—present progressive)
8. We _____ good care of our teeth and toothbrushes. (take—present progressive)
9. My sister _____ braces. (get—present progressive)
10. She _____ the orthodontist. (visit—present progressive)

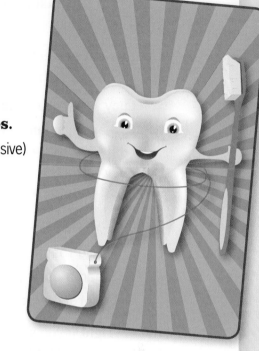

APPLY IT NOW

Be a reporter! Imagine you are at a concert, a sporting event, or a parade. Write four sentences about what is going on around you. Use the present progressive tense in your sentences. Then rewrite the sentences, using the past progressive tense.

5.13 Present Perfect Tense

A verb in the **present perfect tense** tells about an action that happened at some indefinite time in the past. It can also tell about an action that started in the past and continues into the present.

The present perfect tense is formed with *has* or *have* and the past participle.

> Lucy *has traveled* to many states.
>
> She and her family *have taken* a long road trip each year.
>
> Lucy *has kept* a diary of her travels since she was seven.

Crazy Horse, a respected Lakota Indian leader

Which sentence uses the present perfect tense?

A I have read a book about South Dakota.

B I read a book about South Dakota last week.

C I will read a book about South Dakota soon.

You are right if you said sentence A uses the present perfect tense. The present perfect tense is formed with *have* and the past participle. It means that I read the book at some indefinite time in the past.

EXERCISE 1 Find the verb phrase in the present perfect tense in each sentence. Not all the sentences have verbs in the present perfect tense.

1. I have driven through South Dakota with my family.

2. South Dakota has several famous memorials.

3. We have stopped at the Crazy Horse Memorial.

4. Sculptors have worked on the huge Crazy Horse Memorial since 1948.

5. They have not completed it yet.

6. The Black Hills have high peaks.

7. My dad has hiked in those hills.

8. Years of wind, water, and erosion have produced the Badlands.

9. Its peaks and valley have a moonlike appearance.

10. We have gone to several amazing places in South Dakota.

EXERCISE 2 Write the present perfect tense of each verb. Some verbs are irregular. Use the pronoun in parentheses as the subject of the verb phrase.

EXAMPLE **leave (I)   I have left**

1. pack (you)
2. buy (we)
3. drive (he)
4. ask (they)

5. take (it)
6. eat (they)
7. try (she)
8. forget (I)

EXERCISE 3 Complete each sentence with the verb in parentheses. Use the present perfect tense.

1. I _____ to South Dakota with my family. (travel)

2. We _____ to Mount Rushmore. (be)

3. I _____ the huge faces of the four presidents. (see)

4. The amazing sculpture _____ for more than 80 years. (exist)

5. Millions of tourists _____ it. (visit)

6. People _____ the addition of a fifth face—that of Susan B. Anthony, an advocate of women's rights. (propose)

Mount Rushmore

APPLY IT NOW

Write four sentences about places you have been and the things you have seen there. Use the present perfect tense in your sentences.

Grammar in Action.   Find the first use of the present perfect tense on page 362. Hint: It might be hiding a little.

5.14 Past Perfect Tense

Caduceus,
a medical
symbol

A verb in the **past perfect tense** tells about an action that was finished before something else happened in the past.

The past perfect tense is formed with *had* and the past participle.

> I *had finished* my report before I called my friend.
>
> After I *had chosen* Elizabeth Blackwell as the topic of my report, I went to the library to find books about her life.

Which sentence uses the past perfect tense?

A I think Elizabeth Blackwell was strong and courageous.

B I had read two books about Blackwell before I started to write my report.

C The library has several books about Blackwell.

You are right if you said sentence B uses the past perfect tense. *Had read* means I read the books before I did something else—started to write the report.

Which action in this sentence took place first?

> Before Elizabeth Blackwell studied to become a doctor, she had worked as a teacher.

You are right if you said *had worked*. The past perfect tense indicates that one action (working) preceded another action (studying) in the past.

EXERCISE 1 Write the past perfect tense of each verb. Some verbs are irregular. Use the pronoun in parentheses as the subject of the verb phrase.

EXAMPLE **play (I)**   **I had played**

1. visit (you)
2. look (we)
3. talk (he)
4. lose (they)
5. help (she)
6. fall (it)

EXERCISE 2 Find the verb phrases in the past perfect tense. Not all the sentences have phrases in the past perfect tense.

1. I have learned a lot about the life of Elizabeth Blackwell, the first female doctor in the United States.

2. Her family had lived in England before they moved to the United States in the 1830s.

3. She became interested in medicine.

4. At this time the United States had no women doctors.

5. Twenty-nine medical schools had rejected her before one accepted her as a student.

6. After she had graduated first in her class in medical school, she went to Europe.

7. She could not get a job in a hospital after she had returned to the United States.

8. Eventually, she had her own private office in New York.

Elizabeth Blackwell

EXERCISE 3 Complete each sentence with the verb in parentheses. Use the past perfect tense.

1. Before Elizabeth Blackwell, no woman in the United States _____ a diploma as a doctor. (receive)

2. Blackwell helped other women with their medical careers after she _____ a doctor. (become)

3. After she _____ as a doctor in the United States for several years, she went to Europe. (practice)

4. She _____ for almost 40 years as a doctor in England. (work)

5. Because Blackwell _____ the way, it was easier for other women to become doctors. (pave)

APPLY IT NOW

Think of someone you admire. Write three sentences in the past perfect tense about something that this person has done. Include two actions in each sentence. Example: After my mom had graduated from college, she got a job creating computer games.

5.15 Future Perfect Tense

A verb in the **future perfect tense** tells about an action that will have been completed at some time in the future. The future perfect tense is formed by adding *will have* to the past participle of the verb.

> **Corinne** *will have saved* **enough money to go to the movie by Saturday.**

Will have saved tells that Corinne will have completed the action (saving money) before some time in the future (Saturday).

Which sentence uses the future perfect tense?

A **She will have eaten dinner by 7:00 p.m.**

B **He eats dinner every night.**

C **We will have dinner at 6:30 tonight.**

You are right if you said sentence A uses the future perfect tense. *Will have eaten* tells us that she will have completed the action (eating dinner) before some time in the future (7:00 p.m.).

EXERCISE 1 Find the verb phrase in the future perfect tense in each sentence.

1. By tomorrow the committee will have chosen a date for the show.
2. The committee will have announced the date by Monday.
3. By next week many students will have signed up for the show.
4. I will have decided on my act.
5. The committee will have held auditions for the show by next month.

EXERCISE 2 Write the future perfect tense of each verb. Some verbs are irregular. Use the pronoun in parentheses as the subject of the verb phrase.

EXAMPLE **speak (I)**   **I will have spoken**

1. pack (you)
2. schedule (we)
3. drive (he)
4. arrive (they)
5. stop (it)
6. wait (they)
7. move (it)
8. sit (I)

EXERCISE 3 Complete each sentence with the verb in parentheses. Use the future perfect tense.

1. Sophia _____ the tickets to us by tomorrow. (give)
2. If we're late, Elizabeth _____ by the time we arrive. (dance)
3. Nicholas _____ by now. (sing)
4. We _____ the first act. (miss)
5. Spencer _____ by the final act. (doze)
6. Some people _____ before the end of the show. (leave)

EXERCISE 4 Find the verb phrase in the perfect tense in each sentence. Tell if the verb is present perfect, past perfect, or future perfect.

1. Once I had heard about the show, I was excited.
2. I have decided on my act for the talent show.
3. My mother will have made me a costume by next week.
4. My friends have chosen a dance to perform.
5. Connor had planned a hip-hop act, but he changed his mind.

APPLY IT NOW

Imagine you are leaving for a trip. Write four sentences that tell the things that will have happened by the time you leave. Use the future perfect tense in each sentence.
Example: Before I leave, I will have taken the cat to my neighbor's house.

5.16 Subject-Verb Agreement

A subject and verb must agree, whether the verb is a helping verb or the main verb.

	PRESENT	PAST
I	am, do	was, did
you, we, they	are, do	were, did
he, she, it	is, does	was, did

SINGULAR SUBJECT	VERB	
The *girl*	*is* petting	the dog.
That *dog*	*does*	tricks.

PLURAL SUBJECT	VERB	
Kevin and Kurt	*are* brushing	the dog.
They	*were*	at the dog show.

Which verb correctly completes this sentence?

Several breeds _____ shown at the dog show.

A is

B are

C was

You are right if you said B. The subject *breeds* is plural and needs the verb *are*.

A collective noun is considered a singular noun even though it refers to more than one person or thing.

The *litter* of puppies includes one black pup.

EXERCISE 1 Complete each sentence with the verb in parentheses that agrees with the subject.

1. We (is are) bringing our dogs to the dog show.
2. Our wolfhound (was were) a winner last year.
3. He (do does) all sorts of tricks.
4. I (am is) nervous.
5. (Does Do) you know where to go?
6. The girls (is are) grooming their dogs.
7. My dog (is are) always excited at shows.
8. All the dogs (was were) on leashes.
9. A group of judges (was were) looking over the dogs.
10. (Do Does) your dog bark a lot?

EXERCISE 2 Complete each sentence with am, is, are, was, were, do, or does.

1. The dog show _____ at the kennel club every year.
2. A funny dachshund _____ in line as the dogs paraded across the stage.
3. _____ this collie follow commands?
4. _____ you think the spaniel will win?
5. Those Great Danes _____ large dogs.
6. A poodle _____ the winner of last year's show.
7. The winner of this year's show _____ a tiny Chihuahua.
8. Photographers _____ taking pictures of all the dogs earlier.
9. Rex _____ a mixed breed.
10. I _____ coming to the show next year.

APPLY IT NOW

Use three of the following words in different sentences about animals kept as pets: *am, is, are, was, were, do, does.* Make sure the subjects and verbs agree.
Example: The lizard was in the aquarium.

5.17 *There Is and There Are*

When a sentence starts with *there is, there are, there was,* or *there were,* the subject follows the verb. The verb must still agree with the subject.

	VERB		SINGULAR SUBJECT	
There	*is*	a	*sea*	around Japan.

	VERB		PLURAL SUBJECT	
There	*are*	many	*islands*	in Japan.

In the first sentence, the singular subject *sea* comes after the verb *is.* In the second sentence, the plural subject *islands* comes after the verb *are.*

What is the subject in this sentence? Which verb correctly completes it?

There _____ noisy monkeys called macaques in Japan.

A **is**

B **are**

C **was**

You are right if you said B. *Monkeys* is the subject, and it is plural. The verb *are* is needed to agree with *monkeys.*

EXERCISE 1 Find the subject and the verb in each sentence. Tell whether the subject is singular or plural.

1. There are four main islands in Japan.
2. There is a beautiful mountain, Mount Fuji, an inactive volcano.
3. There are many people in Japanese cities.
4. There was much pollution in the past.

Mount Fuji

EXERCISE 2 Find the subject of each sentence. Complete each sentence with *is* or *are* so that the verb agrees with the subject.

1. There _____ some active volcanoes in Japan.

2. There _____ a red sun on the Japanese flag.

3. There _____ three branches in the Japanese government.

4. There _____ a big fishing industry in Japan.

5. There _____ also big electronic firms in Japan.

6. There _____ fast trains in Japan.

7. There _____ many holidays in Japan in early May in a period called Golden Week.

8. There _____ a big holiday for children during that time.

9. There _____ four different writing systems in Japan.

10. There _____ school on Saturday in Japan.

Samurai

EXERCISE 3 Complete each sentence with ***there is, there are, there was,*** or ***there were.***

1. _____ emperors in Japan in the past.

2. _____ still an emperor today.

3. _____ a prime minister too.

4. _____ once fierce warriors in Japan called samurai.

5. _____ tea at nearly every meal in Japan even today.

6. _____ raw fish in some sushi, a popular Japanese food.

7. _____ arcades with games in Tokyo.

8. Every year for New Year's, _____ a big festival.

9. _____ many earthquakes in Japan.

10. Did you know that _____ a major earthquake in Japan in 1920?

APPLY IT NOW

Write four sentences about things in your city or town. Begin your sentences with *There is, There are, There was,* and *There were.*

Tech Tip With an adult, research your city or town online.

Verbs • 139

Verb Review

5.1 Find the action verb in each sentence.

1. The family traveled to California.

2. They strolled along Monterey Bay.

5.2 Find the verb in each sentence. Tell if it is a being verb or an action verb.

3. Alicia Markova was a famous British ballerina.

4. She danced with many ballet companies.

5.3 Find the linking verb and the subject complement in each sentence.

5. The giraffes are tall.

6. Their home is Africa.

5.4 Tell whether the underlined verb is a helping verb or a linking verb.

7. Most of the melons <u>were</u> ripe by Labor Day.

8. Dad <u>has</u> cut the watermelon into slices.

5.5 Find the helping verb and the main verb in each sentence.

9. I am walking my dog.

10. He will fetch the newspaper every morning.

5.6 Complete each sentence with the form of the verb in parentheses.

11. The boy and his father _____ in the Boundary Waters. (canoe—past)

12. He is _____ faster than his father. (paddle—present participle)

13. They _____ the canoe onto the shore. (pull—present)

5.7 Complete each sentence with the form of the verb in parentheses.

14. The man _____ how to pitch well. (know—present)

15. We are _____ our gloves to the game. (bring—present participle)

16. We _____ a cheer when our team won. (do—past)

5.8 Complete each sentence with the form of the verb in parentheses.

17. Mrs. LaRosa _____ a lesson about hibernation last month. (teach—past)

18. Each group is _____ its own animal to study. (choose—present participle)

19. We always _____ our own partners. (choose—present)

5.9 Complete each sentence with the verb in parentheses.

20. The figure skaters (glide glides) over the ice.

21. She (complete completes) the move successfully.

5.10 Complete each sentence with the verb in parentheses. Use the simple past tense.

22. Ben Franklin _____ an efficient stove. (make)

23. Franklin also _____ *Poor Richard's Almanac.* (write)

5.11 Find the verb or verb phrase in each sentence. Tell the tense of each verb.

24. The pen pals are going to write letters to each other.

25. Antonia wrote often.

5.12 Write the present progressive tense and past progressive tense of each verb. Use the pronoun in parentheses as the subject of the verb phrase.

26. change (I)

27. learn (you)

5.13 Complete each sentence with the verb in parentheses. Use the present perfect tense.

28. Many people _____ the Grand Canyon. (visit)

29. Flash floods _____ through the canyon. (rush)

5.14 Complete each sentence with the verb in parentheses. Use the past perfect tense.

30. Before John Ferris, no engineer _____ such a lofty invention. (attempt)

31. At the previous World's Fair in Paris, the French _____ the Eiffel Tower. (build)

5.15 Complete each sentence with the verb in parentheses. Use the future perfect tense.

32. The animals _____ their winter dens by then. (leave)

33. Birds _____ from warmer climates in spring. (return)

5.16 Complete each sentence with the verb in parentheses.

34. My aunt Agnes (is are) throwing salt.

35. (Do Does) you know it's bad luck to break a mirror?

5.17 Complete each sentence with the verb in parentheses.

36. There (is are) eight planets and three dwarf planets in our solar system.

37. There (is are) much water on Earth.

 Tech Tip Go to www.voyagesinenglish.com for more activities.

Verb Challenge

Read the paragraph and answer the questions.

1. This fall our class went on a field trip to a farm. 2. It was the first time many of us had visited a farm. 3. First, we took a hayride. 4. Our host told us about the farm crops while we were riding through the fields on a wagon pulled by a tractor. 5. Next, we walked through a maze in a cornfield. 6. There was a winding path between tall stalks of corn. 7. I was the first out, but next time I am going to find the way out even faster! 8. The best part of the trip was a stop at the pumpkin patch. 9. We each chose a pumpkin to take home. 10. My mom has helped me carve mine, and the jack-o'-lantern is sitting on a table in our front window. 11. Maybe we can return to the farm for our spring field trip.

1. In sentence 1 is *went* an action, a being, or a helping verb?
2. In sentence 2 what is the tense of the verb *had visited*?
3. In sentence 3 is *took* a regular or an irregular verb? What are its principal parts?
4. In sentence 4 what is the tense of the verb *were riding*?
5. In sentence 5 is *walked* a regular or irregular verb? What are its principal parts?
6. In sentence 6 what is the verb? What is the subject?
7. In sentence 7 what is the verb phrase in the future tense?
8. In sentence 8 what is the linking verb?
9. In sentence 10 what is the tense of the verb phrase *has helped*?
10. In sentence 10 what is the tense of the verb phrase *is sitting*?
11. In sentence 11 what is the helping verb?

Adverbs and Conjunctions

6.1 Adverbs of Time and Place

6.2 Adverbs of Manner

6.3 Adverbs That Compare

6.4 More Adverbs That Compare

6.5 *Good* and *Well*; Negative Words

6.6 Coordinating Conjunctions

Adverb and Conjunction Review

Adverb and Conjunction Challenge

6.1 Adverbs of Time and Place

An **adverb** tells more about a verb. An adverb can tell when, how often, or where.

- An **adverb of time** answers the question *when* or *how often*.
- An **adverb of place** answers the question *where*.

When: He will bring his lunch *tomorrow*.

How often: I *always* bring my lunch.

Where: She ate *outside*.

Study the lists of some common adverbs of time and place.

ADVERBS OF TIME	ADVERBS OF PLACE
again	above
already	ahead
always	away
before	back
immediately	below
late	down
never	far
now	forward
often	here
sometimes	in
soon	inside
then	near
today	out
tomorrow	overhead
usually	there
yesterday	up

Mmmm!

EXERCISE 1 Tell whether each adverb tells when, how often, or where.

1. immediately
2. below
3. far
4. now
5. above
6. near
7. always
8. never
9. up
10. sometimes

EXERCISE 2 Find the adverb of time or place in each sentence. There may be more than one answer.

1. Yesterday my sister and I decided to make apple pancakes.
2. We had never made them.
3. We got the ingredients out.
4. Soon we started mixing ingredients.
5. Then I knocked over the bag of flour.
6. The flour flew everywhere.
7. We immediately started to clean.
8. We didn't have any flour left to make the batter again.
9. We put everything back.
10. Today we went to a restaurant and ate pancakes there.

EXERCISE 3 Complete each sentence with an adverb of time or place. Tell which kind each adverb is.

1. I _____ take a peanut butter sandwich and an apple to school for lunch.
2. _____ I decided to make a different kind of sandwich.
3. I opened the refrigerator, and I looked _____.
4. I found some cheese _____.
5. _____ I saw some pickles.
6. I _____ decided to make a cheese sandwich.
7. _____ I made my sandwich.
8. I opened my lunch box, and I put the sandwich and pickles _____.
9. I put the bread and cheese _____ in the refrigerator.
10. During lunch at school, I got _____ my lunch box and ate the sandwich.

APPLY IT NOW

Think of an activity you like to do with your family or friends on the weekend. Write five sentences about it, using adverbs of time and place in each sentence. Circle the adverbs you use.

Grammar in Action. Name the first adverbs of time and place used in the excerpt on page 400.

6.2 Adverbs of Manner

An adverb can tell how an action takes place. An **adverb of manner** answers the question *how* about a verb. Many adverbs of manner end in *ly,* but some—such as *fast, well,* and *hard*—do not end in *ly.*

The wind blew *strongly.* (How did the wind blow?)
The kite flew *gracefully.* (How did the kite fly?)
We ran *fast* **across the field.** (How did we run?)

Strongly, gracefully, and *fast* answer the question *how.* They are adverbs of manner.

Study the list of some common adverbs of manner.

ADVERBS OF MANNER

carefully	happily	quickly
clearly	kindly	rapidly
courageously	noisily	slowly
easily	patiently	smoothly
forcefully	politely	thoughtfully

Which sentence uses an adverb of manner?

A **The string hung loosely.**
B **The string is white.**
C **The string tangled again.**

You are right if you said that sentence A has an adverb of manner. *Loosely* tells how the string hung.

Which of the following is not an adverb of manner?

A **fast**
B **greedily**
C **recently**

You are right if you said C. *Recently* is an adverb of time.

EXERCISE 1 Find the adverb of manner in each sentence.

1. Chuck ran quickly.
2. He held the kite string tightly.
3. A breeze blew lightly across the porch.
4. He hastily tossed the kite into the air.
5. It floated gently to the ground.
6. Chuck ran fast the next time.
7. He launched the kite excitedly.
8. It flew perfectly.

EXERCISE 2 Complete each sentence with an adverb of manner. Choose from the following adverbs. Use each adverb only once.

patiently   attentively   enthusiastically

lightly   strongly   similarly

1. Mr. Ellerbruch _____ explained how kites work.
2. The students listened _____.
3. Kites work _____ to sailboats.
4. The wind should not blow too _____ or too _____.
5. Heather and Sarah talked _____ about kite flying.

EXERCISE 3 Find the adverbs of time, place, or manner in these sentences. Tell what kind each adverb is.

1. Fly your kite only when you can safely control it.
2. Do you see power lines near?
3. Never fly your kite in that situation.
4. Ask people politely not to stand nearby.
5. Be alert because the force and direction of the wind can change suddenly.
6. Always act responsibly and sensibly when your kite is in the air.

APPLY IT NOW

Write four sentences about what you did last weekend. Use an adverb of manner in each sentence describing how you did something.
Example: I played soccer. I played soccer skillfully and enthusiastically.

Grammar in Action.   Name the last adverb of manner used in the excerpt on page 400.

6.3 Adverbs That Compare

Many adverbs can be used to make comparisons. Adverbs can compare the actions of two or more people or things. To compare the actions of two people or things, *-er* is often added to an adverb. To compare three or more people or things, *-est* is often added to an adverb.

Juanita wakes up early.

COMPARING THE ACTIONS OF TWO PEOPLE

Juanita wakes up *earlier* than her brother.

COMPARING THE ACTIONS OF MORE THAN TWO PEOPLE

Of all the family members, Mom wakes up *earliest*.

Earlier compares the actions of Juanita and her brother. It compares the actions of two people. Note that *-er* forms are often used with *than*. *Earliest* compares Mom's action to those of all the other family members.

Which sentence uses an adverb that compares an action?

A **Mom takes a shower first.**

B **Dad showers fastest of all the family members.**

C **Juanita always sings in the shower.**

You are right if you said sentence B. The adverb *fastest* compares Dad's action to those of the other family members.

Which sentence uses an adverb that compares an action?

A **Dad leaves the house sooner than my brother.**

B **I leave the house next.**

C **Mom leaves the house last.**

You are right if you said sentence A. The adverb *sooner* compares Dad's action to those of my brother.

EXERCISE 1 Complete the chart.

Adverb	Compares Actions of Two	Compares Actions of Three or More
1. deep	_____	_____
2. high	_____	_____
3. hard	_____	_____
4. fast	_____	_____
5. late	_____	_____
6. long	_____	_____

EXERCISE 2 Find the adverb that compares in each sentence.

1. The wind blew harder today than it had yesterday.
2. Ali arrived earliest at the field for a kite-flying lesson.
3. To launch his kite, Ali ran fastest of all the learners.
4. His kite rose higher than mine did.
5. Once the kite was up, it stayed in the air longest.
6. Ali held his string tightest of all the kite flyers.

EXERCISE 3 Choose the correct adverb that compares to complete each sentence.

1. I worked (harder hardest) of all my friends at learning how to fly a kite.
2. I worked (harder hardest) at learning how to fly a kite than learning to play soccer.
3. I learned how to dribble a basketball (faster fastest) than how to fly a kite.
4. I used the (smaller smallest) kite of my friends.
5. Every time I tried to fly, the kite stayed in the air (longer longest) than the time before.
6. Today my kite flew (higher highest) than the week before.

APPLY IT NOW

Write three sentences using different adverbs that compare. Use your family as the topic. Underline the adverbs.

6.4 More Adverbs That Compare

Some adverbs that compare are not formed by adding *-er* or *-est*. Instead, these adverbs use *more* or *most* to make comparisons.

- Use *more* or *most* for adverbs ending in *ly*.

  clearly   **more clearly**   **most clearly**

- Use *more* or *most* for adverbs of three or more syllables.

  clumsily   **more clumsily**   **most clumsily**

More is used when the actions of two people or things are compared. Adverbs with *more* are often used with *than*. *Most* is used when the actions of three or more people or things are compared.

Jennie stood *more steadily* on the balance beam than Katie did. (compares the actions of two people)

Of all the gymnasts, Amelia stood on the balance beam *most steadily*. (compares the actions of three or more people)

Which sentence uses an adverb that compares?

A **David tumbled most frequently of all.**

B **David did well on the rings.**

C **David practiced frequently.**

You are right if you said sentence A. *Most frequently* compares David's actions to those of two or more other gymnasts.

EXERCISE 1 **Complete the chart.**

Adverb	Compares Actions of Two	Compares Actions of Three or More
1. diligently	_____	_____
2. thoughtfully	_____	_____
3. tirelessly	_____	_____
4. easily	_____	_____
5. quietly	_____	_____
6. loudly	_____	_____
7. brightly	_____	_____

EXERCISE 2 **Choose the correct adverb that compares to complete each sentence.**

1. Of all the campers, Ellie tells stories (more effectively most effectively).

2. Matt can put up a tent (more quickly   most quickly) than Henry can.

3. Jane and Jessica row across the lake (more rapidly most rapidly) than any other pair.

4. Isabel paddles a kayak (more skillfully   most skillfully) of all.

5. Of all the archers, Kevin hits the target (more frequently most frequently).

EXERCISE 3 **Complete each sentence with the correct form of an adverb that compares. Use the adverb in parentheses.**

1. Mia ties knots _____ of all the campers. (skillfully)

2. Rihanna sings _____ of all the people around the campfire. (enthusiastically)

3. Julia observes animals in the woods _____ than I do. (carefully)

4. She moves through the woods the _____ of all the campers. (quietly)

5. Kyle can make a fire _____ than Carlos can. (easily)

APPLY IT NOW

Write three sentences using different adverbs that compare. Use your friends or neighbors as the topic. Use a thesaurus to choose descriptive adverbs. Underline the adverbs.

Tech Tip With an adult, use an online thesaurus.

6.5 *Good* and *Well;* Negative Words

The word *good* is an adjective; it describes a noun. *Good* usually tells what kind. The word *well* is an adverb; it describes a verb. *Well* tells how.

> **Maria made a *good* meal.** (tells what kind of meal)
>
> **Maria cooks *well*.** (tells how Maria cooks)

Well can be used as an adjective, but only about a person's health.

> **Ben was *well* enough to ride his bike today.**

Which word completes the sentence correctly?

> **Joe demonstrated his skateboarding skills** (good well).

You are correct if you chose *well*. *Well* is an adverb that describes the verb *demonstrates*.

A **negative** idea can be formed in one of several ways.

- By using *never* or *not* before the verb. *Not* is sometimes part of a contraction: *didn't, won't, wouldn't.*

> **I *never* eat candy.**
>
> **Let's *not* make soup on this hot day.**

- By adding *no* before a noun.

> **There is *no* milk in the refrigerator.**

Use only one negative word in a sentence to express a negative idea. Is this sentence correct?

> **I don't never eat ice cream.**

The sentence is incorrect because it has two negative words—*don't* and *never*. To correct it, remove one of the negative words: *I don't eat ice cream* or *I never eat ice cream.*

EXERCISE 1 Complete each sentence with *good* or *well*.

1. My sister bakes _____.
2. Her homemade bread is very _____.
3. I can make fruit smoothies _____.
4. I operate the blender _____.
5. I mix the ingredients _____.
6. Everyone says that my smoothies are _____.

EXERCISE 2 These sentences are incorrect because they contain more than one negative word. Rewrite each sentence.

1. Angelina doesn't never eat rutabagas.
2. I don't never bring my lunch to school.
3. Brianna doesn't never have pizza for breakfast.
4. The cafeteria doesn't have no soup today.
5. I don't put no bananas on my cereal.
6. My friends don't never get their lunches from the cafeteria.
7. We don't never have hamburgers on Monday.
8. I don't have no money to buy milk.

EXERCISE 3 Correct the sentences that use *good* or *well* or negative words incorrectly. Not all sentences contain mistakes.

1. My little sister never makes her own lunch.
2. She cannot spread the jelly good.
3. My brother never puts no mustard on his sandwiches.
4. There are no apples in the fruit bowl.
5. There isn't no more juice in the cabinet.
6. My mom makes lunches good.

APPLY IT NOW

Write three sentences about something that you don't like to do. Use *good* and *well* in at least one sentence.
Examples:
I don't like to dance.
I don't dance well.
I may practice to become a good dancer.

6.6 Coordinating Conjunctions

A **coordinating conjunction** joins two words or groups of words. The words *and, but,* and *or* are coordinating conjunctions. They are used to join words or groups of words that are similar. In these sentences the similar words and groups of words connected by the coordinating conjunctions are underlined.

And: Paige <u>buys</u> *and* <u>trades</u> baseball cards.

But: Horatio <u>plays football</u> *but* <u>collects baseball cards</u>.

Or: Do you like <u>football</u> *or* <u>baseball</u>?
       Do you keep your cards <u>in boxes</u> *or* <u>in bags</u>?

Which sentences have coordinating conjunctions? What do the conjunctions join?

A Michael and Rose like photography.

B I want to take a picture too.

C James smiled but blinked during the shot.

You are right if you said A and C. In sentence A *and* joins *Michael* and *Rose.* In sentence C *but* joins *smiled* and *blinked.*

EXERCISE 1 Find the coordinating conjunction in each sentence.

1. Magic can be a fun and entertaining hobby.

2. It is a good idea to get books or DVDs with magic tricks.

3. With them you can study or watch magic tricks.

4. You can do tricks with simple objects such as cards and coins.

5. A wand and a top hat are common props for magic acts.

6. They are nice but not necessary for your magic tricks.

EXERCISE 2 Find the coordinating conjunction in each sentence. Identify the words or groups of words the conjunction joins.

EXAMPLE **Some stamps are <u>rare</u> <u>and</u> <u>valuable</u>.**

1. Stamp collecting can be an exciting but expensive hobby.
2. People collect new or used stamps.
3. Many stores buy and sell stamps.
4. You can get used stamps from letters or from packages.
5. You might ask friends and relatives to give you used stamps.
6. Use tweezers or special tongs to peel off the stamps.
7. After you remove a stamp with water, dry and press it.
8. Many stamps show flowers or birds.
9. Some stamps honor famous people or events.
10. The value of a stamp is determined by its rarity and condition.
11. Is this stamp common or rare?
12. Keep your stamps in envelopes or in albums.

First Moon Landing, 1969

Probing the Planets

USA 18c

EXERCISE 3 Complete each sentence with a coordinating conjunction that makes sense.

and   but   or

1. Knitting is fun _____ difficult.
2. Before you use needles, you can learn stitches with your fingers _____ with a spool.
3. Tanya knitted mittens _____ a scarf.
4. She will use the purple _____ the green yarn.
5. She finished the scarf _____ didn't wear it.
6. Should I make a blanket _____ a sweater?

APPLY IT NOW

Write three sentences about a hobby. Use the conjunctions *and*, *but*, and *or* in your sentences. Example: Cooking is difficult but fun.

Tech Tip   On the class blog, tell your class about your hobby.

Adverb and Conjunction Review

6.1 Find the adverb of time or place in each sentence.

1. Yesterday I filled the bird feeder.

2. Greedy squirrels often try to eat the birdseed.

3. Two squirrels immediately started to climb the pole.

4. I chased the squirrels away.

5. They ran down.

6. They didn't try to climb the pole again.

7. Later I checked the feeder.

8. The squirrels hadn't come back.

9. Birds were feeding there.

10. Tomorrow the feeder will need more birdseed.

6.2 Find the adverb of manner in each sentence.

11. Daedalus expertly made wings from feathers and wax.

12. He and his son learned to fly effectively.

13. They flew gracefully through the sky.

14. They successfully escaped from Crete.

15. Icarus was flying through the air joyfully.

16. The wind blew gently.

17. Icarus foolishly flew close to the sun.

18. The hot sun quickly melted the wax.

19. Icarus abruptly fell into the sea.

20. Daedalus helplessly watched him fall.

6.3 Write the two forms for each adverb to compare the actions of two people and to compare the actions of three or more people.

21. slow

22. fast

23. loud

24. late

25. high

26. early

27. soon

28. near

6.4 Choose the correct adverb that compares to complete each sentence.

29. Grace ran the obstacle course (more quickly   most quickly) than Spencer.

30. Lamar ran through the tires (more carefully   most carefully) than Amber did.

31. Of all the contestants, Liz practiced running the course (more frequently most frequently).

32. Peter practiced (more tirelessly most tirelessly) than his brother Ben.

33. It was Jonathan's goal to run the course (more accurately most accurately) than his brother.

34. Kristy ran the course (more smoothly most smoothly) of all the children.

35. Kara climbed the rope (more rapidly most rapidly) than Eliza.

36. Jude ran the course (more determinedly most determinedly) during the event than he did in practice.

6.5 Choose the correct word to complete each sentence.

37. Chloe is a (good well) gardener.

38. Roberto takes (good well) care of his garden.

39. That plant goes (good well) next to the garden gate.

40. I don't want (any no) weeds in my garden.

41. There are (no not) lemons on my lemon tree.

42. The vegetables taste (good well).

43. There aren't (any no) blueberries left to sell.

44. There are (any no) raspberries either.

45. Carrots and beans sell (good well).

46. I don't want (any no) pests on my plants.

6.6 Find the coordinating conjunction in each sentence. Identify the words or groups of words the conjunction joins.

47. Do you like to ride bikes or skateboards?

48. Pedro wants a bike and lock for his birthday.

49. Make sure to wear helmets and knee pads when riding your skateboard.

50. I'm tired but happy after playing outside all day.

51. I like going to the bike path or the skate park.

52. Skateboarding can be exciting but dangerous if you are not careful.

53. His bike is in the garage or at the bike rack.

Tech Tip Go to www.voyagesinenglish.com for more activities.

Adverb and Conjunction Challenge

Read the paragraph and answer the questions.

1. Finally, the wild animal acts were completed.
2. Now it was time for the main event of the circus.
3. The new act was exciting but dangerous. 4. The famous acrobat would swing skillfully above the heads of the crowd. 5. She approached the ladder, climbed up quickly, and smiled down at the vast audience. 6. The drums rolled loudly and then were silent. 7. The figure grasped the bar tightly, swung forward, and then let go. 8. She gracefully twirled in the air, seemed to hang momentarily suspended in space, and then smoothly reached for the trapeze at the other side. 9. The crowd breathed easily again. 10. They applauded more enthusiastically for her than for any other circus performer. 11. Everyone was thrilled and amazed by the acrobat's skill.

1. In sentences 1 and 2, find the adverbs of time.
2. In sentence 3 what is the coordinating conjunction?
3. In sentence 3 what two words does the conjunction connect?
4. In sentence 4 what is the adverb of manner?
5. In sentence 5 what are the two adverbs of place?
6. Name the two adverbs in sentence 6. What kind is each?
7. Name the adverb of place in sentence 7.
8. Name the two adverbs of time in sentence 8.
9. Name the two adverbs in sentence 9. What kind is each?
10. In sentence 11 what is the coordinating conjunction?
11. In sentence 11 what two words does the conjunction connect?
12. Find the adverb that compares in the paragraph.

Punctuation and Capitalization

7.1 End Punctuation

7.2 Capitalization

7.3 Titles of Works

7.4 Abbreviations

7.5 Personal Titles

7.6 Commas: Part I

7.7 Commas: Part II

7.8 Apostrophes

7.9 Addresses

7.10 Direct Quotations

Punctuation and Capitalization Review

Punctuation and Capitalization Challenge

7.1 End Punctuation

End punctuation helps make writing clear. It shows where one sentence ends and the next one begins.

- A declarative sentence makes a statement. Use a period at the end of a declarative sentence.

  Michael Jordan played basketball.

- An imperative sentence gives a command. Use a period at the end of an imperative sentence.

  Throw the ball to me.

- An interrogative sentence asks a question. Use a question mark at the end of an interrogative sentence.

  Did she make the basket?

- An exclamatory sentence expresses strong or sudden feeling or emotion. Use an exclamation point at the end of an exclamatory sentence.

  What a shot he just made!

Which punctuation mark goes at the end of this sentence?

  There are five players on a basketball team

You are right if you said a period. The sentence, which makes a statement, is a declarative sentence. It must end with a period.

EXERCISE 1 Tell whether each sentence makes a statement, gives a command, asks a question, or expresses a strong feeling or emotion. Use the end punctuation as a clue.

1. James Naismith invented basketball.
2. Let's give three cheers for James Naismith!
3. Why did he invent the game?
4. He wanted a game that could be played indoors during winter.
5. Tell us how he did it.

EXERCISE 2 Rewrite these sentences, using the correct end punctuation. Tell whether each sentence is declarative or interrogative.

1. Basketball is more than 100 years old
2. When did Naismith invent basketball
3. He invented basketball in 1891
4. What was Naismith's job
5. He was a sports instructor

EXERCISE 3 Rewrite these sentences, using the correct end punctuation. Tell whether each sentence is imperative or exclamatory.

1. Please give me more information about Naismith
2. What an inventive man he was
3. Don't stop telling the story of James Naismith
4. It is very interesting
5. What a great game basketball is

James Naismith

EXERCISE 4 Rewrite these sentences, using the correct end punctuation. Tell whether each sentence is declarative, imperative, interrogative, or exclamatory.

1. James Naismith used a soccer ball and two peach baskets for hoops in his new game
2. That was very clever
3. Explain the nature of the early games
4. The peach baskets didn't have holes at the bottom
5. The game stopped every time the ball went into the basket
6. How strange that sounds
7. What is the size of a basketball today
8. Is basketball a popular sport around the world

APPLY IT NOW

Tell about a sport you have played or seen. Write four sentences, one of each type. Be sure to use the three kinds of end punctuation.
Examples: The Tour de France takes place every summer. Where is it held? Look at that bike. Wow, it's amazing!

7.2 Capitalization

A sentence begins with a **capital letter.**

Some words always begin with a capital letter.

- The first word in a sentence
- Names of people and pets

Jane Goodall	Benjamin Franklin
Aunt Mary	Rachel
General Anderson	Koko

- Names of streets, cities, states, and countries

Market Street	Texas
Dallas	Canada

- Names of days, months, and holidays

Thursday	August	Columbus Day

- The personal pronoun *I*

Which word group needs capital letters?

A **a day at the beach**
B **thanksgiving day in new york city**
C **brunch with the family**

You are right if you said B. *Thanksgiving Day* and *New York City* need capital letters. These word groups name a specific holiday and a specific city.

EXERCISE 1 Tell why each word or word group needs one or more capital letters.

1. William
2. September
3. Carroll Avenue
4. Valentine's Day
5. Tuesday
6. Moscow
7. Oregon
8. Nigeria
9. New Year's Day
10. my cat, Buttercup

EXERCISE 2 Rewrite each sentence, adding capital letters where needed.

1. the first monday in september is labor day.

2. canadians celebrate thanksgiving in october.

3. my family and i once celebrated pioneer day with relatives in utah.

4. we learned that flag day is in june.

5. in japan, children's day is celebrated on may 5.

6. a marathon is held in boston on patriot's day.

7. My cousin michael ran in the marathon last april.

8. in vietnam, tet, the holiday that marks the start of a new year, is celebrated in late january or early february.

9. in mexico, independence day is in september.

10. in canada, people celebrate family day on the third monday in february.

11. grandma barbara always calls us from toronto on that day.

12. my cousin katie celebrates anzac day in new zealand.

I love turkey!

EXERCISE 3 Complete each sentence with a word that begins with a capital letter.

1. My birthday is in _____.

2. My favorite holiday is _____.

3. The first day of school is usually in _____.

4. The street my school is on is _____.

5. The capital of my state is _____.

6. The Statue of Liberty is in _____.

7. If I had a hamster, I'd name it _____.

8. The Eiffel Tower is in _____.

APPLY IT NOW

Write four sentences about what you and your family do on holidays. Use capital letters correctly.

Tech Tip With an adult, research a holiday online.

7.3 Titles of Works

There are special rules for writing the titles of books, poems, and other published works.

- Each important word in the title begins with a capital letter.
- The first word and the last word of a title always begin with a capital letter.
- Some short words, such as *and, of, to, for, a, an,* and *the,* are not capitalized unless they are the first or last word in the title. Verbs such as *is* and pronouns such as *it* are capitalized.
- Titles of books and magazines are italicized when they are typed and underlined when they are handwritten.
- Titles of poems, stories, and magazine articles have quotation marks around them.

Book:	*Tales of a Fourth Grade Nothing* by Judy Blume or Tales of a Fourth Grade Nothing by Judy Blume
Magazine:	*National Geographic Kids* or National Geographic Kids
Poem:	"If I Could Grant a Wish for You" by Elizabeth Harris
Story:	"The Happy Prince" by Oscar Wilde
Article:	"Explore the Fantastic Forest!" by Peter Mandel

Which of these is a poem? How do you know?

A *Abel's Island* by William Steig

B *Saffy's Angel* by Hilary McKay

C "Until I Saw the Sea" by Lilian Moore

You are right if you said C. The title of a poem has quotation marks around it.

EXERCISE 1 Tell whether each is the title of a book or a poem.

1. *Ginger Pye* by Eleanor Estes
2. "Fog" by Carl Sandburg
3. *How to Eat Fried Worms* by Thomas Rockwell
4. *More Than Anything Else* by Marie Bradby
5. *Amber Brown Wants Extra Credit* by Paula Danziger
6. "The Lesson for Tonight" by John Ciardi

EXERCISE 2 Rewrite each title, using capital letters where needed.

1. *a single shard* by Linda Sue Park
2. *my side of the mountain* by Jean Craighead George
3. "birthday wish" by Diane Z. Shore
4. *wayside school gets a little stranger* by Louis Sachar
5. "adventures of isabel" by Ogden Nash
6. *the mouse and the motorcycle* by Beverly Cleary
7. *pippi longstocking* by Astrid Lindgren
8. "it's dark in here" by Shel Silverstein

Marie Bradby

EXERCISE 3 Write each title correctly.

1. who has seen the wind? by Christina Rossetti (poem)
2. the new kid on the block by Jack Prelutsky (poem)
3. diary of a wimpy kid by Jeff Kinney (book)
4. the light of independence by Clifford Jones (magazine article)
5. help! i'm a prisoner in the library by Eth Clifford (book)
6. catch a little rhyme by Eve Merriam (poem)
7. sports illustrated for kids (magazine)

APPLY IT NOW

Make a list of five books and poems you have read. Include the authors. Be sure to follow the correct rules for the titles.
Examples:
Pippi Longstocking by Astrid Lindgren
"Flies" by Ogden Nash

Tech Tip · Use italics if typing book titles on a computer.

7.4 Abbreviations

A short form of a word is called an **abbreviation.** Abbreviations usually end with periods.

DAYS OF THE WEEK

Sunday—Sun.   Thursday—Thurs.
Monday—Mon.   Friday—Fri.
Tuesday—Tues.   Saturday—Sat.
Wednesday—Wed.

MONTHS OF THE YEAR

January—Jan.   September—Sept.
February—Feb.   October—Oct.
March—Mar.   November—Nov.
April—Apr.   December—Dec.
August—Aug.

May, June, and *July* are not abbreviated.

ADDRESSES

Street—St.   Avenue—Ave.   North—N.   East—E.

Postal abbreviations have two capital letters and no periods.

POSTAL ABBREVIATIONS FOR STATES

Alaska—AK   Kentucky—KY

Abbreviations for units of measure do not begin with capital letters. Do not add *s* to abbreviations for plural measures: *8 ounces = 8 oz.* Periods are not used in metric measures.

UNITS OF MEASURE

inch—in.   pint—pt.   pound—lb.
yard—yd.   quart—qt.   mile—mi.
liter—l   kilometer—km   centimeter—cm

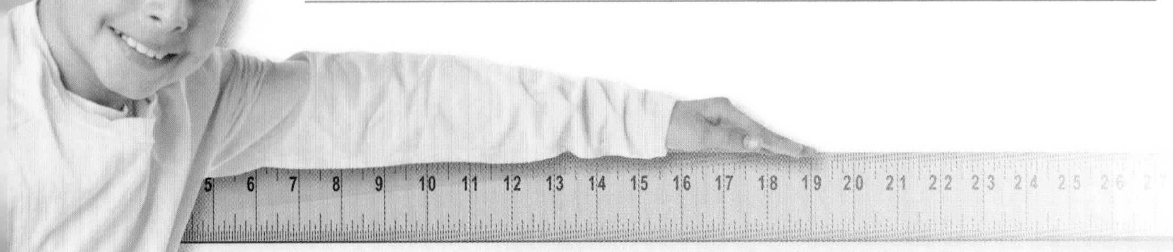

EXERCISE 1 Write the word each abbreviation stands for. Use a dictionary or other reference book if you need help.

1. Wed.
2. cm
3. Blvd.
4. S.
5. Jan.
6. km

7. qt.
8. Apr.
9. Ave.
10. E.
11. IL
12. CA

Lake 3 km
Camp 4 mi.

EXERCISE 2 Rewrite each word group, using the abbreviation for each word in italics.

1. *South* Third *Avenue*
2. one *pint* of berries
3. Miami, *Florida*
4. *Thursday, April* 15
5. a *yard* of cloth

6. one *liter* of water
7. *North* Front *Street*
8. Austin, *Texas*
9. Peterson *Boulevard*
10. *Friday, February* 10

EXERCISE 3 Change the words that can be abbreviated to abbreviations in this person's to-do list.

Friday, April 30
• Go shopping with Dad to buy Mom a Mother's Day gift.
• Get two yards of ribbon to wrap gifts at Superstore on North Washington Street.

Saturday, May 1
• Remind Mom to buy five pounds of apples for the apple-bobbing game.
• Send birthday card to Aunt Gwen. Her address is 912 East Center Avenue.

APPLY IT NOW

Find five examples of abbreviations of a date, an address, and a unit of measure around your house. Mail, newspapers, and food packaging are good sources. Write the abbreviations and report back to the class.

Grammar in Action

Find the abbreviation used on page 439.
What does the abbreviation stand for?

7.5 Personal Titles

Titles such as *Mr., Mrs., Ms., Dr., Sgt.,* and *Gov.* are abbreviations that go in front of people's names. Each one begins with a capital letter and ends with a period.

Mr. **Mark Holzer**   Dr. **Mary Carter**

Mrs. **Juanita Cruz**   Sgt. **Phil Harmon**

Ms. **Fern Beamon**   Gov. **Ron Adams**

A person may use an initial in place of a name. An initial is a capital letter followed by a period.

John F. **Kennedy**   J. R. R. **Tolkien**

Robert E. **Lee**   J. K. **Rowling**

Some countries and organizations occasionally use initials in place of a name. The initials are usually followed by periods.

U.S.A.   **United States of America**

B.S.A.   **Boy Scouts of America**

Which name is not written correctly?

A **Sgt. Gerald J. Joyce**

B **Ms. S Marcin**

C **Dr. K. Loftus**

You are right if you said B. A period is needed after the initial *S.*

EXERCISE 1 Rewrite these names, using periods and capital letters where needed.

1. dr simon f cook
2. cpl sue t marks
3. mrs juliette g low
4. mr h r ruiz
5. pres w wayne noble
6. dr jill m greef
7. ms lily k wisdom
8. gov virginia c castro

Girl Scouts of the U.S.A.

EXERCISE 2 Rewrite these sentences, using initials for the italicized words.

1. John *Fitzgerald* Kennedy was the 35th *United States* president.
2. William *Dickson* Boyce was the founder of the *Boy Scouts of America*.
3. *Phineus Taylor* Barnum ran a circus.
4. *Elwyn Brooks* White wrote about a pig and a spider.
5. *Clive Staples* Lewis wrote fables and fairy tales for children.

EXERCISE 3 Rewrite these sentences, using periods and capital letters where needed.

1. mrs richards is my art teacher.
2. the writer of our class play was c j chang.
3. gov adam b davidson is going to visit our town.
4. the sign on the door read "dr jane s quincy."
5. the actor playing pres lincoln was a p taylor.
6. capt edgar w martinez spoke to our class about fire safety.
7. I address letters to my uncle in this way: capt kevin c rourke.
8. The teachers organizing the field trip are ms jones, mr chin, and mrs lenski.
9. Our government officials include gov christine r campbell and sen lisa madison.
10. my favorite authors are jean m malone, e l konigsburg, and john d fitzgerald.

William Dickson Boyce

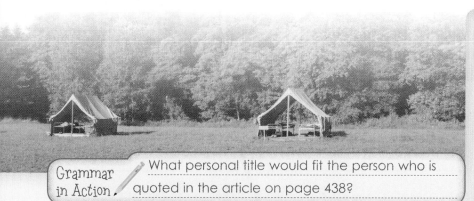

Grammar in Action. What personal title would fit the person who is quoted in the article on page 438?

APPLY IT NOW

Think of people you know who use initials in their names. Write four names, using initials, and tell who the people are.

7.6 Commas: Part I

A **comma** is used to separate words and groups of words so that they are easier to read and understand.

A comma is used before the coordinating conjunctions *and, or,* or *but* to separate two sentences joined into a compound sentence. Commas are used in compound sentences but not in compound sentence parts.

Petra raised her hand*,* *but* John shouted the answer.

Which sentence uses commas correctly?

A **We practiced our Spanish, and hoped to use it in Mexico.**

B **Elizabeth bought postcards and her sister bought souvenirs.**

C **I packed my suitcase, and Dad loaded it into the van.**

You are right if you said sentence C. A comma is used before *and* in a compound sentence.

Three or more words or groups of words of the same kind written one after another are called a **series.** Often part of the series is connected by the coordinate conjunction *and* or *or.* Commas are used to separate words in a series.

Ana, Christopher, and Otto **raised their hands.**

Which sentence uses commas correctly?

A **Salzburg, Barcelona, and, Galway are my favorite European cities.**

B **Krista wanted to hike ski and shop on her vacation.**

C **I took pictures of the coastline, mountains, and plants.**

You are right if you said sentence C. The words *coastline, mountains, and plants* are in a series and a comma comes before the coordinating conjunction *and.*

EXERCISE 1 Rewrite these sentences, adding commas where needed.

1. For some time the family had wanted to go to England and they planned their trip carefully.

2. She packed an umbrella a raincoat and a waterproof hat.

3. Anna didn't forget her boots and she reminded Finn to bring his.

4. We want to visit London Oxford and Cambridge.

5. The tourists visited Big Ben Buckingham Palace and Windsor Castle.

6. We tried to visit the British Museum but it was closed.

7. The restaurant served tea scones and a variety of jams.

8. A scone is somewhat like a biscuit with raisins in it and it goes well with a cup of tea.

9. Should we go now to Kensington Market or should we wait until tomorrow?

10. John or Margaret will go to the museum again but Spencer will see the Thames River.

Big Ben and the London Eye

EXERCISE 2 Rewrite these sentences so that they use commas correctly.

1. We did not have good weather but we still had a good time.

2. We had fog, rain and sleet, on the same day.

3. We traveled by taxi bus, and boat.

4. Highlights of our trip were Buckingham Palace, Big Ben and the Tower of London.

5. The London Eye is like a giant Ferris wheel but its cars are big glass booths.

6. Josephine, Audrey and Lilianne, enjoyed the Shakespeare play but Emily liked watching the soccer games more.

APPLY IT NOW

Write five sentences about a trip you took. Tell about places you visited, what you did and saw, and what you ate. Use commas correctly.

7.7 Commas: Part II

Speaking directly to a person and using that person's name is called **direct address.** Commas set off words in direct address to separate the name of the person spoken to from the rest of the sentence.

- Use one comma to separate the name if it is at the beginning or the end of a sentence.

    Carmen, **please hand in your paper.**

    This is your final report of the year, *Alex.*

- Use two commas to separate the name if it is in the middle of a sentence. A comma appears before and after the name.

    Do you think, *Ethan,* **that you should staple your paper?**

A comma is used after the word *yes* or *no* when it introduces a sentence.

    Yes, **you are correct.**

    No, **you may not use a pen on your test.**

Which sentence uses commas correctly?

A **We studied, Mrs. Paulson, using our textbooks and notebooks.**

B **No I did not know that we could use our map.**

C **Dad can you help me study for my geography test?**

You are right if you said sentence A. It has commas used before and after the name of the person in direct address.

EXERCISE 1 Rewrite these sentences, adding commas to set off the words in direct address.

1. Henry what are you going to do this summer?
2. I think Joe that I'm going to a soccer camp.
3. What about you Daniela?

4. I hope I get to go to an art camp and swim in my spare time Henry.

5. You will be surprised to hear this Mr. Cortez but I am asking my parents if I can go to a summer camp that teaches Chinese.

6. Are you kidding Joe about learning Chinese?

7. Joe I am so proud of you!

8. Daniela is planning to join you Joe.

EXERCISE 2 Rewrite these sentences, adding commas where needed.

1. No I will not be going on any vacations this summer.

2. Yes I will be swimming and playing at the park.

3. Yes Jim and his family have a pool in their backyard.

4. Yes I hope to be invited to his pool often.

5. No they do not have a diving board.

EXERCISE 3 Rewrite the sentences so that they use commas correctly.

1. Class let's take out a sheet of paper, and write a paragraph.

2. No it will not be about what we did over the weekend.

3. Yes I would like for you, class to write about what you want to do during summer vacation.

4. Your paragraph can be about camps, vacations or sports.

5. Nora please include your name date and title of your paragraph on your paper.

6. The bell rang and, the students turned in their paragraphs.

Chinese characters'
meaning (left to right):
learning, summer,
happiness, and bravery

APPLY IT NOW

Imagine a short conversation between you and a friend. Write four sentences of your conversation. Use *yes* or *no* and direct address. Be sure to use commas correctly.

7.8 Apostrophes

An **apostrophe** is used

- **to form the possessive of a noun**

  The room belongs to Marco.

  It is *Marco's* room. (possessive noun)

  Adding an apostrophe and the letter *s* to the name *Marco* shows that the room is his.

- **to show that one or more letters are left out of a contraction**

  Matthew will not clean his room.

  Matthew *won't* clean his room.

  Common contractions are *isn't, aren't, wasn't, weren't, doesn't, didn't, can't, won't,* and *I'll.*

Which sentence uses an apostrophe to show possession? How are the other apostrophes used?

What a mess!

A **Paige's room is messy.**

B **She couldn't find her shoes.**

C **She doesn't know where to look.**

You are right if you said sentence A. The apostrophe and *s* added to the name *Paige* shows that the room belongs to her. Both sentences B and C use apostrophes in contractions.

EXERCISE 1 Tell whether the apostrophe in each sentence shows possession or helps make a contraction.

1. Liam's brother sleeps on the top bunk.
2. His brother didn't make his bed.
3. Please don't leave dirty socks on the floor.
4. All the toys and rumpled clothes are under Dillon's bed.
5. Doesn't my room look nice?

EXERCISE 2 Rewrite the sentences, adding apostrophes where needed.

1. Lets rearrange our bedroom.
2. Well need help to move the furniture.
3. Sams desk should go here.
4. I dont want my computer over there.
5. Be careful with Uncle Arthurs lamp.
6. I cant move the heavy bookcase.
7. Dads old globe looks good on the desk.
8. Im also going to clean my closet.
9. The room isnt ready yet.
10. We didnt clean under the beds.
11. I cant reach the top shelf of the closet.
12. We can use Lucys ladder.
13. Shell get the ladder.
14. The ladder wasnt in the kitchen.
15. I dont need it because Dad helped me.
16. Sam doesnt like the new room arrangement.

EXERCISE 3 Replace the italicized words in each sentence with a contraction.

1. My room *is not* messy.
2. My sister *does not* keep her room neat.
3. I *do not* leave clothes lying around.
4. My shoes *were not* under the bed.
5. I *cannot* finish cleaning now.
6. I *did not* do my homework yet.
7. I *will not* have time tonight for cleaning.
8. *I will* finish cleaning on Saturday.

APPLY IT NOW

Write five sentences about how you might rearrange a room in your home. Use a word with an apostrophe in each sentence. Circle those words.

7.9 Addresses

Capital letters and commas are used in writing addresses. An address is written like this.

Name
Street Address, Apartment or Floor Number
City, State Abbreviation Zip Code

In an address capitalize the first letter of every title, word, and abbreviation. Capitalize both letters of a state's postal abbreviation.

Dr. Charles Turner
1312 E. Main St., Apt. 2
Gatesville, TX 76528

If there is an apartment or a floor number, it is separated from the street address by a comma. A comma always separates the names of the city and the state, but there is never a comma between the state abbreviation and the zip code.

Is this address written correctly?

Jamie Jones
6700 N. Arrowhead Drive, Apt. 12
Urbana, IL 61820

You are right if you said yes. The first letter of each word is capitalized. Both letters of the postal abbreviation are capitalized. Commas are used between the street address and the apartment number and between the names of the city and the state.

EXERCISE 1 Rewrite each address, using capital letters where needed.

1. mr. tom gannon
   100 vine st., apt. 6
   cordale, ga 31015

2. mrs. becky ritter
   10 n. cherry blvd.
   towanda, pa 18848

EXERCISE 2 Rewrite each address, using commas and periods where needed.

1. Mrs Lynne Calvino
   399 W Oak Rd Apt D
   Concord MA 01742

2. Dr Bahir L Sihab
   107 E 81 St 2nd Floor
   New York NY 10028

EXERCISE 3 Rewrite each address, using commas, capital letters, and periods where needed.

1. mr. antonio p. rodriguez
   5500 reflections blvd.
   lutz fl 33558

2. dr. shelly klickstein
   10 e. tripp ave. apt. 3
   Benton ak 72015

3. ms tina m polanski
   1568 fairview ave
   missoula mt 59801

4. mr samuel w miller
   211 s virginia st
   reno nv 89501

APPLY IT NOW

Imagine you have written a letter to a friend. Draw an envelope. Write your name and address in the upper left corner for the return address. Write your friend's name and address for the mailing address.

7.10 Direct Quotations

A **direct quotation** contains the exact words a person says. Quotation marks are used before and after the words of a speaker. A comma is used to set off what is said from the rest of the sentence.

COMMA   DIRECT QUOTATION

Lucy said, "I know some interesting facts about Russia."

DIRECT QUOTATION   COMMA

"Please tell us something about Russia," requested Louis.

The name of the person speaking can go in the middle of a direct quotation. Two sets of quotation marks and two commas set off a divided quotation.

"The capital of Russia," remarked Terry, "is Moscow."

Which sentence tells Lucy's exact words?

A **Lucy said that Russia is the largest country.**

B **Lucy said, "Russia is the largest country."**

C **Lucy says her grandparents miss Russia.**

You are right if you said sentence B. This sentence includes a direct quotation. Lucy's exact words are inside the quotation marks. A comma sets off what she said from the rest of the sentence.

EXERCISE 1 Rewrite each sentence. Use a comma to separate what is said from the rest of the sentence.

1. Mr. Thompson said "More than a hundred languages and dialects are spoken in Russia."

2. "Russian, however, is the official language" he added.

Russian nesting dolls

3. Susie exclaimed "That's a great many languages!"

4. Chris asked "Does anyone speak most of the languages?"

5. "That's an interesting question" Mr. Thompson replied.

EXERCISE 2 Rewrite each sentence. Put quotation marks around the exact words of the speaker.

1. Some students in our school come from Russia, said Mr. Thompson.

2. He asked, Mikhail, will you tell the class about Russia?

3. The summer months are beautiful, Mikhail said.

4. Tina exclaimed, I thought it was freezing in Russia!

5. Many places here can be just as cold, said Mikhail.

6. The daylight in summer, he continued, lasts a long time.

EXERCISE 3 Rewrite each sentence. Use commas to separate what is said from the rest of the sentence. Put quotation marks around the exact words of the speaker.

1. Mr. Thompson asked What are some facts you learned about Russia?

2. Moscow is the capital of Russia Erin quickly replied.

3. It is also she continued Russia's largest city.

4. The country James added used to be called the USSR.

5. Katie said Russia is famous for its arts.

6. Russia was important for ballet she continued.

7. One special food is caviar said Thomas which is actually fish eggs.

8. Russia is so big Amber exclaimed that it takes seven days to cross it by train!

9. Megan said Eastern Russia is often called Siberia.

10. The winter there is very cold she added.

APPLY IT NOW

Interview a friend or a parent about where he or she would like to travel. Write four sentences that contain that person's exact words. Use commas and quotation marks correctly.

Grammar in Action. In what paragraph is a direct quotation used in the article on page 438?

Punctuation and Capitalization Review

7.1 Rewrite these sentences, adding the correct end punctuation.

1. Can you find India on the map of the world

2. India is located south of Pakistan

3. Name the capital of India, please

4. How impressive the Taj Mahal is

5. India is made up of states, just like the United States

7.2 Rewrite these sentences, adding capital letters where needed.

6. thanksgiving always falls on a thursday.

7. my friend mae lived on arbor avenue.

8. i have relatives who once lived in ecuador.

9. my best friend's birthday is january 12.

10. we are going to visit rome in june with our friend marina.

7.3 Rewrite each title correctly.

11. diary of a worm by Doreen Cronin (book)

12. ranger rick (magazine)

13. fireflies in the garden by Robert Frost (poem)

14. world's tallest bridge opens in france (article)

15. sadako and the thousand paper cranes by Eleanor Coerr (book)

7.4 Rewrite each word group, using the abbreviation for each underlined word.

16. one <u>quart</u> of strawberries

17. <u>Thursday</u>, <u>December</u> 9

18. 50-<u>yard</u> dash

19. 881 <u>North</u> Fremont <u>Avenue</u>

20. Quincy, <u>Illinois</u>

7.5 Rewrite these sentences, using abbreviations or initials for the underlined words.

21. <u>Doctor</u> Martin Luther King was a civil rights leader.

22. A portrait of Susan <u>Brownell</u> Anthony has been on coins and stamps.

23. Franklin <u>Delano</u> Roosevelt served as United States president for 12 years.

24. Lewis <u>Comfort</u> Tiffany created art with colored glass.

25. <u>Sergeant</u> York was a famous hero in World War I.

7.6 Rewrite these sentences, adding commas where needed.

26. Sonja wanted fruit salad but there was none in the refrigerator.

27. She washed grapes strawberries and blueberries.

28. Sonja shared the fruit salad with Rebecca Kevin and Omar.

29. Everyone enjoyed the fruit salad and Sonja wants to make it again soon.

7.7 Rewrite these sentences, adding commas where needed.

30. Can we go camping Mom?

31. Yes that is a great idea.

32. Do you know Mom if it is supposed to rain?

33. No I have not checked the weather Web site yet.

7.8 Rewrite these sentences, adding apostrophes where needed. Tell whether the apostrophe shows possession or helps make a contraction.

34. Liam plans to stay at his grandmothers house for the weekend.

35. Hes packing pajamas, clothes, and a toothbrush in a bag.

36. Liam wont bring any toys.

37. His dad loaded Liams bag into the car.

38. The car trip didnt take long.

39. His grandmother doesnt live far away.

7.9 Rewrite these addresses, using capital letters, periods, and commas where needed.

40. ms lola pierce
6260 n oak rd apt 7
jamesville ny 13078

41. dr shelby harter
812 woodruff place
wapakoneta oh 45895

7.10 Rewrite these sentences, using commas and quotation marks where needed.

42. Rivers can hold only so much water said Mr. Hanks.

43. After heavy rains or a lot of snowmelt he explained a river may overflow.

44. I live near a river announced Marcy.

45. Mr. Hanks asked Has your basement ever flooded?

46. No Marcy replied but we have used sandbags to keep water out several times.

Tech Tip

Go to www.voyagesinenglish.com for more activities.

Punctuation and Capitalization Challenge

Read the paragraphs and answer the questions.

1. It was Monday afternoon at Jefferson Elementary School. 2. Jerry listened carefully as their guest speaker, Mr. Mark Gray, told the class about birds of prey. 3. "Birds of prey come in all shapes and sizes," the speaker said. 4. "They're amazing creatures." 5. Jerry discovered that birds of prey include falcons, hawks, eagles, and vultures.

6. "Mr. Gray, are owls also birds of prey?" Jerry asked.

7. "Yes, they are," Mr. Gray answered.

8. Jerry then learned that owls are the only birds of prey that hunt primarily at night. 9. He was amazed that the wingspan of some birds of prey is almost 10 feet. 10. Did you know that birds of prey have three eyelids? 11. They have an upper eyelid, a lower eyelid, and an eyelid that moistens the eye. 12. Their eyesight is sharp, and they can see much better than humans, especially in dim light. 13. Yes, Jerry and his class learned a great deal from Mr. Gray's talk about those magnificent birds.

1. In sentence 1 why do *Monday* and *Jefferson Elementary School* begin with capital letters?
2. What kind of sentence is sentence 2?
3. In sentence 3 why are quotation marks used?
4. In sentence 4 why is an apostrophe used?
5. In sentence 5 why are commas used?
6. In sentence 6 name a word in direct address.
7. In sentence 7 what are the exact words of Mr. Gray?
8. In sentence 7 why is a comma used after the word *are*?
9. What kind of sentence is sentence 10?
10. In sentence 11 why are commas used?
11. In sentence 12 why is the first comma used?
12. In sentence 13 why is the comma used?
13. In sentence 13 why is the apostrophe used?
14. What is the abbreviation used several times in these paragraphs? What kind of abbreviation is it?

Diagramming

8.1 Subjects and Verbs

8.2 Direct Objects

8.3 Possessives and Adjectives

8.4 Subject Complements

8.5 Adverbs

8.6 Compound Subjects and Predicates

8.7 Compound Direct Objects

8.8 Nouns as Compound Subject Complements

8.9 Adjectives as Compound Subject Complements

8.10 Compound Sentences

8.11 Diagramming Practice

Diagramming Review

Diagramming Challenge

8.1 Subjects and Verbs

A **diagram** is a drawing that shows how the parts of a sentence are related. The most important parts of a sentence are the subject and the predicate. The simple subject of a sentence is a noun or a pronoun. The simple predicate is a verb.

A sentence with a simple subject and a simple predicate is diagrammed in this way.

Let's do an example: **Students learn.**

1. Draw a horizontal line.
2. Write the simple predicate—the verb *learn*—on the line at the right.

learn

3. Think: *Who or what learns? Students* is the subject. Write *Students* on the line to the left of *learn.*
4. Draw a vertical line to separate the subject and the predicate. This vertical line goes through the horizontal line.

Here is another example: **Teachers help.** Can you tell what word is the predicate? Can you tell what word is the subject?

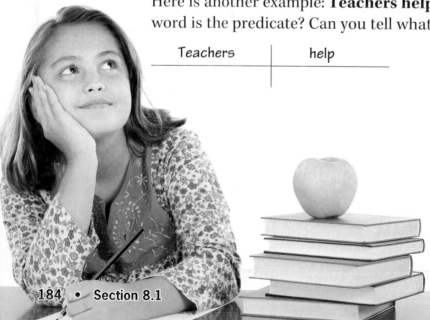

EXERCISE 1 Complete each diagram by adding a subject or a verb. Choose from these words.

athletes   clap   experiment   passengers

1. Scientists _____|_____

2. _____|_____ train

3. Fans _____|_____

4. _____|_____ ride

EXERCISE 2 Diagram each sentence.

1. Tourists sightsee.
2. We swam.
3. Scissors cut.
4. Maria cooks.
5. Clocks tick.
6. I skate.
7. Children play.
8. Bloggers write.
9. Computers calculate.
10. Friends help.
11. He paints.
12. Lilies bloom.
13. Hens cackle.
14. Carlos hikes.
15. She agrees.

Scientist Isaac Newton experimented with gravity.

APPLY IT NOW

Write three sentences about people you know and what they do. Use a subject and a predicate in each sentence. Diagram each sentence.
Example: Amy writes.

8.2 Direct Objects

The **direct object** is the noun or pronoun that completes the action of the verb. To find the direct object or direct objects in a sentence, ask *whom* or *what* after the verb.

A sentence with a simple subject, a simple predicate, and a direct object is diagrammed in this way.

Let's do an example: **Monkeys climb trees.**

1. Draw a horizontal line.
2. Write the simple predicate *climb* on the line at the right. Write the simple subject *Monkeys* on the line at the left. Draw a vertical line to separate the subject and the predicate.

Monkeys	climb

3. Think: *Monkeys climb what? Trees* is the answer. It is the direct object. Write *trees* on the line after *climb*. Draw a vertical line to separate the predicate and the direct object. Do not draw it through the horizontal line.

Monkeys	climb	trees

EXERCISE 1 Complete each diagram with a direct object. Choose from these direct objects.

milk   oatmeal

1. | Cows | give |

2. | Janet | dislikes |

Am I seeing things? Is that a monkey?

EXERCISE 2 Diagram each sentence.

1. Chris wears sunglasses.
2. We played checkers.
3. Yolanda delivers newspapers.
4. Octopuses squirt ink.
5. Pioneers built cabins.
6. Eleanor flies kites.
7. Bees gather nectar.
8. Windmills produce energy.
9. I drink juice.
10. Will has drums.
11. Grant grows tomatoes.
12. We recycle paper.
13. They ride horses.
14. Tourists visit California.
15. Computers process information.

APPLY IT NOW

Add direct objects to the sentences that you wrote for the Apply It Now on page 185. Then diagram the sentences.
Example: Amy writes poems.

Grammar in Action   Find the first direct object used in the excerpt on page 480.

8.3 Possessives and Adjectives

A **possessive noun** shows who possesses, or owns, something. Possessive nouns end in *'s* or just in an apostrophe: the *baby's* toy, the *babies'* toys. The noun that follows a possessive noun names the thing that is owned.

In a diagram a possessive noun is written on a slanted line under the noun it goes with. The possessive adjectives *my, your, his, her, its, our,* and *their* are diagrammed the same way.

Let's do an example: **Kate's horse trots.**

1. Write the predicate *trots* and the simple subject *horse* on the line with a vertical line between them.
2. Think: *Who owns the horse?* Kate owns the horse. It is Kate's horse. Write *Kate's* on a slanted line under *horse*.

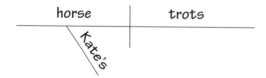

An **adjective** describes a noun. An adjective can tell how much or how many. The articles *a, an,* and *the*—which point out nouns—are also adjectives. In a diagram an adjective is written on a slanted line under the noun it goes with.

Let's do an example: **Wild horses gallop.**

1. Write the predicate *gallop* and the subject *horses* on the line with a vertical line between them.
2. Think: *What kind of horses gallop? Wild* is an adjective that tells more about horses. Write *Wild* on a slanted line under *horses*.

EXERCISE 1 Complete each diagram with the possessive or adjective given.

1. Tanya's

balloon	popped

2. Red

lights	flashed

3. an

We	saw	eagle

EXERCISE 2 Diagram each sentence.

1. Sam's bike broke.
2. Busy bees buzz.
3. Ralph likes warm pretzels.
4. Andrea's performance received loud applause.
5. A frog eats insects.
6. Lucia writes long e-mails.
7. His parrot talks.
8. Josh wears red socks.
9. Jeff writes funny stories.
10. The trees have pink flowers.
11. Loud music blared.
12. My cat has long whiskers.
13. Libby's mom makes great lemonade.
14. The long movie bored us.
15. Hawks have powerful eyesight.

APPLY IT NOW

Write two sentences about your family using possessive nouns and two sentences using adjectives. Then diagram the sentences.
Example: Anna's dog has black spots.

8.4 Subject Complements

A **subject complement** comes after a linking verb. Some linking verbs are *is, are, was,* and *were.* Nouns or adjectives can be subject complements. A noun used as a subject complement renames the subject. An adjective used as a subject complement describes the subject of the sentence.

In a diagram the subject complement is written on the horizontal line to the right of the verb. A slanted line that points back to the subject separates the verb and the subject complement.

Let's do an example: **Lassie is a dog.**

1. Write the linking verb and the subject on the horizontal line.

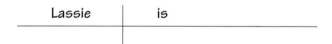

2. Think: *What is Lassie?* Lassie is a dog. *Dog* is a noun that renames the subject *Lassie.* Draw a slanted line after the verb *is* that points back to *Lassie.* Write *dog* on the horizontal line after the linking verb. The article *a* is an adjective that goes with the noun *dog.* Write *a* on a slanted line under *dog.*

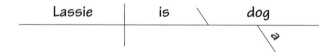

Let's do another example: **Rainbows are colorful.**

1. Write the linking verb and the subject on the horizontal line.

Rainbows | are

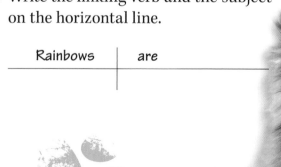

2. Think: *What are rainbows?* Rainbows are colorful. *Colorful* is an adjective that tells more about the subject *rainbows*. Draw a slanted line after the verb *are* that points back to *Rainbows*. Write *colorful* on the line after the verb.

Rainbows	are \ colorful

EXERCISE 1 Complete each diagram by adding the noun or adjective given as a subject complement.

1. fruit

Oranges	are

2. excited

Inez	was

EXERCISE 2 Diagram each sentence.

1. Whales are mammals.
2. The trees were cypresses.
3. Mom's specialty is cornbread.
4. The supermarket was a busy place.
5. A submarine is a sandwich.
6. The photos are great.
7. My jacket is warm.
8. He is British.
9. Hudson was an explorer.
10. The cocoa was delicious.
11. Kendra is my friend.
12. Mandolins are musical instruments.
13. Samantha was enthusiastic.
14. Nick's pastime is soccer.
15. A kangaroo is a marsupial.

APPLY IT NOW

Write four sentences about people or animals you know. Use two nouns and two adjectives as subject complements to tell more about each person or animal. Diagram your sentences.
Example: Javier is a friend. Spot is loyal.

Grammar in Action. Find the first subject complement in the excerpt on page 476.

8.5 Adverbs

An **adverb** tells more about a verb. An adverb tells when, how often, where, or how. Add an adverb to a diagram by writing it on a slanted line under the verb that it tells more about.

Let's do an example: **Jess walked quickly.**

1. Write the predicate and the subject on the line.

2. Think: *How did Jess walk?* The answer is *quickly. Quickly* is an adverb that tells how about the verb *walked.* Write *quickly* on a slanted line under *walked.*

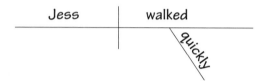

Here is another example. Can you tell how each word is used? Is it the subject, verb, or direct object? Is it an adjective, an adverb, or a possessive noun?

Did you identify *sometimes* as an adverb? It is an adverb that tells how often about the verb *chases.* It is written on a slanted line under *chases.*

EXERCISE 1 Copy each diagram. Finish it by adding the adverb given.

1. badly

Lewis	plays	soccer

2. often

Babies	cry

EXERCISE 2 Diagram each sentence.

1. The flowers wilted quickly.
2. I often eat raspberries.
3. The stars shine brightly.
4. The turtle crawled inside.
5. Julie cautiously petted the horse.
6. Yuri carefully opened the package.
7. Our hearts beat regularly.
8. The bus arrived late.
9. The teacher answers questions clearly.
10. The volcano erupted violently.
11. We hastily packed our suitcases.
12. My team won again!
13. The river flooded yesterday.
14. The children played outside.
15. The helicopter rose slowly.

APPLY IT NOW

Write four sentences about what people do on weekends. Use an adverb to tell where, when, how often, or how people do what they do. Use descriptive adverbs. Then diagram your sentences.
Examples: We sometimes play basketball.
We play aggressively.

 With an adult, use an online thesaurus.

8.6 Compound Subjects and Predicates

A sentence may have more than one subject. A sentence may also have more than one predicate. These are called **compound subjects** and **compound predicates.** In a diagram they are placed on separate parallel lines that are connected by a dashed line for the conjunction.

Let's do an example: **Airplanes and helicopters fly.** (compound subject)

1. Draw two short, parallel horizontal lines. Write a subject on each line.
2. Connect the subjects as shown. Write the conjunction *and* on the dashed line. Complete the diagram.

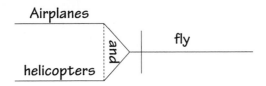

Let's do an example: **She smiled and waved.** (compound predicate)

1. Draw a short horizontal line. Write the subject on the line.
2. Draw a vertical line to separate the subject from the predicate. Draw two short, parallel horizontal lines. Write a verb on each line.
3. Connect the verbs as shown. Write the conjunction *and* on the dashed line.

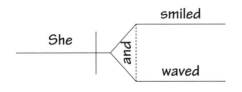

I can fly!

EXERCISE 1 Copy each diagram. Finish it by adding the compound subject or predicate given.

1. Catchers and pitchers

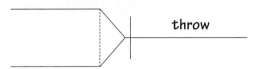

2. float and bob

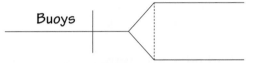

EXERCISE 2 Diagram each sentence.

1. Briony and Liam joined our club.
2. Tyler swims and bikes.
3. Sarah and I run.
4. Carrots and pretzels crunch.
5. Carlos and Ann swept and dusted.
6. Lewis and Clark were explorers.
7. Frogs and toads are amphibians.
8. The refrigerator shook and rattled.
9. Rap and hip-hop are musical styles.
10. Candles flicker and burn.
11. Ostriches and kiwis are flightless birds.
12. The tourists stopped and rested.
13. Endive and radishes are vegetables.
14. Carlos's robot walks and talks.
15. Almanacs and atlases are useful books.

Lewis and Clark

APPLY IT NOW

Write four sentences about a sporting event, two with compound subjects and two with compound predicates. Diagram your sentences.
Examples: The players and the coaches arrived.
The crowd stood and cheered.

8.7 Compound Direct Objects

A sentence may have more than one direct object. A direct object completes the action of the verb. To find the direct object or direct objects in a sentence, ask *whom* or *what* after the verb. In a diagram a compound direct object is placed on parallel horizontal lines connected by a dashed line for the conjunction.

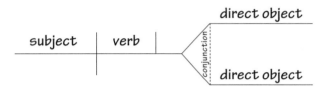

Let's do an example: **We cooked eggs and pancakes.**

1. Write the verb and the subject on the line with a vertical line between them.
2. Think: *What did we cook?* The answer is *eggs* and *pancakes.* The two nouns form a compound direct object. Write *eggs* and *pancakes* on two short, parallel horizontal lines after the verb *cooked.* Put the conjunction *and* on a dashed line between the nouns. Add a vertical line between the verb and the compound direct object.

EXERCISE 1 Copy the diagram. Finish it by adding the compound direct object given.

tulips and daffodils

Charlie | picked

EXERCISE 2 Diagram each sentence.

1. I often eat salad or soup.
2. Bob likes soccer and basketball.
3. The acrobats juggled balls and rings.
4. Lilian wore jeans and a T-shirt.
5. Jacob plays the guitar and the piano.
6. We study math and science.
7. Mom bought apples and grapes.
8. My sister writes stories and poems.
9. My brother studies French and Spanish.
10. I usually drink water or juice.
11. The flag has stars and stripes.
12. We recycle glass and plastic.
13. African nations include Mali and Morocco.
14. The ocean has currents and tides.
15. Dad always watches sports and the news.

8.8 Nouns as Compound Subject Complements

A sentence may have more than one **noun used as a subject complement.** In a diagram a compound subject complement is placed on parallel horizontal lines connected by a dashed line for the conjunction.

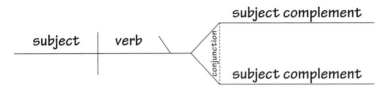

Let's do an example: **Popular sports are baseball and football.**

1. Write the linking verb and the subject on the line.
2. Think: *What are popular sports?* The answer is *baseball* and *football.* The nouns form a compound subject complement that renames the subject *sports.* Draw a slanted line after the linking verb that points back to the subject *sports.* Then draw two parallel horizontal lines after the linking verb. Write *baseball* and *football* on the lines and connect them with a dashed line. Write the conjunction *and* on the dashed line. *Popular* is an adjective that describes *sports.* Write *Popular* on a slanted line under *sports.*

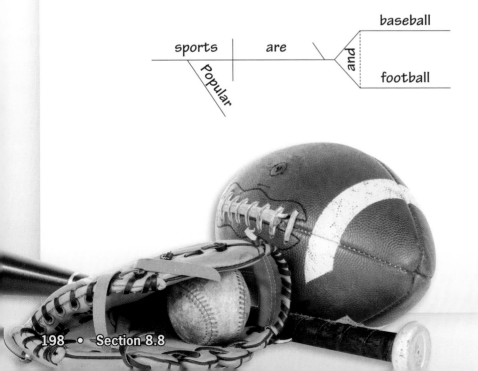

EXERCISE 1 Copy the diagram. Finish it by adding the nouns given as a compound subject complement.

dancers and singers

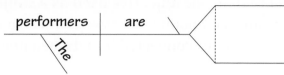

EXERCISE 2 Diagram each sentence.

1. Olympic sports are gymnastics and skating.
2. The main characters are a frog and a toad.
3. Her topic is birds or flowers.
4. The partners are Jason and Alex.
5. The books are mysteries and biographies.
6. My cousins are skaters and skiers.
7. Jenna's pets are a frog and some fish.
8. Her gifts were a sweater and a scarf.
9. He is an author and an illustrator.
10. My favorite fruits are peaches and cherries.
11. Unusual pets are snakes or ferrets.
12. The winners were Ava and Ethan.
13. Our choices are lasagna or macaroni.
14. Common names are Madison and Emily.
15. The soup is chicken and dumplings.

APPLY IT NOW

Complete these sentences with nouns as compound subject complements. Diagram the sentences.
Example: Students' favorite foods are pizza and hot dogs.
Popular games are . . .
Good writers are . . .
Good friends are . . .

8.9 Adjectives as Compound Subject Complements

A sentence may have more than one **adjective used as a subject complement.** In a diagram a compound adjective complement is placed on parallel horizontal lines connected by a dashed line for the conjunction.

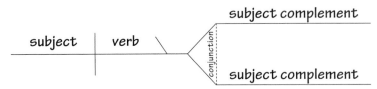

Let's do an example: **Cheetahs are sleek and fast.**

1. Diagram the subject and the linking verb.
2. Think: *What are cheetahs?* Cheetahs are *sleek* and *fast.* The adjectives form a compound subject complement that describes the subject *cheetahs.* Draw a slanted line after the linking verb that points back to the subject *Cheetahs.* Then draw a line for each adjective as shown. Connect these lines with a dashed line for the conjunction *and.*

EXERCISE 1 Copy the diagram. Finish it by adding the adjectives given as a compound subject complement.

sticky and sweet

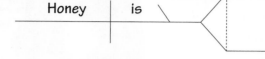

EXERCISE 2 Diagram each sentence.

1. Elephants are big but gentle.
2. The soup was hot and salty.
3. The cave was dark and gloomy.
4. Frogs' skin is green or brown.
5. The gems were small but expensive.
6. The sky was gray and cloudy.
7. The bonfire was warm and colorful.
8. Paul's kitten is cute and curious.
9. The trail was long and steep.
10. The sky was blue and cloudless.
11. The stadium was crowded and noisy.
12. Summer was hot but rainy.
13. The flowers were red or yellow.
14. The players were enthusiastic and hardworking.
15. Mountains are tall and majestic.

APPLY IT NOW

Write two sentences about a vacation or a place you would like to visit. Use adjectives as compound subject complements in each sentence. Then diagram the sentences. Examples: Our vacation was long and enjoyable. Hawaii is fun and exciting.

8.10 Compound Sentences

A **compound sentence** is made of two smaller sentences. A compound sentence is diagrammed as two separate sentences, with each sentence on a separate horizontal line, one above the other. The lines are connected by a dashed line for the conjunction *and, or,* or *but.*

subject	verb

conjunction

subject	verb

Notice that each sentence has its own subject and its own verb.

Let's do an example: **Callie sleeps late, but Colin wakes early.**

1. Diagram each smaller sentence on a horizontal line. Put one horizontal line above the other. Be sure to place each adverb under the appropriate verb.
2. Draw a dashed line to connect the sentences. Write the conjunction *but* on the dashed line.

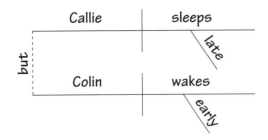

EXERCISE 1 Copy the diagram. Finish it by adding the sentence given. Use the conjunction *but*.

Veronica watches TV.

Will	reads	books

EXERCISE 2 Diagram each sentence.

1. Simon is happy, but Sherry is sad.
2. I got a camera, and I now take many photos.
3. Temperatures soared, and we went outside.
4. I play the guitar, but I rarely practice.
5. Kara finished the book, and she then wrote a report.
6. A chameleon is a lizard, and it changes color.
7. Tom was excited, but Leo was bored.
8. Mom cleaned the garage, and Dad washed the car.
9. Carrie made hamburgers, and we ate outdoors.
10. Sheila is my friend, and we talk often.
11. We did the experiment, and we reported the results.
12. Marla likes animals, and she loves zoos.
13. Friends are important, and I have good friends.
14. Botanists study plants, but zoologists study animals.
15. Heroes are important, and I admire great presidents.

APPLY IT NOW

Write two compound sentences about what you like to do in the summer. Trade your sentences with a partner. Diagram each other's sentences.

8.11 Diagramming Practice

You have learned to diagram sentences that have compound parts. Can you match the correct diagram with each of these sentences? The diagrams do not include describing words.

1. Mira had a cold, and she ate hot soup.
2. Homemade soup is delicious and healthful.
3. Martha and Mary make good pies.

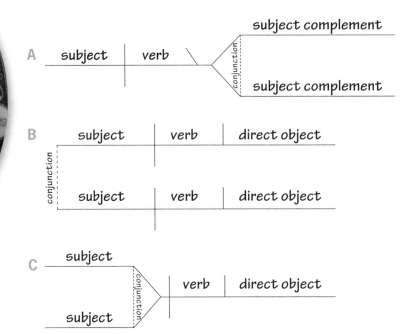

You are right if you matched sentence 1 with B, sentence 2 with A, and sentence 3 with C.

EXERCISE 1 Match each sentence with one of the diagrams above—A, B, or C.

1. Louis and Thomas fed hamsters.
2. Dogs are friendly and affectionate.
3. We wanted snow, but we got rain.
4. Supermarkets are busy and crowded.
5. Edison and Frank collect coins.

EXERCISE 2 Write out the sentences.

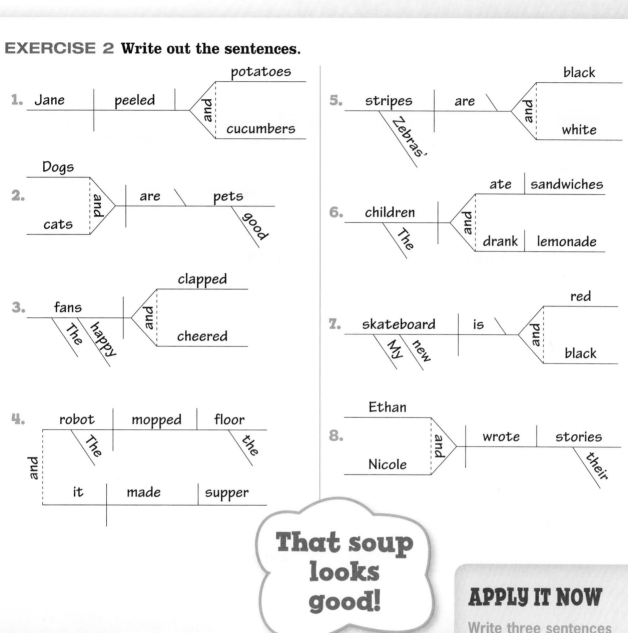

1. Jane | peeled | potatoes **and** cucumbers

2. Dogs **and** cats | are | pets (good)

3. The fans (happy) | clapped **and** cheered

4. The robot | mopped | the floor **and** it | made | supper

5. Zebras' stripes | are | black **and** white

6. The children | ate | sandwiches **and** drank | lemonade

7. My skateboard (new) | is | red **and** black

8. Ethan **and** Nicole | wrote | stories (their)

That soup looks good!

APPLY IT NOW

Write three sentences about food. Make one sentence a compound sentence. The other two sentences should have either a compound subject or a compound subject complement. Diagram your sentences.
Example: Dori and Mia like sticky rice.

Diagramming Review

Diagram each sentence.

8.1

1. Caterpillars crawl.
2. Mom bakes.
3. Dan reads.

8.2

4. Cats chase mice.
5. Dogs chew bones.
6. Squirrels gather acorns.

8.3

7. Cecilia's mom called.
8. Yellow daffodils bloom.
9. Sawyer's fish nibbled the food.

8.4

10. Cinnamon is a spice.
11. Gelatin is wiggly.
12. Yogurt is creamy.

8.5

13. The car stopped suddenly.
14. She watches TV often.
15. The wind blew harshly.

8.6

16. Fred and Ginger danced.
17. Judy sang and acted.
18. Dean and Jerry joked.

8.7

19. I ate waffles and pancakes.
20. Mom fixed spaghetti and meatballs.
21. Sally wants bacon and eggs.

8.8

22. He is an actor or a singer.
23. Healthful snacks are apples and oranges.
24. Warm states are Florida and California.

25. My shoes were black and shiny.

26. The sauces are sweet or sour.

27. The meeting was long but interesting.

28. A warbler is a bird, and it sings sweetly.

29. Sylvia likes peanuts, but she has allergies.

30. Theo plays the flute, and he practiced today.

8.11 **Write out the sentences.**

31.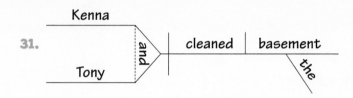

32.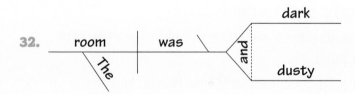

33.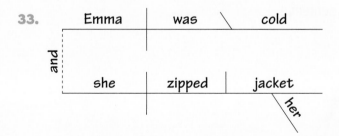

Diagramming Challenge

Study the diagram and answer the questions.

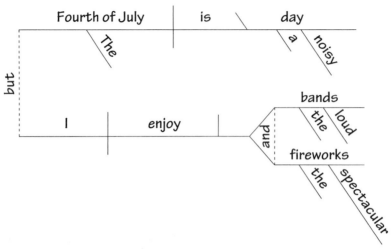

1. What kind of sentence is this?
2. What are the subjects?
3. What are the verbs?
4. What compound sentence part is there?
5. What are the adjectives and articles? What noun does each describe or point out?
6. What is the subject complement? How do you know?
7. What are the direct objects? How do you know?
8. Write out the sentence.

WRITTEN AND ORAL COMMUNICATION

Chapters

1 Personal Narratives

2 Formal Letters

3 Descriptions

4 How-to Articles

5 Persuasive Writing

6 Creative Writing: Fables

7 Expository Writing

8 Research Reports

Personal Narratives

LiNK ## Through My Eyes

by Ruby Bridges

When we were near the school, my mother said, "Ruby, I want you to behave yourself today and do what the marshals say."

. . . As we walked through the crowd, I didn't see any faces. I guess that's because I wasn't very tall and I was surrounded by the marshals. People yelled and threw things. I could see the school building, and it looked bigger and nicer than my old school. When we climbed the high steps to the front door, there were policemen in uniforms at the top. The policemen at the door and the crowd behind us made me think this was an important place.

It must be college, I thought to myself.

> Ruby Bridges shares her personal experience of what it was like attending an all-white school in 1960. The story is shared from her own point of view.

THROUGH MY EYES

RUBY BRIDGES

WE SHALL OVERCOME

Martin Luther King Jr.

CHAPTER 1

Welcome Home Holly

Claire J.
Room 206

The ad in the paper said "free puppies to a good home." We called the number to ask a few questions. My brother and sister and I had always imagined getting a yellow-haired dog. The owners said "yellowish." When we pulled into the driveway, my family and I were surprised to see brown dogs. Since we drove so far, we decided to get out of the car and take a look at the puppies. I wasn't even halfway to the pen when I made my decision—we had to get one.

My mom and my brother and sister were picking up the playful, roly-poly puppies. There were 10 in all. But I held on to one in particular. She was brown and soft and sleepy. I was in love.

As I looked around to show my mom, I saw my sister Katie trying to pick up two puppies, but one slid through her arms onto the wet grass. Katie panicked, but the puppy got up and ran to its mother.

Max walked around with a giant smile on his face, picking one up after another and brushing his cheek against their floppy ears. He was laughing at them falling over themselves, chasing one another. He was overwhelmed with the puppies' sweetness.

After an hour of playing with all the puppies, my mom asked which one we should choose. Max, Katie, and I all had an opinion, so Mom tried to help us out with the decision. She couldn't stop gushing about how precious they all were. We finally decided to get the sleepy one that I still held in my arms since the moment we arrived. The owner said we had to wait another two weeks before we could take Holly home. We pulled slowly out of that long driveway, keeping our eyes on the puppies playing in the grass until we went around the bend.

BE KIND TO ANIMALS

2011 DOG TAG TOWNSHIP OF HOPE 0000

What Makes a Good Personal Narrative?

A narrative is a story. A personal narrative is a true story about something that happened to the writer. It could be a journal entry about the first day of school. It could be a letter describing an exciting trip. Ruby Bridges wrote her personal narrative *Through My Eyes,* sharing her experience in Louisiana in the 1960s. Here are some ideas for what makes a good personal narrative.

LiNK

Through My Eyes

On Sunday, November 13, my mother told me I would start at a new school the next day. She hinted there could be something unusual about it, but she didn't explain.... All I remember thinking that night was that I wouldn't be going to school with my friends anymore, and I wasn't happy about that.

Ruby Bridges

Topic

Anything that really happened to you can be a good topic for a personal narrative. It should be something you remember clearly. The topic might be something funny, exciting, or unusual.

Audience

The people who will read your story are your audience. Think of them when you choose your topic. Your friends might want to hear how you beat the newest video game. Your grandparents might be more interested in hearing about a family trip.

A student hugs a stand-up display of Ruby Bridges.

Point of View

Point of view shows who is telling the story. In your personal narrative, you are telling the story. This is called the first-person point of view. Use words such as *I, me, my, we,* and *our.*

ACTIVITY A Read the personal narrative on page 211 and answer these questions.

1. How can you tell that this is a personal narrative?
2. Why do you think the writer chose this topic?
3. Who is the audience of this narrative?
4. What is the point of view of this narrative?
5. What words are used to show the point of view?
6. What are the main events in the narrative?
7. What are the most interesting details?

ACTIVITY B Decide which topics would make good personal narratives.

1. the day I found a $20 bill
2. my first piano recital
3. my brother's trip to the zoo
4. a train ride I'll never forget
5. the day I was born
6. what I'd do if I were an astronaut
7. my unlucky day at the beach
8. a boring afternoon
9. my summer vacation to the Grand Canyon
10. when I broke my arm
11. my first trip in an airplane
12. the day of the big snowstorm
13. how to build a bird house
14. my plans for college
15. the most helpful person I know

WRITER'S CORNER

Write three things that happened to you that would make good personal narratives.

Time Order

The events in a personal narrative are told in the order that they happened. Tell what happened first near the beginning and what happened last near the ending. Use time words such as *first, next, after, then, finally,* and *last* to show the order of the events. Here is an example.

First, I got out of bed.

Then I got dressed.

After getting dressed, I ate breakfast.

Next, I waited on the corner for the bus.

Finally, the bus arrived.

ACTIVITY C Below is a personal narrative about a trip to school in the morning. The first two sentences are given, but the other sentences are in the wrong order. Put the sentences in time order in paragraph form.

I woke up late this morning. I should have just stayed in bed.

1. After breakfast I headed for the bus.
2. When I looked in my closet, I found that all my favorite shirts were in the laundry.
3. I finally picked out a shirt, but I spilled juice on it at breakfast.
4. Next, I missed my bus by a few seconds.
5. It was too late to finish eating.
6. When I got to school, I remembered that my homework was back at home.
7. I had to leave the bus stop when I realized I'd forgotten my lunch.
8. I begged my brother to drive me to school.

ACTIVITY D Here are two paragraphs that fourth graders wrote. The first paragraph is about planting a garden. The second paragraph is about a snowstorm. Choose from the time words in the list to help show the order in which things happened.

Finally   First   Next   Then

1. I was excited about planting a garden. _____, I chose a nice sunny spot. _____, I dug up the soil. _____, I fertilized it. _____, I planted the seeds and watered them. I can't wait for the flowers to grow.

2. The weather report was for a big snowstorm for the next day, and school was canceled. We woke up early that day. The snow was coming down quickly in huge, fluffy flakes. Dad wanted to go to the garage and try to take out the car. _____, we shoveled the area in front of our door. _____, we started to shovel the walk to the garage. _____, we looked back, and we couldn't see the walk. What we had just shoveled was a blanket of snow. _____, we decided to go back into the house to have hot chocolate.

ACTIVITY E Revise the paragraph. Put the sentences in time order. Add at least two time words to show the order.

My brothers and I were stuck inside for yet another rainy day. She made an announcement. My mother was getting tired of our yelling. We spent the morning chasing one another around the house. "It's mud day!" she called out. We spent the next hour rolling in the mud and getting as dirty as we could. She told us to run upstairs and find our oldest clothes. When we finally came inside and changed our clothes, we were ready for a nap. She sent us to the backyard, where the rain had turned our lawn into a mud puddle.

WRITER'S CORNER

Choose one of your personal-narrative ideas from the Writer's Corner on page 213. Write five sentences about it, using time words to show the order of events.

Grammar in Action • Add sentence variety by using compound sentences. See Section 1.10.

Introduction, Body, and Conclusion

Through My Eyes

When I was six years old, the civil rights movement came knocking at the door. It was 1960, and history pushed in and swept me up in a whirlwind. At the time, I knew little about the racial fears and hatred in Louisiana, where I was growing up.

Ruby Bridges

A personal narrative has three main parts: the introduction, the body, and the conclusion. These are the beginning, middle, and ending of your story. Here are some tips for writing each part of a personal narrative.

Introduction

The introduction of your personal narrative is your chance to grab your reader's attention. The introduction should make the reader want to know more. You might want to ask a question, or you might make an interesting statement that will make the reader want to read the rest of your story. Does the introduction to *Through My Eyes* grab your attention?

Body

The body, or middle, of your personal narrative tells what happened. It describes the events in time order, including everything important that happened. It should not include details that are not related to your personal narrative. It should contain interesting details.

Conclusion

The conclusion of your personal narrative should tell how the story ended. You might tell something you learned or explain how you felt.

ACTIVITY A Choose the most effective introduction for each personal narrative.

1. I was doing well until I found myself at the top of a hill. Before I could stop, I was flying down the slope. Then my wheel hit a rock. Bam! Down I went! I bruised my leg and scraped my elbow, but luckily I wasn't hurt badly. Now I know why I should always wear a helmet.

   a. I was riding my skateboard down Acorn Street.

   b. I had never tried to skateboard before.

   c. I was zooming along on my skateboard and feeling confident—maybe too confident!

2. My class went on a sleepover at the Museum of Natural History. First, we explored an ancient Egyptian tomb by flashlight. It was really eerie! Next, a troupe of African dancers performed. Then we curled up in our sleeping bags next to the skeleton of a real dinosaur. I was fascinated by its sharp teeth. I decided then and there that I want to study dinosaurs when I grow up.

   a. I had an exciting weekend.

   b. Have you ever slept near a dinosaur? I have.

   c. Here's how I decided what I want to be when I grow up.

ACTIVITY B For each group choose the sentence that is part of the introduction, the sentence that is part of the body, and the sentence that is part of the conclusion.

1. I caught three big fish in just one hour.

   I never thought I would like fishing.

   After that experience, I can't wait to go fishing again.

2. By the time it was over, I realized it was the best Saturday of my life.

   We played in the fountains and went down the water slide.

   I got a big surprise from my parents last weekend.

WRITER'S CORNER

Write a one-sentence introduction to the personal narrative you wrote for the Writer's Corner on page 215. Remember to grab the reader's attention.

Details

The body of a personal narrative should be filled with details. Good details make a personal narrative clearer and more real to the reader. However, details unrelated to the story can distract the reader. Make sure all your details add something to your personal narrative.

ACTIVITY C **Which two details in each group are not related to the same topic as the rest?**

1. My parents said we could get a dog.

   My sister once had a goldfish.

   We went to the animal shelter.

   Our neighbor is allergic to cats.

   There were a lot of dogs waiting to be adopted.

   There were some cats waiting to be adopted too.

   A little black and white dog was wagging her tail.

   We all fell in love with that dog on the spot.

   We bought her a new red leash and took her home.

2. I went into the submarine.

   We went below the surface of the water.

   I like to water-ski.

   There were many tropical fish.

   I could see oyster beds.

   I could see sea urchins and sea horses.

   I have a poster of sea horses on my bedroom wall.

   Some of the sea urchins were brightly colored.

   The moray eel was strange-looking.

ACTIVITY D Choose one personal narrative and find the unrelated detail. Then write a conclusion that explains how things ended.

A.   The day after we moved to Minnesota was the most surprising day of my life. Until that day I had never seen snow. As soon as I woke up, I put on my warmest clothes, ran outside, and jumped into a drift. I couldn't believe how wet and cold it was! My brother and I played in the snow all morning. He's two years older than I am. Mom gave us socks to put on our hands so we could make a snowman. We used an old cardboard box to slide down a hill.

B.   Dad has told me a million times to close the door of the hamster cage, and I usually remember to do it. Last Tuesday I forgot. The first thing Dad does when he comes home from work is change his clothes and shoes. On Tuesday when he picked up his shoe, he saw a ball of fluff curled up inside. It was Magpie, my hamster! Dad was so startled that he dropped the shoe. Magpie woke up and scooted under the bed. The bed was covered with my favorite blanket. I had to crawl under it and pull him out.

C.   Sometimes after a disappointment, things do work out. I really wanted tickets to the kids' concert in the park. My favorite band was going to play. My dad was going to go online early and get tickets before he left for work. That day the weather was beautiful. When he got up, the computer connection was down. When he tried later at work, all the tickets were gone. I was so disappointed. Later, my dad told the story to someone at work. The person had gotten some extra tickets, and he offered them to my dad.

WRITER'S CORNER

Exchange with a partner the sentences you wrote for the Writer's Corner on page 215. Read your partner's sentences, offering suggestions where details would be helpful. Review your partner's comments.

Time Lines

A time line is one tool that writers use to organize their ideas. It can help you think of all the important events in a personal narrative. A time line can also help you put your ideas in time order.

A time line is created by drawing a long line on a sheet of paper. The line can be drawn either up and down, diagonally, or across the paper. On one side the line is divided into equal periods of time. On the other side, important events are listed in time order.

Here is a time line one student, Ernesto, made for his personal narrative about tubing on the Delaware River.

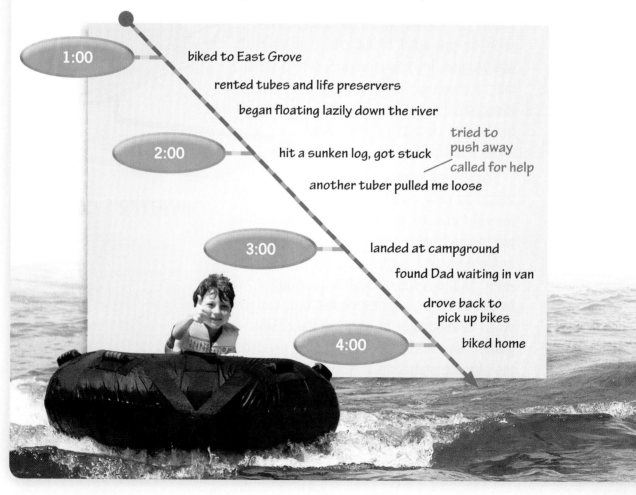

1:00 — biked to East Grove

rented tubes and life preservers

began floating lazily down the river

2:00 — hit a sunken log, got stuck — tried to push away / called for help

another tuber pulled me loose

3:00 — landed at campground

found Dad waiting in van

drove back to pick up bikes

4:00 — biked home

Look at Ernesto's time line. On the left side, he divided it by hours, listing each hour at an even distance. On the right side, he listed all the important events where they belonged on the line.

Do the same thing when you create your time line. On one side divide the line into equal periods of time, such as by minutes, hours, or days. On the other side, put the events where they belong in time order. For example, if an event happened at 1:20, put it closer to 1:00 than to 2:00.

ACTIVITY A Copy and complete the following time line about what you did one recent evening. Add more times if necessary. Add events on the other side.

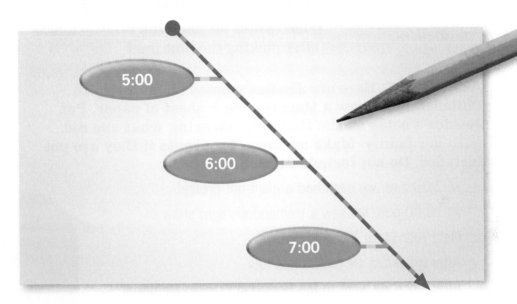

5:00

6:00

7:00

ACTIVITY B Imagine you are Ernesto writing a personal narrative. Using the time line on page 220, write two sentences about each part of your tubing adventure: starting the trip, getting stuck on the log, and ending the trip. Use time words to connect your ideas.

WRITER'S CORNER

Make a time line of the classes that you have today. Make the opening bell your first event and the closing bell your last event.

Tech Tip Use an online tool to create your time line.

Through My Eyes

I spent the whole first day with Mrs. Henry in the classroom. . . . My mother sat in the classroom that day, but not the next. When the marshals came to the house on Wednesday morning, my mother said, "Ruby, I can't go to school with you today, but don't be afraid. The marshals will take care of you. Be good now, and don't cry."

Ruby Bridges

Revising a Time Line

Once you finish a time line, it is a good idea to go back over it. Ask yourself the following questions: Did each event occur at the time shown on the time line? Should I rearrange any events? Have I included all the important details? Are there missing details I should add or unneeded details I should take out? Make any changes to the time line that you think are necessary. Notice the order of events in the excerpt on the left.

Look at Ernesto's time line on page 220. What details do you think Ernesto added after making the time line?

ACTIVITY C Here are Jessica's notes about a trip to Philadelphia. Draw a time line on a sheet of paper. Put Jessica's notes on the time line, showing what she did with her family. Make up times for events if they are not included. Do not include unneeded details.

At 2:00 p.m. we each had a giant hot pretzel.

At 10:30 p.m. we saw a tremendous light show.

Next year we're going to Boston.

After breakfast we took a bus tour.

After lunch we went to the Benjamin Franklin Memorial.

Betsy Ross lived in Philadelphia.

When the tour was over, we went to Independence Hall.

At 9:00 a.m. we ate breakfast at a coffee shop.

We didn't have time to see the Liberty Bell.

For lunch we had Philly cheese steaks.

We went back to our hotel for dinner.

Philadelphia is called the "City of Brotherly Love."

Ruby Bridges, age 6

ACTIVITY D Put these steps for making muffins into the time line. Leave out the unneeded detail. Then write the steps in paragraph form. Use time words.

6:10   I put the muffins into a 350° oven.

6:05   I stirred until the batter was smooth.

6:25   I checked on the muffins as they baked.

6:03   I added the milk and eggs.

6:08   I poured the batter into the muffin tins.

6:20   My brother came home.

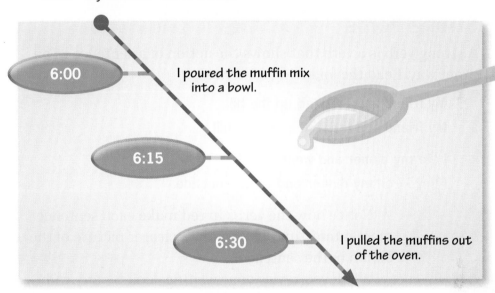

6:00 — I poured the muffin mix into a bowl.

6:15

6:30 — I pulled the muffins out of the oven.

ACTIVITY E What did you do last Sunday? Make a time line. Start with waking up in the morning. End with going to bed. Read over your time line. Add any missing details. Take out any unneeded details.

WRITER'S CORNER

Use the time line you made in Activity E to write four or five sentences for the body of a personal narrative about what you did last Sunday. Use time words to connect the details.

Exact Words

A writer paints a picture with words. If you use exact words, such as strong verbs and colorful adjectives, you will paint a clearer picture. When you use exact words, readers will enjoy your writing more.

Strong Verbs

A strong verb is a verb that shows the action of a sentence in an exact way. Read the following sentences:

My friend and I walked up the hill.

My friend and I *marched* up the hill.

I ate my dinner and went outside.

I *devoured* my dinner and *darted* outside.

Notice how the verbs in red make each sentence more interesting. They paint a clearer picture of the action in the sentence.

When you revise your writing, look for any verbs that are too general or dull. Replace them with strong verbs.

ACTIVITY A Think of a strong verb to replace each verb below. Using three of the verbs you thought of, write a sentence using each verb.

1. said
2. break
3. go
4. cry
5. get
6. ran

ACTIVITY B Replace the italicized verb in each sentence with a strong verb from the list.

| bragged | rattled | slid |
| grumbled | scooted | demanded |

1. The train *moved* along the track.

2. The playful otters *went* down the muddy riverbank.

3. Sean *said*, "I can't move this box."

4. I *ran* around the corner to hide from him.

5. "I scored the winning run!" *said* Mia.

6. The coach *asked* that the players try harder.

ACTIVITY C Revise the paragraph. Change at least four verbs to strong verbs.

The engine sounded, and the boat went. I held on to the rope and went across the water on my water skis. "Look at me!" I said. My heart was beating fast. A spray of water hit my face. Then, as the boat turned, I lost my balance and went through the air. I hit the water and let go of the rope. As the boat came around to pick me up, I said, "May I go again?"

ACTIVITY D Complete the sentences with strong verbs.

1. Jane _____ across the park to catch up to her friends.

2. The puppy _____ his food quickly.

3. A fuzzy caterpillar _____ slowly through the grass.

4. The kite _____ in the wind and then _____ to the ground.

5. At the playground Connor _____ and _____ with his brother.

WRITER'S CORNER

Write four sentences describing what you did this past weekend or after school. Then exchange papers with a partner and suggest strong verbs to replace each verb that was used.

Colorful Adjectives

Just like strong verbs, colorful adjectives can bring your writing to life. Colorful adjectives describe something in an exact way. Colorful adjectives paint a clear picture of what is being described.

The mean dog jumped at the gate.

The *snarling* dog jumped at the gate.

Notice how the colorful adjective *snarling* makes the second sentence more interesting. When you revise your writing, look for places to add colorful adjectives.

ACTIVITY E **Replace the adjective in italics in each sentence with a colorful adjective from the list.**

enormous	jagged	velvety
blinding	thrilling	rundown
charming	silent	booming

1. Suddenly, the call of a crow echoed through the *quiet* forest.
2. The campers listened to the *good* story.
3. I tried to take a bite of the *big* sandwich.
4. He stroked the kitten's *soft* fur.
5. The forest ranger had a *nice* smile.
6. We tiptoed past the *old* shed.
7. The *loud* thunder scared everyone.
8. She tripped on the *rough* rock.
9. I had to squint in the *bright* sun.

LiNK

Through My Eyes

As I sat quietly huddled with Mrs. Henry, mobs of protestors roamed the streets. People threw rocks and bricks at passing cars. Some even tossed flaming bottles of gasoline.

Ruby Bridges

Angry protestors outside Ruby Bridges's school in 1960

ACTIVITY F Complete the sentences with colorful adjectives. Be as creative as you can.

1. The _____ sailboat glided on the _____ blue water.
2. A _____ squirrel darted behind a _____ tree.
3. Charlie's _____ pet scared his neighbors.
4. The _____ boys marched up the _____ hill.
5. Her _____ baby waved her _____ hands in the air.
6. The _____ smell of popcorn made me hungry.
7. One by one we dove into the _____ water of the _____ lake.
8. The _____ girls were lost in the _____ fog.

ACTIVITY G Complete the paragraph by using exact words. The word in parentheses tells whether to use a strong verb or a colorful adjective.

The air grew thinner as we __(verb)__ up the mountain. __(Adjective)__ trees gave way to smaller plants. The __(adjective)__ wind was cold, and we __(verb)__ in our thin cotton jackets. __(Adjective)__ clouds threatened overhead. In the distance we could hear an eagle __(verb)__. Suddenly, there was a __(adjective)__ clap of thunder, and lightning __(verb)__ the sky. Because of the __(adjective)__ storm, we __(verb)__ for shelter.

ACTIVITY H Paint a clearer picture for each sentence by replacing each italicized word.

1. I *went* down the ramp on my *new* skateboard.
2. The *tasty dessert* was *eaten* after school.
3. We had a *nice* time *playing* at the fun fair.
4. Spencer and Alonzo *walked* up the *big* mountain.

WRITER'S CORNER

Write a short paragraph about something that happened to you last week. Use strong verbs and colorful adjectives to form a clear picture.

Grammar in Action. To add variety to your paragraph, use at least one compound sentence. See Section 1.10.

Contractions with Pronouns

Sometimes two words can be combined to make one word called a contraction. The contraction is shorter than the two words because one or more letters are left out. An apostrophe takes the place of the missing letter or letters.

Some contractions are formed by joining a pronoun and a verb. Study this list of contractions. Name the missing letter or letters in each contraction.

I am	I'm	I have	I've
he is	he's	you have	you've
she is	she's	we have	we've
it is	it's	they have	they've
we are	we're	he has	he's
you are	you're	she has	she's
they are	they're	it has	it's
I will	I'll	I would	I'd
he will	he'll	you would	you'd
she will	she'll	we would	we'd
it will	it'll	they would	they'd
we will	we'll	he would	he'd
you will	you'll	she would	she'd
they will	they'll		

ACTIVITY A Match each pair of words in Column A with their contraction in Column B.

	Column A		Column B
1.	they have	a.	I'll
2.	I would	b.	we'll
3.	we will	c.	I'm
4.	she is	d.	they've
5.	I have	e.	we're
6.	I am	f.	you've
7.	it is	g.	she's
8.	I will	h.	I've
9.	we are	i.	it's
10.	you have	j.	I'd

ACTIVITY B Use a contraction in place of the words in italics in each sentence.

1. *I have* never seen a pink flamingo.
2. *She is* going to eat split pea soup.
3. In the play, *I am* a talking rabbit.
4. *We are* playing on the trampoline.
5. *I would* rather meet a cat than a tiger.
6. If you start to walk, *they will* follow you.
7. I think *it is* the same color as mine.
8. If we can, *we will* be there.
9. *They are* making a dragon kite.
10. *He has* learned his lines in the play.
11. *They would* like to go to the art fair.
12. *You will* be late if you don't get up now.
13. *I will* take a pound of red cherries.

WRITER'S CORNER

Think of a movie you have seen or a book you have read recently. Write three sentences using different pronouns and describe the characters. Use a contraction in each sentence.

Formal and Informal Language

Sometimes writing should be formal. You use formal writing when you write a letter to a business or a report for your teacher. At other times your writing can be informal, such as in an e-mail to a friend.

One way to make your writing formal is to avoid contractions. Informal writing often uses contractions, but formal writing does not. Think of your audience and your purpose before you write. If you are writing something formal, do not use contractions.

ACTIVITY C Make each sentence more formal by taking out the contraction.

1. You said you'd help me.
2. She'll be there right after school.
3. I'd like more information about your book club.
4. We've never done this before.
5. I think it's going to rain.

6. She's requesting a refund.
7. I thought they'd be here by now.
8. They're not going to accept the offer.
9. It's been sunny all week.
10. He's going to finish the project by Friday.
11. I'm not going to be at the meeting.
12. You'll need permission from your teacher to attend.
13. They'll call the airline to make the reservation.
14. We're going to make the changes.
15. It's been a long time since I talked to them.

ACTIVITY D These paragraphs are from a friendly letter. Make them less formal by adding contractions. Words used to make contractions with pronouns are underlined.

<u>We are</u> having a great time here in North Conway. <u>I am</u> so excited! Today <u>we will</u> be going on the water slides. <u>I have</u> also gone swimming in the lake, and <u>we have</u> all had fun playing mini golf. <u>You will</u> wish that you had come. Do not worry. <u>I will</u> be sure to bring home pictures.

Tomorrow <u>we will</u> go hiking in the morning, and <u>I will</u> go water-skiing in the afternoon. <u>I have</u> only been water-skiing once, but I want to try it again. The next day <u>we are</u> going horseback riding. <u>I have</u> never been horseback riding before. <u>It is</u> going to be scary, but <u>I will</u> try to do my best. Maybe <u>I will</u> like it.

ACTIVITY E These paragraphs are from a thank-you letter. Make it more formal by taking out the contractions.

I'm writing to thank you for visiting our class last week. It's always a pleasure to talk to a real firefighter. I'm sure you're a busy person, and we're honored that you decided to visit our class. You're always welcome in our classroom.

You've inspired many of us to become firefighters when we grow up. If possible, we'd like to visit you at the fire station. It would be interesting to see the fire trucks and other equipment up close.

ACTIVITY F Complete each sentence with the items in parentheses that would be more appropriate.

1. (You'd   You would) enjoy visiting our town, Mr. President.
2. My sister says (she'll   she will) go bananas at the dance party.
3. I (can't   cannot) wait until summer break.
4. If (you're   you are) practicing soccer after school today, can you come over tomorrow?
5. (I'd   I would) like to inform you that your payment is late and (you'll   you will) get a fine.

WRITER'S CORNER

Write a four- or five-sentence formal note requesting something from your teacher or principal. Use formal language and avoid contractions.

Oral Personal Narratives

When you get home from school, do you tell your family what happened during the day? At school do you tell your friends what you did over the weekend? When you do, you are giving an oral personal narrative.

An oral personal narrative has the same parts as a written personal narrative. Keep the same tips in mind.

Introduction

Your opening should grab your listeners' attention. You might start with a question or a sentence that hints at what your personal narrative is about.

Body

Tell the main part of your personal narrative in time order so your listeners can follow it easily. Add enough details to make your story interesting, but do not include things that aren't important. Details that are not important to the story will distract your listeners.

Conclusion

Be sure to let your listeners know that the story is finished. Tell them how the experience ended and how you felt about what happened.

Voice

Change your tone of voice to make parts of your personal narrative sound exciting or important. You might speak faster or louder at an exciting part. You might speak slower or softer at a scary part. Remember that this is your own story. Let your personality shine through.

ACTIVITY A Think of something good that happened to you at school recently. Write an interesting opening sentence for an oral personal narrative about the event. Practice saying the sentence in different tones of voice.

ACTIVITY B Read each sentence aloud twice with a partner. Show a different emotion each time. You might read it as if you were happy, surprised, frightened, angry, or sad.

1. It's just around the corner.

2. I didn't expect that.

3. Is that really for me?

4. I think it's going to be here soon.

5. I don't think you should do that.

ACTIVITY C Read aloud the personal narrative on page 211. Use your voice, face, and body movements to show the feelings of the person who wrote the narrative.

ACTIVITY D Reread the personal narrative on page 210. Practice reading the narrative aloud. What emotions does the narrative bring up?

SPEAKER'S CORNER

Tell a partner about the experience you chose for Activity A. Include all the details that you think are important. Ask your partner which details he or she thinks are the most interesting. Do the same for your partner's experience.

Practice

Speaking in front of the whole class can be scary. One way to calm your nerves is to practice ahead of time. The better you know your story, the calmer you will feel.

Write your introduction and conclusion on note cards. Write each detail of your personal narrative on a separate card. Use keywords and phrases to help you remember the details. Put the cards in time order. Read them over carefully to make sure all the details are important.

Practice telling your story several times. You might stand in front of a mirror, or you might ask a friend or family member to listen to you. Look at your note cards to help you remember what you want to say, but don't just read them aloud. Use a tone of voice that shows how you felt about the experience.

Listening Tips

In an oral personal narrative, the listener is as important as the speaker. Follow these tips when you listen to another student's personal narrative:

- Look at the speaker so he or she knows you are paying attention.
- Listen to the introduction and try to guess what the narrative will be about.
- Picture the story in your mind as the speaker talks.
- Listen for the speaker's tone of voice to know how he or she felt about the experience.
- Give the speaker some positive feedback at the end of his or her presentation.

ACTIVITY E Choose one of these ideas. Think of a good introduction that would grab the attention of your audience. Think of a conclusion that tells how the experience ended. Write the introduction and conclusion on note cards. Then think of important details for the body and write them on separate note cards.

A. a time you surprised your family

B. something exciting that happened on vacation

C. making something with a friend or your family

D. something that didn't turn out as you expected

E. a funny thing a pet did

F. some unusual weather you experienced

G. a time you were lost or lost something

H. a contest when you won something

ACTIVITY F Work with a partner. Take turns telling each other about the experience you chose in Activity E. When it is your turn to talk, practice using your voice in different ways to show different emotions. When it is your turn to listen, help your partner decide which tone of voice worked best to tell his or her story.

SPEAKER'S CORNER

Prepare to tell about the event you chose in Activity E. Be sure your notes are in time order. Practice using your voice to make the story interesting. Finally, present your personal narrative to the class.

Prewriting and Drafting

What funny, exciting, or strange things have happened to you? What stories from your life do you like to tell? One way to share these stories is to write a personal narrative.

Prewriting

Prewriting is the time a writer spends exploring ideas and planning. Will, a fourth

 grader, spent time prewriting before writing

a personal narrative. He brainstormed to help himself choose a topic, freewrote, and then made a time line.

Brainstorming

Brainstorming is listing ideas quickly. Will began choosing a topic by brainstorming a list of things that had happened to him. Here is his list.

getting lost on the way home from school

getting an A on my math test

hanging out with my friends over
   the summer

making a bird sanctuary with my mom

going to the beach

After Will had completed his list, he thought about each topic. He wanted to write a narrative with a beginning that gets readers' attention and a clear ending. He also wanted a story that would be interesting to his audience, his classmates. He decided to write about making a bird sanctuary with his mother. Since some of his friends had seen his sanctuary and asked him about it, he thought they would be interested in reading about it.

Your Turn

Brainstorm a list of interesting things that have happened to you. Did you go on an exciting trip? Did you do something you are proud of? When you have completed your list, choose a topic that you will enjoy writing about. Your topic should also be interesting to your audience, your classmates.

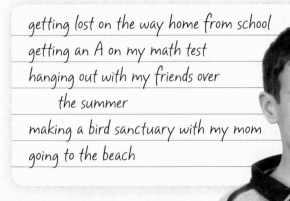

Freewriting

After choosing a topic, Will spent five minutes freewriting. He wrote all the ideas and details he remembered about his topic. He wrote in words and phrases.

Your Turn

Spend some time freewriting. List all the ideas and details about your experience you can think of. Write quickly. Pay attention to your ideas.

Making a Time Line

After freewriting, Will decided to organize  his ideas with a time line. He drew his time line across a sheet of paper. On one side he divided his line into hours.

On the other side, he filled in the important events in the narrative from his freewriting.

When he was finished, he reviewed his time line. He added a detail that seemed important and crossed out one detail that did not seem important. The time line he made is below.

Your Turn

Make a time line to organize your notes. What happened first? What happened next? How did the experience end? Put your notes in order on the time line.

Read your time line. Can you think of any important details you forgot? Are there any details that are not related to your topic? Revise your time line if necessary.

10:00 — went to garden center, picked out birdbath and two bird feeders, looked at plants and flowers

12:00 — put birdbath under tree
put bird feeders in tree ——added seeds, nuts, fruit
filled birdbath with water
~~ate peanut butter~~
~~sandwiches for lunch~~

2:00 — birds came to eat and drink

Prewriting

Drafting

Content Editing

Revising

Copyediting

Proofreading

Publishing

Drafting

Will was ready to write the first draft of his narrative. He used his time line to guide his writing. As he typed, he thought of more details to add. He used time words to help  his readers understand his narrative. Will wanted his readers to know how much he enjoyed working on his bird sanctuary.

My Bird Sanctuary

This sumer my mom and I made a bird sanctuary in our backyard. First, we went to the garden center. We picked out a nice birdbath. We bought two bird feeders too. We looked at a lot of plants and flowers, but we didn't buy any.

When we got home, we put the birdbath under a tree by the hedge the birds can hide in the hedge. Next, I put the bird feeders in the tree. I put seeds, nuts, and fruit in the feeders. Then my mom got the hose and filled the birdbath with water. The sanctuary was ready

Later that afternoon my mom called me to the window. There were birds eating at the feeders. A bluebird was taking a drink from the birdbath. I was happy that w'ed made the sanctuary. The birds seemed happy too.

Your Turn

Look over your notes and your time line. Then begin writing your draft.

- Write an introduction that grabs your reader's attention.
- In the body give details in time order about what happened.
- Write a conclusion that tells what you learned from your experience or how you felt about it.

As you write, add details to make your narrative more interesting. Do not include any details that do not relate to your topic.

Writer's Tip Double-space your narrative so you will have room to edit and make changes later.

Writing a Title

Have you ever read a book or an article because the title caught your attention? A good title catches a reader's attention and gives a hint about the topic.

A good title should be short but interesting. Use strong and colorful words that make a reader want to know more. Try using words that start with the same sound to give your title punch. For example, "Bobby's Birthday Blast" sounds better than "Bobby's Party."

Grammar in Action

Find the run-on sentence in Will's draft. See Section 1.11 for more information.

Prewriting

Drafting

Content Editing

Revising

Copyediting

Proofreading

Publishing

Content Editing

Will enjoyed writing his first draft, but he knew he could make it better. First, he checked the ideas and details in his draft by content editing.

Content editors read a draft to make sure that all the important ideas are included. They also make sure there are no unnecessary details. Will made his corrections with a red pencil so that the changes would be easy to see.

After looking over his draft, Will asked his friend Kaitlin to read it. Because Kaitlin had not heard about his bird sanctuary, she would notice if any important details were missing. Kaitlin used this Content Editor's Checklist to help her.

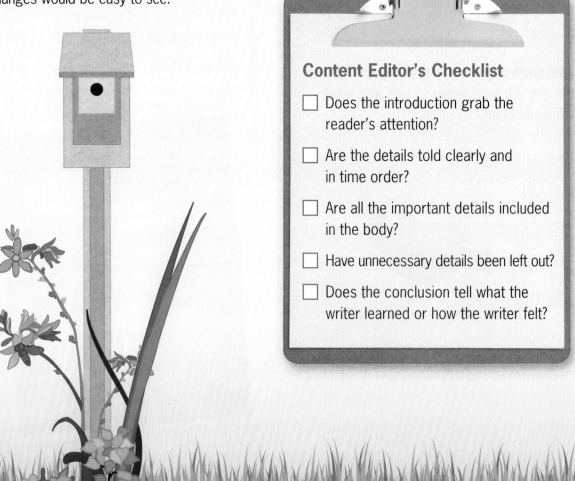

Content Editor's Checklist

☐ Does the introduction grab the reader's attention?

☐ Are the details told clearly and in time order?

☐ Are all the important details included in the body?

☐ Have unnecessary details been left out?

☐ Does the conclusion tell what the writer learned or how the writer felt?

Kaitlin read the draft once all the way through. Then she read it more carefully, checking each item on the checklist. She read the introduction to see if it grabbed the reader's attention. As she read the body, she looked for details that were unnecessary or out of order. She checked the conclusion to see if it was effective. Kaitlin shared her suggestions with Will.

Kaitlin first told Will what she liked about his personal narrative. She found the topic very interesting. She liked the conclusion and found that all the details were in time order. Then she gave Will these suggestions:

- The introduction tells what your topic is, but it didn't really grab my attention.
- I don't think you need to tell that you didn't buy any plants or flowers.
- Maybe you could tell why you put different kinds of food in the bird feeders. I thought all birds eat seeds or insects.
- It might be interesting to know what kind of tree you put the bird feeders in.

Will thanked Kaitlin for her suggestions. He liked most of them and knew that he would use her ideas when he revised his draft.

Your Turn

Read your draft, looking carefully at the Content Editor's Checklist.

- Write your ideas on your draft. Then work with a partner and read each other's narratives.
- Take notes on a separate sheet of paper.
- Meet with your partner and respectfully make suggestions for improvement. Remember to share what you like about your partner's work.

After hearing your partner's suggestions, decide which ones you want to use in your revision.

Writer's Tip Check one item from the Content Editor's Checklist at a time.

Prewriting

Drafting

Content Editing

Revising

Copyediting

Proofreading

Publishing

Writer's Workshop

Revising

This is how Will used Kaitlin's suggestions and his own ideas to revise his narrative.

My Backyard Bird Sanctuary

Watching birds in the wild can be fun, but why not make the birds come to you?
This sumer my mom and I made a bird sanctuary in our backyard. First, we went to the garden center. We picked out a nice birdbath. We bought two bird feeders too. ~~We looked at a lot of plants and flowers, but we didn't buy any.~~

When we got home, we put the birdbath under a tree by the hedge the birds can hide *from other animals* in the hedge. Next, I put the bird feeders in the tree. *Different kinds of birds eat different kinds of food, so* I put seeds, nuts, and fruit in the feeders. Then my mom got the hose and filled the birdbath with water. The sanctuary was ready

Later that afternoon my mom called me to the window. There were ~~birds~~ *some chickadees and a cardinal* eating at the feeders. A bluebird was taking a drink from the birdbath. I was happy that w'ed made the sanctuary. The birds seemed happy too.

Look at what Will did to improve his personal narrative.

- He took Kaitlin's suggestion about his introduction. What did he add?
- What sentence did he remove because it wasn't necessary in his narrative?
- Will didn't think that telling the kind of tree was important. Instead, what did he decide to add about his feeder?
- Kaitlin wrote that the introduction didn't grab her attention. How did Will fix this? Did the new introduction grab your attention?
- Kaitlin at first wondered why Will put different kinds of food in the bird feeders. What did Will add in the second paragraph?
- How did Will change the last paragraph? Why do you think he made the change?

Will looked over his draft again. He decided to add the phrase *from other animals* to explain why the birds would want to hide.

The last thing Will did was to improve his title. He thought the two *b* sounds gave it real punch.

Your Turn

Use your partner's suggestions and your own ideas to revise your narrative. When you have finished, go over the Content Editor's Checklist again. Be sure you can answer yes to all the questions.

Prewriting

Drafting

Content Editing

Revising

Copyediting

Proofreading

Publishing

Copyediting and Proofreading

Copyediting

When you copyedit, you check every sentence to make sure it is clear and makes sense. Copyeditors also check that all the words have been used correctly.

Will knew that his revisions had improved his writing. His new introduction would interest readers, and the body included all the important details. He knew, however, that he could make his draft better by copyediting.

As Will copyedited his draft, he used this Copyeditor's Checklist.

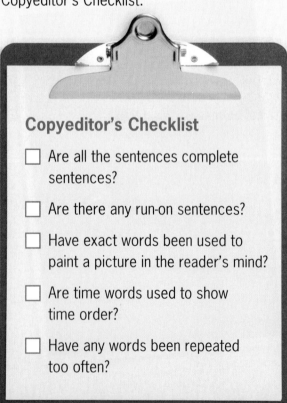

Copyeditor's Checklist

- ☐ Are all the sentences complete sentences?
- ☐ Are there any run-on sentences?
- ☐ Have exact words been used to paint a picture in the reader's mind?
- ☐ Are time words used to show time order?
- ☐ Have any words been repeated too often?

Will found some changes he wanted to make. He noticed that he had used the word *nice* to describe the birdbath. He decided to use colorful adjectives to help the reader picture the birdbath. He also noticed that he had used the verb *put* three times in the second paragraph. He changed one of them to *hung,* which was a stronger verb.

Word Choice

Will also noticed a run-on sentence and corrected it by turning it into two separate sentences. Can you find the run-on sentence in his narrative?

Sentence Fluency

Your Turn

Read your personal narrative again and copyedit it, using the Copyeditor's Checklist.

Proofreading

After copyediting, Will asked his classmate Santiago to proofread his draft. Proofreading is checking a draft for mistakes in grammar, spelling, capitalization, or punctuation. Writers always ask someone else to proofread their work. Santiago used the Proofreader's Checklist as he read Will's draft.

Proofreader's Checklist

- ☐ Are the paragraphs indented?
- ☐ Have any words been misspelled?
- ☐ Is the grammar correct?
- ☐ Are capitalization and punctuation correct?
- ☐ Were any new mistakes added during editing?

Santiago was happy to proofread Will's narrative. He realized the word *summer*

Conventions

was misspelled. He also found a missing period and a misplaced apostrophe. Can you find them?

Your Turn

Read your draft carefully, using the Proofreader's Checklist. Continue question by question through the list. Use proofreading marks to make changes.

When you have finished proofreading your own narrative, trade papers with a partner. Go over your partner's paper in the same way.

Prewriting

Drafting

Content Editing

Revising

Copyediting

Proofreading

Publishing

Common Proofreading Marks

Symbol	Meaning	Example
¶	begin new paragraph	over. ¶Begin a new
⊂	close up space	close u͡p space
∧	insert	students think (*should*)
ℛ	delete, omit	that the ~~the~~ book
/	make lowercase	Mathematics
∼	reverse letters	reve(sr)e letters
≡	capitalize	washington
⌄ ⌄	add quotation marks	ˇI am,ˇ I said.
⊙	add period	Marta drank tea⊙

Writer's Workshop

Publishing

Will was almost ready to share his personal narrative with his audience. He checked it over once more before printing out his personal narrative. He put the title in the top center of the paper with his name below it. After printing it out, he posted it on a bulletin board for his classmates to read.

My Backyard Bird Sanctuary

by Will Jazinski

Watching birds in the wild can be fun, but why not make the birds come to you? This summer my mom and I made a bird sanctuary in our backyard. First, we went to the garden center. We picked out a shallow stone birdbath. We bought two bird feeders too.

When we got home, we put the birdbath under a tree by the hedge. The birds can hide from other animals in the hedge. Next, I hung the bird feeders in the tree. Different kinds of birds eat different kinds of food, so I put seeds, nuts, and fruit in the feeders. Then my mom got the hose and filled the birdbath with water. The sanctuary was ready.

Later that afternoon my mom called me to the window. There were some chickadees and a cardinal eating at the feeders. A bluebird was taking a drink from the birdbath. I was happy that we'd made the sanctuary. The birds seemed happy too.

A publisher prints a written work and then sells or distributes it to the public. Completing Presentation the final version of something that will be published is a writer's last step in the writing process. This is your opportunity to share your work with your classmates, friends, and family.

There are many ways you can publish your personal narrative.

 Create a class book or scrapbook. Put together all the personal narratives from your class. Use a digital camera to add photos. You might also include original illustrations or souvenirs.

 Film your personal narrative. Present it by using a video of each student reading his or her narrative aloud and showing it at Parents' Night to an even larger audience.

 Post your personal narrative to a Web site that publishes student writing. Work with an adult to find an appropriate site.

 Make a pop-up book. Add illustrations by drawing them yourself or using a digital camera.

Your Turn

Print out or neatly handwrite your final copy. Then, along with your teacher and classmates, choose one of the publishing options.

- Place the title in the top center of the paper and put your name under the title.
- Check over your personal narrative one final time.
- Make sure that all your mistakes have been corrected and that no new mistakes have been made.

If you are creating a book, add visuals to draw readers into your narrative and to help them picture in their minds what happened.

Reading your classmates' personal narratives may teach you some surprising things about your classmates. When your classmates read your personal narrative, they may learn something surprising about you.

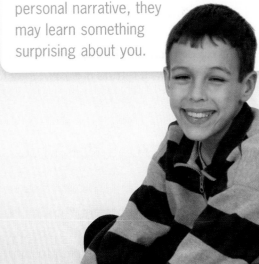

Prewriting

Drafting

Content Editing

Revising

Copyediting

Proofreading

Publishing

Formal Letters

2495 Crescent Drive
Columbus, Ohio 43215

November 22, 2005

Ms. Rachel Montgomery
Vice President of Operations
ABC Company
One International Drive
Columbus, Ohio 43215

Dear Ms. Montgomery:

On November 20, I purchased a package of your
Scrumptious pudding cups. The label said that it
contained three different flavors—chocolate, vanilla,
and tapioca. However, when I opened the box, I was
disappointed to find that all the pudding was tapioca. . . .

I have enclosed the store receipt and the pudding label.
Please send me a refund of $3.49. I look forward to your reply.

Sincerely,

Keisha Bright

Keisha Bright

> This formal letter from *You Can Write a Business
> Letter* by Jennifer Rozines Roy and Sherri Mabry
> Gordon applies the correct format, uses formal
> language, and avoids the use of contractions.

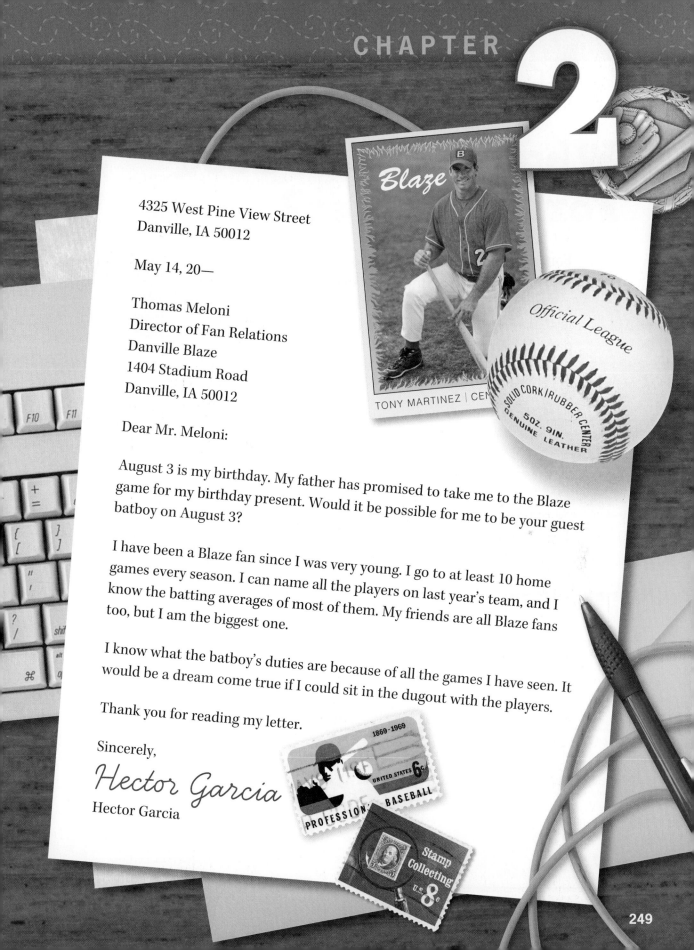

4325 West Pine View Street
Danville, IA 50012

May 14, 20—

Thomas Meloni
Director of Fan Relations
Danville Blaze
1404 Stadium Road
Danville, IA 50012

Dear Mr. Meloni:

August 3 is my birthday. My father has promised to take me to the Blaze game for my birthday present. Would it be possible for me to be your guest batboy on August 3?

I have been a Blaze fan since I was very young. I go to at least 10 home games every season. I can name all the players on last year's team, and I know the batting averages of most of them. My friends are all Blaze fans too, but I am the biggest one.

I know what the batboy's duties are because of all the games I have seen. It would be a dream come true if I could sit in the dugout with the players.

Thank you for reading my letter.

Sincerely,

Hector Garcia

Hector Garcia

What Makes a Good Formal Letter?

Formal letters are used when companies or people write about business matters. Formal letters present information in a specific way. In formal letters all writing starts at the left side of the page. Here are the parts of a formal letter.

The **heading** is your address with the date below it. The heading goes at the top left corner of the letter.

4325 West Pine View Street
Danville, IA 50012

May 14, 20—

Thomas Meloni
Director of Fan Relations
Danville Blaze
1404 Stadium Road
Danville, IA 50012

The **inside address** shows the name of the person receiving the letter and that person's job title. The inside address also shows the name and address of the company that the person works for.

The **greeting** should begin with *Dear* followed by the person's name. If you don't know the person's name, the greeting should be *Dear Sir or Madam*. All greetings should end with a colon (:).

Dear Mr. Meloni:

August 3 is my birthday. My father has promised to take me to the Blaze game for my birthday present. Would it be possible for me to be your guest batboy on August 3?

The **body** is the main part of the letter. It explains your reason for writing.

I have been a Blaze fan since I was very young. I go to at least 10 home games every season. I can name all the players on last year's team, and I know the batting averages of most of them. My friends are all Blaze fans too, but I am the biggest one.

I know what the batboy's duties are because of all the games I have seen. It would be a dream come true if I could sit in the dugout with the players.

Thank you for reading my letter.

The **closing** of a formal letter should be short and polite. You can use *Sincerely* or *Respectfully*. The closing ends with a comma. If you are typing, skip several lines and type your name.

Sincerely,

Hector Garcia
Hector Garcia

Always sign your name after the closing. If you type your letter, add your **signature** between the closing and your typed name. Include both your first and last names.

The Body

The body is the main part of the letter. First, you should explain your problem or situation. Next, you should ask the reader to help you. Explain what you would like the company or organization to do. Finally, you should thank the reader for his or her help.

ACTIVITY A Match each part of a formal letter with its description.

1. closing
2. greeting
3. inside address
4. heading
5. signature
6. body

a. gives the receiver's address
b. gives the message
c. comes after the closing
d. ends with a colon
e. Sincerely yours,
f. gives the sender's address

ACTIVITY B Arrange each list in the proper order for the heading of a formal letter.

1. St. Louis, MO 63139; 275 E. King Street; May 10, 20—
2. June 7, 20—; 1830 Birch Road; Akron, OH 45210
3. 8122 Copper Street; Calumet, MI 49913; July 2, 20—
4. your own address, today's date

ACTIVITY C Rewrite each greeting using correct capitalization and punctuation.

1. Dear sir or madam:
2. Dear Ms Guzman;
3. dear dr Thomas—
4. Dear mr. hughes,

WRITER'S CORNER

Write parts of a formal letter from your school to your family, but leave the body blank. Use your school's address and today's date for the heading. Write your own address as the inside address. Write the name of a family member in the greeting. Sign your own name in the closing.

Using Formal English

In a formal letter, it is important that the reader understand exactly what the writer needs. That is why formal letters use language that is understood by most people. American businesses use formal English when they communicate in writing.

Formal English is polite. It uses proper grammar and correct spelling. *Lots of* and *thanks* are examples of informal language that should not be used in formal writing. You also should avoid contractions such as *I'm, I'll, you're,* or *you've.*

Formal English avoids words that are slang. Slang is informal language that people use in speaking or writing. For example, the words *cool* and *awesome* to say something is good are slang. If you are not sure about a word, check a dictionary. If a word is labeled slang or if it is not in the dictionary, don't use it in a formal letter.

LiNK

Dear Master Lippincott:

I am delighted that you and your little friends are interested in the matter of salting the streets, and that you are eager to put a stop to such cruelty.

In the first place, you can help by telling every one about it, and by getting people, old and young, interested. Do you know that not one person to whom I have spoken about it—aside from Dr. Johnson, the people at the A.S.P.C.A., and Mr. Harison—knew anything about it? Strange, was it not? . . .

ACTIVITY D **The following sentence pairs should not be in formal letters. Some are impolite, and some are not in formal language. Rewrite the sentences so that they can be used in formal letters.**

1. Your kids' museum is wicked good! Do you give tours to fourth-grade classes?

2. The dumb directions are impossible to follow. It took me forever to figure them out.

3. Me and my buddies shop at your store a lot. You need to start selling Thor basketball shoes.

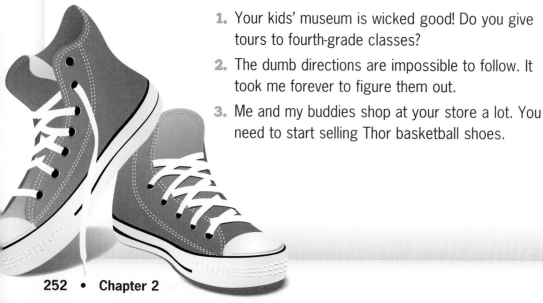

4. I want my money back. Your ad didn't say the model plane was made out of crummy cardboard.

5. I'm writing a report on the Alamo. Send me all the free stuff you have about that battle.

ACTIVITY E The formal letter below is filled with mistakes. There is a mistake in the heading, the inside address, the greeting, and the closing. See if you can find them all. Then read the body. Find two sentences that do not use formal English.

2404 Oak Terrace
Roman, OK 73013

Juan Marquez
Ardmore Eraser Company
2500 Francis St.
Ardmore, OK 73050

Dear Mr. Marquez,

I am writing to request new erasers for our class. The erasers we bought are totally bad. They leave black marks on the paper when we try to erase.

Our class bought 30 erasers from your store. Can't you send us some new erasers or something? If not, please refund us the $14 we spent on the erasers.

Thank you for your help.

Sincerely
Melanie McLaughlin
Melanie McLaughlin

WRITER'S CORNER

Using four or five sentences, write the body of a short formal letter to your teacher. You might ask for something special for you or your class, such as less homework or a change in seats. Use formal English.

Grammar in Action. When using a collective noun, such as "class," use a singular verb. See Section 2.7.

Types of Formal Letters

There are two main types of formal letters that you might write. You might write to a company to complain about a product, or you might write to an organization to request information. Both types of formal letters follow the rules that you learned in Lesson 1.

Letters of Complaint

You might write a letter of complaint to a company because a product that you purchased from them does not work or is incomplete. In the body of your letter, first state what the problem is. Then explain how you would like the company to solve the problem.

Remember that this is a formal letter. You should use polite language, even if you are unhappy with the company. Successful businesses usually try to keep their customers happy and will work to solve your problem.

ACTIVITY A Read the name of each product. What kind of problem might you have with that product? Tell why you might write a formal letter about each one.

1. box of cereal
2. MP3 player with headphones
3. backpack with several pockets and zippers
4. soccer cleats
5. cell phone

ACTIVITY B In this letter of complaint, the writer has used language that will not make the business eager to help. Rewrite the letter using formal language.

143 Twain Lane
Hannibal, MO 63407

December 22, 20—

Director
City Bookstore
124 Main Street
Hannibal, MO 63407

Hey:

What kind of cheesy operation are you running? On November 29 I placed an order at your shop for *The Hawk That Dare Not Hunt by Day* by Scott O'Dell. The clerk promised it would be sent to me within 10 days, but I haven't received it yet. What's going on?

I want to give this book as a birthday gift. I was hoping to give it for my friend's birthday this year, not next year. You better call me as soon as possible to tell me when I'll get my book. My phone number is 606-555-6342.

A really mad customer,

Rico Jones
Rico Jones

Ugh!
(I'm so mad.)

WRITER'S CORNER

Think of a product that didn't work as you expected it would. Write answers to these questions: *What is the product? What is the problem? To whom can you write to solve the problem? If you don't know, how can you find out?*

Tech Tip With an adult, research your product information online.

Letters of Request

You may sometimes need information for a school project or for a family vacation. Often you can find what you need on the Internet. If you cannot find exactly what you need there, you may have to write to someone who can give you more personal help. Government agencies or other organizations supply this type of information for free. You could write one of them a letter of request. Businesses will typically give information on their products or services for people who may be future customers.

As in all formal letters, first state the reason that you are writing. Then tell how you would like the agency or organization to help you. Keep your letter short and polite.

ACTIVITY C Choose two of the following situations. Write the body of a formal letter for each product or service needed. Explain clearly and formally what you would like. Be sure to thank the person for helping you.

A. Your family will be driving across South Dakota. You would like information about Custer State Park.

B. Your school chorus wants to have T-shirts made. You would like to know the price for printing 35 T-shirts.

C. Your school band wants to travel to a concert in a nearby town. You would like to know how much it costs to charter a bus and how many passengers each bus holds.

D. Your favorite toothpaste is offering a free book of knock-knock jokes. You must send in four proof-of-purchase seals and a stamped, self-addressed envelope.

E. Your school sports team was the subject of an article in a local newspaper a few weeks ago. You would like to get some extra copies of the newspaper to give to some of your relatives.

Buffalo are one of the attractions of South Dakota's Custer State Park.

ACTIVITY D Some of the following sentences are from letters of complaint. Some are from letters of request. Read each sentence and decide which is which.

1. Please send me a copy of the latest Tangerine Man comic book.

2. The problem is that the wheels of the skateboard are lopsided.

3. I hope you will find the time to send me an autographed picture.

4. I found that the bookshelf kit did not come with directions for putting it together.

5. I have not yet received the Perfect Gloss shellac I ordered a month ago.

6. I would be grateful if you would send me some information about places to stay near Mount Washington.

7. I am looking for copies of old CDs. Can you tell if you have any Cold Play in stock at the moment?

8. The hamster toy wheel I ordered is missing a part.

ACTIVITY E These are writers' first drafts of letters of request. The language is too informal. Rewrite the letters to make the language formal and polite.

1. Hi. How's it going? My soccer team will be visiting Prairie City for the tournament next week. Any chance we can take a tour of your dairy while we're in town? There will be about 25 of us. Thanks.

2. Hello. I got an MP3 player from my mom for my birthday. It's model SPX, and it's really cool. I use it a lot. But I've lost the case that it came in. I'd like a new case. I can pay for it. Don't worry. Send me a bill.

WRITER'S CORNER

Think of the product you wrote about in the Writer's Corner on page 255. In three or four sentences, clearly and politely explain the problem for a letter of complaint.

Grammar in Action. Make sure the proper nouns are capitalized in your letter of complaint. See Section 2.2.

Compound Sentences

Some writers use too many short sentences in their writing. Writing is more interesting when the sentence lengths are varied. Often two short sentences with related ideas can be combined, or joined, to make a longer sentence. The longer sentence is called a compound sentence. The short sentences can be combined by using a comma and a conjunction such as *and, but,* or *or.*

Here are some sentence pairs that have been combined to make compound sentences. Notice how the compound sentences are more interesting and less choppy.

One leg is missing. The top is scratched.
One leg is missing, and the top is scratched.

I changed the batteries. It still doesn't work.
I changed the batteries, but it still doesn't work.

We can go Tuesday. Friday is OK if that's better for you.
We can go Tuesday, or Friday is OK if that's better for you.

Where are we going? How do we get there?
Where are we going, and how do we get there?

Should we wait until the movie ends? Would you rather go now?
Should we wait until the movie ends, or would you rather go now?

ACTIVITY A Write each compound sentence with correct punctuation.

1. I read all the instructions but I still have a few questions.
2. You can mail the tickets to us or we can pick them up at the box office.
3. I enjoy reading your magazine and I would like to order a subscription.
4. We would like to take the tour but we will not arrive until the afternoon.
5. We will be there for five days and we would like some information on nearby parks.

ACTIVITY B Combine each pair of sentences to form a compound sentence. Use the conjunction in parentheses.

1. The basket is new. The handle broke off. (but)
2. I will send it back. You can pick it up. (or)
3. The bottle cap is closed. The liquid leaks out. (but)
4. The plastic is cracked. The color is faded. (and)
5. My mom called. My dad sent a fax. (and)
6. I've called for help. I only get a busy signal. (but)
7. The switch is on. The toy will not start. (but)
8. You can fix it. You can send me a new one. (or)
9. I wanted to buy your game. The store had run out. (but)
10. You can send me a new copy. You can refund my money. (or)

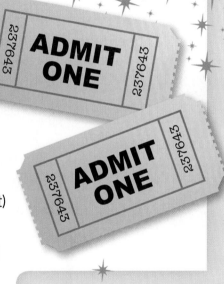

WRITER'S CORNER

Write two compound sentences for each of the conjunctions *and*, *or*, and *but*.

Choosing the Correct Conjunction

You can combine sentences only when they are about related ideas. There are different ways that ideas can be related. You need to use the conjunction that shows how the ideas are related.

Study this chart to know when to use *and, but,* and *or.*

and	**connects ideas that are alike in some way**
	Carla can swim, *and* she can ride a bike.
but	**connects ideas that are different**
	Tomás can swim, *but* he can't ride a bike.
or	**connects ideas that give a choice**
	Later I will go swimming, *or* I will ride my bike.

ACTIVITY C Combine the first part of each compound sentence in Column 1 with the correct second part in Column 2. Write the sentences using the correct conjunctions.

Column 1

1. Dad must use sunscreen,
2. John has a fever,
3. Todd took the bus,
4. We were going to play tennis,
5. Fido slipped out of his collar,
6. The baby must have his blanket,
7. We wanted to see the film,
8. We can walk to the game,

Column 2

a. he still went to school.
b. he met us at the museum.
c. it started to rain.
d. he will get burned.
e. we can take our bikes.
f. it took an hour to catch him.
g. the tickets were sold out.
h. he will start to cry.

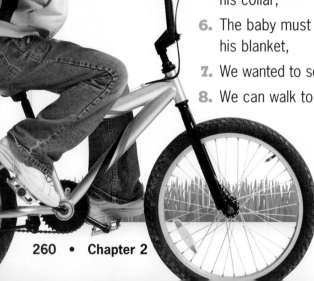

ACTIVITY D There is a conjunction missing in each of these sentences. Tell the best conjunction that could complete each sentence.

1. You can call me, _____ you can send me an e-mail.
2. I like the jacket, _____ the buttons are too large.
3. The lamp works, _____ the bulb is burned out.
4. The pearls are real, _____ they are expensive.
5. We can go there by car, _____ we can take a bus.

ACTIVITY E Write each pair of sentences as a compound sentence.

1. The backpack is new. The zipper ripped out.
2. The bag is closed. The pieces fall out anyway.
3. The clock is slow. The alarm doesn't work.
4. The chain fell off. The paint is scratched.
5. We can eat our big meal now. We can have it tonight.
6. Come visit us anytime. Be sure to call first.
7. I like to garden. I have never grown squash before.
8. Would you like some tea? Would you like coffee?
9. I have a new puppy. I need information on caring for it.
10. We can sleep in a cabin. We can stay at the lodge.

ACTIVITY F Complete each compound sentence. Use a related idea that goes with the first part.

1. I didn't write the correct address on the envelope, and _____.
2. I ordered a special card, but _____.
3. We can buy the video game at the store, or _____.
4. The game was inexpensive, but _____.
5. I can save this money, or _____.

Mailing a Formal Letter

Addressing the Envelope

Formal letters are most effective when they are clear, neat, and get to the right person. It is important to address the envelope correctly. Look at the envelope below.

Your return address goes on the top left corner of the envelope. Write your name, street address, city, state, and zip code. If the letter cannot be delivered, the Postal Service will know where to return it.

In the middle of the envelope, write the name and the address of the person receiving the letter. This is the mailing address. Copy this information from the inside address on your letter, using the same capitalization and punctuation.

Return Address (the letter writer's address)

Mailing Address (the receiver's address)

Stamp (Always attach one in the top right corner.)

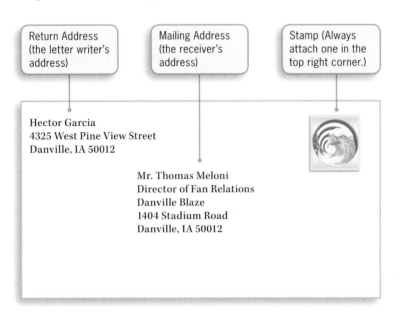

Hector Garcia
4325 West Pine View Street
Danville, IA 50012

Mr. Thomas Meloni
Director of Fan Relations
Danville Blaze
1404 Stadium Road
Danville, IA 50012

State Abbreviations

State	
Alabama	AL
Alaska	AK
Arizona	AZ
Arkansas	AR
California	CA
Colorado	CO
Connecticut	CT
Delaware	DE
District of Columbia	DC
Florida	FL
Georgia	GA
Hawaii	HI
Idaho	ID
Illinois	IL
Indiana	IN
Iowa	IA
Kansas	KS
Kentucky	KY
Louisiana	LA
Maine	ME
Maryland	MD
Massachusetts	MA
Michigan	MI
Minnesota	MN
Mississippi	MS
Missouri	MO
Montana	MT
Nebraska	NE
Nevada	NV
New Hampshire	NH
New Jersey	NJ
New Mexico	NM
New York	NY
North Carolina	NC
North Dakota	ND
Ohio	OH
Oklahoma	OK
Oregon	OR
Pennsylvania	PA
Rhode Island	RI
South Carolina	SC
South Dakota	SD
Tennessee	TN
Texas	TX
Utah	UT
Vermont	VT
Virginia	VA
Washington	WA
West Virginia	WV
Wisconsin	WI
Wyoming	WY

State Abbreviations

The United States Postal Service has assigned abbreviations to the names of the states. The abbreviations are listed on page 262. Use them to help the Postal Service deliver your mail.

ACTIVITY A Put the following return addresses in the correct order. Write them as they should be written on envelopes.

1. Juliet F. Jefferson; Honolulu, Hawaii 96800; 724 Palm Street

2. Keokuk, Iowa 52632; Charles Singh; 14 Front Street

3. 314A Gross Point Road; Anne Gray; Big Bar, Idaho 83678

4. Lombard, Pennsylvania 60015; 23N52 18th Avenue; Lilly Cappin

5. Nicholas Harrington; 11 14th Street; Boston, Massachusetts 22098

ACTIVITY B Put the following mailing addresses in the correct order. Write them as they should be written on envelopes.

1. Director of Customer Service; Mr. Khalid Azarra; Skaters' World; 664 Hampton Road; St. Louis, Missouri 63197

2. Ms. Hannah Morgan; President; 67 Natchez Boulevard; Loopy Toy Company; Los Angeles, California 90048

3. Mr. John Cicero; Lagrange, Texas 40525; Cicero Canoes; Manager of Customer Relations; 12 Lake Street

4. Chicago, Illinois 60618; Ms. Ann Marcic; Green Architecture; 4018 N. Sawyer Ave.; Lead Architect

WRITER'S CORNER

Draw an envelope on a sheet of paper. Address the envelope to your school principal. Add your return address and draw a stamp in the correct corner.

Folding Your Letter

There is a correct way to fold a formal letter. First, fold the bottom third of the paper a little more than half the way up. Then fold the top third down. Be sure to keep the left and right edges even. Place the letter into an envelope with the last fold on the top.

Preparing the Envelope on a Computer

For formal letters, it is recommended that the return address and the mailing address be typed.

If you are preparing your letter on a computer, word-processing programs generally have a feature that makes it easy for you to prepare an envelope. All you need to do is type the return address and the mailing address in the correct places. Most printers have a place where you can put envelopes to be printed.

Have you ever printed an envelope? If not, perhaps you can ask a classmate or family member to show you how to do this.

ACTIVITY C Use the list of state abbreviations on page 262. Write the state or district that each of the following abbreviations stands for.

1. ND	12. GA	23. CO	34. CT	45. KS
2. FL	13. TX	24. KY	35. IA	46. PA
3. MO	14. WV	25. HI	36. OR	47. WY
4. LA	15. AK	26. AZ	37. MN	48. ID
5. IL	16. CA	27. IN	38. NH	49. VA
6. SC	17. MI	28. WI	39. AL	50. NE
7. AR	18. WA	29. DE	40. NM	51. DC
8. OK	19. NJ	30. UT	41. OH	
9. NV	20. VT	31. MS	42. MT	
10. TN	21. ME	32. MD	43. MA	
11. NY	22. RI	33. SD	44. NC	

ACTIVITY D The information in each of these addresses is not in the correct order. Draw envelopes on a sheet of paper. Address the envelopes correctly. Design and draw your own stamps.

Return Address	Mailing Address
1. 501 Adams Avenue Kelly Schmidt New Orleans, LA 70101	672 South High Street Advertising Director Mrs. Ann Saldo Happy Toy Company Arlington, VA 22213
2. Dewar, IA 50623 Pat Parker 656 West George Street	P.O. Box 6789 Ms. Jean Jaklin Portland, OR 97228 Vice President Skateboards Plus
3. Frank Martineau Edison NJ 08816 342 Lincoln Lane	Business Manager Krafts for Kids Phoenix, AZ 20190 Mr. Carlos Suarez 1150 Briar Square

WRITER'S CORNER

Look at the Writer's Corners on pages 255 and 257. Write the address for the company on an envelope. Then fold your letter and insert it into the envelope.

Tech Tip Print the address on your envelopes using your printer.

Antonyms

Antonyms are pairs of words that have opposite meanings. Here are some antonyms.

wide/narrow	**thick/thin**	**fixed/broken**
poor/rich	**yes/no**	**better/worse**
fast/slow	**true/false**	**tidy/messy**

You might use antonyms when you write a letter of complaint. Antonyms can describe what is wrong with a product. They can also describe how you want the problem to be solved. Here are some examples.

The coat looks *thick* in your ads, but it's really very *thin*.

The toy arrived *broken*, and I'd like to have it *fixed*.

I thought the roses would be *real*, but they were *artificial*.

ACTIVITY A Read each word. Give an antonym for it.

1. tight	7. sweet	13. off	19. noisy
2. sharp	8. over	14. wrong	20. dark
3. happy	9. high	15. loud	21. buy
4. kind	10. open	16. bent	22. long
5. strong	11. dry	17. cloudy	23. easy
6. warm	12. little	18. stop	24. sleepy

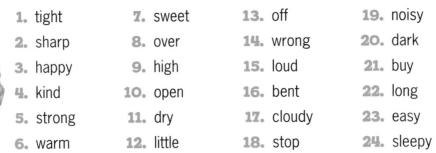

ACTIVITY B Match each word in Column A with its antonym in Column B. Use a dictionary if you need help.

Column A

1. large
2. high
3. right
4. old
5. awake
6. rare
7. difficult
8. bright
9. busy
10. give

Column B

a. common
b. asleep
c. young
d. easy
e. dim
f. take
g. low
h. idle
i. small
j. left

ACTIVITY C Write *yes* if the underlined words in each item are antonyms. Write *no* if they are not.

1. The <u>hilly</u> road became <u>flat</u> when we got to the desert.
2. We left a <u>neat</u> cabin, and it was <u>clean</u> when we got back.
3. A <u>fast</u> car is no help when traffic is <u>slow</u>.
4. I thought the leather would be <u>real</u>, but it is <u>fake</u>.
5. The opening is too <u>wide</u> and <u>long</u>.
6. The directions were <u>complicated</u>, and they were <u>difficult</u> to follow.
7. The colors of the T-shirt had been <u>bright</u>, but they became <u>faded</u> after it was washed.
8. The printer was <u>old</u>, but I thought it was <u>new</u>.
9. The tube of glue in the kit was almost <u>empty</u>, but it should have been <u>full</u>.
10. Our cat is <u>fat</u> and has <u>plump</u> legs.

WRITER'S CORNER

Choose four words from the list below. Find an antonym for each word and write a sentence for each antonym.

walk	friend	huge
tired	boring	top
quiet	smooth	hot

ACTIVITY D Choose an antonym for each underlined word from the words in parentheses.

1. The <u>rich</u> man could not afford a ticket. (poor happy honest)
2. My shirt is too <u>big</u>. (wrinkled dirty small)
3. Conner spilled juice on the <u>old</u> rug. (green new tattered)
4. The clay is not supposed to <u>soften</u> so quickly. (grow break harden)
5. The lid will not <u>shut</u>. (open bend twirl)
6. Let the soup <u>heat</u> for five minutes. (burn cool cook)
7. I thought the bat would be <u>heavier</u>. (lighter smaller bigger)
8. Maria <u>lost</u> her book in the park. (read bought found)
9. We cheered when the player <u>dropped</u> the ball. (caught threw held)
10. The <u>gentle</u> rain cooled down the runners. (icy hard blowing)

ACTIVITY E Finish each compound sentence. Use an antonym for the underlined word.

1. Backpacks are supposed to be <u>light</u>, but _____.
2. The ad showed a shirt with <u>long</u> sleeves, but _____.
3. I thought the model car would be <u>fast</u>, but _____.
4. We need a <u>bright</u> flashlight for camping, but _____.
5. James asked for a <u>sweet</u> drink, but _____.
6. The sweater was <u>loose</u> before it was washed, but _____.
7. Those batteries should last a <u>long</u> time, but _____.
8. The frozen dinner was supposed to taste <u>good</u>, but _____.
9. The fish tank looked <u>huge</u> in the photo, but _____.
10. That bookcase seemed <u>sturdy</u>, but _____.

ACTIVITY F Use an antonym in place of each underlined word. Write the new sentence.

1. The alarm is too <u>quiet</u>.
2. Our mail delivery was <u>early</u>.
3. The left wheel is <u>crooked</u>.
4. That manager was <u>polite</u>.
5. This is the <u>best</u> meal I ever had.
6. I was <u>disappointed</u> with the jacket I ordered.
7. My ice skates were <u>expensive</u>.
8. The bread was <u>stale</u>.
9. My neighbor <u>received</u> a box.
10. The address on the envelope was <u>wrong</u>.

ACTIVITY G Some words have more than one antonym. Choose the best antonym for the underlined word to complete each sentence.

1. The lever is <u>hard</u> to pull, and we asked for one that is (soft   easy   simple).
2. Dad can eat only <u>mild</u> foods, but the soup was (strong   sharp   spicy).
3. I need <u>strong</u> tent poles, but these (weak   feeble   sick) poles bent the first time I used them.
4. The bag of markers was <u>full</u>, but the box for the cards was (vacant   blank   empty).
5. Our dancers ordered <u>long</u> skirts, but you sent (short   wide   brief) ones.
6. The blender was <u>convenient</u> for mixing, but cleaning it was (untimely   easy   awkward).
7. The amount of red paint in the kit was <u>insufficient</u> to complete the project, but the amount of blue paint was (abundant   adequate   passable).
8. The game was supposed to be <u>entertaining</u>, but my friends found it (boring   sad   exciting).

WRITER'S CORNER

Using three objects, write a sentence for three letters of complaint. Use a pair of antonyms in each sentence.

Oral Complaints and Conflicts

Everyone gets angry once in a while. Sometimes we get hurt feelings or have a reason to complain. Yet if you have heard friends disagree, you probably know that talking about complaints and conflicts is difficult. Here are some ways to resolve conflicts by talking things over.

Cool Off

Take a deep breath. Before you try to talk about a conflict, take some time to clear your head. Think about what happened and why it happened. Take a walk around the block. Let your feelings quiet down. You'll be glad you did.

Use Ground Rules

Ask a grown-up to help you both come up with rules that you can follow to keep your conversation positive. Here are some rules that work pretty well.

- Be respectful.
- Wait your turn to speak.
- Work together for a fair solution.
- Tell the truth.

Remember, both people in a conflict think that they are right. Try to be polite to the other person.

Win/Win Guidelines

How do you talk with a person about a problem? Try these guidelines.

Use "I Messages."

Use "I messages" to say how you feel without putting blame on the other person. Your "I message" can be an appeal for help or understanding from the other person. For example, if you were mad at your younger brother because he lost your basketball, you might say "I'm angry that my brother lost my ball. I wish he'd have asked me if he could borrow it first."

Try to see the other person's point of view.

Put yourself in the other person's shoes. You might say "I guess I never let you borrow anything, and you did need a ball to try out for the team."

Know you were part of the problem.

Knowing how you were part of the problem might help you understand how the problem started and how another problem might be avoided in the future.

ACTIVITY A Choose a side for each conflict and write an "I message."

1. Robert drops his pencil during a test. Simon picks it up and starts using it because his own pencil is broken.

2. Chad has his science project on his desk. Kate accidentally knocks it over with her backpack.

3. After music class, Allison teases Earl about his singing.

4. Jo forgets to ask Jenny to come to her birthday party.

SPEAKER'S CORNER

Plan a conflict-resolution skit with a partner. Come up with a problem that two students might face. Plan your presentation that includes the win/win guidelines and a solution that you are both happy about.

Coming to a Solution

Now that you're talking, you can talk about a solution, or compromise, that works for both of you. In the case of the lost basketball, the younger brother might agree to save up to buy his older brother a new basketball. The older brother might agree to let his younger brother borrow the basketball in the future as long as he asks first.

Tips for a Resolver

On a different day, you might become part of a conflict and not even be involved in the problem. Two friends might ask you to help them solve a conflict that they are having. Or you might be asked to be on a conflict-resolution team. Here are some tips to help you.

- Pay attention to both people.
- Be sure you understand the problem.
- Focus on the problem and don't get off the subject. Don't talk about other problems these people might have had in the past.
- Be fair. Don't take sides.
- Speak calmly and politely.
- Work toward a solution.

If a problem is too big for you to help resolve, make sure you ask for help from a teacher or another adult.

ACTIVITY B Pretend that you are either Simon, Kate, Allison, or Jo in each of the situations in Activity A. Write how you might be responsible for the problem. Then meet with a partner and practice saying how you are responsible for the problem.

ACTIVITY C Read this story written from Matthew's point of view. Pretend that you are Matthew and follow the win/win guidelines. Write "I messages," how you think Xavier sees the problem, and how you think you might be part of the problem.

My best friend Xavier won a chance to meet our favorite snowboarder after his Saturday competition. Xavier was allowed to bring a guest, and he asked me to come along. I said yes and I told my soccer coach that I would not be able to play in the game on Saturday. Then on Saturday morning Xavier told me that his parents wanted him to take his sister Francesca instead. I didn't get to meet the snowboarder. Even worse, I was not allowed to start in the soccer game because my coach had told another player that he could start in my place. I am mad at Xavier, and I haven't talked to him for three days.

SPEAKER'S CORNER

Practice your skit from the Speaker's Corner on page 271. Then present it to your classmates.

Tech Tip Record your skit when practicing.

Prewriting and Drafting

When you buy a product, you expect it to work. If it doesn't, you should tell the company that made it or sold it to you. Then the company can fix the problem. A good way to tell the company is in a formal letter of complaint.

Prewriting

Before writing a formal letter, a writer spends time prewriting to gather ideas. The prewriting steps include choosing a topic and planning the letter.

Choosing a Topic

Audrey is a fourth-grade student who was asked to write a letter of complaint for a class  assignment. She began by making a list of things she had bought or received recently. Then she listed any problems she had found with them.

Audrey had bought a camera that didn't take very good pictures in the dark. She had also received some socks that had worn out quickly. Then she thought of an I Go Bingo game she had bought while visiting cousins in New Jersey. When she opened it, she saw that the game was missing its playing cards. She decided to write a letter to the Timely Toy Company.

Your Turn

Make a list of things you have bought or received recently. Try to think of things that had problems with them. Make a T-chart to organize your list. Begin by drawing a large *T* on a sheet of paper. List the products down the left side of the chart. List the problems on the right side. When your chart is complete, circle one that you'd like to write about.

If none of the things you listed had any problems, imagine a problem that one of them might have had. Use this idea to start your letter of complaint.

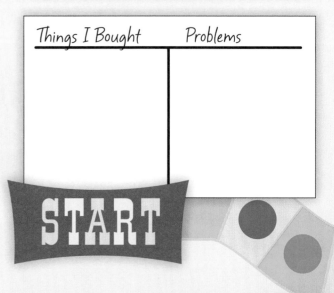

Things I Bought | Problems

START

Planning the Letter

After choosing her topic, Audrey began planning her letter. She started by writing the address of the Timely Toy Company from the game box. She wasn't sure to whom she should send her letter, so she decided to address it to the Customer Service Department. This is the address Audrey wrote.

Customer Service Department
Timely Toy Company
99 Highpoint circle
Cypress, PA 90630

Next, Audrey wrote her writing plan. She knew her letter would have three sections: a beginning, a middle, and an ending. She wrote ideas for each section in her plan.

For the beginning she took notes about the problem or situation. For the middle she

 Organization explained how she wanted the

company to fix the problem. For the ending she thanked the company for its help. Here is Audrey's writing plan.

Your Turn

Write an address for your letter. Look for it in the package or instructions for the product. If you do not find it, you might search the Internet for the address. If you cannot find the company's address, use your school's address and use your teacher's name. Next, make a writing plan for your letter.

- For the beginning write ideas describing the situation or problem.
- For the middle write suggestions for fixing the problem.
- For the ending write what you will say to thank the company for its help.

Beginning
Problem: bought I Go Bingo while visiting cousins in New Jersey. Game was missing deck of cards. Can't take it back to store.

Middle
Suggestions for fixing problem: send deck of cards or refund money to buy a new game

Ending
Thank you for your help.

Drafting

Audrey wrote her letter to the customer service department of a big toy company. It was a formal letter, so she used formal language.

She wrote a first draft, using her writing plan as she worked. She double-spaced lines to leave room for changes and corrections when she revised her writing.

October 5, 20—

Customer Service Department
Timely Toy Company
99 Highpoint circle
Cypress, PA 90630

Dear Sir or Madam:

I was visiting my cousins in New Jersey. We played your I Go Bingo game. I liked it so much that we went to Max's Toy City in the Century Mall, and I bought my own I Go Bingo. When I got back home to Cincinnati, I opened the box the deck of cards was missing.

I can't play I Go Bingo without the cards. I'm writing to ask that you either send me the cards or refund my money so I can buy I Go Bingo at another store. I cannot take the game back to the store where I got it. It is in New Jersey and I live in Ohio.

Please respond as soon as you can so I can begin to enjoy your teriffic game. Thank you for your help.

Sincerely
Audrey Morrissey

Your Turn

Look at your writing plan and write your first draft. Keep in mind that you will probably rewrite your letter several times.

Remember your audience as you write. Be sure your writing is clear and to the point. Include details that the person needs to know.

- The beginning of your letter should state the situation and the problem.
- The middle should tell how you want the problem solved.
- The ending should thank the person for taking the time to help you.

Using Details to Make Your Message Clear

When you write a letter of complaint, it is important to be brief. Do not add unnecessary details, but do not leave out important details. Be sure that you include details that will help the company solve your problem quickly and the way you want. The following information will make your message clear to the reader:

- the exact problem with the product
- the date you bought the product
- ways you have tried to solve the problem
- suggestions for how to solve the problem

Writer's Tip Double-space lines so you will have room to make changes later.

Editor's Workshop

Content Editing

Audrey knew that she would revise her letter before she mailed it. The first thing she wanted to be sure of was that the content of her letter was correct. Did she include all the parts of a letter? Does the letter explain the problem clearly? Did she say what she wants the company to do?

Audrey used a checklist like this as she read over her letter. She also used a different pencil color so that she could see her changes more easily. Audrey read over the first draft of her letter. It looked good, but she was afraid she might have missed something. Audrey wanted a friend to read the first draft of her letter. She asked Katie to read it.

Katie and Audrey often studied together and checked each other's homework. They both knew that they should point out problems to make the writing better, not to make their partner feel bad.

Katie read Audrey's letter through a few times and checked it against the Content Editor's Checklist. Then she and Audrey met.

First, Katie told Audrey about things that she liked. Her letter clearly explained the problem. She also suggested ways to solve the problem. But Katie saw some ways that Audrey's letter could be improved. Here are her comments.

- When did you buy the game? If it was a long time ago, they might not help you. Add this detail.

- You don't need to tell them that Max's Toy Store is in the Century Mall. They just need to know that it is not in Ohio.

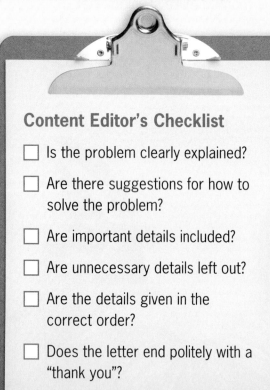

Content Editor's Checklist

☐ Is the problem clearly explained?

☐ Are there suggestions for how to solve the problem?

☐ Are important details included?

☐ Are unnecessary details left out?

☐ Are the details given in the correct order?

☐ Does the letter end politely with a "thank you"?

- How much did you pay for your game? Do you have a receipt? You should send a copy of the receipt with your letter.

- I think the detail about not being able to return the game to the store should go earlier in the letter. It's part of the problem, not what you want the company to do.

Audrey knew that Katie's suggestions were good ones, so she decided to follow most of them. She revised her draft, using Audrey's ideas and some of her own.

Grammar in Action

Can you find the run-on sentence in Audrey's letter? See Section 1.11.

Your Turn

- Read over your first draft and check it, using the Content Editor's Checklist. Write your ideas on your draft.

- Trade letters with a partner. Read your partner's letter several times, using the Content Editor's Checklist.

- When you have finished reading your partner's first draft, give your honest opinion of how you think the letter could be improved. Be sure to comment on the good things that you read. Your partner will do the same for you.

Prewriting

Drafting

Content Editing

Revising

Copyediting

Proofreading

Publishing

Writer's Workshop

Revising

Here is Audrey's revision of her letter.

October 5, 20—

Customer Service Department

Timely Toy Company

99 Highpoint circle

Cypress, PA 90630

Dear Sir or Madam:

Last week
^I was visiting my cousins in New Jersey. We played your I Go Bingo game. I liked it

so much that ~~we went to Max's Toy City in the Century Mall, and~~ *the next day* I bought my own

I got it at a store near my cousins' house.
I Go Bingo. When I got back home to Cincinnati, I opened the box ^ the deck of

cards was missing.

I enjoy your game, but I can't play it
^~~I can't play I Go Bingo~~ without the cards. I'm writing to ask that you either send me

the cards or refund my money so I can buy I Go Bingo at another store. I cannot

take the game back to the store where I got it. It is in New Jersey and I live in Ohio. ^
I am including a copy of my receipt. As you can see, I paid $9.47 for the game.

Please respond as soon as you can so I can begin to enjoy your teriffic game.

Thank you for your help.

Sincerely

Audrey Morrissey

Audrey did some things to improve her letter.

- How did Audrey change the first sentence?
- How did she change the information on where she bought the game?
- What two things did Audrey add to the second paragraph?
- Did she take Katie's suggestion about moving the detail about the store being too far away to take back the game?

The last thing Audrey did was to make her letter a bit more polite. She mentioned that she  wanted the cards because she really enjoyed playing I Go Bingo. She hoped this would encourage her reader to respond quickly.

Your Turn

Use your own ideas and the suggestions that you got from your content editor to revise your letter. Like Audrey, you don't have to follow all of your partner's suggestions. Follow only the suggestions that make your letter better.

When you have finished, go over the Content Editor's Checklist again. Can you answer yes to each question?

Prewriting

Drafting

Content Editing

Revising

Copyediting

Proofreading

Publishing

Copyediting and Proofreading

Copyediting

Audrey saw that her letter was greatly improved by following Katie's suggestions. She was sure that it contained all the necessary information. Now Audrey had to make sure she followed the correct form for a formal letter.

 Word Choice She wanted to be sure that she used formal language and that her sentences flowed together smoothly. She used the following checklist.

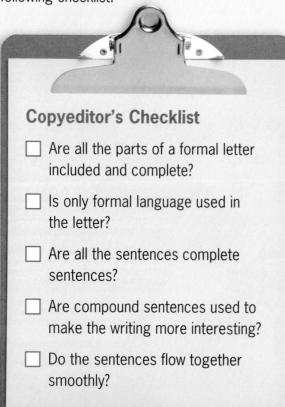

Copyeditor's Checklist

- [ ] Are all the parts of a formal letter included and complete?

- [ ] Is only formal language used in the letter?

- [ ] Are all the sentences complete sentences?

- [ ] Are compound sentences used to make the writing more interesting?

- [ ] Do the sentences flow together smoothly?

Audrey checked over her letter to make sure all the important parts were there. Most of one part was missing. Review Audrey's letter. Do you know which part it was?

Audrey was missing most of the heading. She forgot to put in her own address. She added it above the date:

> 456 Wyomiss Lane
> Cincinnati, OH 45201

Audrey saw that she had used some contractions. She replaced them to make her letter more formal.

Audrey checked to make sure her sentences were correct and varied. She didn't

 Sentence Fluency like the way the first two sentences sounded. How would you combine them?

Audrey also spotted the run-on sentence and fixed it.

Your Turn

Look over your revised draft. Be sure that all the parts of the letter are there. A good way to catch these mistakes is to compare your letter with one that you know is correct. Use the Copyeditor's Checklist to copyedit your draft.

Proofreading

Before writing the final copy of her letter, Audrey proofread the draft to check for correct spelling, punctuation, capitalization, and grammar.

Audrey used this checklist to help her proofread.

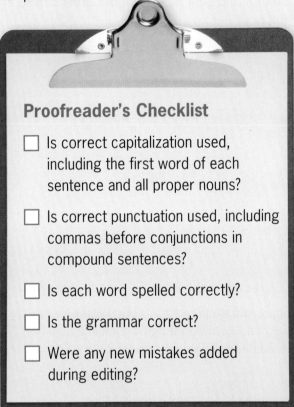

Proofreader's Checklist

- ☐ Is correct capitalization used, including the first word of each sentence and all proper nouns?
- ☐ Is correct punctuation used, including commas before conjunctions in compound sentences?
- ☐ Is each word spelled correctly?
- ☐ Is the grammar correct?
- ☐ Were any new mistakes added during editing?

Writers usually ask someone else to proofread their work for spelling, grammar, capitalization, and punctuation mistakes. A proofreader will often catch mistakes that the writer missed.

Audrey asked another classmate, Finn, to proofread her letter. Finn followed the Proofreader's Checklist. He found that the word *circle* in the inside address should have been capitalized. He found that the closing needed a comma. He also found a misspelled word. See if you can find it.

Conventions

Your Turn

Read your letter carefully against the Proofreader's Checklist. Answer each question on the list separately.

When you have gone through the whole checklist, trade letters with a partner. Go through your partner's letter in the same way.

Writer's Tip Be sure to use a dictionary if you are unsure of the spelling of a word.

Prewriting

Drafting

Content Editing

Revising

Copyediting

Proofreading

Publishing

Publishing

Audrey revised her letter several times. Each time she made it better. When she felt that her letter was ready, she carefully typed it onto a clean sheet of paper and signed it. She addressed an envelope, placed the letter and a copy of her receipt inside, added a stamp, and sent it. A deck of cards arrived in the mail just six days later!

456 Wyomiss Lane
Cincinnati, OH 45201

October 5, 20—

Customer Service Department
Timely Toy Company
99 Highpoint Circle
Cypress, PA 90630

Dear Sir or Madam:

Last week I was visiting my cousins in New Jersey, and we played your I Go Bingo game. I liked it so much that the next day I bought my own I Go Bingo. I got it at a store near my cousins' house. When I got back home to Cincinnati, I opened the box, but the deck of cards was missing.

I enjoy your game, but I cannot play it without the cards. I am writing to ask that you either send me the cards or refund my money so I can buy I Go Bingo at another store. I cannot take the game back to the store where I got it. It is in New Jersey, and I live in Ohio. I am including a copy of my receipt. As you can see, I paid $9.47 for the game.

Please respond as soon as you can so I can begin to enjoy your terrific game. Thank you for your help.

Sincerely,

Audrey Morrissey

Audrey Morrissey

There are many ways you can publish your letter. As a class, decide if you will publish your letters using the same publishing method or do them differently. However you choose to publish your letters, be sure it is clear and appealing to your audience.

 Mail or e-mail your letter. If you mail it, see below how to address an envelope. Don't forget to sign your letter.

 Make a classroom newsletter. Include your letter and your classmates' in a Letters of Complaint section.

 Post your letter on a bulletin board. Label the board "Reply Hall of Fame" and post your letters along with your classmates' letters. As the letters are answered, display the replies next to the original letters.

 Post your letter on your classroom's wiki, blog, or Web site. You can receive comments about your letter and review others' work.

Your Turn

Any time you share writing with your audience, it is publishing. Once you drop a formal letter into a mailbox or e-mail it, you can no longer correct mistakes. You want to be sure that everything in your letter is correct.

Look over your draft one more time to make sure all the mistakes have been corrected, and then print out or neatly handwrite your final copy. Choose one of the publishing methods.

Presentation

If you choose to mail your letter, address the envelope. The address on the envelope should match the inside address. Then place your letter inside the envelope, stamp it, and mail it.

Prewriting

Drafting

Content Editing

Revising

Copyediting

Proofreading

Publishing

Audrey Morrissey
456 Wyomiss Lane
Cincinnati, OH 45201

Customer Service Department
Timely Toy Company
99 Highpoint Circle
Cypress, PA 90630

FINISH

Descriptions

LiNK **The View from Saturday**

by E.L. Konigsburg

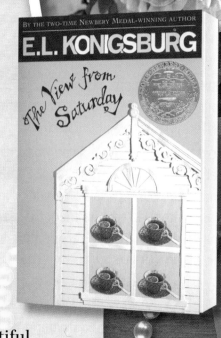

Wedding cakes are not baked as much as they are built. In the real world, people don't build wedding cakes. They order in. If you are going to build it yourself, it is not done in a day. It takes three. On the first day, Grandma Sadie baked the layers. On the second, she constructed the cake, using cardboard bases and straws for supports, and made the basic icing to cover the layers. On the third day, she made the designer icing for the rosebuds and put the little bride and groom on top. Fact: The cake was beautiful.

. . . Unfortunately, he didn't see the wagon handle, so he tripped on it, slid on the wet concrete, fell in the puddle of melted ice and, unfortunately, toppled the wedding cake.

> The excerpt from *The View from Saturday* shows key elements of a description. It uses time order and visual sensory language to help create a picture in the reader's mind.

CHAPTER 3

The Burrowing Owl

by Olivia M., Room 213

The burrowing owl is about 9 inches long. Its back, head, and wing feathers are brown with white spots. Its belly feathers are whitish with brown stripes. It has yellow eyes and a dark band around its neck.

This owl's long legs and bullet-shaped head give it a strange appearance. Its stilt-like legs serve a purpose. They allow the owl to peek up over the grass that covers the prairies where it lives. They help it to run down the insects on which it feeds. The bird also eats small rodents. That is why farmers welcome this "ground owl" in their fields.

Although the owl is capable of digging its own nest, the bird usually seeks out holes made by prairie dogs, badgers, and other small mammals. It then lines the holes with grasses, roots, and dung. The female deposits 7 to 10 eggs near the bottom of the hole.

This owl has many different calls. The main song is a hoo–hooo–uh, hoo–hooo–uh, which the male uses to attract a mate. Other common calls are a raspy chuckle and a screech similar to car brakes squealing. When they sense danger, owlets in the nest make a sound that resembles a rattlesnake's warning.

The burrowing owl is native to southern Canada and the plains of the western United States. It has become endangered in some areas because of the destruction of its habitat.

What Makes a Good Description?

People write descriptions for many purposes. You can read descriptions in books, advertising, and newspapers. Lively descriptions often use sensory language to help readers picture the people, places, things, and events in stories.

Descriptions usually have a beginning that names the topic, a middle that provides most of the details, and an ending that sums up the main idea or completes the information about the topic.

Choose a Topic

It is important to choose a topic that you know well. Your topic should be something you have seen, heard, smelled, touched, or tasted.

Choose a topic that is broad enough for you to write a description of more than one or two sentences. However, your subject should be limited enough to describe in the time that you have for writing.

Picture the Topic

Form a picture of your topic in your mind. Think about everything that you see, hear, smell, taste, and touch. Then describe the topic in as much detail as you can. Use sensory language.

Think About Your Audience

Remember your audience when you choose a topic. Will your readers be grown-ups or children? Will they know a lot about your topic, or will they know nothing about it? Keep these things in mind when you choose a topic.

Also remember your audience when you choose your words and phrases. Language that is too difficult or too simple can make readers lose interest in what you have to say. You want to catch their interest right away and hold it. Choose words that match your audience.

ACTIVITY A **Read each of the following pairs of topics. Choose which of the two is a better topic for a description. Then tell whether the other topic is too limited or too broad to be a good topic for a description.**

1. a. Grandfather's old dog
   b. hunting dogs

2. a. how I like my pancakes
   b. my idea of a good breakfast

3. a. my favorite beach
   b. things that I brought to the beach

4. a. outside my bedroom window
   b. my hometown

5. a. my favorite musical performer
   b. rock 'n' roll music

6. a. the stores in my neighborhood
   b. the bakery on my block

7. a. my costume in the school play
   b. the costumes in the school play

8. a. the rides at the amusement park
   b. my favorite ride at the amusement park

WRITER'S CORNER

Make a list of five topics like those in Activity A. Then decide who the audience would be for each topic. Share your list with a classmate. Ask whether he or she agrees with you about the audience.

LiNK

The View from Saturday

At lunchtime, I sat on the end of the bench. Noah took a seat next to me. Nadia came from the food line carrying her tray and found no vacant seat at any of the girls' tables, so she sat next to Noah. Julian, who had brought his lunch, was seated at a table at the far end of the room, all alone.

E.L. Konigsburg

Organizing Your Description

Decide on the way that you want your audience to see what you are describing. Readers can more easily picture a description in their minds if it is written in an organized way. Here are some ways to organize descriptions.

Space Order

When you use space order, you describe things from one direction to another; for example, from left to right, from top to bottom, or from near to far. When you organize by space order, keep the details in order. Don't jump back and forth. Can you picture the scene from the description in the excerpt on the left?

Time Order

When you are writing about an event, organize your description by the order that things happen or in the order that you notice them. If you write about a trip to a bakery, you might notice the smells first, then the displays of baked goods, then the taste of the treat that you buy.

ACTIVITY B Tell how best to organize a description of the following subjects. Would you use space order or time order?

1. the American flag
2. making breakfast
3. your family kitchen
4. a baseball diamond
5. a birthday party
6. your favorite animal
7. the clothes you wore to school today
8. washing a car or a pet

ACTIVITY C The following sentences describe Mr. Jones. Write the sentences so that the description is organized in space order, from top to bottom.

1. He wears a bright red bandana around his neck.
2. He usually wears cowboy boots.
3. Mr. Jones has copper-red hair.
4. A shiny gold tooth gleams in his mouth.
5. He always wears jeans.
6. All his shirts are plaid flannel.
7. His bushy moustache is also red.

ACTIVITY D The following sentences describe a sleepover birthday party. Write the sentences so that the description is organized in time order.

1. After we put all our sleeping bags in the family room, we played with Madeline's new karaoke game.
2. After hours with the karaoke game, we ate pizza and watched movies.
3. When breakfast was over, we packed up our things and thanked Madeline for a great party.
4. I got to Madeline's house for her sleepover birthday party at 6 p.m.
5. We finally fell asleep around midnight.
6. Madeline's parents made pancakes for breakfast.

ACTIVITY E Decide if the following topics are better for grown-ups or for children. Then tell if they should be described using space order or time order. Explain why.

1. the latest video game
2. a worker's toolbox
3. a classical music performance

WRITER'S CORNER

In five sentences describe your bedroom or what you do after school. Decide if you will use space order or time order.

Grammar in Action. Try using object pronouns instead of renaming your object in your sentences. Review Section 3.6.

Sensory Language

Our five senses tell us about the world. Seeing tells us about rainbows and clouds. Hearing tells us about music and barking dogs. Touching tells us about kittens' fur. Smelling tells us about pies in the oven. Tasting tells us about cherries in our mouths.

Many of the things that you know you learned from your five senses. When you describe things, use words that appeal to the five senses to help people understand what you already know. The more senses you appeal to in your description, the more your audience can picture what you describe. In the excerpt on page 293, you can picture how the character felt at the end of the bus ride.

Read these two sentences.

A **The old gate opened noisily.**

B **The rusty gate creaked loudly and scraped on the cracked sidewalk.**

In sentence A the writer tells you what happened. In sentence B the writer not only tells you what happened, but also how it happened. Which sentence makes you feel more like you are there? Can you name the senses that the writer appealed to in sentence B?

ACTIVITY A Tell which senses you would use to describe these subjects. Tell how each sense adds to the description.

1. making a fresh salad
2. toasting marshmallows over a campfire
3. wrapping presents
4. walking in the rain
5. building a sand castle on the beach
6. shopping at a farmer's market
7. baking cookies
8. riding a roller coaster
9. watching the seals at the zoo
10. hiking in the woods

ACTIVITY B Write the sense that you think would be used most in a description for each of the locations.

1. a bowling alley
2. a tennis court
3. a flower shop
4. the lobby of a movie theater
5. a sandy beach on a hot day
6. an amusement park
7. a parade route
8. an autumn day
9. a water park
10. a petting zoo

LiNK

The View from Saturday

When the bus picked up the last passengers from the last stop in The Farm, I lifted my leg off my backpack. My foot had fallen asleep, and it felt heavy as I lowered it. I rested it on the floor and allowed the pinpricks of blood to tease their way back up my leg.

E.L. Konigsburg

ACTIVITY C Use the sense in parentheses to write one sentence that describes each item.

1. an ostrich (sight)
2. bacon (smell)
3. a water faucet (sound)
4. you, as you run (sound)
5. a woman's purse (sight)
6. the wind (smell)
7. water in a swimming pool (taste)
8. burnt toast (taste)
9. buttered popcorn (touch)
10. rain (touch)

WRITER'S CORNER

Choose a location from Activity B. Write five sentences using sensory words that describe it. Try to use all the senses to make your description come alive.

ACTIVITY D Tell which sense each sentence appeals to.

1. The new shoes gave my foot a painful blister.
2. Red and blue kites wheeled and bobbed in the sky.
3. Paulo's stomach ached from hunger.
4. Those gym socks need to be washed.
5. Their tasty hamburgers are cooked just right.
6. The skateboards' wheels rumbled on the sidewalk.
7. The sour milk ruined my cereal.
8. Only six or seven coins rattled in the bank.
9. My clothes got all smoky from the burning leaves.
10. The cup of hot chocolate warmed my numb fingers.

ACTIVITY E Match each sensory word in Column A with the subject in Column B that the word could describe. Tell what sense each word appeals to.

Column A	Column B
1. spicy	a. photograph
2. icy	b. apples
3. jagged	c. water
4. stinky	d. garbage
5. jingling	e. caramel
6. musty	f. fire
7. blurred	g. bells
8. sour	h. basement
9. sticky	i. pizza
10. crackling	j. mountaintops

294

ACTIVITY F The underlined sensory words in the following paragraphs got mixed up. Rewrite the sentences that have the misplaced words. Put the sensory words in the correct places. Use each sensory word just one time.

We dropped our <u>blood-curdling</u> backpacks onto the ground. I was hungry from hiking all morning, and I was looking forward to a <u>scared</u> lunch. We found a <u>hungry</u> spot to have a picnic. Just as we were unpacking our sandwiches, we heard a <u>crooked</u> growl coming from the bushes. Eddie jumped to his feet and ran back down the trail, yelling, "Bear!"

I didn't know if he was right or not, but I was too frightened to take any chances. I jumped up and followed Eddie back down the <u>heavy</u> path. We flew down the <u>tasty</u> hill like <u>steep</u> rabbits. I passed Eddie. Then he passed me. We both passed another group of hikers <u>stampeding</u> up the hill. Eddie yelled again, "Bear!" Soon there were eight of us <u>trudging</u> down the path. By the time we got back to the trail head, there were almost 20 of us.

Tomorrow Eddie and I may go back for our backpacks if we feel a little braver than we do right now. We'll be on the lookout for any more <u>shady</u> bears, however.

ACTIVITY G Write a sentence to describe each item below. Include as many sensory words as you can.

1. a sunrise
2. your favorite meal
3. a puppy
4. a beach
5. kites in the sky
6. a bonfire

WRITER'S CORNER

Write a paragraph with five sentences, describing a place that you enjoy. Use at least five sensory words and underline them.

Grammar in Action. Show variety in your writing by combining short sentences with conjunctions. See Section 1.

Suffixes

A suffix is a word part added to the end of a base word. A suffix changes the meaning of the base word or makes a new word. Be sure to use suffixes correctly in your writing. Using the correct suffix can make your writing clear. Using the wrong suffix can confuse a reader.

Study the chart of common suffixes. Look at each suffix and its meaning. Notice how the base word changes when the suffix is added.

COMMON SUFFIXES

Suffix	Meaning	Base Word	Example
-ful	full of	cheer	cheerful
-less	without	help	helpless
-y	like; full of	thirst	thirsty
-er	person who	bake	baker

Read the paragraph below. Find the suffixes in the words in red. Can you explain how each suffix changes the meaning of the base word?

> Martin is a rock *climber*. He is *careful* to follow all the rules he learned in his training. Martin knows that he is not just *lucky* when he has a good climb. Following safety rules is the key. Martin is not *careless*, so he has many good climbs.

ACTIVITY A Look at the words in the paragraph above and the meanings of the suffixes in the chart. Then complete the chart below.

1. climb + er = _____ climbs
2. care + ful = _____ care
3. luck + y = _____ luck
4. care + less = _____ care

ACTIVITY B Find the word with a suffix in each sentence. Then underline the suffixes.

1. My dad is a builder of homes.
2. Kia is thankful for your help.
3. The child's parents were hopeful that he would get well.
4. Exercise keeps me healthy.
5. The nurse said that the shot is painless.
6. I feel guilty when I tell lies.
7. The orange grower lost his crop.
8. It was a cloudy day.
9. Gina is a fearless athlete.
10. Are you a football player?
11. The doctor's advice was helpful.
12. She is blameless in this situation.

ACTIVITY C With a partner take turns naming the base word in the words you found in Activity B. Explain how the meaning of the base word changes when the suffix is added.

ACTIVITY D Write a word with a suffix for each of these meanings.

1. full of snow
2. a person who gardens
3. full of skill
4. full of curls
5. without clouds
6. full of grace
7. a person who sings
8. without noise
9. full of pain
10. a person who leads

WRITER'S CORNER

Skim through a book of fiction for five words containing suffixes from the chart on page 296. List the words. Find the base word. Include the name of the book you used.

Spelling Changes

Sometimes the base word changes its spelling when a suffix is added. Be sure to check a dictionary if you want to add a suffix to a word and you are unsure of the spelling.

SUFFIX	BASE WORD	EXAMPLE
-ful	beauty	beautiful
-less	penny	penniless
-y	fog	foggy
-er	run	runner

ACTIVITY E Add the suffix to each base word. Change the spelling as needed. Use a dictionary if you need help.

1. bag + -y
2. plenty + -ful
3. ice + -y
4. dance + -er
5. program + -er
6. mercy + -less

ACTIVITY F Choose a word from the list to replace the words in parentheses. Write each new sentence.

teacher   hopeless   thirsty   beautiful
greedy   graceful   timeless   helper

1. The dancer was (full of grace).
2. That story is (without time).
3. I like my (person who teaches).
4. Jane's mom is a lunchroom (one who helps).
5. After running, he was (full of thirst).
6. The wedding gown was (full of beauty).
7. King Midas was (full of greed).
8. Paul felt (without hope) as he looked at his messy bedroom.

ACTIVITY G Add the correct suffix to the base word in italics in each sentence. Change the spelling of the base word if necessary. Write each new sentence. Use a dictionary if you need help.

1. When I grow up, I want to be a *write*.
2. Kendra is the most *power* hitter on our team.
3. My shoes got *mud* in the rain.
4. His pale face was almost *color*.
5. Latrel is a good *swim*.
6. Mozart was a great *compose* from Vienna.
7. I'm hoping for a *sun* afternoon.
8. The baby is quite a *cry*.
9. The peach was sweet and *juice*.
10. We are *hope* that our team will win the championship.
11. The ring isn't made of gold, and it is almost *value*.
12. It is best to be *truth* and admit when you make a mistake.

King Midas
counting gold

ACTIVITY H Add *-ful, -less, -y,* or *-er* to each word. Then write a sentence for each word.

1. care
2. wind
3. use
4. storm
5. peace
6. mind
7. play
8. clue

WRITER'S CORNER

In four or five sentences, describe a picnic or a snack you enjoyed outside. Tell about some of the wonderful things that you saw, heard, smelled, touched, or tasted. Use three or more words with suffixes.

Similes and Metaphors

Similes

You can use sensory language to describe people or things. Another way to describe people or things is by comparing them to other people or things.

A simile uses the words *like* or *as* to compare two different things. Can you find the simile in the excerpt on page 301?

Read the sentences below. What does each sentence say about Ramona? What does she do well?

A **Ramona runs like a deer.**

B **Ramona is as fast as lightning.**

Sentence A compares the way that Ramona runs to the way that a deer runs. We know that a deer runs fast, so Ramona must run fast too. In sentence B Ramona is compared to lightning. Lightning is so fast that it is over almost as soon as it starts. Both sentences say that Ramona is fast.

Be careful when you choose the thing that you compare your subject with. Choose something that is different from your subject except for the part you want to point out. If you say your parakeet eats like a bird, readers will think that is a silly thing to say. All parakeets eat like birds. If you say that Ramona eats like a bird, readers will know that Ramona does not eat a lot.

Readers should also know enough about the two things being compared to understand what is meant. Most people know that a deer runs fast. However, many people haven't seen a zebra run. If you write that Ramona runs like a zebra, your readers might not understand what you mean.

ACTIVITY A Tell what two people or things are being compared in these similes.

1. Willie was as hungry as a bear.
2. Mr. Jones laughs like a hyena.
3. The hungry workers ate like starved wolves.
4. The lake is as smooth as glass.
5. You're as lazy as a slug.
6. The floor was as cold as ice cubes.
7. All the windows reflecting the sun were like sheets of gold.
8. The falling leaves were like dancers doing movements in the air.
9. His heavy suitcase was like a bag of bricks.
10. The diver posed at the end of the board was as still as a statue.

ACTIVITY B Match each subject in Column A with an idea in Column B to make a simile. Then write three descriptive sentences using three of the pairs.

Column A	Column B
1. children arguing	a. a roller coaster
2. sweaty gym shoes	b. leather
3. icicles	c. dirty marshmallows
4. cheering friends	d. glowing emeralds
5. fear	e. a skunk
6. cat eyes	f. chattering monkeys
7. tough steak	g. a knot in the stomach
8. storm clouds	h. beautiful music
9. a hilly road	i. a glass necklace

LiNK

The View from Saturday

The large center hall of the Sillington house had a staircase that curved upward like a stretch of DNA. To the right of the hall was a living room that had a huge fireplace. . .

E.L. Konigsburg

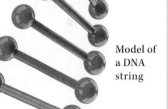

Model of a DNA string

WRITER'S CORNER

Write three similes to describe things that you saw or did this past weekend. Try to paint a word picture with each simile.

Metaphors

Like a simile, a metaphor describes by comparing. A metaphor is different from a simile because a metaphor does not use the words *like* or *as*. "Ed's car is a pile of junk" is a metaphor. It compares Ed's car to a pile of junk.

As with similes, the two things being compared in metaphors must be different. "Mr. Wong is a clever old bird" is a metaphor. "The crow is a clever old bird" is not a metaphor.

ACTIVITY C What two people or things are being compared in these metaphors?

1. Ellie is a pro on the tennis court.
2. The candidate was a pit bull in the debate.
3. Adil is an Einstein in science class.
4. The sun was a blazing torch in the sky.
5. After the heavy rains, our yard was a lake.
6. The football player was a ram, pushing into the solid line of opposing players.

ACTIVITY D Complete each sentence. Use a word from the list that would make a good metaphor for each sentence.

mountain	king	stain	heaven
music	pretzel	window	

1. The fantasy book is a _____ into another world.
2. This lasagna is a piece of _____.
3. The winding road was a _____.
4. Yesterday's absence was the only _____ on my attendance record.
5. The snowdrift was a white _____ on the sidewalk.
6. The sound of the car pulling up was _____ to my ears.
7. My dog Bo is the _____ of the neighborhood.

ACTIVITY E Tell what two things are being compared. Then tell if the description is a simile or a metaphor.

1. Clouds floated in the ocean of the sky.
2. The cat's fur stood up like porcupine quills.
3. The corn was as sweet as candy.
4. The bulldozer was a giant dinosaur with dirt in its jaws.
5. The skyscrapers make downtown a concrete canyon.
6. Shadows stretched like fingers across the lawn.
7. The kitten's teeth were tiny needles jabbing my fingers.
8. The leafless trees moving in the wind were rattling skeletons.
9. The coach's angry voice was like thunder.
10. The houses are like tiny boxes when you see them from a plane.

ACTIVITY F The following sentences have similes and metaphors. Write new sentences using the underlined part of each simile or metaphor. The first one is done for you.

EXAMPLE **Seeds dropping from the branches whirled like tiny helicopters.**

Hummingbirds hovered beside the flowers like tiny helicopters.

1. The fireflies were stars that escaped from the night sky.
2. A squirrel, holding her acorn like a trophy, chuckled loudly.
3. In the distance a dog howled out a sad song.
4. The old man's hands were as twisted as tree roots.
5. The toddler moved like a tornado, scattering toys and clothes around the house.

WRITER'S CORNER

Choose a person or thing to describe. Write one sentence that uses a simile and one that uses a metaphor. Read your description to the class.

Tech Tip Post your description on the class wiki or blog.

Graphic Organizers

When you write a description, it helps to picture in your mind what you want to describe. Think about how it looks and how it sounds. Remember how it feels, how it smells, and how it tastes. Write the details you remember. That way you will be less likely to forget them when you write your description. There are two good ways to organize the information. You can make a five-senses chart, or you can make an idea web.

Five-Senses Chart

A five-senses chart lets you gather details according to each sense. This chart is for a cherry soda.

CHERRY SODA				
SIGHT	SOUND	SMELL	TASTE	TOUCH
tall glass with bubbling red soda ice cubes straw sticking up	fizzing clinking of ice cubes in glass	hint of cherry aroma	deep cherry flavor sweet	cold and wet fizz tickles the nose

A cherry soda appeals to all five senses, so each column has something written in it. Many topics will not have something in every column. Some topics will have many items listed under one sense. For example, a five-senses chart for a music CD could have many sounds in the sound column but nothing in the smell or taste columns.

ACTIVITY A The details in this five-senses chart are mixed up. Put the details in the correct columns.

FOOTBALL GAME				
SIGHT	SOUND	SMELL	TASTE	TOUCH
cheers and boos crisp autumn air	hot dogs hard seats players moving up and down the field	whistles cheerleaders jumping up and down	thud of players crashing together excited fans	soft drinks crowd jumping up football flying through the air

ACTIVITY B Add at least one detail to each column in the chart.

CAFETERIA				
SIGHT	SOUND	SMELL	TASTE	TOUCH
students sitting at tables with trays	the chatter of many discussions	frying onions	spicy pizza	the hot cup of soup on my tray

ACTIVITY C Draw a five-senses chart to record details about a food court at a shopping mall. Think of the many food choices offered and the way the foods are presented. Think about the sights and sounds of the dining area. Add as many sensory details as you can.

WRITER'S CORNER

Work with a partner. Decide on a topic to describe. Make a five-senses chart for that topic.

Tech Tip Use a spreadsheet to create your chart.

Idea Web

Another way to gather details is to use an idea web. Idea webs can help you organize ideas when you write.

First, write your topic in a box in the center of a sheet of paper. Think of ideas that the topic suggests to you. Write the main ideas in ovals around your topic. Space out the ovals so that you will have room to add other ovals with more information.

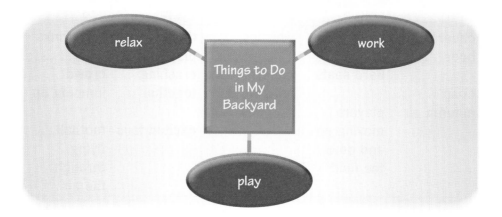

Surround each main-idea oval with supporting details.

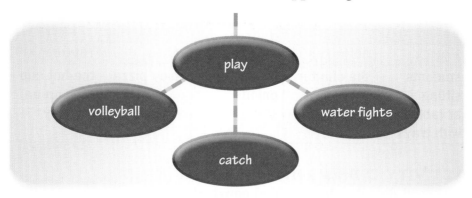

Details in one oval can remind you of more details.

ACTIVITY D Copy the idea web for the topic Favorite Breakfasts. Use the words in the list to fill in ideas and details.

whole wheat   veggie

apple cinnamon   buttermilk

bacon and onions

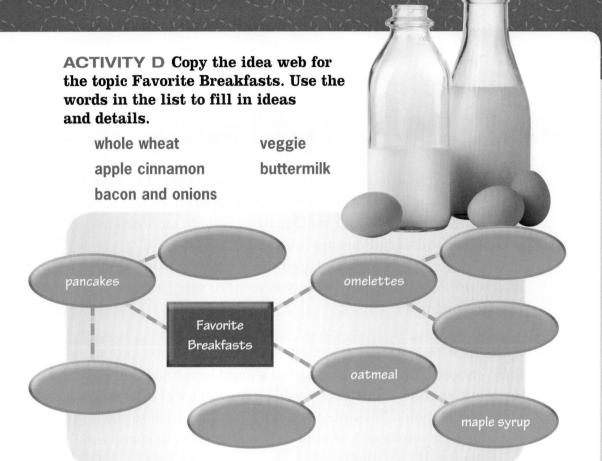

ACTIVITY E Fill in the ovals with details related to a school gym.

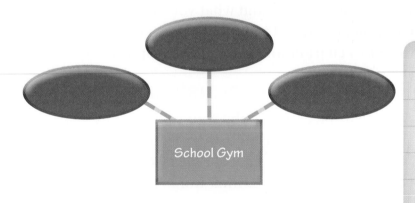

WRITER'S CORNER

Make an idea web for the topic that you and your partner chose for the five-senses chart on page 305. When you have finished, compare the two graphic organizers.

Tech Tip Use an online tool to create your idea web.

Oral Descriptions

You probably describe several things every day even if you don't realize it. You might describe a television program or movie to friends. You might tell your mother what you ate for lunch in school. These descriptions are informal.

Oral descriptions in school are more formal. For this kind of description, you prepare what you want to say. Then you practice saying it.

Choose a Topic

First, choose a topic to talk about. It should be a topic that you are familiar with. Your topic should be one that will interest your audience. It should be limited enough that you can describe it in the time that you have. It should be broad enough to spend time describing it.

Picture the Topic

Once you have chosen a topic, gather your information. Picture your topic. Remember what you see and what you hear. Think about what you feel, smell, and taste. Write what you can remember. A five-senses chart or an idea web can help you.

Organize the Information

Decide if you can describe your topic best by using space order or time order. Copy your notes from the five-senses chart or idea web onto note cards in the order you think works best.

Practice

Use your notes as you practice your oral description. Don't try to remember everything you wrote word for word. Use note cards to help you remember the main ideas. Practice your description many times until you feel comfortable. As you practice, think about these things.

- Speak loudly enough for everyone to hear.
- Look at your audience as you speak.
- Stand up straight. Do not move around too much.
- Look at your note cards if you forget what to say.

ACTIVITY A Tell which of these topics would be good for an oral description and which would not. Explain why.

1. a family car
2. London
3. a best friend
4. a bicycle
5. favorite socks
6. a park in the city
7. a baseball bat
8. a street performer
9. a view from a window
10. houseboats

ACTIVITY B Make a five-senses chart or an idea web for your favorite breakfast. Include as many senses as you can. Then organize the information into time order. Use note cards.

SPEAKER'S CORNER

Use the notes that you wrote for Activity B. Practice giving your description at least three times. Present it to a partner. Then listen to your partner's description.

Listening Tips

It is hard to stand up in front of a group of people and give a talk. It is even harder if the audience is not paying attention. That is why it is important for the audience to be polite. Here are some things to remember when you are listening to someone speak.

- Pay attention to the speaker. Take notes of interesting things the speaker says or interesting words he or she uses.
- Sit still. Do not move around in your seat.
- Do not talk. You would bother the speaker and the other people in the audience.
- Try to picture in your mind what the speaker is describing. Listen for sensory words, similes, and metaphors.
- If you have a question, wait until the speaker has finished. Then raise your hand to ask your question.

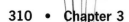

ACTIVITY C Take turns with a partner. Choose an object in the classroom. Don't tell your partner what you chose. Describe the object. When you have finished, your partner will draw a picture of your object. Discuss your partner's picture. Did you give a complete description? Did your partner listen closely to what you said?

ACTIVITY D Think of an event you were at recently, such as a parade, a sporting event, or a party. In a small group, give a brief description of your event. Listen to your classmates' descriptions.

ACTIVITY E Use the chart below to prepare a short oral description of your favorite restaurant. Add at least six details to the chart. Organize your description by time order or space order. Write your notes on note cards. Practice saying your speech. Be prepared to present your description to a partner.

MY FAVORITE RESTAURANT				
SIGHT	SOUND	SMELL	TASTE	TOUCH

ACTIVITY F Take turns describing your favorite restaurant with a partner, using the notes you took in Activity E. Then ask questions to help your partner think of new sensory details. For example, you might ask, "Is the restaurant noisy or quiet?" or "What do the hamburgers taste like?" Use your partner's questions to help you think of sensory details. Add the new sensory details to your note cards.

ACTIVITY G Think back on the events you discussed in Activity D. Using the one you described, prepare a five-senses chart like the one in Activity E. Add details to the chart. Decide on an order in which to give an oral description. Write notes on note cards. Practice giving your oral description. Be prepared to present your description to the class.

SPEAKER'S CORNER

Present to the class the description that you prepared in Activity G. Listen to new suggestions from your classmates, and offer suggestions to your classmates' descriptions.

Prewriting and Drafting

It is time to use the writing process to write a description. You may choose to describe a person, a place, a thing, or an event. Your audience will be your classmates.

Prewriting

Prewriting is the time that you explore topics that you could write about. It is the time to decide how you want to organize your description.

Choosing a Topic

Carmen is a fourth-grade student. The students in her class have been given an assignment to write a description of a summertime experience. Carmen had done so many things over the summer that she had trouble deciding what to write about. Her family had visited the state capital. She had gone to summer camp. Relatives from Costa Rica had come to visit for a week. Carmen felt that she didn't know enough about the state capital to write a good description. Besides, she thought it was boring. She didn't think that her classmates would be interested in hearing  about her relatives. There wasn't enough time to write everything about her stay at the summer camp. After she thought for a while, Carmen decided to write about one activity at the camp. She would write about the canoe trips she took.

Your Turn

Think about people, places, things, or events that are interesting to you. Consider them in the same way that Carmen thought about the topics that she could write about.

- Which ones do you know well enough to write about?
- Which ones are limited enough to write a good description in the time that you have?
- Which ones will be interesting for your classmates to read?

When you have narrowed your list, choose the topic that interests you the most.

Organizing Ideas

Carmen had many memories of her canoe trips. She wanted to be certain that she included all the important details in her description.

Carmen created a five-senses chart to help her think of sensory details. The chart helped organize her ideas into sight, sound, smell, taste, and touch.

Once she had gathered her details, Carmen thought about how she would organize her  description. She decided to use space order. She would start with the first lake the canoers paddled on and then describe the second and third lakes.

Your Turn

Think of all the details you can about your topic. To help you think of sensory details, use a five-senses chart like the one Carmen created or use an idea web to help you think of more details.

Once you have thought of plenty of sensory details, think of how you will organize your description. Will it be easier to describe your topic in time order or space order?

FIVE NATIONS CANOEING TRIPS					
	SIGHT	SOUND	SMELL	TASTE	TOUCH
first lake	bass, muskie	campers' noises			icy water
second lake	deer, beavers, raccoons, woodchucks	wild turkeys, crows, woodpeckers		wild raspberries	prickly thorns
third lake		croaking frogs	decaying plants		

Prewriting

Drafting

Content Editing

Revising

Copyediting

Proofreading

Publishing

Drafting

Carmen used her five-senses chart to write the first draft of her description. She double-spaced her lines to leave room for changes when she revised her writing.

My favorite activity at Five Nations Summer Camp is canoeing. The camp used to be an old rock quarry. When they dug out the stone, they left three deep holes that became lakes. The water is deep. It is icy cold and as dark as ink. You can't swim in it, but if you take out a canoe, you will see some beautiful scenery.

It takes about 20 minutes to paddle across the first lake. You won't see as much wildlife here as in the other lakes. There are a lot of fish, such as bass and muskie. You won't see them, though, unless they go after bugs on the water's surface. When you get to the end of the first lake, you have to portage your canoe.

Now you begin to see and hear more wildlife. In the distance you can often hear three or four different woodpeckers. They are the drummers of the forest. You can hear their rat-a-tat pounding. They are looking for bugs in the oak trees that surround the lakes. You can also hear the calls of other birds echoing through the trees. You'll recognize the cawing of crows and the "gobble gobble" of the wild turkeys. Besides birds, you may also see deer, raccoons, beavers, and woodchucks.

The portage to the third lake is pretty long. Several patches of wild raspberries make the hike worthwhile. It is easy to spend a half hour or so cramming the delightfuly sweet fruit into your mouth. By the time you are full, your hands will be stained a dark red. Be careful, though. Raspberry bushes have needle-sharp thorns. It's too bad there aren't wild blueberries. They don't have thorns.

Prewriting

Drafting

Content Editing

Revising

Copyediting

Proofreading

Publishing

The third lake has a shallower shoreline than the first two lakes have. The tall grass and cattails around the edges make an ideal hiding place for thousands of frogs. Late in the day they join in a croaking chorus that fills the air. Something else fills the air here. There is a rotten stink along the shore.. After 15 minutes in the foul air, most campers are ready to turn around and head back home. The entire trip lasts only four hours, but you will remember it your whole life.

Your Turn

Use your idea web or five-senses chart to write your first draft. Keep your audience in mind as you write. Use words that your readers will understand and that will hold their interest.

Writer's Tip Double-space your lines so that you will have room to make changes later.

Similes and Metaphors

Most good descriptions include similes and metaphors. They are not used in every

 Voice

sentence, however. Too many similes and metaphors can confuse the reader. A writer should choose the most memorable similes and metaphors, ones that paint clear pictures in the reader's mind.

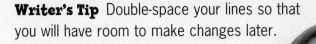

Editor's Workshop

Content Editing

When writers complete their first draft, they want to make sure that all the important information is included and that it is correct. It is just as important to be certain that unnecessary information is left out and that the ideas are presented in an order that is easy to follow.

Content Editor's Checklist

☐ Will the audience be interested in the topic?

☐ Are sensory details included?

☐ Is all the necessary information included?

☐ Is unnecessary information left out?

☐ Are the details presented in an order that is easy to follow?

☐ Are similes or metaphors used to help the reader picture the description more easily?

☐ Does the ending sum up the description?

Carmen used the Content Editor's Checklist to make sure that her description did all these things.

Carmen asked her friend Mathias to look over her paper. Mathias and Carmen often checked each other's writing. She trusted his opinions and knew that he would make good suggestions.

Mathias used the checklist to go over Carmen's description. He made a list of ways that he thought Carmen could improve her description. Then they met to discuss what he found. Mathias told Carmen that he really enjoyed her description and thought her audience would be interested in the topic.

 Word Choice

He thought the description was well organized and full of sensory details, including similes and metaphors. He also thought the ending summed up the description nicely.

Then Mathias made these suggestions for improvement.

- The opening doesn't say what your paper is about. Your description is about nature, but it sounds like you will be talking about canoeing.
- Why don't you see much wildlife around the first lake?
- What do you mean when you say you must portage your canoe?
- You say that the reader will recognize the cawing of crows and the gobbling of wild turkeys. Not everyone will know how these birds sound. Maybe you should leave that part out.
- The sentences about wild blueberries aren't necessary if you don't see them on the trip.
- What causes the rotten stink along the shore of the third lake? Are there skunks nearby?

Carmen was pleased with Mathias's suggestions. She could see that they would improve her paper, so she decided to follow most of them. She didn't agree with the suggestion about dropping the birdcalls. Carmen decided to leave that sentence as it was.

Your Turn

Reread your first draft several times. Use the Content Editor's Checklist to help you remember what to look for. When you feel that your description is as good as you can make it, trade papers with a classmate.

- Look over your partner's paper as carefully as you did yours.
- Use the Content Editor's Checklist. Write notes about ways that you think your partner's paper could be improved.
- Meet with your partner to suggest your improvements.
- Be sure to point out the good things as well as things you think should be changed.

Writer's Tip Don't try to check all the items on the Content Editor's Checklist at once. Look for one item at a time.

Prewriting
Drafting
Content Editing
Revising
Copyediting
Proofreading
Publishing

Writer's Workshop

Revising

This is how Carmen revised her description, using Mathias's suggestions and her own ideas.

The best way to see nature up close is from a canoe. I learned how to canoe last year
~~My favorite activity~~ at Five Nations Summer Camp ~~is canoeing~~. The camp used to be an old rock quarry. When they dug out the stone, they left three deep holes that became lakes. The water is deep. It is icy cold and as dark as ink. You can't swim in it, but if you take out a canoe, you will see some beautiful scenery.

It takes about 20 minutes to paddle across the first lake. You won't see as much wildlife here as in the other lakes. *The activity around the camp scares most of it away.* There are a lot of fish, such as bass and muskie. You won't see them, though, unless they go after bugs on the water's surface. When you get to the end of the first lake, you have to portage your canoe. *That means you must carry it over a stretch of land to the next lake.* Now you begin to see and hear more wildlife. In the distance you can often hear three or four different woodpeckers. They are the drummers of the forest. You can hear their rat-a-tat pounding. They are looking for bugs in the oak trees that surround the lakes. You can also hear the calls of other birds echoing through the trees. You'll recognize the cawing of crows and the "gobble gobble" of the wild turkeys. Besides birds, you may also see deer, raccoons, beavers, and woodchucks.

The portage to the third lake is pretty long. Several patches of wild raspberries make the hike worthwhile. It is easy to spend a half hour or so cramming the delightfuly sweet fruit into your mouth. By the time you are full, your hands will be stained a dark red. Be careful, though. Raspberry bushes have needle-sharp thorns. ~~It's too bad there aren't wild blueberries. They don't have thorns.~~

The third lake has a shallower shoreline than the first two lakes have. The tall grass and cattails around the edges make an ideal hiding place for thousands of frogs. Late in the day they join in a croaking chorus that fills the air. Something else fills the air here. There is a rotten stink along the shore. *Dead plants are decaying and causing the smell.* After 15 minutes in the foul air, most campers are ready to turn around and head back home. The entire trip lasts only four hours, but you will remember it your whole life.

Prewriting

Drafting

Content Editing

Revising

Copyediting

Proofreading

Publishing

Carmen revised her description in several ways. Try to answer these questions.

- How did Carmen change the beginning of her description? Why does her change better introduce the topic of her description?
- Look at the second paragraph. Carmen added two sentences. What helpful information does the first sentence give? What helpful information does the second sentence give?
- Look at the third paragraph. Why do you think that Carmen took out the last two sentences?
- Look at the last paragraph. Find the sentence that Carmen added. What helpful information does the sentence give?

Your Turn

Use your partner's comments and your own ideas to revise your draft. When you have finished, go over the Content Editor's Checklist again. Can you answer yes to each question?

Copyediting and Proofreading

Copyediting

When you copyedit, you make sure that you have used the right words for what you want

 Sentence Fluency

to say. You also want your sentences to flow smoothly. There shouldn't be too many long sentences or too many short ones.

Carmen used the Copyeditor's Checklist to finish editing her description. Carmen read her paper aloud and listened to how the sentences sounded. The first two sentences in the paragraph about the raspberries didn't sound quite right. Carmen decided to combine them to make a compound sentence. How would you combine the two sentences? She also decided to combine two of the sentences about woodpeckers to make the writing flow more smoothly.

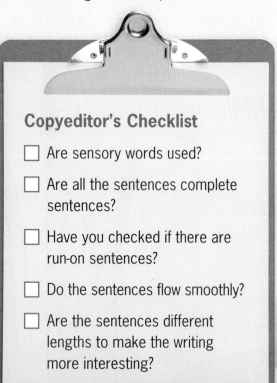

Copyeditor's Checklist

☐ Are sensory words used?

☐ Are all the sentences complete sentences?

☐ Have you checked if there are run-on sentences?

☐ Do the sentences flow smoothly?

☐ Are the sentences different lengths to make the writing more interesting?

Your Turn

Look over your revised description. Use the Copyeditor's Checklist to make sure that your writing is interesting and easy to read. Read your description aloud or ask someone else to read it aloud while you listen.

Grammar in Action

Add descriptive adjectives to help your audience create a picture of your description. Review Section 2.1.

Proofreading

Incorrect capitalization, punctuation, or grammar make readers think that a writer is

careless. After you have finished editing and revising your work and you feel that your sentences and ideas are clear, you are ready to proofread. A checklist can help you catch all these mistakes.

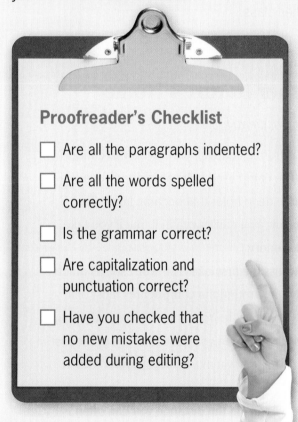

Proofreader's Checklist

☐ Are all the paragraphs indented?

☐ Are all the words spelled correctly?

☐ Is the grammar correct?

☐ Are capitalization and punctuation correct?

☐ Have you checked that no new mistakes were added during editing?

Carmen used the checklist to proofread her description. She caught one misspelled word, *delightfuly*. What is the correct spelling of this word? Then Carmen saw a paragraph that needed to be indented. Can you spot it?

Carmen was pleased that she found the mistakes. Now she wanted her friend Deana to give her description one final proofreading. It is a good idea to have another person proofread your paper after you have proofread it yourself.

Deana read Carmen's description three times, using the Proofreader's Checklist. She found a sentence with two periods. Can you find this mistake?

Your Turn

Read your paper carefully, using the Proofreader's Checklist.

- Look for only one kind of mistake at a time. You might not see some mistakes if you look for too many things at once. If you read your paper several times, you have more opportunities to catch mistakes.
- Use the proofreading marks that you learned in Chapter 1 to mark changes on your paper.
- When you have finished proofreading your description, trade papers with a partner. Proofread your partner's paper and use proofreading marks to point out corrections.

Prewriting

Drafting

Content Editing

Revising

Copyediting

Proofreading

Publishing

Writer's Workshop

Publishing

Publishing is the time that you share your finished work with an audience. You know it is your best work. You might read it aloud in class, put it on a bulletin board, or turn it in to your teacher.

Carmen had revised her description several times. She had copyedited and proofread it herself and asked a classmate to proofread it also. After all the work, Carmen added a title and was eager to share her description with her class.

Paddling into Mother Nature's Home

by Carmen Vieira

The best way to see nature up close is from a canoe. I learned how to canoe last year at Five Nations Summer Camp. The camp used to be an old rock quarry. When they dug out the stone, they left three deep holes that became lakes. The water is deep. It is icy cold and as dark as ink. You can't swim in it, but if you take out a canoe, you will see some beautiful scenery.

It takes about 20 minutes to paddle across the first lake. You won't see as much wildlife here as in the other lakes. The activity around the camp scares most of it away. There are a lot of fish, such as bass and muskie. You won't see them, though, unless they go after bugs on the water's surface. When you get to the end of the first lake, you have to portage your canoe. That means you must carry it over a stretch of land to the next lake.

Now you begin to see and hear more wildlife. In the distance you can often hear three or four different woodpeckers. They are the drummers of the forest. You can hear their rat-a-tat pounding as they look for bugs in the oak trees that surround the lakes. You can also hear the calls of other birds echoing through the trees. You'll recognize the cawing of crows and the "gobble gobble" of the wild turkeys. Besides birds, you may also see deer, raccoons, beavers, and woodchucks.

The portage to the third lake is pretty long, but several patches of wild raspberries make the hike worthwhile. It is easy to spend a half hour or so cramming the

Prewriting

Drafting

Content Editing

Revising

Copyediting

Proofreading

Publishing

delightfully sweet fruit into your mouth. By the time you are full, your hands will be stained a dark red. Be careful, though. Raspberry bushes have needle-sharp thorns.

The third lake has a shallower shoreline than the first two lakes have. The tall grass and cattails around the edges make an ideal hiding place for thousands of frogs. Late in the day they join in a croaking chorus that fills the air. Something else fills the air here. There is a rotten stink along the shore. Dead plants are decaying and causing the smell. After 15 minutes in the foul air, most campers are ready to turn around and head back home. The entire trip lasts only four hours, but you will remember it your whole life.

There are many ways you can publish your description. Give these ideas a try. Whichever way you choose to publish, be sure you are presenting your best material.

 Post it on your classroom's wiki, blog, or Web site. Have classmates read your description and comment on it.

 Create a class magazine. Decorate the margins with photographs or small pictures of things representing the descriptions.

 Film it. If your description is of a place nearby, film it and add music that lends itself to the mood of your description. You can also narrate it with your descriptive writing.

 Create a class book for a younger grade. Decorate the margins with small pictures of things representing the descriptions.

Your Turn

Look over your draft one last time to make sure there are no mistakes. If

 Presentation

you can, use your computer's spell-checker. Use your neatest handwriting or a computer to make the final copy. Then choose one of the publishing ideas.

Take time to read some of your classmates' descriptions. Good writers read other writers' work for ideas to improve their own work.

How-to Articles

LiNK

Make a Groovy Lava Lamp
National Geographic Kids

The secret behind the lamp's "lava" is science. Oil is lighter, or less dense, than water, so it rises to the surface. Salt is heavier, or more dense, than water, and sinks to the bottom. When you add the salt, blobs of oil attach to the grains and sink. Then the salt dissolves, and the oil returns to the top. The result? A liquid show for the eyes.

YOU WILL NEED

• Clear jar with lid • Vegetable oil • Glitter
• Water • Salt
• Food coloring • Flashlight

Fill the jar three-quarters full of water. Add drops of food coloring until you like the color you see. A few drops go a long way! Sprinkle in glitter for extra sparkle. Fill the jar almost to the top with vegetable oil and let the mixture separate. Pour salt into the jar until you see the cool lava lamp effect. When the bubbles stop, add more salt to see it again. Shine a flashlight behind the jar to watch your lava lamp really glow!

> This how-to article's introduction informs and catches the reader's attention. The body contains the necessary materials, and the steps are written in time order.

CHAPTER 4

Emma J., Room 112

Make Your Own Kazoo

It takes years of experience and great skill to make a guitar or a violin. However, it takes just a few minutes to make a homemade kazoo.

To make your kazoo, you will need a cardboard tube, a sheet of wax paper, a rubber band, and a pair of scissors.

First, cut a square piece of wax paper that's about three inches larger than the opening of the cardboard tube. Wrap the wax paper over one end of the tube.

Next, put the rubber band over the wax paper to fasten it to the tube. Finally, put the open end of the cardboard tube up to your mouth and hum a tune. Notice how the kazoo buzzes and vibrates, changing the sound of your humming.

Play your kazoo for anyone who will listen. Now you have a new instrument to delight (or annoy) your friends!

What Makes a Good How-to Article?

A how-to article teaches the reader how to do something. The instructions for a board game are a kind of how-to article. So is a set of directions to your school. Here are some things to remember when you write a how-to article.

Introduction

The introduction of a how-to article tells what the reader will learn from the article. The introduction should be informative. It might even be catchy if the writer thinks the audience needs to be "hooked."

Body

The body of a how-to article tells how to complete the task. All the necessary materials are listed. Next, the steps are clearly explained in time order. The body should not include any unnecessary information. Each step is written as an imperative sentence, which is a sentence that gives a command. Notice how imperative sentences are used in "Finding Direction with a Watch" on page 327.

Conclusion

The conclusion of a how-to article sums up what has been taught. It might also tell how the information will help the reader.

ACTIVITY A Look over the how-to article "Make Your Own Kazoo" on page 325. Then answer the questions below.

1. Which paragraph makes up the introduction?
2. Which paragraph tells what materials are needed?
3. Are all the important steps included? How many steps are involved in making your own kazoo?
4. Which paragraph makes up the conclusion?
5. Think of another introduction or conclusion the writer might have used for this article.

ACTIVITY B Decide which of the following sentences would make a good introduction for a how-to article about model airplanes. Explain your answers.

1. Never build a model airplane without an adult's help.
2. Model airplanes are made of plastic.
3. Building a model airplane is easy and fun.
4. I'm afraid to ride in airplanes.
5. With a little patience and work, you can build a model airplane that looks just like the real thing.

ACTIVITY C Complete each of these sentence starters as an introduction to a short how-to article that you would like to write.

1. Think about the fun you could have if _____.
2. Before you plant a garden, you need to _____.
3. Playing _____ is easier than it looks.
4. If you are tired of the same old lunch, try making _____ instead.
5. Have you ever wanted to _____?
6. You may have always wondered how _____.

LiNK

Finding Direction with a Watch

A watch with two hands can tell the direction. It must have the correct local time . . . .

In the northern hemisphere, hold the watch horizontally. If it's summer, wind it back an hour; if it's winter, wind it forward an hour.

(continued on page 329)

WRITER'S CORNER

Write a list of three easy things that you know how to do. Choose one and write two or three sentences for an introduction for a how-to article about that topic.

Grammar in Action. To make your introduction more catchy, use a variety of sentences. See Section 1.10.

Time Order

The body of a how-to article tells how to do something step-by-step. The directions are given in time order. If some of the directions are out of order, your readers might get confused. They may not be able to complete the task. Would you be able to find direction in the excerpt on page 329 if you did not follow the steps in the correct order?

The body of a how-to article on writing a letter is written below. Can you find the steps that are out of order?

> **Fold your letter into three parts. Write the heading and the inside address at the top of the page. Then write the closing and sign your name. Write your greeting and the body of your letter. Put the letter into an envelope. Seal the envelope and drop it in a mailbox. Write the receiver's address and your address on the envelope and add a stamp.**

ACTIVITY D Revise the paragraph above, using time order. The first sentence has been done for you.

Write the heading and the inside address at the top of the page.

ACTIVITY E Arrange the steps for taking down a flag in the correct order.

1. Unhook the flag from the flagpole.
2. Fold the flag carefully with your partner.
3. With a partner hold the flag by the corners.
4. Put the flag in a safe place.
5. Bring the flag down the flagpole.

ACTIVITY F The following sentences are from a how-to article about making a sock puppet. Decide which sentence is the introduction and which is the conclusion. Then arrange the steps in time order.

1. Draw a face around the eyes and glue the yarn above them for hair.
2. Now you're ready to put on a show for your friends.
3. Making a sock puppet is simple and fun.
4. Then glue the googly eyes to the front of the sock.
5. Put your hand into the finished sock puppet.
6. Gather a sock, two googly eyes, some yarn, and a permanent marker.

ACTIVITY G Choose one of the topics below. Write three steps for the body of a how-to article about this topic. Use time order.

A. how to take a photograph
B. how to make a turkey and cheese sandwich
C. how to play hopscotch
D. how to make your bed
E. how to wrap a present
F. how to make a scrapbook
G. how to give your dog a bath
H. how to make a paper hat
I. how to do a card trick
J. how to make pancakes
K. how to sew on a button
L. how to make an animal balloon

LiNK

Finding Direction with a Watch

(continued from page 327)

Point the hour hand at the sun. Bisect the angle between the hour hand and 12 to give you a north-south line. In the southern hemisphere, point 12 at the sun, and the midpoint between 12 and the hour hand will give a north-south line.

The Dangerous Book for Boys
by Conn Iggulden and Hal Iggulden

WRITER'S CORNER

Reread the steps that you wrote for a how-to article in Activity G. Add any steps that are missing.

With an adult, research your how-to topic online.

Important Details

A how-to article should be complete. This means that all the necessary information should be included. If an important detail is left out, the reader may not be able to complete the task. Notice the details in the skateboarding excerpt on page 331.

As you write a how-to article, you should also make sure that you leave out any details that are not necessary. Any unimportant details will distract your reader.

Read the how-to paragraph below. Can you find any details that are not needed?

Dive Away!

Diving off a diving board is not as hard as you might think. First, stand at the end of the diving board with your toes coming just off the edge. It could be an indoor pool or an outdoor pool. Bend your knees and lean your head forward. Raise your hands over your head. You won't be doing one of those fancy dives like you see in the Olympics. Push off with your legs and lean forward so that you go headfirst into the water. When you come up, you'll be glad you took your first dive.

The sentence "It could be an indoor pool or an outdoor pool" is not needed. It distracts the reader. The sentence "You won't be doing one of those fancy dives like you see in the Olympics" is also unnecessary.

ACTIVITY A Each group of sentences below is from a how-to article. Which sentence in each group is not an important detail?

1. a. When you hear a fire alarm, get up from your seat.
   b. Line up single file.
   c. Walk calmly and quietly out the door.
   d. Many fire alarms are drills, not real fires.

2. a. Put all the dirty dishes in the dishwasher.
   b. Using a dishwasher is easier than washing the dishes yourself.
   c. Put soap in the dishwasher.
   d. Close the door and turn the knob to "wash."

3. a. To train for a marathon, you should start at least six months before.
   b. The Boston Marathon is one of the most famous marathons.
   c. Start by running just a few miles each day.
   d. Increase your runs by about one mile every week.

4. a. Points from basketball free throws can really add up.
   b. Position the ball and bend your legs like you are going to jump.
   c. Then extend your legs up.
   d. Keep your eyes on the basket and aim with the ball.

ACTIVITY B Identify the unclear information in each sentence. Tell how you would make the directions clearer.

1. Put enough dirt in the pot before you plant the flowers.
2. Cut out many shapes for the art project.
3. Add a small amount of mayonnaise to the salad.
4. You can collect a lot of stuff on a nature walk.

LiNK

Learning How: Skateboarding

. . . Many skaters want to do an ollie. The best way to describe an ollie is jumping up in the air with the skateboard. When an ollie is done well, the skater is suspended in the air with the skateboard underfoot. . . .

To do an ollie, you push your feet down as hard as you can on the tail of the skateboard. You can hear the tail hit the ground. When it hits, you push your front foot forward, which brings the tail off the ground.

Jane Mersky Leder

WRITER'S CORNER

Trade with a partner the how-to article that you used for the Writer's Corner on page 329. Read your partner's how-to article to see if any important details are left out.

Being Specific

The details you give in a how-to article should always be specific. This means telling your readers exactly what they need to know. When giving travel directions, be sure to tell whether to turn right or left. In a recipe tell how much of each ingredient to add and how long to cook the dish.

What specific information is missing from this paragraph?

> **To get to the police station, go down Haverhill Street and turn. Go straight down Winston Street for a while until you reach the store. Turn at the store and go down the hill. Pass a few stop signs and turn right on Main Street. The police station will be on the side of the street.**

This paragraph is missing important details. The writer does not say which direction to turn from Haverhill Street or which way to turn at the store. The writer does not give the name of the store or tell which side of the street the station is on. Phrases such as "a while" or "a few" are also not helpful. Instead, the writer should say exactly how far to go or how many stop signs to pass.

ACTIVITY C The how-to article below is missing some specific information. Discuss what details should be more specific in order to make the fruit smoothie.

Here's what you need to do to make a fruit smoothie. You will need a blender, milk, yogurt, and fruit. First, pour the milk, the fruit, and the yogurt into the blender. Then turn on the blender. Set it high enough to make the smoothie. When you know it's done, pour it into a glass.

ACTIVITY D The note below is a how-to article written for someone who took over a friend's paper route. Read the list of details after the note. Which details should be included in the note? Decide where each important detail should go.

Thank you for offering to help deliver my papers this week! Here's what you need to do. Get the newspaper sections from the driveway and put the papers together. Put all the newspapers into your newspaper sack. Go to each house on the list and deliver the newspapers. Pick up any money envelopes you see and put them in the sack. Hold on to them until I get back.

Thanks again!

Danny

1. Lots of people have signed up for the newspaper this year.
2. Put the papers together by sliding the sports section inside the main sections.
3. I just got a new newspaper sack a month ago.
4. Put the newspaper inside the screen door of each house.
5. The envelopes are usually taped to the door.
6. With any luck all the customers will leave big tips in their envelopes.
7. You should start at 6:30 a.m.

WRITER'S CORNER

Think of a game you like to play. Write the directions for playing the game. Be sure to give specific details.

Prefixes

A prefix is a word part that is added to the beginning of a base word. A prefix changes the meaning of the base word. Three common prefixes are *dis-*, *pre-*, and *under-*.

Here are the definitions of these prefixes and examples of how they are used. Can you use each example word in a sentence?

PREFIX	MEANING	BASE WORD	EXAMPLE
dis-	not, opposite of	like	dislike
pre-	before, earlier	cook	precook
under-	below, less than	foot	underfoot

Sometimes you might come across an unfamiliar word that has a prefix. If you know what the prefix and the base word mean, you might be able to guess what the word means.

ACTIVITY A Think of a word that fits each meaning. Each word should begin with the prefix *dis-*, *pre-*, or *under-*.

1. not allow
2. view before
3. make a line below
4. pay before
5. not favor
6. arrange before
7. not appear
8. below the proper age
9. below the ground
10. not obey

Argh!

(I'm so displeased.)

ACTIVITY B Answer these questions. Use the chart on page 334 if you need help with the meanings of the underlined words.

1. What kinds of activities do children do in <u>preschool</u>?

2. Why might people want to explore <u>undersea</u>?

3. Why would a store <u>discontinue</u> selling a toy?

4. Why do you take the <u>precaution</u> of wearing your seat belt?

ACTIVITY C Add the prefix *dis-*, *pre-*, or *under-* to each word in parentheses to complete the sentence.

1. When Samantha said she had not taken the money, she was being (honest).

2. When we first turned on the radio, we found that some stations had been (set).

3. Remember to wear a button-up shirt on top of your (shirt).

4. The submarine took the crew on their first (sea) adventure.

5. Mr. Jones tried not to (judge) who had told the truth before he knew all the facts.

6. Because we were given less time to take the test, we had a (advantage).

7. The tiny rabbit hid from the fox by hiding in the (brush).

8. The band of trolls plotted their attack from their (ground) hideout.

9. We thought the TV show was being shown live, but the truth is that it was (recorded).

10. My dog Rex may not be smart, but he is never (loyal) or (obedient).

WRITER'S CORNER

Choose five words with prefixes that you wrote from Activity B or C. Use each word in a sentence.

ACTIVITY D Choose the word from the list that best completes each sentence below.

disagree	preheat	underdress
disbelief	prehistoric	underfoot
disconnect	preschool	underhand
displease	preteen	undersized
disrespect	preview	underwater

1. Before starting kindergarten, my brother has to go to _____.

2. The _____ catcher's mitt is too small to fit on my hand.

3. The umpire says that the ball went through the goal, but I _____.

4. Before you put the roast in the oven, be sure to _____ the oven for two hours.

5. After the amazing magic trick, we all shook our heads in _____.

6. Because I hurt my shoulder, I could only throw the ball _____.

7. The student's rude comment to the teacher was a sign of _____.

8. The bones in the cave show that there was a group of _____ settlers in the area.

9. It will _____ Ruana to find out that you forgot her birthday.

10. The class of fifth graders looked for books intended for a _____ audience.

11. Remember to hold your breath when swimming _____.

12. You will _____ for the wedding if you do not wear a jacket and tie.

13. Our teacher will _____ the movie before she shows it to us.

14. I tripped on our cat because it is always _____.

15. The worker will _____ the plug from the wall socket so he won't get a shock.

ACTIVITY E Write the meaning of each word below.

1. underweight
2. disbelieve
3. predate
4. disprove
5. underarm

6. dishonor
7. premix
8. underpay
9. pregame
10. disobey

ACTIVITY F Read the paragraphs below and find the words with the prefixes *dis-, pre-,* or *under-.* Choose five of the words and write the meaning of each word.

Mr. McSweeney wondered what had happened to all his apricots. Before jumping to a conclusion, he took the precaution of counting them. When he did, he knew that he had not underestimated how many there had been. Some of the apricots had disappeared.

His first thought was that one of his customers had been dishonest. He did not want to prejudge his customers and accuse them of something they did not do. Mr. McSweeney thought about asking his customers to prepay before he let them buy any fruit. He could also prearrange for a police officer to watch over his store. The idea that a customer would steal really displeased him.

Then Mr. McSweeney sat in disbelief as he saw a squirrel dart out from the underbrush near the fruit stand. It hopped up from the underside of the stand, took an apricot, and ran off. Mr. McSweeney was glad to find that the thief was a squirrel and not a disloyal customer.

WRITER'S CORNER

Look through a book for five words with the prefixes from this lesson. Write a sentence for each word.

Grammar in Action. Make your sentences more interesting by using descriptive adjectives. See Section 4.1.

Dictionary

Do you know what a quark is? What about sassafras? The best way to find out what a word means is by looking in a dictionary. A dictionary can tell you the meanings of words. It can also tell you where the word comes from, how it is spelled, and more.

Alphabetical Order

A dictionary is arranged in alphabetical order. This makes it easy to find the word you are looking for. When you look for a word, think of the part of the alphabet that the first letter of the word is in: the beginning, the middle, or the end. Flip to that part of the dictionary to look for your word.

Guide Words

Guide words can help you find a word in the dictionary. Two guide words are found at the top of each page. They tell you the first and last words on that page. To find your word, look for the guide words that are closest to your word in alphabetical order. If your word fits between the two guide words, you will find it on that page. Here is the top section of a dictionary page with guide words.

141 lightning • locate

light•ning (līt´nĭng) *n.* A flash of electricity in the sky.

lights (līts) *n. pl.* The lungs of sheep, pigs, etc., used as food for animals

ACTIVITY A Arrange each list of words in alphabetical order.

1. below
   over
   after
   toward

2. street
   crosswalk
   traffic
   light

3. cloud
   star
   moon
   horizon

4. cup
   bowl
   saucer
   knife

ACTIVITY B Arrange each list of words in alphabetical order. If the first letter is the same, use the second letter. If the first two letters are the same, use the third letter.

1. pizza
   pancakes
   potatoes
   peanuts

2. hymn
   harp
   hoard
   hefty

3. spear
   spin
   spot
   spread

4. breakfast
   brand
   bring
   brook

ACTIVITY C Look at the sample guide words below. Decide whether each word would be on that page, before it, or after it.

Guide Words: ligament • lofty

1. lamp
2. train
3. limp
4. mast
5. love
6. look
7. kind
8. lint
9. jewel
10. lose
11. lure
12. load

WRITER'S CORNER

Turn to a page in a dictionary and write five words in random order. Trade lists with a partner. Put your partner's list in alphabetical order. Then find your partner's page in the dictionary. Write the guide words used on that page.

Dictionary Meanings

The most important part of a dictionary entry is the meanings. Some words have just one meaning, while others have more than one. Often a dictionary will give a sample sentence to help you understand the meaning. Look at the dictionary entry below. How many meanings does the word have?

> **jog** (jŏg) **1** *v.* to move by shoving or bumping. *She jogged her friend to see if she was awake.* **2** *v.* to shake up and remember, especially a memory. *The photograph jogged my memory.* **3** *v.* to run at a steady, slow pace. *I jog around town to keep in shape.* **4** *n.* a steady, slow trot. *We went for a jog.*

Did you know all the meanings of the word *jog*? Reading a dictionary entry can help you learn more about a word. It can also help you become a better reader, writer, and speaker. The more words and meanings you know, the easier it will be for you to say what you mean.

ACTIVITY D Look at the entry above for the word *jog*. Decide which meaning is being used in each sentence below.

1. The woman jogged me when the subway train suddenly stopped.

2. I was worn out after jogging for two miles.

3. The smell of wildflowers jogged my memory of the walk in the woods.

4. The football players start off every morning with a jog around the park.

5. When Brian started daydreaming, Stacy jogged his arm to make him pay attention.

6. Finding my old tennis racket jogged my memory of the many hours that I'd spent practicing my serve.

ACTIVITY E Find each word in a dictionary. Tell how many meanings each word has. Then choose two words and write a sentence that uses each word.

1. exercise
2. needle
3. crank
4. outline
5. steel
6. handle
7. strain
8. muddy

ACTIVITY F Look up each word in a dictionary. Write the meaning of the word. Choose two words and use each in a sentence.

1. jest
2. plateau
3. scuttle
4. bewilder
5. replenish
6. graffiti
7. abandon
8. dawdle

ACTIVITY G With a partner find a word in the dictionary that is new to both of you. Write the meaning of the word. Then make up a second meaning for the word. Trade your word with another pair of students. Ask them to tell which meaning is correct. Have them look up your word to check their answer.

WRITER'S CORNER

Find a word in a dictionary that has at least three meanings. Write three sentences, each using a different meaning. Trade sentences with a partner. See if you can guess the meaning of the word in each of your partner's sentences.

Tech Tip With an adult, use an online dictionary.

Time Words

Have you ever read a paragraph in which the sentences did not seem to fit together? If so, the paragraph might have needed time words. Time words help a writer connect ideas so that they flow together. These kinds of words are often placed at the beginning of a sentence. Here are some examples.

after	**finally**	**later**	**second**	**third**
before	**first**	**next**	**then**	**while**

Read the following paragraphs. Notice how time words help the sentences flow more smoothly in the second paragraph.

Here's how to do the laundry. Put all the laundry into a basket and take it to the washing machine. Separate the white clothes from the dark clothes. Open the washing machine and add one cup of detergent. Put the white clothes into the machine. Turn the knob to "wash." Wait about 25 minutes for the machine to wash your clothes.

Here's how to do the laundry. First, put all the laundry into a basket and take it to the washing machine. Separate the white clothes from the dark clothes. Next, open the washing machine and add one cup of detergent. Put the white clothes into the machine. Then turn the knob to "wash." Finally, wait about 25 minutes for the machine to wash your clothes.

ACTIVITY A Use the time words on page 342 to help these two groups of sentences flow together.

Group 1

_____ Kim saw a kitten.

_____ she picked it up.

_____ she stroked its fur.

Group 2

_____ John dropped the birthday cake.

_____ he looked up at everyone.

_____ he started laughing.

ACTIVITY B Add time words to this how-to article.

Here's how to make a pompon ant. You will need three pompons, four craft stems, two googly eyes, some craft glue, and scissors.

_____ glue two pompons together, using just a bit of glue. This will make the body of the ant. _____ glue a third pompon to the other pompons to make the head.

_____ cut four craft stems so that they are each about four inches long. Glue one underneath the front of each pompon. Curl them so they look like legs sticking out each side.

_____ bend the fourth craft stem in the middle and curl each end upward. Glue it to the top of the head to make two antennae.

_____ glue the googly eyes to the front of the head.

_____ put your pompon ant in a special place to amuse you and your friends.

WRITER'S CORNER

Describe in four or five sentences what you do when the school day ends. Use time words. Read your sentences aloud. Then read them without the time words. Which sentences sound better?

Tech Tip Use an online audio recorder when reading aloud.

ACTIVITY C Choose one of the paragraphs below. Revise it by adding at least three time words.

A. To make chicken soup, you will need a can of soup, a can opener, a pot, some water, and crackers. Open the can with the can opener. Pour the soup into the pot. Fill the can with water and add the water to the pot. Put the pot on the stove and turn the knob to "medium." Stir the soup often. After about five minutes, pour the soup into a bowl. Crumble some crackers over the top of the soup.

B. Here's how to brush your teeth. Take your toothbrush out and run the brush under cool water. Spread toothpaste on the brush. Make sure you squeeze the tube from the bottom! Gently brush your teeth for three minutes. Start with your front teeth and work your way to the back. Spit the toothpaste into the sink. Take a sip of water to rinse out your mouth. Rinse off the brush and put it away.

C. To make s'mores at a campfire, you will need graham crackers, a chocolate bar, marshmallows, and a stick. Break a graham cracker into two equal squares. Break off a piece of chocolate and put it on one cracker. Slide a marshmallow onto the stick and hold it over the campfire. Hold it there until it turns a golden brown. Press the marshmallow onto the chocolate. Put the other graham cracker on top like a sandwich and slide the stick out. Be sure to eat the s'more while it's still warm.

D. It's easy and fun to make your own pizza. You will need a 10-inch pizza crust (the ready-made kind works fine), tomato sauce, shredded cheese, and whatever toppings you like, such as mushrooms, pepperoni, sausage, or olives. Spread the tomato sauce on the pizza crust. Sprinkle some cheese on top of the sauce. Put the toppings on. Add another layer of cheese. Put the pizza in the oven, and bake it according to the directions on the pizza crust package. The pizza is done when the cheese turns golden and bubbly.

ACTIVITY D Put these sentences from a story in time order. Add time words. The first sentence of the story is given.

For space-traveler extraordinaire Jenna Moonbeam, it was time to say good-bye.

1. She radioed to the control tower to begin the countdown.
2. She put on her helmet and stepped toward the ship.
3. Zach gave her the signal that he was ready to fly.
4. As the engines roared, she listened to the countdown over the radio.
5. Jenna looked out the window as the earth grew smaller and smaller in the distance.
6. Jenna took her seat at the controls and fastened her seatbelt.
7. The countdown ended, and she could feel the ship lifting off.
8. "We hear you, Moonbeam," came the voice from the tower.
9. Jenna heard the sound of the engines firing up beneath her.
10. She zipped up her space suit and kissed her family good-bye.
11. Her copilot, Zach Solaris, followed behind her as she stepped inside.

ACTIVITY E Choose one of the following suggestions. Write a paragraph as directed. Use at least three time words.

1. You have organized a bike trip for your family. Tell about the route you plan to take.
2. You have developed a new game for gym class. Tell how to play the game.
3. You have won a contest for your new healthful snack recipe. Tell how to make it.
4. You have discovered a new animal that becomes your pet. Tell how to take care of it.

WRITER'S CORNER

Revise the paragraph you chose from Activity C, using different time words. Which paragraph is better?

How-to Talks

Have you ever taught someone how to play a game? Have you told a friend how to get to your home? When you tell someone how to do something, you are giving a how-to talk. Here are some tips for giving a good how-to talk.

Topic

When you plan a how-to talk, choose a topic that your audience might not know but will be interested in learning about. Choose something that is easy to explain in a few steps.

Introduction

Begin your talk by telling what you will teach. You might also want to get your audience's attention with a question or a catchy first sentence.

Body

In the body go through all the steps needed to complete the task. Begin by listing anything your audience will need, showing examples if you can. If possible, show how to complete the task by doing it yourself as you explain. If not, you might show a picture, diagram, or other visual aid.

Conclusion

The conclusion of your talk should sum up what has been taught. You might show your audience what you made or did. Leave time for questions at the end.

ACTIVITY A Which of the topics below do you think would be most interesting to a class of fourth graders?

1. how to play dodge ball
2. how to tie your shoes
3. how to peel a banana
4. how to change the oil in a car
5. how to build a house
6. how to use a video camera
7. how to plan a party
8. how to pack a suitcase

ACTIVITY B Choose two topics below. List three steps you might include in a how-to talk about each topic. Describe how you would show the steps, such as by using a visual aid.

A. how to hard-boil an egg
B. how to sharpen a pencil
C. how to do a cartwheel
D. how to get to the library
E. how to make lemonade
F. how to play miniature golf
G. how to arrange flowers
H. how to hang a picture on a wall

SPEAKER'S CORNER

Think of a topic for a how-to talk you would like to give. Make a list of the steps needed to complete this task. Think of a way to show the steps during your talk.

Prepare

To prepare for a how-to talk, first list all the important steps. Think of an informative introduction and a good conclusion for your talk. Write your introduction and conclusion on separate note cards. Then write each step on a separate note card. Also make notes of when to show your visual aids.

Next, prepare any visual aids. If you will be showing a picture or drawing, make it big enough for everyone to see. If you are bringing in materials, gather everything you need.

Practice

Before giving your how-to talk, practice in front of a friend or family member. Try to look at the person and not just read from your note cards. Remember to speak slowly and clearly.

Practice with your visual aids if you're using them. If you will be showing how to follow the steps in your talk, go through them a few times. Practice each step until you can do it smoothly.

As you practice your talk, ask yourself these questions:

- Am I speaking slowly and clearly?
- Am I speaking loudly enough?
- Does my introduction catch my audience's attention?
- Have I included all the necessary materials?
- Have I included all the important steps?
- Do I show my visual aids at the right time?
- Does my conclusion sum up what has been taught?

Listening Tips

When someone gives a how-to talk, it is important to be a good listener. Keep in mind these points as you listen to your classmates' talks:

- Look at the speaker to show that you are listening.
- Have a pencil and a sheet of paper ready in case you want to take notes.
- Listen for the introduction to find out what is being taught.
- If you cannot see a visual aid or do not understand a step, raise your hand. Politely ask the speaker for help in seeing the visual aid or in understanding the step.
- After the talk, ask the speaker any questions you have.
- Tell the speaker one thing you liked about the talk.

ACTIVITY C Prepare and practice the how-to talk you chose for the Speaker's Corner on page 347. Write on note cards the introduction, the steps, and the conclusion. Prepare your visual aids. Then present the talk to a partner. Talk about ways you could improve your talk. Listen to your partner's talk and give suggestions for improving it.

SPEAKER'S CORNER

Present your how-to talk to the class. Remember to speak slowly and clearly. Show any visual aids so that everyone can see them. When you have finished, invite your audience to ask questions or to make comments. When your classmates give their talks, keep in mind the listening tips.

Prewriting and Drafting

What things do you know how to make or do? Can you build a snow fort or make a necklace? By writing a how-to article, you can share your skills with others.

Prewriting

Brigitte was asked to write a how-to article for her fourth-grade class. Before she began writing, she did prewriting. First, she chose a topic. Then she organized her ideas by listing the materials needed and the steps.

Choosing a Topic

Brigitte had lots of ideas for how-to articles. She had made all sorts of crafts at summer camp.

Ideas Her older sister Claire had taught Brigitte how to play lots of games. She made these lists of all the fun things she knew how to make and do.

Crafts	Games
friendship bracelets	checkers
place mats	tick-tack-toe
jigsaw puzzles	Crazy Eights
snow globes	hopscotch
kites	musical chairs

After looking at her lists, Brigitte decided that a craft would be more fun to describe. Her favorite thing to make was friendship bracelets. However, she thought that it would be much easier to show how to make them. Some of the steps would be hard to describe in writing.

Brigitte also liked making snow globes. She

Voice knew she could clearly and confidently explain how to make them. It would be easy to do in a how-to article. She decided that this would be the topic of her article.

Your Turn

1. Make a list of things that you know how to make or do. You could list crafts and games, as Brigitte did. You could list food that you know how to cook. You could list anything else that you know how to make or do.

2. Look over your list. Choose one topic that would be fun and easy to explain. Choose a topic that you think would interest other people too.

Organizing Your Ideas

After she chose her topic, Brigitte made Organization a list of all the materials needed for making a snow globe. Then she wrote all the important steps.

Materials needed:

jar with lid

small plastic toy
   or other object

silicone sealer

glitter

corn syrup

paints

Steps:

1. Pick out a plastic object to go inside the snow globe.

2. Glue it to the jar lid

3. Fill the jar most of the way with corn syrup.

4. Sprinkle glitter inside the jar.

5. Screw the lid on tight.

6. Spread a strip of silicone sealer around the top of the jar.

7. Paint the top of the globe if you want.

8. Turn over the jar so the lid is the base and the toy is right-side up.

Brigitte looked at her lists. First, she looked to see if she had forgotten anything from the list of things needed. She saw that glue was used in the second step. She added it to the materials list.

Next, Brigitte looked at her steps. She tried to imagine making the snow globe. She realized that the silicone sealer needed to be added before screwing on the lid. She changed the order of the steps.

Your Turn

1. Make a list of all the materials needed for the topic you chose.

2. Write all the important steps.

3. When you have finished, read over what you have written. Make sure you have included all the materials. Check that all the important steps are included and are in the right order.

4. Make changes to your list if you find any mistakes.

Prewriting

Drafting

Content Editing

Revising

Copyediting

Proofreading

Publishing

Drafting

Brigitte was ready to turn her prewriting notes into a first draft. She wrote her steps out in sentence form, adding an introduction and a conclusion.

How to Make a Snow Globe

A snow globe is a pretty decaration, did you know that you can make one yourself? Here's how to do it.

You will need a jar and lid, glue, corn syrup, glitter, silicone sealer, paint, and a plastic toy that fits inside the jar. Choose a plastic toy that would look nice inside a snow globe.

To make the globe, glue the plastic toy to the jar's lid. Fill the jar most of the way up with corn syrup. Pour in some glitter.

You could use eggshells instead of glitter, but that's messier and doesn't look as nice. You would have to boil the eggs. Then you would have to peel the eggshells and break them up to look like snow. I would just use glitter.

Spread some silicone sealer over the top of the jar. Screw the lid on tightly. If you want, you can paint the top or bottom of your globe to make it more colorful.

Turn over the jar so the lid is the base and the toy is right-side up. To test the globe, shake it.

Prewriting

Drafting

Content Editing

Revising

Copyediting

Proofreading

Publishing

Your Turn

1. Look at the prewriting notes you made for your how-to article. Think of an introduction that tells what you will be teaching. You might want to think of a catchy first sentence to get your readers interested.

2. Write the body of your how-to article in time order. Start by listing any materials that are needed. Then list the steps in paragraph form. Use time words to help the sentences fit together.

3. Add a conclusion. Sum up what you taught. You might want to tell the result of following the steps. For example, you might tell your readers what they can do with what they made.

Being Specific

When you write a how-to article, it is important to be specific. It can be easy to forget that your audience might not know what you mean.

If you list materials in your how-to article, look at how you describe them. Could your readers misunderstand and use the wrong materials?

For example, Brigitte said a jar was needed for her snow globe. However, she forgot to mention that the jar needs to be a clear glass jar. Try to think of any important adjectives you should use when describing your materials.

Read over each step to make sure it is clear. Try to think of any way your audience could get the step wrong. If you can think of one, you will need a clearer way to say what you mean.

Grammar in Action

What kind of sentence is the first one in the second paragraph of Brigitte's draft? What kind of sentence is the last one in the draft? See Sections 1.2 and 1.3 for a review.

Editor's Workshop

Content Editing

Brigitte liked the draft she had written. However, she knew she could make it better by editing. She read her draft again, seeing if it was clear, complete, and correct. As she edited, she used this Content Editor's Checklist.

After editing her draft, Brigitte gave it to her friend Justin. Since he had never made a snow globe, she thought he would be able to find any missing steps.

Justin read Brigitte's draft twice. He read it through all the way once. Then he used the checklist to look it over more carefully. He took notes on what changes Brigitte might make. Then he shared his notes with her.

Content Editor's Checklist

- [ ] Does the introduction tell what is being taught?
- [ ] Does the body list all the materials that are needed?
- [ ] Does the body include all the important steps?
- [ ] Are the steps given in time order?
- [ ] Have all unimportant details been left out?
- [ ] Are all the details specific and clear?
- [ ] Does the conclusion sum up what has been taught?

Justin began by telling Brigitte how interesting he thought her topic was. He had never heard of someone making a homemade snow globe.

He told her that all the materials seemed to be listed and most of the steps were clear and in time order. He also liked the introduction. Then Justin gave Brigitte these suggestions.

- Can you give an example of what kind of plastic toy might look nice in a snow globe?
- I don't know if kids would have silicone sealer. Where can you buy it?
- I don't think you need all the stuff about eggshells. If you don't use them, why tell about them?
- Shouldn't you let the glue dry before you put the lid on?
- I think the end comes too fast. You might want to add a better conclusion.

Brigitte listened to Justin's suggestions. She thought he had some good ideas. She thanked Justin and decided to use his ideas when she revised her draft.

Prewriting

Drafting

Content Editing

Revising

Copyediting

Proofreading

Publishing

Your Turn

Read your draft carefully and answer the questions on the Content Editor's Checklist. Take notes of the changes you would like to make.

Trade drafts with a partner. Read your partner's draft and answer the questions on the checklist. You might want to read the draft more than once. Think of any ideas that might improve your partner's draft. Then share your ideas with your partner by giving some ideas of what your partner might change.

Listen to your partner's ideas for your draft. Make any changes that you think will improve your draft.

Writer's Tip When you share your ideas with your partner, start by telling what you like about the draft.

Snow Globeville

Revising

Here are the changes that Brigitte made after meeting with Justin.

How to Make a Snow Globe

A snow globe is a pretty decaration, did you know that you can make one
yourself? Here's how to do it.

You will need a jar and lid, *clear glass* glue, corn syrup, glitter, silicone sealer, paint, and
a plastic toy that fits inside the jar. Choose a plastic toy that would look nice inside
a snow globe *, such as a person, an animal, or a tree. You can find silicone sealer at a hardware store.*

To make the globe, glue the plastic toy to the jar's lid. Fill the jar most of the
way up with corn syrup. Pour in ~~some~~ *one teaspoon of* glitter.

~~You could use eggshells instead of glitter, but that's messier and doesn't look as
nice. You would have to boil the eggs. Then you would have to peel the eggshells
and break them up to look like snow. I would just use glitter.~~

Spread some silicone sealer over the top of the jar. Screw the lid on tightly. *You should let the glue dry first.* If
you want, you can paint the top or bottom of your globe to make it more colorful.

Turn over the jar so the lid is the base and the toy is right side up. To test the
globe, shake it. *The glitter should float inside the globe and fall down slowly like snow. Find a
special place where you can put your homemade snow globe.*

Look at some of the ways Brigitte revised her how-to article. She used Justin's ideas as well as her own to improve her how-to article.

- What examples did Brigitte add to help explain what would look nice in a snow globe?
- Where did she add the information about where to buy silicone sealer?
- How did Brigitte decide to handle the unimportant detail about eggshells?
- What step did Brigitte realize that she should add?
- What did she decide to add to the conclusion?

Finally, Brigitte made a few other changes that she thought were important. She decided to be more specific by telling the audience to use one teaspoon of glitter. She also decided to describe the jar as a "clear glass jar."

Your Turn

Look at your partner's suggestions and your own ideas for improving your draft. Choose the ones you think will make it better. Make the changes to your draft. When you finish, go over the Content Editor's Checklist again.

Writer's Tip Be sure you can answer yes to each question on the Content Editor's Checklist.

Prewriting

Drafting

Content Editing

Revising

Copyediting

Proofreading

Publishing

Editor's Workshop

How-to Articles

Copyediting and Proofreading

Copyediting

Brigitte thought her revisions had made her draft better. However, she knew there was more to do. She still had to copyedit her draft to make sure every sentence was written clearly and correctly. She used this Copyeditor's Checklist to help her.

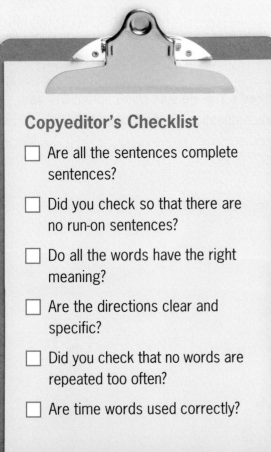

Copyeditor's Checklist

☐ Are all the sentences complete sentences?

☐ Did you check so that there are no run-on sentences?

☐ Do all the words have the right meaning?

☐ Are the directions clear and specific?

☐ Did you check that no words are repeated too often?

☐ Are time words used correctly?

Brigitte found more changes to make. Her first sentence was a run-on sentence. She made it into two sentences.

In the second paragraph, she thought she didn't need to use the word *plastic* twice. She took it out of the second sentence.

Next, she thought that some of her directions were not specific enough. Saying <u>👀 Word Choice</u> that the silicone sealer went on the "top of the jar" seemed confusing, so she called it the "rim." Just to be sure, she said that the rim was where the lid goes.

Finally, Brigitte noticed that she had not <u>👀 Sentence Fluency</u> used any time words. She added the words *then* and *next* to make the sentences fit together better.

Your Turn

Read your how-to article again. Copyedit it, using the Copyeditor's Checklist. Look for any incomplete sentences or run-on sentences.

Make sure that you have used words that mean exactly what you want. See if there are any places where you can add time words to make the sentences fit together better.

Proofreading

Brigitte was glad she found so many ways to improve her article. She knew that a  proofreader might find any mistakes she had missed. Brigitte asked a classmate, Tomás, to check her draft for spelling, grammar, and punctuation. He used this Proofreader's Checklist.

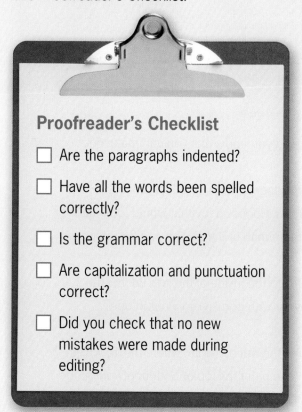

Proofreader's Checklist

☐ Are the paragraphs indented?

☐ Have all the words been spelled correctly?

☐ Is the grammar correct?

☐ Are capitalization and punctuation correct?

☐ Did you check that no new mistakes were made during editing?

Tomás enjoyed reading Brigitte's article about snow globes. He thought he might make one himself. He also noticed a few mistakes that Brigitte had made in her draft.

First, Tomás noticed that the word *decaration* looked strange. He checked a dictionary and found that it was spelled *decoration*.

Tomás thought that Brigitte should say to which side of the lid the toy should be glued. Brigitte wished she had noticed that mistake herself during copyediting. However, she was glad Tomás noticed it now.

Finally, Tomás saw a mistake in one of Brigitte's changes. The sentence about waiting for the glue to dry was not in time order. He thought she should add it earlier in the how-to article.

Your Turn

Read your draft, using the Proofreader's Checklist. Look for any mistakes you may have made. Then give your draft to someone else to check. Listen to the changes your proofreader suggests. Make the changes that improve your draft.

Prewriting

Drafting

Content Editing

Revising

Copyediting

Proofreading

Publishing

Publishing

Brigitte's how-to article was almost completed. She looked it over one more time. Then she typed it on her computer.

She typed the title at the top and put her name below it. Then she printed out her how-to article.

How to Make a Snow Globe

By Brigitte Walsh

A snow globe is a pretty decoration. Did you know that you can make one yourself? Here's how to do it.

You will need a clear glass jar and lid, glue, corn syrup, glitter, silicone sealer, paint, and a plastic toy that fits inside the jar. Choose a toy that would look nice inside a snow globe, such as a person, an animal, or a tree. You can find silicone sealer at a hardware store.

To make the globe, glue the plastic toy to the inside of the jar's lid. Let the glue dry. Then fill the jar most of the way up with corn syrup. Pour in one teaspoon of glitter.

Next, spread some silicone sealer over the rim of the jar, where the lid will go. Screw the lid on tightly. If you want, you can paint the top or bottom of your globe to make it more colorful.

Turn over the jar so the lid is the base and the toy is right-side up. To test the globe, shake it. The glitter should float inside the globe and fall down slowly like snow. Find a special place where you can put your homemade snow globe.

There are many ways you can publish your article. As a class decide how you will Presentation publish the articles. You might choose different ways, depending on your topic.

 Film it. Use your how-to article as a script and videotape yourself. You might ask some friends to help you.

 Do a PowerPoint presentation of your how-to article. Add clip art for items, such as your materials and the finished product.

 Create a class how-to manual. Put everyone's articles together. Arrange them by subject in alphabetical order. Number the pages and create a table of contents that lists the featured subjects. Then make a cover. Choose a title such as *The Fourth-Grade How-to Manual*. Decorate the cover and place the manual in a binder or a report cover. Display the manual in the school library. Then everyone in the school will be able to read your how-to article.

 Post it to an online how-to manual. You might also take digital photos of each step and include the images with your article.

Prewriting
Drafting
Content Editing
Revising
Copyediting
Proofreading
Publishing

Your Turn

Look over your draft one more time. Make sure all the changes have been made correctly.

Add a title and your name at the top if you haven't already done this. Print out your article on a computer or write it neatly on a sheet of paper. Then choose a way to publish your article.

The Fourth-Grade How-to Manual

Persuasive Writing

LiNK **Why Exercise Is Wise**

KidsHealth.org

You've probably heard countless times how exercise is "good for you." But did you know that it can actually help you feel good, too? Getting the right amount of exercise can rev up your energy levels and even help improve your mood.

Rewards and Benefits

Experts recommend that teens get 60 minutes or more of moderate to vigorous physical activity each day. Here are some of the reasons:

Exercise benefits every part of the body, including the mind. . . .

Considering the benefits to the heart, muscles, joints, and mind, it's easy to see why exercise is wise. And the great thing about exercise is that it's never too late to start. Even small things can count as exercise when you're starting out—like taking a short bike ride, walking the dog, or raking leaves. . . .

> This persuasive article states the author's point of view in the introduction, then gives reasons to support it, and concludes by restating the point of view.

Recycling Rocks!

Alonzo Rodriguez

Did you throw something away at lunch today? A wrapper? A can? A bottle? You may think that is no big deal. But when 500 students at our school are doing it every day, it adds up to a lot of trash! I believe it is time for Robert Collins School to start a recycling program.

Our town's landfill is filling up quickly. Using our valuable land to bury trash hurts our environment. People and animals are forced to look elsewhere to build their homes. If we take the time to recycle, garbage does not go into the landfill. Instead the garbage is made into something useful.

Recycling saves energy. Making new products from recycled material uses less energy. For example, recycling six aluminum cans could save enough energy to drive a car five miles. I wonder how many cans the people at our school throw away each day.

If we don't recycle, we will use up our natural resources. For example, recycled paper is used to make new paper products. When this happens, beautiful trees are saved from being cut down for the same purpose.

Our school should make a difference and help the environment. Setting out large bins to collect paper, plastic, and aluminum cans during lunch is just the start. Let's show our town that the kids at Collins School care!

What Makes Good Persuasive Writing?

Persuasive writing tries to convince readers to think or act in a certain way. Sometimes it is used to get people to buy a particular product or to urge people to vote for a political candidate.

Choosing a Topic

When writing a persuasive article, it is important to choose a topic that has two sides. For example, your topic might be your school's music program. The way you feel about the topic is your point of view. You feel strongly that your school should continue to fund the music program. You play the piano and hope to be part of a famous orchestra someday.

Recycling wastes time.

Introduction

State your topic and point of view clearly in the introduction. Write what you want your readers to believe or how you want them to act. In "Recycling Rocks!" on page 363, Alonzo wants the students in his school to start a recycling program.

Body

In the body give reasons to support your point of view. Reasons help the audience understand why you feel a certain way. They convince your readers that your point of view is correct. Some reasons are facts and some are opinions. Alonzo says that recycling helps the environment and saves money.

Conclusion

Sum up your persuasive article with your strongest reasons. Don't add any new reasons in the conclusion, but restate your point of view in a clear and positive way. Your conclusion might include things your readers can do if they agree with you.

Recycling reduces waste.

ACTIVITY A Read each topic and decide if you are for or against it. Write your point of view about the topic.

1. wearing school uniforms
2. eliminating homework
3. exploring space
4. limiting cell phone usage
5. being a vegetarian
6. recycling
7. protecting our natural forests

ACTIVITY B The following are possible points of view. Decide if each point of view is appropriate or inappropriate for a persuasive article.

1. Boys and girls should be allowed to play together on the same sports team.
2. My grandmother really knows how to make great chicken soup.
3. The town should fix the potholes on Oakley Avenue.
4. Life on Mars would be fun.
5. The local library ought to have more computers.
6. My cat, Belford, is the best cat in the world.
7. People should walk instead of drive their cars at least one day a week.

WRITER'S CORNER

Write three topics that you have strong feelings about. After each topic explain why it is important to you.

LiNK

Making Money: Why Should You Work?

This is where you might be saying, "But I'm just a kid! I shouldn't have to work!" That's right; you probably don't have to, but here are some reasons why you may want to:

Earning is learning. By working to earn your own money, you'll be learning skills you'll need to succeed in the world....

pbskids.org

Audience

It is necessary to know your audience when writing a persuasive article. The reasons and language you use will change depending on who you are writing for. Alonzo's persuasive article is aimed at teachers and students at his school. The reasons he gives for recycling are important to them. Who do you think is the audience for the excerpt on this page?

ACTIVITY C Each of the following pairs of sentences is from an advertisement. The audience is either adults or students. Decide for what audience you think each reason is aimed.

1. **a.** The Iso-wheel bicycle is comfortable and easy to pedal.

   b. The awesome Iso-wheel bicycle will blow your friends away.

2. **a.** Watch Channel 6 News for the latest high school basketball scores.

   b. Channel 6 News gives the rush-hour travel times every 12 minutes.

3. **a.** Chill out in South Carolina on the hottest beaches along the Atlantic coast.

   b. Visit historic South Carolina and experience a taste of the Old South.

4. **a.** HiForce energy bars provide essential vitamins and minerals.

   b. HiForce energy bars give you the power to play like a champion.

5. a. The Igloo jacket has cool colors and is maxed out with pockets for all your gear.

b. The Igloo jacket comes in many colors and has more pockets than any other jacket available.

6. a. Winston Park is a world-famous amusement center with activities for all members of the family.

b. Winston Park has thrilling rides, awesome food, and crazy games to play with your friends.

ACTIVITY D Read the following persuasive article. Then answer the questions.

On Saturday a group of students and teachers is going to meet in the vacant lot across the street from our schoolyard. Our plan is to pick up the trash that has made the lot an eyesore in the neighborhood. We will also put a trash can at the entrance to the lot. Mr. Soca and other local residents have complained about the mess. Students from our school have added to the litter there. They often throw on the ground the wrappers from the snacks they eat before and after school. We helped make the mess, and we should clean it up. The project won't take long if a lot of energetic students show up. Please come and help beautify the neighborhood on Saturday at 10:00 a.m.

1. Who is the intended audience for this persuasive article?

2. What is the topic?

3. What is the writer's point of view?

4. What does the writer want the audience to do?

5. What reasons does the writer give to persuade the audience?

6. What facts does the writer give to support the topic?

WRITER'S CORNER

Choose one of the three topics that you wrote about in the Writer's Corner on page 365. Use the Internet or reference books to look for reasons to support your point of view. Write a short explanation telling why the topic might be important to someone else.

Tech Tip With an adult, use an Internet search engine.

Fact and Opinion

Both facts and opinions are used as reasons in persuasive writing. A fact is a statement that can be proved. You can check facts on the Internet or at the library. Here is an example of a fact.

Puerto Rico is a territory of the United States.

An opinion is a statement of a person's judgment, belief, or feeling about a topic. Opinions cannot be proved true or false. Words such as *should, could, believe,* and *feel* often signal opinions. Can you identify an opinion in the excerpt on page 369? The opinions in a persuasive article should be supported by facts. Here is an example of an opinion.

Puerto Rico should be made a state.

The point of view in a persuasive article states the writer's opinion about the topic. A writer should use facts to support that opinion. If a writer uses only opinions to persuade, the argument will be weak and may not convince readers.

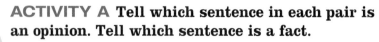

ACTIVITY A Tell which sentence in each pair is an opinion. Tell which sentence is a fact.

1. **a.** I believe that parrots are intelligent birds.

   b. There is a parrot that can say 950 different words.

2. **a.** Maple trees lose their leaves every fall.

   b. Every neighborhood should have maple trees.

3. **a.** I think that Vincent Van Gogh was a great artist.

   b. Vincent Van Gogh sold only one painting in his life.

4. **a.** I feel that Fremd's basketball team is the most exciting team in the conference.

   b. The Fremd Panthers have a record of 14 wins and 3 losses.

ACTIVITY B Identify each statement as a fact or an opinion. Explain your answer.

1. Construction workers put up new buildings.
2. Construction is exciting work.
3. Machines called bulldozers dig and dump dirt.
4. All boys want to drive bulldozers.
5. Both men and women can be construction workers.
6. Construction sites are dangerous.
7. Construction workers wear hard hats on the job.
8. Carpenters and plumbers work in construction.
9. Construction workers are paid by the hour.
10. Construction workers like to work overtime.

ACTIVITY C Read each point of view. Write an opinion that supports each one.

1. Young children should eat fruit instead of candy.
2. Theaters should not show ads before the movie.
3. Smoking at any time should be against the law.
4. Everyone should recycle his or her trash.
5. Girls and boys should be allowed to play on all school teams.
6. Our town needs a stoplight at Summit Street and Grand Avenue.
7. Every child should be allowed to watch only one hour of TV a day.
8. Children should receive an allowance each week that is based on the chores they do.

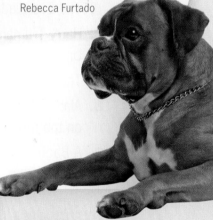

WRITER'S CORNER

Think of an interesting topic and write two or more facts about it. Then write your opinion about the topic. Discuss with a partner what you wrote. How could you prove each fact? What clues show that the other statements are opinions?

Checking Facts

When you write to persuade, make sure that all your facts are correct. If readers know that one statement is not true, they could decide that your work is not believable. You can check your facts by looking them up in books or on the Internet. You could also talk to an expert.

ACTIVITY D Check each statement in a reference book or on the Internet. Tell which are facts and which are false.

1. The song "Satin Doll" was written by Duke Ellington.
2. The 2008 Olympic Games were held in Berlin, Germany.
3. Parts of Lake Superior are over 1,000 feet deep.
4. Michigan was the 15th state to join the United States.
5. The Everglades are in Arizona.
6. Harry Truman served as both vice president and president of the United States.
7. The Nile is a river in South America.
8. Alan B. Shepard Jr. was the first American astronaut to walk on the moon.
9. A Bactrian camel has two humps.
10. Cyan is a shade of red.

Duke Ellington performing with other jazz musicians in 1942

ACTIVITY E Read each point of view below. Tell whether the sentence that supports it is a fact or an opinion. Discuss how you could check each fact.

1. Students should not have to wear school uniforms. Uniforms are too expensive.

2. Schools should not serve soft drinks in cafeterias. Milk has more vitamins than soft drinks do.

3. Classes should start later in the morning. Students will have more time to prepare for school.

4. Schools should be in session throughout the year. I believe a three-month summer vacation is too long.

5. Classes should have no more than 20 students. Teachers will have more time for each student.

ACTIVITY F Reread "Recycling Rocks!" on page 363. Find two opinions and two facts. Write them. Discuss what words signaled opinions. Discuss how you could check each fact.

ACTIVITY G Read the following paragraph from a persuasive article. Answer the questions.

I should receive more allowance. I pay for my own lunch. The cost of lunch has gone up, but my allowance has stayed the same. Now I have less money to spend on things I want. Grown-ups get raises when prices of things go up. I should get a raise too. It's only fair.

1. What is the writer trying to persuade the reader to do?

2. Which sentences are facts?

3. Which sentences are opinions?

4. Does the writer do a good job of supporting her opinions? Explain your answer.

WRITER'S CORNER

Choose one pair of sentences from Activity E. Add two or three other facts and opinions to support the topic.

Post your persuasive writing on a class blog.

Synonyms

Synonyms are words that have the same or almost the same meaning. Here are some pairs of synonyms that you might use when you write.

sleepy/tired	price/cost	dull/boring	angry/upset
scared/frightened	icy/cold	silly/foolish	right/correct
victory/win	big/enormous	good/bad	easy/hard

Writers sometimes use synonyms to replace words that are used too often. Synonyms can make your writing more interesting or more precise.

ACTIVITY A Some synonyms are more precise than others in certain sentences. Choose the synonym that fits better in each sentence below.

1. The toy (starts begins) when you push the button.
2. Dogs can be trained to (lead guide) people who are blind.
3. The suitcase is (empty vacant).
4. The pioneers had to cross many (thick wide) rivers.
5. My watch seems to be running (quickly fast).
6. The bus was (late tardy) this morning.
7. We crossed the Illinois (edge border) and entered Iowa.
8. The bread was baked (new fresh) this morning.

ACTIVITY B Read the lists of words. Match each word in Column A to its synonym in Column B.

Column A	Column B
1. pretty	a. fast
2. angry	b. beautiful
3. laugh	c. stroll
4. walk	d. mad
5. quick	e. giggle

ACTIVITY C Tell whether the underlined words in each sentence are synonyms.

1. A nice man <u>returned</u> the book I <u>lost</u>.

2. The team wanted to <u>win</u>, but they <u>tied</u>.

3. Gabriela's <u>grin</u> looked like a clown's <u>smile</u>.

4. The <u>dirt</u> in our yard is good <u>soil</u> for plants.

5. A <u>narrow</u> bridge crossed over the <u>wide</u> river.

6. The large body of <u>water</u> was a <u>lake</u>.

7. This <u>delicious</u> soup is almost as good as the <u>tasty</u> stew.

8. Jake is <u>pleased</u> with the idea and <u>happy</u> to help.

9. His pants were <u>dirty</u>, and his shoes were <u>filthy</u>.

10. This is an <u>actual</u> Roman coin, a <u>real</u> treasure.

11. The <u>rain</u> was a refreshing <u>shower</u> on such a hot day.

12. If you <u>scrub</u> the kitchen floor, I'll <u>vacuum</u> the hall carpet.

13. Meg felt <u>calm</u> as she watched the <u>tranquil</u> waves coming to shore.

14. The worker has to <u>attach</u> the wires to each other before he can <u>remove</u> them.

15. My brother <u>hates</u> to eat asparagus, and my sister <u>despises</u> corn.

Mississippi River

WRITER'S CORNER

Describe a person or place you saw recently. Write five sentences. Then choose five words from your description and replace them with synonyms. How did your synonyms change your description?

Grammar in Action Use vivid adjectives to add to your description. See Section 2.

Synonyms can add variety to your writing. A paragraph that has variety does not use the same words over and over again. Read the following paragraph. Does it have variety?

> A big dog chased me up a big hill. I was lucky because there was a big tree at the top. I climbed up and sat on a big branch. The dog jumped up and ripped a big piece out of my pant leg. After awhile the dog left and I climbed out of the tree.

It is easy to understand what is happening in the paragraph. However, most people would not enjoy reading it. Even though the word *big* is used correctly, it is used too often. The paragraph doesn't have variety. Read the following paragraph with synonyms replacing the word *big*.

> A huge dog chased me up a high hill. I was lucky because there was a tall tree at the top. I climbed up and sat on a thick branch. The dog jumped up and ripped a large piece out of my pant leg. After awhile the dog left and I climbed out of the tree.

The second paragraph tells the same story as the first. The second paragraph is more interesting, though, because it has more variety.

ACTIVITY D Write the sentences below. Replace each word in italics with a synonym from the list. If you need help, use a dictionary to check word meanings.

> quarrel   liberty   tardy   bushes   twine

1. I tied the sticks together with *string*.
2. Abraham Lincoln gave enslaved people their *freedom*.
3. Let's not *argue* today.
4. Kylie was *late* for class.
5. We lost the ball in the *shrubs*.

Arf!

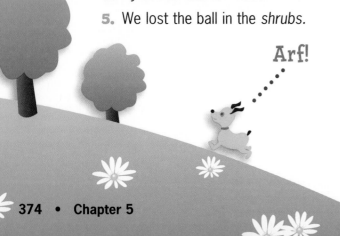

ACTIVITY E Complete the chart by adding antonyms and synonyms. The first one is done for you.

Tiny

WORD	ANTONYM	SYNONYM
tiny	**huge**	**small**
1. fix		
2. sadness		
3. good		
4. honest		
5. shack		
6. come		
7. above		
8. brave		
9. smile		
10. night		

Huge

ACTIVITY F Rewrite the paragraph. Replace five words with synonyms. Underline the synonyms you use.

Nick is afraid that his sister, Sonya, is going to be late for Marta's surprise party. He is afraid that if Sonya is late, Marta might come to the party at the same time. Then the surprise would be ruined. Nick is also afraid that the guests will be noisy. If the guests are too noisy, Marta will hear them. That could also ruin the surprise. We need to help Nick so he won't be afraid.

WRITER'S CORNER

Think of a word that has several synonyms, such as *big*, *good*, or *happy*. Write five synonyms for the word. Use each word in a sentence.

Tech Tip With an adult, use an online thesaurus.

Dictionary

Imagine that you read in a book that an army has set up a bivouac outside of town. If you have never seen the word *bivouac* before, you could look it up in a dictionary and learn that a bivouac is a military camp.

You know that you can use a dictionary to find the meanings of words that you do not know. Dictionaries also have other uses.

When you learn a new word, try to use it in your writing. Also use it in your everyday speech whenever you can. However, you want to be sure that when you say the word, you pronounce it correctly. A dictionary shows the correct way to pronounce words. Look at this sample entry for the word *bivouac*.

biv•ou•ac (biv′ oo ak′) *n.* a temporary camp set up for soldiers in the field.

Syllables

The dots in the entry word show how the word is divided into syllables. A syllable is a word part that can be pronounced separately. How many syllables are in the word *bivouac*?

Below: Civil War bivouac for Union soldiers

Dictionary Respelling

In parentheses right after the entry word is the dictionary respelling. The respelling shows how to pronounce the word. Sometimes you can figure out how a word is pronounced just by looking at the respelling. Other times you may have to check the pronunciation key.

Pronunciation Key

The dictionary respelling for *bivouac* shows that the first syllable is *biv.* You know that *b* and *v* are always pronounced the same, but *i* can be pronounced in different ways. How can you decide the correct way to say *biv*? You can use the pronunciation key. Look at the pronunciation key on the right.

a	cat	u	up
ā	ape	ʉ	fur
ä	cot, car	ch	chin
e	ten	sh	she
ē	me	th	thin
i	fit	*th*	then
ī	ice	zh	measure
ō	go	ŋ	ring
ô	fall, for	ə—a *in* ago
oo	look	e *in* agent
ōō	tool	i *in* pencil
oi	oil	o *in* atom
ou	out	u *in* circus

Key reprinted by permission from *Webster's New World™ Student's Dictionary.* Copyright © 1996 by Hungry Minds, Inc. All rights reserved.

Look for the letter *i* in the key. There are two of them. One is an ordinary *i,* and the other is an *i* with a bar over it (ī). The ordinary *i* is next to the word *fit.* That means it is pronounced the same way as the *i* in *fit.* Because the *i* in *biv* is an ordinary *i,* you know that it stands for the sound of *i* in *fit.* Look at the second and third syllables in *bivouac.* How would you pronounce them?

ACTIVITY A Tell which two words in each row rhyme. Use dictionary respellings to help you pronounce each word.

1. grown   gown   faun   dawn
2. squall   brawl   fowl   knoll
3. slough   bough   beau   gruff
4. brown   known   hewn   sewn
5. ballet   mallet   wallet   chalet

WRITER'S CORNER

Use a dictionary to find five words that you do not know how to pronounce. Write the words and their respellings.

Tech Tip With an adult, use an online dictionary.

Accent Marks

A dictionary respelling uses special marks to show how to say a word. There are also marks to show which syllables are pronounced with more stress. Look at the dictionary respelling for *bivouac.*

(biv′ $\overline{oo}$ ak′)

The marks after *biv* and *ak* are called accent marks. They show that these syllables are stressed more than the second syllable. Because the accent mark after *biv* is darker than the one after *ak,* the stress is heavier on the first syllable. Often respellings have only one accent mark. That syllable is given more stress than the others. The other syllables are given equal stress.

ACTIVITY B Say these words softly to yourself. Write the words. Write how many syllables each word has. Then draw an accent mark after the syllable that you think is stressed the most. Check a dictionary to see if you were correct.

1. generation
2. responsible
3. university
4. electricity
5. refrigerator

6. opportunity
7. manufacture
8. veterinarian
9. magnificent
10. illustration

ACTIVITY C Write the dictionary respellings of these words. Use accent marks.

1. plateau
2. crochet
3. guffaw

4. loquacious
5. sallow

ACTIVITY D Find each underlined word in a dictionary and write its dictionary respelling. Pronounce the word softly to yourself.

1. We watched the <u>dirigible</u> fly over our heads.
2. The curtain was moved by a warm May <u>zephyr</u>.
3. Aunt Rhoda wears <u>pince-nez</u> glasses when she reads.
4. A lightning storm is a terrifying <u>phenomenon</u> to experience.
5. The woman's <u>chauffeur</u> picks her up every day at four.
6. Did you listen to the <u>rhythm</u> of the drums?
7. I like this team's <u>enthusiasm</u>.
8. An ear infection can affect a person's <u>equilibrium</u>.
9. The <u>rambunctious</u> puppy always wants to play.
10. A <u>geranium</u> was blooming in the planter.

ACTIVITY E Use a dictionary to find the word in each pair that is pronounced the way that the respelling shows. Then write a sentence using that word.

1. mə ral′   morale/moral
2. fi nal′ ē   finally/finale
3. dē sent′   decent/descent
4. pʉr sə nel′   personal/personnel
5. i ras′ ə bəl   erasable/irascible
6. def′ ər əns   difference/deference
7. di zərt′   dessert/desert
8. fär′ thər   farther/further

WRITER'S CORNER

Write five sentences using words from this lesson that you did not know before. Write sentences that show the meanings of the words.

Compound Subjects and Predicates

You can make your writing more interesting if you vary the lengths of your sentences. Readers can become bored reading a lot of short, choppy sentences. Often, short sentences can be combined to make longer, more interesting sentences.

Compound Subjects

One way to make longer sentences is by using compound subjects. You can make compound subjects when you have two or more subjects doing the same thing.

> **Parents support Irma Batz for senator. Teachers are also for Irma Batz.**
>
> **Parents and teachers support Irma Batz for senator.**

Notice that the ideas in the two sentences are not worded exactly the same way. As long as the action is the same in the sentences, the subjects can be combined.

Subjects can be combined if the sentences have being verbs instead of action verbs.

> **My uncle is a veteran. My cousin is also a veteran.**
>
> **My uncle and my cousin are veterans.**

The conjunction *or* can also be used to make a compound subject.

> **Mom or Dad will pick you up at the station.**

Questions can have compound subjects too.

> **Will Hank and Fiona try out for the band?**

ACTIVITY A Tell which sentences contain compound subjects. Identify the compound subjects.

1. Tina and her dog are in the backyard.
2. Janine or Frieda will be our next class president.
3. The twins misbehaved all day long.
4. You and I can beat these guys.
5. Mark, Eric, and Laura missed the bus.
6. John and his brother were at the party.
7. Jerzy took Melissa to the doctor.
8. Two runners tied for second place.
9. Do the dog and cat have fresh water?
10. Five people boarded the train.

ACTIVITY B Decide if each pair of sentences can be combined into one sentence with a compound subject. If a pair can be combined, write the new sentence.

1. Harrison plays tennis. Charlotte plays the flute.
2. Do you like to watch old movies? Does your sister like them too?
3. I was sick on Monday. My sister was also ill.
4. Tina likes her steak rare. She likes her hamburgers well done.
5. Mr. Li is learning English. Mrs. Gomez is learning it too.
6. My mom went to the grocery store. My brother went with her.
7. Connor played soccer on Saturday. Luke played soccer on Saturday too.
8. I took my dog for a walk after school. Then I finished my homework.
9. Katarina asked for more chores. She wanted to earn more money to buy an MP3 player.

WRITER'S CORNER

Write four sentences describing things in nature. Use sentences with compound subjects. Then divide each sentence into two sentences. Do the longer sentences sound better than the short ones?

Compound Predicates

Another way to combine sentences is when the same subject is doing two or more things at the same time. You can write the two actions as a compound predicate.

The old cat sat in the sun. It purred contentedly.

The old cat sat in the sun and purred contentedly.

Just as with compound subjects, the conjunction *or* can be used to make compound predicates.

Terri may sing for us. She may play her flute instead.

Terri may sing or play her flute for us.

Compound predicates can be made with the conjunction *but*.

I pushed hard but couldn't budge the car.

Just as with compound subjects, compound predicates can be used in questions.

Will you help us and vote for clean air?

ACTIVITY C Identify the compound predicate in each sentence. Not every sentence contains a compound predicate.

1. Ernest forgot to wear a hat and caught a cold.
2. The car ran out of gas and sputtered to a stop.
3. Are you cooking tonight or should I?
4. I just started piano lessons, but my brother has played for years.
5. Mom will leave early and get there before noon.
6. Cesar divided the money between Eric and Molly.
7. Noah watched two birds circling overhead.
8. Emil lost his bus pass and had to walk home.
9. Who drove the car but didn't fill the gas tank?
10. Allison found the gloves that she lost yesterday.

Purrrrrr

ACTIVITY D Decide if the two sentences in each pair can be combined into one sentence with a compound predicate. If they can be combined, write the new sentence.

1. Jack fell down. He broke his crown.
2. Marya fell off her horse. She takes riding lessons on Saturdays.
3. Donna took off her shoes. She walked across the waxed floor.
4. The young tree bent. It did not break.
5. She served my pizza piping hot. I'll eat it cold too.
6. George opened the refrigerator. He took out a jar of pickles.
7. I could buy new shoes. I could save for a video game.
8. Mandy takes great photographs. She got a new camera.
9. The gardener trimmed the bushes. He also mowed the lawn.
10. At recess we can play basketball. We can run around the track.

ACTIVITY E Tell whether the following sentences have a compound subject or a compound predicate.

1. Keesha and Leona got good grades on the test.
2. Beatrice practiced every day and became a good dancer.
3. The flowers wilted and died.
4. I grabbed by backpack but forgot my lunch.
5. Squirrels and hamsters are rodents.
6. The mothers and daughters prepared a special lunch.
7. The baby laughed and played with the ball.
8. Jake or his brother will try out for the basketball team.

WRITER'S CORNER

Write three pairs of sentences, each pair using the same subject but a different predicate. Combine each pair to make one sentence.

Grammar in Action. See Section 5.1 for help in using action verbs in your predicates.

Oral Persuasion

Oral persuasion is a common form of communication. You hear it every day when you listen to TV and radio commercials. You probably use it yourself to try to convince people to agree with you. This morning you might have tried to persuade someone to drive you to school. Maybe you asked for some extra spending money for after school.

Choosing a Topic

Give an oral presentation to persuade your audience to buy a product or service. Your audience will be your classmates. Choose a product your audience might be interested in purchasing. You might choose a bike-washing service or a video game.

Introduction

Clearly state your point of view in your introduction. Explain why your audience will want to buy the product or service. You might begin your introduction with a catchy sentence. For example, a presentation about a bike-washing service might begin "If your bike could talk, would it say 'Wash me!'?"

Body

In the body give reasons to support your point of view. Include facts and opinions. A fact about a bike-washing service might be "It costs three dollars." An opinion might be "People will be dazzled by your clean bike."

Conclusion

For a conclusion restate your point of view clearly and positively. Sum up the reasons for using your product or service. Tell the audience how their lives will be improved. End with a sentence that will leave your audience thinking about your product or service.

Planning Your Presentation

When you have decided what you want to talk about, begin planning your presentation. You can plan by writing on separate note cards keywords and phrases for your introduction, body, and conclusion. Think of visual aids you might use in your presentation, such as the product or a picture of it. For example, if your topic is a new baseball mitt, you might bring to class a baseball mitt and point out its features. You might also draw several pictures detailing your product or service. Plan a time during your presentation to show your visual aids.

ACTIVITY A **Imagine you are writing a commercial for a product or service. Choose a topic and write an opening statement or question. Write one fact and one opinion about why the audience might buy the product or service. Then write a closing sentence for the commercial that will convince your audience to buy your product.**

Tech Tip Use a video camera to record your commercial.

Practice

Before giving a speech, it is important to practice. The more you practice, the less nervous you will feel when giving your presentation. Practice in front of a mirror, or in front of a friend or family member. Look at your audience as you talk, but refer to your note cards when you need to jog your memory. Use a tone of voice that shows excitement about what you are selling. Practice showing visual aids. Ask for suggestions to improve your speech.

Listening to Persuasive Speeches

You should listen to the speaker with an open mind. When you listen with an open mind, you wait until the speech is over to decide if you agree or disagree. Be ready to think about what the speaker's opinions are and what the facts are. It is up to you to decide what makes sense and what doesn't.

If you have questions about what a speaker has said, raise your hand after the speech. Ask your question politely. If the speaker used facts that you don't think are true, research them later to see if they are correct.

Whether or not you agree with the speaker's point of view, you should follow the same listening tips that you follow for any presentation.

- Sit still and look at the speaker.
- Pay attention to what the speaker is saying.
- Don't talk to people in the audience.
- Clap when the speaker has finished.

ACTIVITY B Work with a small group. Look through a magazine or think of TV commercials. For each advertisement or commercial, discuss whether it uses any of the following reasons to persuade its audience. Write any other persuasive reasons. Talk about which reasons were most effective and why.

1. This product is better than the competition.
2. You will have fun using this product.
3. This product is less expensive than the competition.
4. Your life will be improved by using this product.
5. You will be healthier if you use this product.
6. You will be like the person speaking if you use this product.
7. You will be popular if you use this product.

ACTIVITY C Think of a product or service that you want to persuade your classmates to buy. Write a catchy opening sentence or question for your introduction. Consider reasons that might persuade your audience. You might choose some of the reasons from Activity B to help you think of ideas. Write a memorable conclusion to sum up your presentation. Record on separate note cards keywords and phrases. Choose a visual aid to use in your presentation.

SPEAKER'S CORNER

Give to the class your presentation that you began in Activity C. Make eye contact with your audience and speak in a clear, lively voice. Be sure that any visual aids can be easily seen. Invite your classmates to ask questions and to give feedback at the end of your presentation. Ask questions and give feedback on your classmates' presentations.

Writer's Workshop

Prewriting and Drafting

Writing to persuade is an important type of writing. Today you will start writing a leaflet to persuade people to do what you want them to do.

Prewriting

Prewriting is the time you choose a topic and organize ideas. It is the time you decide who your audience will be. You usually have strong feelings about the topic, or you have a personal interest in it.

Choosing a Topic

Simeon wanted to make a citizenship leaflet as part of his leadership challenge for  student council. Simeon started by thinking of topic ideas and listing them on a sheet of paper. He considered persuading people to vote in school elections or to be nicer in the hallways, but those ideas didn't spark his interest. Then he thought of the yearly bazaar coming up at his school. Simeon decided to make a leaflet persuading parents to attend the bazaar. He knew that the money from the bazaar would help the school buy the video equipment it needed.

Your Turn

Are you trying to earn money for something special? You might want to persuade people to hire you to do chores. Maybe your cat had kittens that you want to give away. Perhaps there is something that you feel strongly about.

- Brainstorm ideas that you would like to persuade people to act on.
- Choose one idea that would be a good topic for your leaflet.
- Think of a short statement that tells what you want your audience to do. It should be something that you can support with facts as well as opinions.
- Write a statement of your point of view.

Organizing Ideas

Last year's bazaar was a big success. People liked the baked goods so much they bought them all. They also bought over 50 pieces of students' art that were on sale. The games 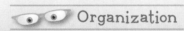 were busy all day. Simeon made an idea web to organize his thinking about reasons that people came to the bazaar.

In Simeon's center box was "Come to the Monroe School Bazaar." He added reasons that people should come. He also added more facts to support the reasons.

Simeon showed his idea web to Mrs. Roth. She said that it was a good beginning, but he had left out the most important reason. He forgot to include making money for Monroe School. Many educational programs were on DVDs, and the school's DVD player is broken. The school also needed a bigger TV to make sure that all the students could see the educational programs. Simeon added another oval to his idea web.

Your Turn

- Read the statement of your point of view that you wrote. Use it as the center idea of an idea web.
- Write in circles around the statement reasons why readers would want to do as you ask. The reasons could be facts or opinions.

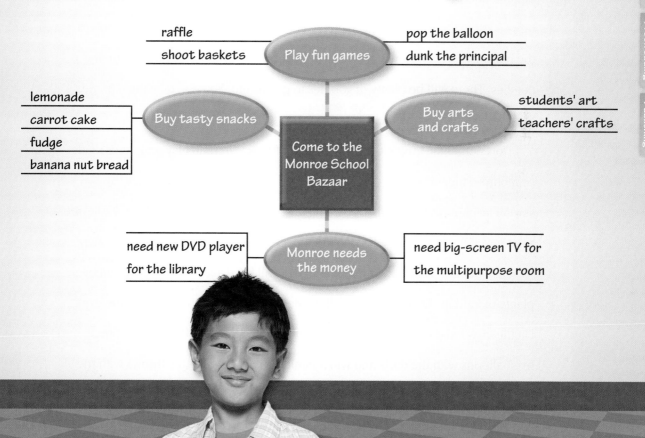

raffle
shoot baskets
Play fun games
pop the balloon
dunk the principal

lemonade
carrot cake
fudge
banana nut bread
Buy tasty snacks

Come to the Monroe School Bazaar

Buy arts and crafts
students' art
teachers' crafts

need new DVD player for the library
Monroe needs the money
need big-screen TV for the multipurpose room

Prewriting
Drafting
Content Editing
Revising
Copyediting
Proofreading
Publishing

Drafting

Simeon used his idea web to help him as he wrote the first draft of his leaflet. He knew that his final copy would be different from this one. He probably would change words and sentences to improve his draft.

Simeon asked Mrs. Roth to read over his writing. She had reminded him to add making money for the school as a reason for parents to come to the bazaar. She would probably have other good suggestions.

Come to the Monroe School Bazaar!

On May ninth, Monroe School is having its yearly bazaar. Come and spend a little of your money to help our school a lot. Buy delicious fudge, carrot cakes, banana nut bread, and other goodies baked by parents of Monroe Students. How do you know the goodies are delicious? Last year we ran out of them way before the bazaar was over. Now our volunteer bakers have promised to double their batches. There will be plenty of goodies to go around. You can take them home. You can eat them at the bazaar.

Don't forget the artwork and crafts! Beautiful pictures and clay sculptures made by Monroe students will be on sale. There will also be knitted goods made by several teachers. A beautiful quilt will be rafled off before the end of the day. Monroe teachers pitched in to make it. Even Principle Losetsky helped to piece it together.

Last, but not least we guarantee that you will have a lot of fun. There will be plenty of loud music to dance to in the cafeteria. There will be games in the gym. Hit the target and dunk Principle Losetsky in the water tank. Break three out of five balloons with the darts and win a bank. Make 3 out of 5 free throws with the basketballs and win a chance to push a cream pie into Mr. Goetz's face. You know you always wanted to do that to a gym teacher.

The best reason to come to the bazaar is that you will help Monroe School to get a new big-screen TV and a DVD player. The 24-inch TV that we have now is too small for students in the back row to see. Our DVD player just broke.

Your Turn

- Review your idea web before you start writing.
- Think about your audience and what you want them to do as you write your first draft.
- State your topic and point of view early in your leaflet.
- Restate your topic and point of view at the end, using different words.

The reasons that you use to support your point of view should appeal to your audience. Be sure to include facts that support your point of view.

Grammar in Action

Find a sentence in the second paragraph that has a compound subject. What is the compound subject?

Prewriting

Drafting

Content Editing

Revising

Copyediting

Proofreading

Publishing

Editor's Workshop

Content Editing

Simeon was happy with his draft. He had chosen an interesting topic and thought of good reasons to support his point of view. He knew, however, that his draft could be improved during content editing.

Simeon used this Content Editor's Checklist for persuasive writing as he read through his leaflet.

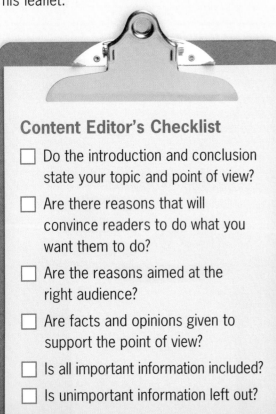

Content Editor's Checklist

- [ ] Do the introduction and conclusion state your topic and point of view?
- [ ] Are there reasons that will convince readers to do what you want them to do?
- [ ] Are the reasons aimed at the right audience?
- [ ] Are facts and opinions given to support the point of view?
- [ ] Is all important information included?
- [ ] Is unimportant information left out?

Simeon thought that he should remind his audience at the end to come to the bazaar.

After writing those sentences, Simeon felt good about his leaflet. However, he knew that there were probably other ways to improve it that he had missed. He asked his friend Chris to take a look.

Chris read over Simeon's work several times. She used the checklist to make sure that she didn't miss anything important. She wrote notes about some ways that Simeon could improve his leaflet.

When she finished, Chris pointed out many good things about the draft. She thought that the introduction clearly stated the topic and point of view. She thought Simeon's reasons were strong. Chris also did not find any information that was unrelated to the topic.

Chris thought that adding the two sentences to restate his point of view at the end was a good idea.

Chris also pointed out ways that Simeon might improve his leaflet.

- You should tell why the students' art we are selling at the bazaar is special.
- You need to remember your audience. Most parents will not be interested in dancing to loud music.
- When you say that people will want to push a pie into a gym teacher's face, you are giving your opinion. Maybe you should leave out that sentence.
- Some parents might not think having a DVD player at school is important. Can you give some reasons for buying a DVD player?

Simeon saw how Chris's suggestions would improve his leaflet and decided to follow most of them.

Your Turn

Reread your first draft carefully several times. Check it against the Content Editor's Checklist. Can you answer yes to all the questions?

Work with a partner. Use the Content Editor's Checklist as you read your partner's leaflet. Would the leaflet persuade you? Talk with your partner when you have both finished.

Writer's Tip When you discuss your partner's leaflet, first point out the strong parts. Then make suggestions that you think will improve the leaflet.

Prewriting

Drafting

Content Editing

Revising

Copyediting

Proofreading

Publishing

Writer's Workshop

Revising

Here is how Simeon revised his leaflet.

Come to the Monroe School Bazaar!

On May ninth, Monroe School is having its yearly bazaar. Come and spend a little of your money to help our school a lot. Buy delicious fudge, carrot cakes, banana nut bread, and other goodies baked by parents of Monroe Students. How do you know the goodies are delicious? Last year we ran out of them way before the bazaar was over. Now our volunteer bakers have promised to double their batches. There will be plenty of goodies to go around. You can take them home. You can eat them at the bazaar.

Don't forget the artwork and crafts! ~~Beautiful pictures and clay sculptures made~~ Several Monroe students have won prizes locally for their drawings and sculptures. They have donated some of their best work to be sold. ~~by Monroe students will be on sale.~~ There will also be knitted goods made by several teachers. A beautiful quilt will be rafled off before the end of the day. Monroe teachers pitched in to make it. Even Principle Losetsky helped to piece it together.

Last, but not least we guarantee that you will have a lot of fun. ~~There will be plenty of loud music to dance to in the cafeteria.~~ There will be games in the gym. Hit the target and dunk Principle Losetsky in the water tank. Break three out of five balloons with the darts and win a bank. Make 3 out of 5 free throws with the basketballs and win a chance to push a cream pie into Mr. Goetz's face. You know you always wanted to do that to a gym teacher.

The best reason to come to the bazaar is that you will help Monroe School to get a new big-screen TV and a DVD player. The 24-inch TV that we have now is too small for students in the back row to see. Our DVD player just broke.

, and we are not able to watch our educational programs. You should keep May 9 open on your calender for our bazaar. We hope to see you there.

Look at the changes that Simeon made to improve his leaflet.
- What did he add about the artwork that is for sale by Monroe students?
- What sentence in the third paragraph did he take out?
- Did Simeon take out or leave in the sentence about the cream pie?
- Where did he explain why Monroe School needs a DVD player?

Simeon was pleased with his leaflet after making the changes. Still he wanted his leaflet to be as persuasive as he could make it, so he kept looking for ways to improve it.

Your Turn

Revise your leaflet. Make improvements so that your writing is clearer and more  Voice persuasive. Use any of your partner's suggestions that you think will help convince your readers. When you have finished, use the Content Editor's Checklist to check your writing one more time.

Win the pie!

Editor's Workshop

Copyediting

Simeon thought his revisions had improved his draft. Next, he started to look more closely at his choice of words and his sentences. He used this Copyeditor's Checklist to help him.

Copyeditor's Checklist

- ☐ Are compound sentences used to vary sentence length?
- ☐ Are sentences with compound subjects or compound predicates used for variety?
- ☐ Is there variety in word choice?
- ☐ Are the words the best ones for persuading the audience?
- ☐ Are prefixes and suffixes used correctly?
- ☐ Are time words used correctly?

Simeon read his leaflet, using the checklist. He caught some things that he wanted to fix.

The last two sentences in the first paragraph could be combined. Simeon  combined them into one sentence with a compound predicate. How would you do this?

Simeon also decided to combine the last two sentences in the second paragraph. He would make these one sentence with a compound subject.

The word *goodies* was used three times in the first paragraph. Simeon replaced two of them with synonyms. He also found two problems with time words. Can you find them?

Writer's Tip When you use the Checklist, look for just one item each time as you read.

Your Turn

Read over your leaflet several times. Use the Copyeditor's Checklist to help you look for ways to vary your sentences.

Proofreading

 **Conventions** Simeon was glad he had found so many ways to improve his draft. He knew his next step would be to proofread his draft for mistakes. He used this Proofreader's Checklist to help him.

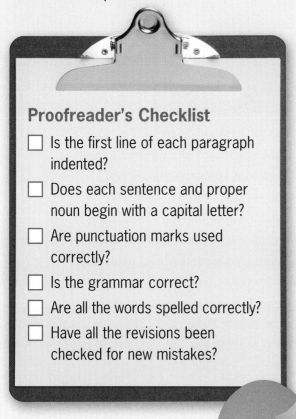

Proofreader's Checklist

☐ Is the first line of each paragraph indented?

☐ Does each sentence and proper noun begin with a capital letter?

☐ Are punctuation marks used correctly?

☐ Is the grammar correct?

☐ Are all the words spelled correctly?

☐ Have all the revisions been checked for new mistakes?

Using the checklist, Simeon found that the word *students* should not have been capitalized in the first paragraph. He also noticed that he had misspelled the word *raffled*.

After Simeon proofread his leaflet, he asked his friend Jules to look it over. Jules used the checklist too, and he found some mistakes that Simeon had missed. First, he noticed that Simeon sometimes spelled out numbers and other times he wrote the numerals. Simeon decided to use numerals every time.

Your Turn

- Proofread your leaflet carefully, using the Proofreader's Checklist. Check it once all the way through for each question on the checklist. This will help you to spot mistakes and to find last-minute improvements.

- After you have finished using the checklist to proofread your own writing, trade your paper with a partner.

- Proofread your partner's writing as closely as you did your own. Mark any mistakes that you find.

Prewriting

Drafting

Content Editing

Revising

Copyediting

Proofreading

Publishing

Writer's Workshop

Publishing

Simeon felt that he had done well and had given parents good reasons to come to the bazaar. He carefully typed his final copy. He felt ready to give it to Mrs. Roth. She would make enough copies for every Monroe School student. When the students' families read the leaflet, it would be published. This is how Simeon's finished leaflet looked.

Come to the Monroe School Bazaar!

On May 9, Monroe School is having its yearly bazaar. Come and spend a little of your money to help our school a lot. Buy delicious fudge, carrot cakes, banana nut bread, and other goodies baked by parents of Monroe students. How do you know the sweets are delicious? Last year we ran out of them way before the bazaar was over. This year our volunteer bakers have promised to double their batches. There will be plenty of treats to go around. You can take them home or eat them at the bazaar.

Don't forget the artwork and crafts! Several Monroe students have won prizes locally for their drawings and sculptures. They have donated some of their best work to be sold. There will also be knitted goods made by several teachers. A beautiful quilt will be raffled off before the end of the day. Principal Losetsky and many Monroe teachers pitched in to make it.

We guarantee that you will have a lot of fun. There will be games in the gym. Hit the target and dunk Principal Losetsky in the water tank. Break 3 out of 5 balloons with the darts and win a bank. Make 3 out of 5 free throws with the basketballs and win a chance to push a cream pie into Mr. Goetz's face. You know you always wanted to do that to a gym teacher.

The best reason to come to the bazaar is that you will help Monroe School to get a new big-screen TV and a DVD player. The 24-inch TV that we have now is too small for students in the back row to see. Our DVD player just broke, and we are not able to watch our educational programs. You should keep May 9 open on your calendar for our bazaar. We hope to see you there.

Whenever you publish your work, your goal is to share your thoughts and experiences with

 Presentation

other people. There are many ways you can publish your persuasive leaflet.

 Post the leaflets on a class bulletin board. Include photographs or drawings of your topic. Make your leaflet have eye-appeal to catch readers' attention.

 Submit your leaflet to the class or school newspaper as an editorial. Perhaps include a survey for students to voice their opinions on the topic.

 Mail your leaflet to someone who might be able to help your cause, such as your mayor, senator, or governor.

 Post your leaflet to a Web site that publishes student writing. Work with an adult to find an appropriate site and share your article with the world.

Your Turn

Before printing out or neatly handwriting your finished leaflet, look it over one more time.

- Be sure that you have made all the necessary corrections and that no new mistakes have been made.
- If your audience will need specific names, dates, addresses, or phone numbers to do what you have suggested, be sure that you have included them.
- You can fold your leaflet in half or thirds and decorate the outside.

Then choose one of the publishing options to present your leaflet.

Prewriting

Drafting

Content Editing

Revising

Copyediting

Proofreading

Publishing

Creative Writing

LiNK **The Three Questions**

by Jon J. Muth
Based on a story by Leo Tolstoy

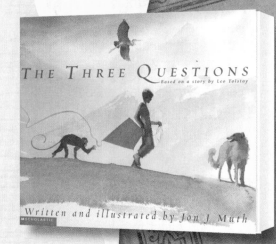

. . . Then, an idea came to him. *I know!* he thought. *I will ask Leo, the turtle. He has lived a very long time. Surely he will know the answers I am looking for.*

Nikolai hiked high up into the mountains where the old turtle lived all alone.

When Nikolai arrived, he found Leo digging a garden. The turtle was old, and digging was hard for him.

"I have three questions and I came to ask your help," Nikolai said.

"When is the best time to do things? Who is the most important one? What is the right thing to do?"

Leo listened carefully, but he only smiled. Then he went on with his digging. . . .

> This fable takes place in a nature environment, uses animals as characters, and has a main character that has a problem to solve. It includes a moral at the end of the story.

The Mouse's New Home
by Jackson McCall
Room 316

A busy mouse was working on his home in a field. He already had a nice, cozy home made of twigs and leaves. He wanted an even bigger home where he could relax in the evenings.

A chipmunk who was walking by watched the mouse taking apart the roof of his old home.

"Can I help you with your work?" asked the chipmunk.

"Oh, no," replied the mouse, who never thought he needed help. "I can do it myself."

Soon the mouse had taken apart the roof and walls. He wanted to build the tallest, biggest home in the field. He started new, higher walls.

Next, a squirrel came by.

"Can I help you finish up?" the squirrel asked. "It looks like a storm's coming." The mouse didn't pay attention to the squirrel or to the dark clouds in the sky. He just kept working.

Just as he was starting to patch on the roof, it started to rain. He looked around to see if anyone could help him, but everyone was gone.

The rain started pouring into his home. It got so wet that the walls he had built all washed away. He realized, a little too late, that he couldn't do everything himself.

What Makes a Good Fable?

A fable is a story that teaches a lesson. It is not a story about real life. In fact the main characters in a fable are usually animals who talk and act like people.

In a fable a main character faces a problem. The problem is solved in a way that teaches the reader a lesson about life. Here are some things to keep in mind when writing a fable.

Setting

The setting of a fable is often a place in nature. It should be a place where the characters in the story might be found. A story about a bird might be set at the top of a tree. A story about a mole might be set underground. The setting you choose can help shape the story you will tell in your fable.

Characters

The characters are an important part of a fable. Each character in a fable might be a different kind of animal. Or all the characters might be the same kind of animal.

A good character in a fable is more than just an animal that does something. Good characters do things for a reason. They have personalities that make them act the way they do.

The story told in a fable often takes place because a character thinks and acts a certain way. A character might make a mistake and learn a lesson. He or she might do something wise that teaches the reader a lesson.

ACTIVITY A Think of a good setting for each of the following characters. Explain why each setting is a good choice.

1. an eagle
2. a mountain goat
3. a bear
4. a seahorse
5. a beaver

ACTIVITY B Think of an animal character that might live in each of the following settings. Describe each animal's home.

1. a cave in the woods
2. the desert
3. an old barn
4. the ocean floor
5. a jungle

ACTIVITY C Choose three characters below. Choose a word on the right that might describe each character's personality. Then write a sentence about the character and its personality.

1. a horse
2. an ant
3. a cat
4. a beaver
5. a snail
6. a fox

a. cunning
b. friendly
c. eager
d. lazy
e. hardworking
f. curious

WRITER'S CORNER

Think of an animal character that you know from a book or a movie. In three sentences, describe the character and his or her personality. Tell how the character's personality affects what the character does.

Grammar in Action

Use one compound predicate in your sentences. See Section 1.7 for review.

Problem

In almost every fable, a character faces a problem. The story in a fable often tells how (or if) the problem is solved. Sometimes the problem might be a danger that the character faces, such as falling into a well or being chased by a hungry wolf. In other cases the problem might be less serious. A character might just be looking for a tasty snack or a chance to cool off in a stream.

Moral

A moral is a life lesson that a character learns. The whole purpose of a fable is to teach the reader this lesson. The moral is usually told at the end of the story, as shown in the excerpt below.

The moral is often shown in the way the problem is resolved. The character might make a mistake that he or she will not forget the next time. Or the character might make a wise decision that the reader can learn from.

The moral of the story is often related to the personality of the character. For example, a selfish hedgehog might learn a lesson about sharing. A patient crow might teach a lesson about not acting too quickly.

LiNK

The Lion and the Mouse

... Unable to free himself, he filled the forest with his angry roaring. The Mouse knew the voice and quickly found the Lion struggling in the net. Running to one of the great ropes that bound him, she gnawed it until it parted, and soon the Lion was free.

"You laughed when I said I would repay you," said the Mouse. "Now you see that even a Mouse can help a Lion."

Aesop's Fable

ACTIVITY D Read the fable on page 401 again and answer these questions.

1. What is the setting of this fable?
2. Who is the main character?
3. What words would you use to describe this character?
4. What problem does the main character face?
5. What is the moral of the story?

I'm mighty!

ACTIVITY E **Read this fable. Then answer the questions.**

The Ant and the Grasshopper

One summer's day a grasshopper was hopping around in a field, chirping and playing games. Along came a hardworking ant who was struggling to carry an ear of corn into his home.

"Don't work so hard," said the grasshopper. "Come play with me!"

"Winter is coming, and I must store food before it gets cold," the ant said. "You should do the same."

"Why worry about the winter?" the grasshopper asked. "Today it is warm, and there is plenty of food to eat."

The ant went on working, and the grasshopper went on playing. Then winter came, and the grasshopper was hungry. He went to the ant, begging for food.

"Don't come to me," said the ant, who was munching on a piece of corn. "You should have gathered your food when you had a chance, but instead you decided to play games."

1. What is the problem in this story?
2. What words would you use to describe the characters?
3. Which character learns a lesson?
4. What is the moral of this fable?

He's tiny!

WRITER'S CORNER

Think of another fable that could have the same moral as "The Ant and the Grasshopper." In a short paragraph, describe the characters of your fable and the problem they might face.

Beginning, Middle, and Ending

When you write a fable, there are many things to keep in mind. You should write your fable in a natural, lively way. You need a good setting and interesting characters. You need a problem for your characters and a moral. You also need to put all these parts together in the right order, with a clear beginning, middle, and ending.

The Velveteen Rabbit

...And about his little soft nose and his round black eyes there was something familiar, so that the Boy thought to himself:

"Why, he looks just like my old Bunny that was lost when I had scarlet fever!"

But he never knew that it was his own Bunny, come back to look at the child who had first helped him to be Real.

Margery Williams

Beginning

The beginning of a fable should describe the setting of the story. It should also describe the main character or characters. It might describe what the main character is doing at the beginning of the story. It should tell the problem that the characters face in the fable.

Middle

In the middle of the story, the characters try to solve the problem. The way they act should fit their personalities. The middle should include all the important events of the story in time order. It might also include dialogue, which is the characters' spoken words.

Ending

At the end of a fable, the problem is resolved. That doesn't mean the ending is always a happy one. Often the story ends badly for the main character.

The end of the story teaches a lesson. Sometimes the main character learns a lesson the hard way. Other times the main character solves the problem, teaching an important lesson to the reader. The writer often states the moral of the story in the last sentence. Notice how the author concludes her fable in the excerpt on page 406. Sometimes a character might state the moral, using dialogue.

ACTIVITY A Tell whether you would find this information in the beginning, middle, or ending of a fable.

1. the moral of the story
2. a description of the setting
3. important events in time order
4. a description of the characters
5. how the problem is resolved

ACTIVITY B Decide which of the following would make good beginnings for fables. Tell what changes you might make to the bad beginnings to improve them.

1. There once was an animal who lived somewhere with his friends. He had a problem that he wanted to solve, but he didn't know how.

2. A little owl who lived in the woods wanted to throw a surprise birthday party for one of his friends.

3. A speedy fish wanted to prove that he was the fastest fish in his school. He challenged the other fish to a race, which he was going to lose. He will learn that too much boasting can get you into trouble.

4. A friendly elephant was cooling off by a river when a rabbit came up to him. "Excuse me," the rabbit said. "Can you help me get across?"

5. A lazy turtle was sitting by the side of the road with nothing to do. But he was happy doing nothing, because he was lazy. Everything was fine with him.

WRITER'S CORNER

Choose one of the beginnings from Activity B that you think should be rewritten. In three or four sentences, write a better beginning for the fable.

Tech Tip Type your sentences on a computer and save them.

ACTIVITY C Decide whether each of these sentences belongs in the beginning, middle, or ending of a fable.

1. "You silly skunk," the raccoon said. "Don't you know that you should never make a promise you can't keep?"

2. The rabbit cried out for help from his spot in the middle of the river.

3. There once was a lonely bear who lived in the forest.

4. You should never save for tomorrow what you can do today.

5. "Excuse me," the fox said to the wolf. "Can you help me? I seem to be lost."

6. A clever sheep was walking through a meadow on a beautiful spring day.

7. "A word to the wise," said Bear. "Never trust strangers!"

8. The sun beat down on slithering Snake as he crossed the desert to his home under a rock.

9. "Help!" cried crow. "My beak is stuck in this tree!"

10. Soon the cat climbed over the sofa to spy on the mouse.

ACTIVITY D The sentences below are from a fable, but they are all mixed up. Put them in the correct order.

1. A fox once fell into a deep well and could not get out.

2. "Next time," the fox said as he walked away, "remember to look before you leap!"

3. The goat jumped in and began to drink.

4. The goat suddenly realized that he had no way out.

5. As the goat was drinking, the fox climbed on his back and jumped out of the well.

6. Along came a goat who looked in the well, hoping for a drink.

7. "The water is delicious. Jump in with me," the fox said.

8. Knowing he had no friends, the fox wondered who would rescue him from the well.

ACTIVITY E Choose one of these ideas for a fable. Write the beginning of this fable. Include words that describe the character and the setting.

A. An ant tries to carry a giant pea back to his hill.

B. A horse wants to go for a run outside the gates of the farm.

C. A bird wants to relax instead of fixing his nest, which has come apart in a storm.

D. A squirrel wants to take all the nuts on the ground for himself.

E. A lizard is warming herself on a rock in the desert, when a hawk approaches.

ACTIVITY F Write an ending for this fable. Show how the problem is resolved. Include a moral.

The Fox and the Crow

A crow was perched at the top of a tree in the woods. She was holding a piece of cheese in her beak. A hungry fox came by and saw the crow. He wanted the cheese for himself.

"That crow is so lovely," the fox called out loudly. "Her black feathers are so beautiful. I wonder if her voice is as fine as her feathers."

The crow was very vain. She wanted the fox to think her voice was beautiful too. She let out a loud caw, and the cheese fell out of her mouth.

WRITER'S CORNER

Look at the new beginning you wrote for the Writer's Corner on page 407.

Add three or four more sentences describing what might happen in the middle of this fable.

 Tech Tip Add these sentences to your saved document.

Homophones

Homophones are words that sound the same but have different spellings and meanings. Writers often misspell a word by writing its homophone. Here are a few common homophones.

HOMOPHONES	EXAMPLES
there	I left my boots over there.
they're	They're leaving without me.
their	Mark and Peter put their hands in the air.
to	Alberto went to the supermarket.
too	The summer is too far away.
two	Two birds were chirping in the tree.
your	Don't count your chickens before they hatch.
you're	Are you sure you're ready?

The best way to avoid using the wrong homophone is to think of the meaning of the word you are using. If you are unsure of which spelling to use, check a dictionary.

ACTIVITY A Choose the homophone that completes each sentence.

1. The fans were glad to see (there their they're) team win.
2. If you ask me to come, I'll be (there their they're).
3. My parents are thrilled that (there their they're) coming.
4. It's raining (to too two) hard to play today.
5. The show will be starting in (to too two) minutes.
6. I don't have money (to too two) pay for the movie.
7. Be sure to pack extra socks for (your you're) trip.
8. (Your You're) not wearing that, are you?
9. Are we going over to (there their they're) house?
10. Bring your new game over (there their they're).

ACTIVITY B Complete the paragraph below by choosing the correct homophones from the list.

their	they're	there
to	too	two
your	you're	

One day a ladybug came to a river that was _____ wide to cross. Near the river _____ was a scorpion, and the _____ creatures began talking. The scorpion offered _____ take the ladybug across on his back. "Promise that _____ not going to sting me," the ladybug said, and the scorpion promised. Once they had made _____ way across the river, the scorpion stung the ladybug. "Why did you break _____ promise?" the ladybug asked. "Ladybugs should know that _____ not supposed to trust scorpions," the scorpion said. "Stinging is in our nature."

WRITER'S CORNER

In four sentences describe a character and setting for a fable. Use three different homophones from these pages. Trade descriptions with a partner. Check that your partner used the correct homophones.

More Common Homophones

The English language is filled with homophones. Because they sound alike, they are often confused in writing. Here are some other homophones to keep in mind when you are writing.

HOMOPHONES	EXAMPLE
peace, piece	The old enemies made peace and shared a piece of cake.
knew, new	We knew from the leaky roof that the house wasn't new.
threw, through	I threw the ball through the hoop.
hole, whole	The leak from the small hole flooded the whole basement.
buy, by	I want to buy a book written by Dr. Seuss.
plain, plane	The small plane gently landed on the grassy plain.
hour, our	We set our alarms to go off in an hour.
hear, here	Come over here so I can hear you.

ACTIVITY C Choose the homophone that correctly completes each sentence.

1. Nobody _____ that climbing the mountain would be so hard. (knew new)

2. After a long battle, the two armies finally made _____. (peace piece)

3. The television program lasts more than an _____. (hour our)

4. We flew to Alaska on a _____. (plain plane)

5. The rain was leaking through a _____ in the roof. (hole whole)

6. I could _____ the sound of the train in the distance. (hear here)

7. Our car will pass _____ a tunnel soon. (threw through)

8. Please put your backpack _____ your desk. (buy by)

9. Claire _____ the ball to her little sister. (threw through)

10. Christopher bought himself a _____ MP3 player from the money he saved. (knew new)

ACTIVITY D Complete the paragraph below. Use the homophones from the list.

knew	our	hear
new	hour	here

The Tortoise and the Hare

Once there was a hare who _____ she could beat anyone in a race. One day a _____ animal came to town—a slow tortoise. The hare challenged the tortoise to a race, and he agreed.

The hare sprinted out far ahead. After an _____ of running, the hare came to a tree where she sat down to rest her legs. "I think I'll stop _____ for a while," the hare said. "The tortoise will never catch up, and besides, all this running can wear you out." The hare fell into a long sleep and didn't _____ the tortoise walking slowly by.

The hare finally woke up just as the tortoise was crossing the finish line. "I guess _____ speed isn't what matters in the end," the tortoise said. "Sometimes slow and steady wins the race."

WRITER'S CORNER

Choose three pairs of homophones below. Look up the meaning of each word in a dictionary. Write a sentence using each word you chose.

ore, oar	bough, bow
root, route	male, mail
rein, rain	soar, sore
vain, vein	peer, pier

Expanding Sentences

A sentence can tell you a little or a lot. Sometimes adding words to a sentence can paint a clearer picture. Adjectives and adverbs are two kinds of words that can add meaning to a sentence. They can make a sentence more detailed and interesting.

Adding Adjectives

Adjectives tell more about a noun in a sentence. Some adjectives describe how something looks, sounds, feels, smells, or tastes. Other adjectives show other qualities; for example, *quick, brave,* and *hungry.* Notice how adjectives add meaning to each sentence below.

> **The wolf howled from the mountaintop.**
> **The old gray wolf howled from the snowy mountaintop.**
>
> **A boy rode his bicycle across the field.**
> **A teenage boy rode his shiny, new bicycle over the grassy field.**
>
> **The turtle looked across the river.**
> **The clever turtle looked across the raging river.**

Adding adjectives helps you give a clearer idea of what is happening in the sentence.

ACTIVITY A Add adjectives to these nouns to make them clearer.

1. butterfly
2. flowers
3. house
4. book
5. car
6. rooster
7. puppy
8. boat

ACTIVITY B Add adjectives to these sentences to make them clearer.

1. Atop the _____ hill stood a _____ dog.
2. The _____ lady wore a _____ hat.
3. A _____ ship sailed through the _____ sea.
4. The _____ basket was filled with _____ apples.
5. Behind the _____ rock I found a colony of _____ ants.

ACTIVITY C Add adjectives to this paragraph to create a clearer picture.

I wrapped myself in a _____ coat and pulled a _____ hat over my head. Then I stepped out the _____ door. The _____ breeze smacked my face. As I walked down the _____ pathway in front of the house, I saw a _____ squirrel scurry up the _____ tree in the yard. A _____ bird looked down at me from a _____ branch. Unlike these animals I was glad I could go back into my _____ house whenever I felt too _____.

ACTIVITY D Write sentences that use each of these adjectives. Look in a dictionary if you are unsure what a word means.

1. clever
2. impatient
3. refreshing
4. spectacular

WRITER'S CORNER

Rewrite the sentences from Activity C again, using different adjectives. Tell how the adjectives changed the meaning of the sentences.

Grammar in Action
Refer to Section 4, adjectives, to help you use adjectives in your sentences.

Adding Adverbs

Adverbs can give a clearer picture of the way people, animals, or things act. Adverbs describe how, when, where, or why something happens.

Some adverbs describe things you see or hear. For example, you can see or hear something happening quickly, quietly, or gracefully. Other adverbs, such as *honestly, kindly,* or *politely,* describe ideas that cannot be seen.

See how adding adverbs changes the sentences below. In each sentence the adverbs give a clearer picture of how, when, where, or why the action takes place.

> **I rubbed my eyes and walked down the stairs.**
> **I rubbed my eyes sleepily and walked slowly down the stairs.**
>
> **"How can you do that?" my sister asked.**
> **"How can you do that?" my sister asked angrily.**
>
> **The frog gazed at the fly resting on the log.**
> **The frog gazed hungrily at the fly resting lazily on the log.**

ACTIVITY E Add adverbs to these sentences to show how, when, where, or why the action takes place.

1. Myra smiled _____ when we asked where she had been.

2. The wolf growled _____ at the intruder.

3. When I did not come _____, my mother called to me _____.

4. Peter _____ displayed the prize he had won.

5. The children watched _____ for the bus to arrive.

6. "Summer's finally here!" Tina called _____.

7. The dancers drifted _____ across the stage.

8. When questioned by the teacher, Nina looked away _____.

9. The dog _____ appeared when its master called.

10. Nobody doubted that the soldier had fought _____.

ACTIVITY F Add adverbs to the paragraph.

Paul and I looked up _____ at the sky. The clouds were coming _____. "We should get going," Paul said _____. We hopped on our bicycles and started pedaling _____ down the street. When we got to the house, I _____ realized I had left my umbrella outside. "Better wait for this storm to let up before going back out there," Paul said _____.

ACTIVITY G Rewrite each sentence by adding both an adjective and an adverb.

1. The boat sailed out to sea.
2. A snake slithered through the grass.
3. The bald eagle sailed through the air.
4. The horse galloped across the field.
5. The music filled the room as the people danced.
6. The bird flew to the tree.
7. Those explorers walked through the jungle.
8. A toad leaped from the rock.
9. The lanterns rocked in the wind.
10. A parrot sang in the shop.

WRITER'S CORNER

Look through a book for five sentences with at least one adverb. Rewrite the sentences, using different adverbs. How did the new words change the meaning of each sentence?

Tech Tip With an adult, use an online thesaurus.

Haiku

Haiku is a Japanese form of poetry. A haiku is short. It is just three lines long and contains seventeen syllables. There are five syllables in the first line, seven syllables in the second line, and five syllables in the third line. (A syllable is a word or part of a word that has a vowel sound. *Snow* has one syllable. *Snowboard* has two syllables. *Snowboarding* has three syllables.)

A haiku does not tell a story. It describes one idea, moment, or feeling. Often it creates a peaceful image of nature. It might describe a quiet spot in the woods or a bird chirping in a tree. It could also describe any other memorable moment, such as the end of a school day, nighttime in a city, or waking up on Sunday morning.

Look at this haiku. The syllables are marked.

> Hot, thick, humid air,
>
> Bare feet running on sidewalk.
>
> Summer is freedom.
>
> —Emma Joyce

Emma, the author of this haiku, does not try to tell a whole story in her poem. Instead, she describes how she feels during the summertime. What feeling do you get when you read this haiku?

ACTIVITY A Which of these might be easy to write a haiku about? Which ones might be hard? Explain your answers.

1. a trip to the moon and back
2. sitting by a stream
3. relaxing on a raft in a lake
4. a movie that you saw recently
5. laughing with a friend
6. what happened on summer vacation
7. a grasshopper sitting on a leaf
8. a new board game
9. walking your dog
10. opening birthday presents

ACTIVITY B Write each haiku. Make a mark above each syllable.

1. Walking into class
   I see my best friend smiling.
   This year could be fun.

2. Sitting in the sun,
   The waves lulling me to sleep—
   I love summertime.

3. Rex sits at my feet
   Hoping for a scrap of food.
   Don't dogs ever learn?

WRITER'S CORNER

Choose an outdoor setting to write about, such as a forest, park, or even your own backyard. Write a list of ideas, moments, or feelings that could be part of your haiku.

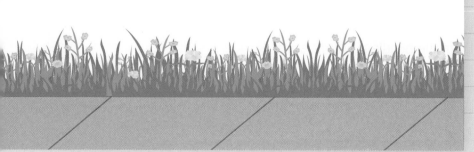

Writing a Haiku

Haiku can be easy and fun to write. Haiku can be the perfect way to show something you saw or imagined. Here are some tips for writing a haiku of your own.

1. Think of an idea. You might close your eyes and let your mind drift. Write the ideas. Then choose an idea that would make a good haiku.

2. Make a list of words related to your idea. Think of words that use your senses. What do you see? What do you hear or smell? How does this idea make you feel?

3. Begin writing your haiku. Write a line that is five syllables long. Use words from your list.

4. Write a second line that is seven syllables long and a third line that is five syllables long. Try to make the second line connect to the first or last line. Often in a haiku, the first two lines form one idea. The third line shows a new idea.

5. Look at the lines you have written. Is there one line you really like? Are there other lines you might change? Try changing your haiku, keeping the lines you like. You might change just one word in a line. Keep working on your haiku until it is just right.

ACTIVITY C Match the first two lines of the haiku on the left with the final lines on the right.

1. Jolted from behind
   I see my brother laughing—

2. A tiny kitten
   Curls up in a sunny spot.

3. Out my bus window
   I see a world waking up.

4. A small voice cries out
   From the bundle in Mom's arms.

a. I like bumper cars.

b. My sister is home.

c. A new day dawning.

d. What a life she has!

Lady Chiyo, a famous haiku poet of the 18th century

ACTIVITY D Choose three haiku beginnings below. Write a final line for each poem.

A. Red and yellow leaves
Scatter across the backyard

B. Cup of hot cocoa
Defrosts my shivering bones

C. Dusty spider webs
Line the slanted attic walls

D. Windowpane rattles,
Raindrops patter on the roof

E. My best friend Lucy
Whispers secrets
in my ear

F. Saturday in bed—
The sun peeks through
my window

G. Squirrel on a branch
Looks up, then darts
through the air

ACTIVITY E Choose a phrase below. Write a haiku, using the phrase as the first or last line.

A. vacation's coming

B. a fly buzzing by

C. waiting for the bus

D. running through a field

E. crickets chirping at night

F. a snowy wonderland

G. flower petals falling

H. soccer ball soaring

I. books lining the shelves

J. jumping in the waves

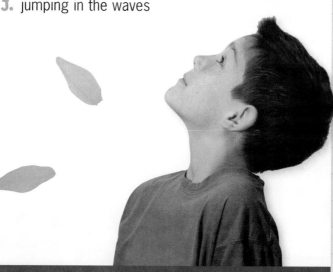

WRITER'S CORNER

Write your own haiku, following the steps from this lesson. Use your idea from the Writer's Corner on page 419. When you have written a first draft, see if there are any words or lines that you can revise. Keep revising until you are happy with your haiku. Share your haiku with the class.

Post your haiku on a class blog or wiki.

Telling a Fable

A fable can be a fun kind of story to tell. Lively, memorable characters do interesting things and can teach your audience an important lesson about life. Here are some tips for telling a good fable.

Audience

Think of your listeners when you choose your fable. Choose a fable they might not have heard. Be sure the fable has a moral that your audience can understand.

Characters and Setting

Poor little kitty!

Think of where your fable takes place. Imagine this setting in detail. Use your mental picture when telling your fable.

Think about the characters. What in the characters' personalities leads them to act the way they do? As you prepare, write a list of words that describe each character.

Beginning, Middle, and Ending

Your fable should have a clear beginning, middle, and ending. The beginning should mention the setting, the characters, and the problem they face. In the middle a character might try to solve the problem.

The ending should tell how the problem is solved or whether it is solved at all. You should also state the moral at the end of the fable.

Make a Chart

As you prepare your fable, you can make a graphic organizer to organize your ideas. Here is an example of a chart you might make.

The Scared Cat

Setting: on a branch of an oak tree

Characters: a scared but cute cat, a clever crow

Main events:

1. The cat asks the crow to help him get down.

2. The crow tells the cat he can get down himself, but the cat says he is too scared.

3. The crow laughs at the cat and starts shaking the branch.

4. The cat gets even more scared and runs down the tree, safe and sound.

Moral: Sometimes you have to do something unpleasant to help someone else.

ACTIVITY A Look at the chart for the fable "The Scared Cat." Think of what each character might say. Then write dialogue for each character. Which character do you think would tell the moral?

SPEAKER'S CORNER

Tell the fable "The Scared Cat" to a partner. Describe the setting and characters in the beginning. Tell the main events in your own words. Use the dialogue you wrote in Activity A. Compare your fable with your partner's.

Using Your Voice

Using your voice well is one of the keys to telling a good fable. You might have an interesting fable with original characters and a good moral. However, if you don't use your voice well, your audience may lose interest. Here are some speaking tips to keep in mind.

- Change your pace for different parts of your story. You might speak slowly at the beginning and ending. Speak more quickly when the fastest action happens.
- Use a different tone of voice for each character. Be sure your tone of voice fits the character. This will help your listeners tell who is speaking. It will also make your characters more interesting.
- Use your voice or an object to make sound effects. You might make a whooshing sound to show the blowing breeze. A ticking noise can remind your audience of a clock.

Practice

It is important to practice telling your fable before you tell it to an audience. Begin by writing on note cards the information about the setting, the characters, the main events, and the moral. Look at the note cards as you practice telling the story to a friend or in front of a mirror.

Try changing your pace as you practice. Use different voices and sound effects. Keep practicing until you feel comfortable telling your fable.

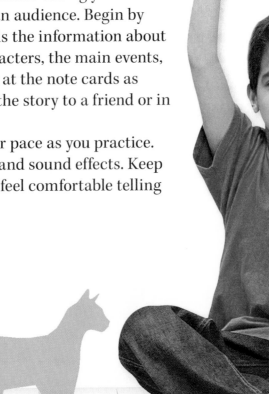

Listening Tips

When you listen to someone else tell a fable, use these tips to help you be a good listener.

- When the setting and characters are described, try to picture them in your mind.
- Listen carefully for what each character says and how he or she says it. How they speak may tell you something about their personalities.
- Listen for any sound effects that can help you imagine the scene.
- Pay attention to the moral of the story at the end. Think of how the moral is shown by the fable.

Give feedback to the speaker at the end of the story. You might say something you liked about the story or ask any questions you have.

ACTIVITY B Think of a fable you would like to tell. You may choose a fable you know or make up one yourself. Make a chart like the one on page 423 that lists the setting, characters, main events, and moral. Then copy the information onto note cards. Practice telling your fable with a partner. Vary the tone of your voice to show different characters. Change your pace to fit the story.

SPEAKER'S CORNER

Tell your fable from Activity B to the class. You might refer to your note cards, but try to speak in your own words. When you have finished, invite your classmates to ask questions or give feedback. When you listen to your classmates' fables, use the listening tips to help you be a good listener.

Writer's Workshop

Prewriting and Drafting

What fables do you know? Do you remember the story of the tortoise and the hare, the fox and the crow, or the ant and the grasshopper? Each is a simple story that teaches a lesson.

Prewriting

For a fourth-grade creative writing project, Anthony decided to write a fable. He began by prewriting. First, he brainstormed a moral. Then he used a graphic organizer to plan his story.

Brainstorming

Anthony began prewriting by brainstorming lessons that he had learned in his life. He made this list of morals he could use in his fable.

Always try hard at things.
Don't wait too long for something, or
   in the end it may be too late.
If at first you don't succeed, try again.
Be nice to people, and they will be nice to you.
Sometimes it's better to be smart than
   to be strong.

The first moral didn't seem very interesting. The second one reminded him of the time he  kept his Halloween candy for later. When he finally went back to it, the candy was stale. Anthony liked this moral better than any of the others.

Your Turn

- Begin prewriting by brainstorming one part of your fable. You might brainstorm a list of morals, as Anthony did, or you might brainstorm a list of characters or settings.
- When you have completed your list, choose your favorite to help you start your fable.

Planning a Story

When he was finished brainstorming, Anthony began planning his fable. He made a chart to keep track of his ideas. He made spaces for his characters, setting, main events, and moral of the story.

> **Organization**

First, Anthony thought of different animals that might be characters. He decided a squirrel would be an interesting character. Anthony thought that the squirrel might be friends with a bird.

Then Anthony thought of the setting. A squirrel and a bird might live in the woods. Since there are lots of nuts, fruits, and berries in the woods, it would be a good place to find food.

Next, he thought about his story. Maybe his characters could find some food but then lose it because they waited too long, just as Anthony had done with his Halloween candy. He decided that the squirrel would find some food but not take it home because he was lazy. Anthony wrote in his chart all the important events for his story.

As he planned his story, Anthony added to his characters and setting sections. He added words to describe the personalities of his characters.

He added an apple tree to the setting because it was an important part of the story. Here is the chart Anthony made.

Characters:
a squirrel who is hungry, friendly, and lazy; a bird who is helpful and smart

Setting:
in the woods, near an apple tree

Main events:
1. A group of squirrels look for food.
2. A bird leads one squirrel to an apple tree.
3. The bird says that the squirrel should take some apples home.
4. The squirrel eats a bunch of apples and falls asleep.
5. Other squirrels find the tree and take the apples while he's asleep.

Moral:
Don't wait too long for something, or in the end it may be too late.

Your Turn

Make a chart for your fable.
- Include the characters and setting.
- Add words to describe the characters' personalities.
- Include all the main events in the fable in time order.
- Write the moral that you want your readers to learn.

Drafting

Anthony used his chart to help him write his fable. Here is the draft he wrote.

Ricky and the Blue Jay

One day a squirrel named Ricky was searching for food with his friends. They each went in there own direction. Ricky went down a path with his friend Jay, who was a blue jay.

Jay told Ricky about a tree he had found that had lots of apples under it. Soon they came to the tree. They had hit the jackpot! Ricky was so hungry. He ate as many apples as he could.

"Let's take some of these back home," Jay said.

"We can do that later. Let's eat some more!" Ricky said. He kept on eating, and soon he was very full. He lay down and fell asleep under the tree.

A few hours later Ricky woke up with a stomachache. He felt sick because he had eaten so many apples. He looked around he found that all the apples were gone! Ricky asked Jay what had happened. "While you were asleep, your friends came and took all the apples away," Jay said.

Anthony wrote his fable, using lively, natural language that would keep his readers interested. He wrote a beginning that introduced his characters, Ricky and Jay. He also mentioned the problem they faced: searching for food.

 Voice

In the middle he told what happened in time order. The events in his story showed what Ricky and Jay did to solve their problem.

In the ending he showed how the problem was solved. Jay's words at the end hint at the moral of the story.

Your Turn

1. Use the chart you made in prewriting to write your fable. Write in a lively voice to keep your audience interested. Start with a beginning that tells about the characters, the setting, and the problem.

2. Next, tell what the characters do to try to solve the problem. Include all the events you need to tell a good story. Write the events in time order.

3. At the end of the fable, if the problem was solved, tell how. The ending should show who learned a lesson. Be sure to tell the moral of the fable in the ending.

Writing Dialogue

Dialogue is the words that your characters speak. Be sure to tell who is speaking after each line of dialogue.

Dialogue can give important information and move the story along. In Anthony's story Jay's final line of dialogue tells the reader what happened to the apples.

Using dialogue in a fable can also help you show the characters and their personalities. For example, Jay's dialogue showed how he liked to plan ahead. Ricky's dialogue showed how impatient he was.

One way to show a character's feelings or personality in dialogue is to add an adverb.

 Word Choice

When Ricky said, "Let's eat!" in Anthony's fable, Anthony could have added that he spoke "greedily" or "excitedly." Use adverbs that show how your characters speak or act.

Writer's Tip Any words that are spoken should begin and end with quotation marks.

Content Editing

Anthony had enjoyed writing his first draft. He liked his characters and thought his fable had a good moral. He knew that he could make his fable better by editing. He read his draft again. He wanted to make sure it made sense and that there was nothing important missing. He wanted to make sure the story was clear and complete. As he edited, he used this Content Editor's Checklist.

After editing his draft, Anthony gave his fable to his classmate Carl. He thought Carl would enjoy reading his fable. Anthony hoped Carl would find some ways to improve his draft.

Carl read Anthony's fable once for fun. Then he read it again more carefully, using the Content Editor's Checklist. He tried to think of ways to improve Anthony's fable. Carl listed his ideas and shared them with Anthony.

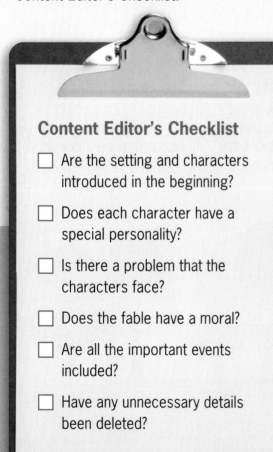

Content Editor's Checklist

- [ ] Are the setting and characters introduced in the beginning?
- [ ] Does each character have a special personality?
- [ ] Is there a problem that the characters face?
- [ ] Does the fable have a moral?
- [ ] Are all the important events included?
- [ ] Have any unnecessary details been deleted?

Carl began by telling Anthony what he liked about the fable. He really liked Ricky's personality, and he thought the problem was a good one. He thought that Ricky had done something many people might do and that he had learned an important lesson. Carl also made these suggestions.

- Where is the setting of this fable? It's probably in the woods, but you should tell that somewhere.
- You should add a sentence telling that other squirrels came to take the apples.
- I think the reader can guess why Ricky had a stomachache, so you don't need that sentence.
- I think I know what the moral of the story is, but you don't really tell it. Can you add that to the ending?

Anthony thanked Carl for his comments. Anthony liked many of his classmate's ideas. He decided to use most of Carl's suggestions as he revised his draft.

Your Turn

- Read over your draft, using the Content Editor's Checklist.
- Trade your draft with a partner. Use the checklist to make suggestions for your partner's draft.
- Share your suggestions with your partner. Remember to tell your partner what you liked about the draft.
- Listen carefully to your partner's suggestions. Thank your partner for his or her comments. Make any changes that you think will make your fable better.

Prewriting

Drafting

Content Editing

Revising

Copyediting

Proofreading

Publishing

zzzzzzzz

Revising

Anthony made several changes after reading his draft again and going over it with Carl. Here are the changes that he made.

Ricky and the ~~Blue Jay~~ Apple Tree

One day a squirrel named Ricky was searching for food in the woods with his friends. They each went in there own direction. Ricky went down a path with his friend Jay, who was a blue jay.

Jay told Ricky about a tree he had found that had lots of apples under it. Soon they came to the tree. They had hit the jackpot! Ricky was so hungry. He ate as many apples as he could.

"Let's take some of these back home," Jay said.

"We can do that later. Let's eat some more!" Ricky said. He kept on eating, and soon he was very full. He lay down and fell asleep under the tree.

A few hours later Ricky woke up with a stomachache. ~~He felt sick because he had eaten so many apples.~~ He looked around he found that all the apples were gone! Ricky asked Jay what had happened.

"While you were asleep, your friends came and took all the apples away," Jay said. "Sometimes if you wait too long to do something, you lose your chance!"

Look at some of the changes Anthony made to his draft. He used his own ideas and some of Carl's suggestions to improve it.

- Anthony realized he had forgotten to include the setting of his fable. Where did he add that information?
- He did not add another sentence about what happened while Ricky was asleep. Do you agree?
- What detail did Anthony decide to take out?
- Where did Anthony add the moral of the story?

After making some of the changes Carl had suggested, Anthony decided to change the title. He didn't think the blue jay was important enough to the story. He wrote a new title that included the apples.

Grammar in Action

Name the adverb of time in the second paragraph. See Section 6.1 for review.

Your Turn

Look at the changes your partner suggested and the ideas you had. Make any changes you think will make your draft better. When you have finished, go over the Content Editor's Checklist again. Be sure you can answer yes to each question.

Prewriting
Drafting
Content Editing
Revising
Copyediting
Proofreading
Publishing

Copyediting and Proofreading

Copyediting

After revising, Anthony was ready to copyedit his draft. He wanted to make sure that he had chosen the right words and written each sentence correctly. He used this Copyeditor's Checklist to help him.

After looking over his draft, Anthony found a few places where he could make changes.

Copyeditor's Checklist

- ☐ Are the sentences complete?

- ☐ Did I look for run-on sentences?

- ☐ Did I look for any sentences that are too choppy?

- ☐ Do all the words have the right meaning?

- ☐ Did I check if any words are repeated too often?

- ☐ Did I check if there are places where adjectives or adverbs could be added to make the story clearer?

First, he realized that there were several short sentences in the second paragraph. This made his paragraph seem choppy. He combined two sentences to help the paragraph flow better.

👁👁 Sentence Fluency

Next, Anthony decided to add a few adjectives to paint a clearer picture. He added the adjective *friendly* to describe Ricky's personality. He added the adverb *excitedly* to show how Ricky spoke.

Finally, Anthony found a run-on sentence in the paragraph about Ricky waking up. He changed the word *he* to *and* to make the sentence correct.

Your Turn

Read your fable again and copyedit it, using the Copyeditor's Checklist.

Proofreading

Anthony thought his fable was coming along nicely. He hoped that by proofreading his draft, he could catch any mistakes that he had missed. Anthony asked his sister Maria to proofread his draft because she was good with details. She used this Proofreader's Checklist.

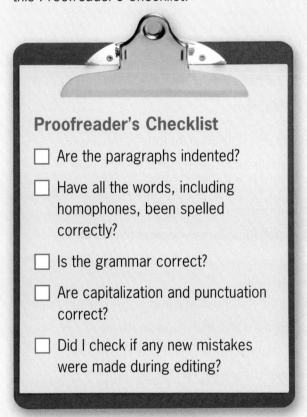

Proofreader's Checklist

☐ Are the paragraphs indented?

☐ Have all the words, including homophones, been spelled correctly?

☐ Is the grammar correct?

☐ Are capitalization and punctuation correct?

☐ Did I check if any new mistakes were made during editing?

Maria liked Anthony's fable, though she was surprised that Ricky would be eating apples instead of nuts. She thought he was a very foolish squirrel. She also found a few mistakes to correct.

First, she noticed that a word was misspelled because Anthony had used the homophone instead. In the second sentence, he should have used the word *their* instead of *there*.

Next, Maria found that Anthony had forgotten to indent the last paragraph, so she reminded him to do that.

Finally, she noticed a mistake in the last sentence he had added. She reminded him that every line of dialogue should begin and end with quotation marks. He had forgotten the quotation marks at the end of the sentence.

Anthony thanked his sister for her help and agreed that all her corrections should be made.

Your Turn

- Ask a partner to proofread your draft, using the Proofreader's Checklist.
- Use the checklist to proofread your partner's draft. Then explain your suggestions politely. Listen to your partner's suggestions.
- Make the changes that you think will improve your draft.

Prewriting

Drafting

Content Editing

Revising

Copyediting

Proofreading

Publishing

Publishing

Anthony's fable was almost complete. He looked it over one more time to make sure that all the changes had been made correctly.

He typed his fable on his computer. He made sure to include a title and his name. Then he printed out his fable.

Ricky and the Apple Tree

by Anthony Stephani

One day a friendly squirrel named Ricky was searching for food in the woods with his friends. They each went in their own direction. Ricky went down a path with his friend Jay, who was a blue jay.

Jay told Ricky about a tree he had found that had lots of apples under it. Soon they came to the tree. They had hit the jackpot! Ricky was so hungry that he ate as many apples as he could.

"Let's take some of these back home," Jay said.

"We can do that later. Let's eat some more!" Ricky said excitedly. He kept on eating, and soon he was very full. He lay down and fell asleep under the tree.

A few hours later Ricky woke up with a stomachache. He looked around and found that all the apples were gone! Ricky asked Jay what had happened.

"While you were asleep, your friends came and took all the apples away," Jay said. "Sometimes if you wait too long to do something, you lose your chance!"

Will Anthony catch it?

Now it is your turn to share your new fable by publishing it. There are many ways you can publish your fable.

 Put together a book of all the fables from your class. Add illustrations. Read some of your classmates' fables. See if you can find any other fables that have the same moral as yours. You might also have your class book on hand for Parents' Night.

 Post your fable on your classroom's wiki, blog, or Web site. Invite other students to review and comment on your work.

 Record yourself reading your fable and upload it as a podcast on the class blog. Use the speaking tips from Lesson 6 when you read your fable. Invite classmates to listen and share their thoughts on the class blog.

 Make your fable come to life. Use computer programs to illustrate and then animate your fable. You can add music and sound effects to round out the story.

Prewriting

Drafting

Content Editing

Revising

Copyediting

Proofreading

Publishing

Your Turn

Read over your draft one more time. Make sure that all the changes have been made correctly. If you typed your fable on a computer, you might use the computer's spell-checker to double-check the spelling.

If you did not type your fable on a computer, write it neatly by hand. Be sure to include

 Presentation

a title and your name at the top. If the fable is more than one page long, number the second page. Then choose a way to publish your fable.

Writer's Tip Remember that a computer's spell-checker will not find incorrect homophones.

Expository Writing

LiNK **Going for the Gold**

Chandler Schaak, *Time for Kids*, Feb. 27, 2009

From February 7 to 13, more than 2,000 athletes with intellectual disabilities competed in the 2009 Special Olympics World Winter Games, in Idaho.

... More than 2,000 athletes from 95 countries took that oath at the opening ceremony of the 2009 Special Olympics World Winter Games. They competed in seven sports, including skiing, skating and floor hockey. ...

Amanda Coviello, 21, won the gold medal in the super-G, a downhill skiing event. "Doctors told us Amanda would never have any motor skills and would have a hard time with language," says Sue Coviello, Amanda's mom. "Now she is a gold medalist and even learned Russian ..."

At the closing ceremony, the Olympic flame was extinguished. But the work of the Special Olympics athletes and volunteers continues.

> This expository article has a topic sentence and includes a statement from an interview.

Melrose Grade School News

How Do You Spell *Winner?*

Fourth grader Josh Franzen may not have taken home a trophy from the National Spelling Bee last week, but his strong showing made his friends proud back at Melrose Grade School.

Josh was the first Melrose student ever to reach the national competition in Washington, D.C. He was eliminated in the fourth round, misspelling *inchoate*, but he was not disappointed.

"It was amazing just to get here," Josh said. "It was an experience I'll never forget."

Getting there certainly was not easy. First, he had to win the local and state spelling bees. He spent hours every night studying words, including many that he had never even heard of.

"There were lots of late nights with the spelling books. He really drove us crazy sometimes," said his mother, Marie Franzen.

As a result of his hard studying, he got to spend four days in the nation's capital. He made friends with some of the best young spellers in the country.

"These people are so smart," Josh said. "I was proud to have gotten as far as I did." ◆

What Makes a Good Expository Article?

Expository writing tells a reader about a real-life topic. It uses facts to describe real people, places, things, or events. Book reports and textbooks are examples of expository writing. Another example is an article in a newspaper. Here are some tips for writing a good expository article.

Introduction

The introduction of an expository article tells what the article is about. Sometimes the article might start with a catchy sentence to grab the reader's attention. In a news article, this sentence is called a "lead." The introduction should also include a topic sentence that states the most important facts about the topic. In the introduction below, the third sentence is the topic sentence.

> **Have you ever wondered how the school's tasty peach crisp dessert is made? Just ask Fran Steele. As the head cook of the cafeteria, she's been cooking delicious meals for students for more than 15 years.**

Body

In the body of an expository article, the writer gives information that supports the topic sentence. The body answers the questions *who, what, when, where, why* and *how.* In a news article, the most important information is told first.

Conclusion

The conclusion of an expository article sums up the article. A good conclusion will leave the reader thinking about the topic. It might end with a quotation or an interesting statement. In a news article, the conclusion is called a "wrap-up."

ACTIVITY A Which of the following makes a good topic for an expository article? Why do you think so?

1. new animals at the zoo
2. how to recognize beings from other planets
3. a brief history of my school
4. how snow forms
5. what I'll do when I become president
6. how chicks hatch
7. your opinion about superheroes
8. what a gazelle is
9. how crayons are made
10. why your dog is the best pet

ACTIVITY B Decide whether each sentence below fits best in the introduction, the body, or the conclusion of an expository article about a class field trip.

1. This was the second field trip this year for Mrs. Parker's class.
2. "The class really enjoyed it," Mrs. Parker said. "It felt as if an ancient culture were suddenly brought to life."
3. A busload of fourth graders saw the wonders of ancient Egypt on a field trip to the Caldwell Museum.
4. Marcos Johnson said his favorite part of the trip was seeing a mummy up close.

WRITER'S CORNER

Think of a museum that you have visited with your class or your family. In three or four sentences, write the introduction for an expository article about that museum. Include a topic sentence and underline it.

Order of Importance

In news articles, facts are given in order of importance. This is because people often do not read the whole article. They might read just the first few sentences. Therefore, the most important information is given first. What information do you get from the first sentence of the excerpt on page 443?

The school newspaper article below is organized in order of importance.

> Carlos Gonzales was elected class president Monday, defeating Courtney Halm by 11 votes.
>
> Tina Bremer was elected vice president. Misha Jacobs won the vote for secretary, and Pauline Paulson was voted treasurer.
>
> Carlos's friends cheered when the announcement was made over the loudspeaker. Even many of the students who voted for the other candidate said Carlos would be a good president.
>
> "He's really smart, and he's a good speaker," said student Maria Higgins.
>
> More than 200 students voted in this year's election.

The news that Carlos was elected president is more important than who won the other offices. The number of students who voted is less important than the students' reactions.

ACTIVITY C Imagine writing an article about a band that is planning to perform in your community. Which facts would be the most important? Which facts are the least important?

1. Many people are excited about the concert, and tickets are selling fast.
2. The concert is sponsored by the local PTA.
3. The band will be performing on Saturday at 8:00 p.m.
4. The band is touring all across the country.
5. The name of the band is "The Crushed Peanuts."

ACTIVITY D Arrange each set of sentences from a news article in order of importance. Explain your choices.

1. **a.** Marsha Haywood was the highest scorer for the Rockets, scoring 10 points.
   b. The Reading Rockets beat the Newton Nuggets 32–28 for their first win of the basketball season Tuesday night.
   c. The Rockets' next game will be on Wednesday against the Palatine Pirates.

2. **a.** The old building will be torn down next May.
   b. Students are excited about the new school. "Everything looks so fresh and clean. It might actually be fun to go to school!" said Mark O'Shea.
   c. The brand-new Marshall Elementary School opened yesterday, as students and teachers carried their books across the street from the old school.

3. **a.** The student council decided to make the eagle the new school mascot Wednesday, replacing the aardvark.
   b. This was the third time in the history of the school that the mascot has been changed.
   c. The decision was made to change the mascot because the eagle is a more exciting animal than the aardvark.

Aardvark

LiNK

Lunar Lander Inventors Win Big

On Thursday, the X Prize Foundation awarded the Northrop Grumman Lunar Lander X Prize at a ceremony in Washington, D.C. Two teams of inventors won a total of $1.5 million for crafting and flying robotic machines that could land on the moon. The prize money for the contest came from NASA.

Scholastic News Online

WRITER'S CORNER

Find an article in your local newspaper and list at least three ideas from the article in the order that they appear. Work with a partner to decide why the writer placed the ideas in that order. Share what you found with the class.

Tech Tip With an adult, find the article online.

Gathering Information

Before you write an expository article, you must gather information about your topic. Anywhere you look for information is called a source. For news articles a reporter often goes to an event, such as a baseball game or a town meeting, to get information. Other sources of information include books, Web sites, and newspapers. An interview with someone connected to the topic can also be an effective source.

Interviewing

Often the best information comes from people who are connected to an event. If your school is buying new computers, your principal can probably tell you why they are needed. If there was a heavy snowstorm, a snowplow driver would know which streets are blocked. Always bring a parent or teacher if you are interviewing someone you don't know. Why is the quotation used in the excerpt on the left?

LiNK

Bee Mystery

Millions of honeybees are vanishing, and their disappearing act has experts stumped.

Honeybees are more important than many people realize. A lot of what we eat is directly or indirectly pollinated by the bees. . .

Bee expert Dennis vanEngelsdorp used to see up to 60,000 of the insects inside every hive. "now many hives have no bees—dead or alive," he says. . . .

National Geographic Kids

Deciding What Is Important

Part of good note taking is deciding which facts are important and which ones aren't. Important facts have an effect after the event is over. If a baseball player drops a ball, but no one scores, the fact is not important. If the home team loses the championship because a player drops a ball, the fact is important.

ACTIVITY A Choose one person to interview for an article about each topic. Explain why you would choose that person.

1. a fire at the local skating rink

   the rink's owner   a firefighter   a skater

2. a teacher who is retiring

   the retiring teacher   another teacher   a student

3. a traffic jam caused by a school bus breaking down

   a student   a police officer   the bus driver

4. an annual marathon in a big city

   the mayor   the winner   a spectator

5. the grand opening of a new restaurant

   the owner   the chef   a customer

ACTIVITY B Read the following newspaper article. Decide which facts are not important enough to include in the article.

The Rosa Parks School custodian was bitten while protecting a student from a dog. John Mayer ran out to the schoolyard when he heard screaming. He had been replacing batteries in the school's smoke alarms. A small poodle had cornered Alicia Tomarz against the playground fence. It may have smelled Alicia's cat on her clothes. Mayer stepped between the poodle and Alicia, and the dog bit him. When the custodian shouted, the dog ran off.

The dog's owner was located and said that the dog had been given all its shots. The poodle's name is Snowball. Mr. Mayer was taken to the hospital. He didn't want to go, but Principal Wicki insisted. A doctor gave him three stitches. Mr. Mayer will be back in school tomorrow.

WRITER'S CORNER

Imagine you are going to interview a classmate about his or her weekend. Write five questions that you might ask.

The Five Ws

The most important facts in a news article should be included near the beginning. The most important facts are told in the topic sentence in the introduction, while the rest are told in the body. These facts should answer questions known as "the five Ws." These questions are *who, what, when, where,* and *why.* The facts might also answer the question of *how* something happened.

Sometimes one of these questions may not be answered in an article. Or it might be answered in a different way than you expect. For example, an article about a tornado may not have a *why.*

ACTIVITY C Look back at "How Do You Spell *Winner?*" on page 439. Answer these questions.

1. Who is Josh Franzen?
2. What did he do?
3. Where did this event take place?
4. When did this event take place?
5. Why was Josh not disappointed?
6. How did Josh get to this event?

ACTIVITY D Use three facts from the following information to write the introduction to an expository article.

Who?	fourth graders Maria Jones and Britney LaPierre
What?	formed a new gardening club
When?	last Friday
Where?	in the garden behind Jefferson School
Why?	to share their love of gardening
How?	by asking classmates to sign a petition and presenting it to Principal McLaughlin

ACTIVITY E Read each introduction to an expository article. Write two questions that the article should answer. Begin each question with *who, what, when, where,* or *why.*

1. A moose escaped from the Stafford County Zoo and has been sighted walking behind people's houses along Main Street.

2. A group of fourth-grade students decided to spread holiday cheer by making box lunches for a shelter in the area.

3. A powerful snowstorm hit the area Monday, knocking out power in some places and forcing some schools to close.

4. One of the teachers in Markham Elementary School announced that she will retire.

5. A student has created a new kind of ball game that many kids around school have started to play.

6. Students performed the play *Stone Soup* in the school gym, and those who attended said they enjoyed the performance.

7. A new study showed that smoking can be especially harmful to those who start when they are young.

8. A local author has written a book about the history of the town. The book will be in bookstores on Tuesday.

9. New bleachers are being installed at the Lane High School athletic field.

10. The Grace Street Fire Station is set to open next week.

WRITER'S CORNER

Think of an event you have recently been a part of, such as a birthday or a wedding. Imagine you are a reporter covering the event. Write six sentences about the event, answering the questions *who, what, when, where, why,* and *how.*

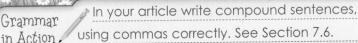

Grammar in Action. In your article write compound sentences, using commas correctly. See Section 7.6.

Negative Words

A word that means "no" is called a negative. Writers use negative words to express the opposite of something in a sentence. For example, if a writer wanted to say the opposite of *Everyone was at the park,* he or she might write *No one was at the park.* The following are common negative words used in writing:

no	**not**	**none**	**nothing**
nobody	**no one**	**never**	**nowhere**

Contractions with *Not*

Contractions with *not* (*n't*) can also be used to express *no.* *Did not* becomes *didn't.* You can give a sentence the opposite meaning by adding a *not* contraction.

> **The children couldn't believe their eyes.** (could + not)
> **Christina hasn't visited Paris.** (has + not)
> **I don't have a ride to baseball practice.** (do + not)

You might have heard the contraction *ain't.* It is sometimes used informally to express *am not, isn't,* or *aren't.* However, *ain't* is a slang term and is not proper English.

Negative Adverbs

Words like *hardly, scarcely, rarely,* and *barely* are negative adverbs. When used with *ever* or *any,* these words express a negative idea.

> **I hardly ever go to the theater.**
> **We have barely any money.**

The Eiffel Tower in Paris

ACTIVITY A Choose a word from the list to fill in each blank. Write each new sentence.

nobody   never   none   nothing   nowhere   not

1. Ann is _____ on time.
2. The driver did _____ know where he was going.
3. _____ wanted to help clean up after the party.
4. I was hoping to see paintings by Picasso at the museum, but there were _____.
5. Jason has _____ to do.
6. The monkey was _____ to be found.
7. Bradley could find _____ interested in buying his tickets.
8. There is _____ to eat in the cabinet.

ACTIVITY B Rewrite the following sentences, using *hardly, scarcely, barely,* or *rarely* with *any* or *ever* instead of *no* or *never.*

1. I never eat junk food.
2. Carrie never goes on vacation.
3. They have no time to go to the store.
4. We never ice-skate in the winter.
5. I was expecting a blizzard, but there was no snow.
6. That shop never has sales.
7. There are no baby animals in the petting zoo.
8. I never want to make my bed in the morning.

WRITER'S CORNER

Write four sentences about yourself, using in each a different negative word from the list on page 448. Use a contraction with *not* in one of your sentences.

Double Negatives

You may have heard that two wrongs don't make a right. In a sentence, however, two negative words often do make a positive. When two negative words are put together in a sentence, they cancel each other out. This is called a double negative.

In most cases it is incorrect to write a double negative. Often, people who use double negatives end up saying the opposite of what they mean. For example:

There wasn't no soup left.

This sentence actually means "There was soup left." To fix this sentence, you might change *wasn't* to *was* or *no* to *any.* Either of these revised sentences are correct:

There wasn't any soup left.

There was no soup left.

When using negative adverbs such as *hardly, scarcely, rarely,* and *barely,* you should also avoid double negatives. Avoid phrases such as *barely never* or *hardly none.* Instead, use *barely ever* or *hardly any.*

In some cases two negative words do not create a double negative. If two negative words are in different parts of a compound sentence, they do not make a double negative. Adding the introductory word *no* at the beginning of a sentence also does not create a double negative. For example:

Tommy isn't going, so I'm not going either.

No, we aren't going to the amusement park.

When you write, keep an eye out for sentences with more than one negative word. Check to make sure that you have not written a double negative.

ACTIVITY C **Choose the word that best completes each sentence. Avoid double negatives.**

1. Marcos didn't invite (anyone   no one) to the birthday party.
2. I have (anything   nothing) to wear to the dance.
3. We've hardly (ever   never) seen a tomato like that.
4. There are barely (any   none) crackers left in the box.
5. I couldn't find (nothing   anything) I wanted to buy.
6. Nobody brought (any   no) lawn chairs.
7. Aiden hasn't (never   ever) seen the Grand Canyon.

ACTIVITY D **Find the sentences that contain double negatives. If a sentence contains a double negative, rewrite it.**

1. I'd never want to live nowhere but here.
2. If Tina can't stay up late, then you can't either.
3. No, I haven't been to Peru.
4. Paulette couldn't scarcely believe what had happened.
5. There aren't no sandwiches left.
6. Margo has never been skiing before.
7. There aren't no photos of your birthday party.
8. No, Kate is not taking her jacket with her.

ACTIVITY E **Revise the following paragraphs by removing the double negatives.**

It wasn't nothing that Detective Hopkins had ever seen before. The money wasn't in the safe, but he didn't know what had happened. He couldn't find nobody who knew the combination. There weren't no fingerprints on the safe, either.

"Don't you have no ideas, Detective Hopkins?" his assistant asked.

"No, I don't," the detective replied.

WRITER'S CORNER

Write a short paragraph using negative words. Avoid double negatives. Trade papers with a partner. Check your partner's paragraph to be sure your partner avoided double negatives.

Rambling Sentences

Have you ever read a very long sentence? When you got to the end, did you wonder what the sentence was about? Sentences that go on too long are rambling sentences.

A rambling sentence contains too many thoughts or ideas. You can often spot a rambling sentence because it contains several conjunctions such as *and, or,* or *but.*

Read this rambling sentence.

> **Students in the fourth grade said art was their favorite subject, mainly because they enjoy painting, and their next favorites were gym, music, and science, and their favorite part of the day was recess because they got to play with their friends.**

Look at all the ideas in the sentence. The writer first names the students' favorite subject, art, and explains why it was chosen. Next, the writer lists students' other favorite subjects. Finally, the writer names students' favorite part of the day and explains why they enjoy it.

The best way to fix a rambling sentence is to break it into separate sentences. You can break it in places where conjunctions are used. Read these revised sentences. Which version is easier to understand?

> **Students in the fourth grade said art was their favorite subject, mainly because they enjoy painting. Their next favorites were gym, music, and science. Their favorite part of the day was recess because they got to play with their friends.**

ACTIVITY A Revise each rambling sentence to make it into two or more shorter, clearer sentences.

1. One day I went skateboarding in my cousin's neighborhood, but I forgot to look where I was going, and some sticks were in my way and I fell.

2. Our class learned how to use a computer the first month of school, and then we learned how to write a computer program, and one group even created a math game.

3. Jeremy built a model of the space shuttle for the science fair, and he was excited when he won first prize, and he received a trophy.

4. The artist unwrapped the wet ball of clay, and she molded it in her hands, and then she used the potter's wheel to make a vase.

5. George picked blueberries on the farm, but he was in a hurry, and he didn't pick them carefully, and he got stains on his shirt.

6. Dogs are one of the most popular pets because they are loving animals, and they are fun to play with, and they can protect your home by scaring away any strangers.

7. Students in Mrs. Pekin's class are happy to be taking part in a book-reading contest, and they said the contest would give them a chance to win some great prizes or at least allow them to read some new books.

8. Yesterday as we were having lunch we heard sirens and we ran to the window and saw an ambulance at the house across the street.

9. There were many stands of fruit on display and Jessica found it difficult to choose a piece of fruit from among them, but she finally selected a mango for her dessert.

WRITER'S CORNER

Write one long sentence combining five things you like to do. Use the conjunctions *and*, *but*, or *or*. Trade your sentence with a partner and revise your partner's sentence by dividing it into more than one sentence. Do the revised sentences sound better?

Revising Sentences

Often there is more than one way to revise a rambling sentence. A rambling sentence with four ideas could be broken into four short sentences. It could be broken into two sentences, or two short sentences and one longer sentence. Read the sentence below.

Hundreds of people attended the game, and they enjoyed the songs played by the marching band, and the crowd cheered hard for the football team but the team lost in overtime.

Here are two ways this sentence could be revised.

Hundreds of people attended the game. They enjoyed the songs played by the marching band. The crowd cheered hard for the football team. The team lost in overtime.

Hundreds of people attended the game, and they enjoyed the songs played by the marching band. The crowd cheered hard for the football team, but the team lost in overtime.

In the first revision, each idea is given its own sentence. In the second revision, two related ideas are included in each sentence. How else could this sentence be revised?

ACTIVITY B Revise one of these paragraphs. Turn the rambling sentences into shorter, clearer sentences.

A. Jenny brushed Pegasus down and threw a saddle blanket and pad over his back before she went to get his saddle from the tack room, but by the time she returned, he had reached around and pulled the pad and blanket off and dropped them on the sawdust-covered floor. "Oh, you're going to be like that," she scolded as she picked them up and brushed them off, but Pegasus wasn't done, and he kicked over the trash can that was directly behind him.

B. Quilts are beautiful bedspreads, and they are made by sewing together many types of cloth patches. Old shirts and dresses and other scraps of colorful clothing are good material for patches, and some people even go to used-clothing stores to buy the fabric for these patches. In the past neighbors, friends, and relatives gave one another scraps of clothing to make the quilts, and so for each scrap there was an interesting story to tell about its owner.

ACTIVITY C Revise each rambling sentence in a way that makes it clearer and easier to read.

1. The motorcyclist stopped at the top of the hill and looked down the hill, and he saw a quiet little village below that he could visit and he headed down the hill.

2. Mrs. Powell said she loves her job as a librarian and she enjoys reading to the students or helping them find books, but as a child she wanted to be a TV star.

3. The town of Williamsville was founded in 1823 and had 200 people by 1840, but a great fire caused many people to move away in 1852.

4. Doctors say that people should eat a balanced diet in order to get all the vitamins they need, and some people take additional vitamins, but it is important to check with a doctor to make sure they're the right vitamins.

5. The black horses were hitched to a large wagon, and they wore ornate harnesses and attracted the attention of all the people at the parade.

6. Gus and I practiced our duet during lunch for over a month and his suggestions really made our song sound better.

7. On one particularly hot summer day, Claudia called a few friends to meet her at the pool so she then packed a lunch and rode her bike to meet them for an afternoon of swimming.

WRITER'S CORNER

Revise your partner's rambling sentence from the Writer's Corner on page 453 by combining some ideas differently. Break the sentence into smaller sentences by removing the conjunctions. Which sentences do you think are more effective?

Library Catalogs

The Library Catalog

How quickly can you find information in the library? The first place to look is the library catalog. It tells you exactly where to find the information you need.

Today most libraries have their catalogs on computer. These electronic catalogs include entries listed by title, author, or subject.

Electronic catalogs are easy to use. All you have to do is type the word into the search box and the computer will give you a choice of entries. With this list you can find the books you need.

When you type in an author's name, for example, the computer will list all the books by the author that are in the library. The computer will also list any books about the author that the library has.

Here is an example of what a student found after typing the word *horses* into the search box.

Barrie Park Library System

Search was: horses

232 keyword matches

2 author matches

38 subject matches

Browse titles beginning with *horses*

Browse authors beginning with *horses*

Browse subjects beginning with *horses*

Enter terms: horses | SEARCH

When the student clicked on *Browse subjects beginning with horses,* she found a list of books on that subject. When she clicked on one of the books, she saw the following screen.

Barrie Park Library System

Search was: horses

Title: Galloping Through History
Author: Johnson, Rose
Call No: 575.84JOH
Publisher: Freestyle Books: Newark, NJ, 2004
197p. illus.
Summary: A survey of the evolution of the horse through history and its domestication by humans.
Subjects: Horses, evolution, mammals, natural selection, domestication

Where to find it:	**Copies:**	**Available:**
North Branch Library	2	1

ACTIVITY A **Use the example electronic catalog entry above to answer the following questions.**

1. What is this book about?
2. Who is the author of this book?
3. At what library can this book be found?
4. How many copies are available?
5. What other words might a person use to search for similar books on this subject?
6. Does this book have illustrations?

WRITER'S CORNER

Choose a topic and write three questions you would like to answer about the topic. Look up books about the topic in the library catalog. List two books that might be helpful in answering your questions.

Finding Information

Fiction books and nonfiction books are kept in separate sections in the library. Fiction books are usually arranged by the authors' last names. Nonfiction books are arranged by subject. Nonfiction books are often used for research.

The library catalog tells you where to find the book you need. Just look for the book's call number.

Call Number

Every book has a call number made up of numbers and letters. A call number is the book's address in the library. It tells you where the book lives on the shelves.

First, find the book's call number in the library catalog. What is the call number for the book *Galloping Through History* on page 457?

Write the call number. You will see it on the label on the spine of the book you are looking for.

Dewey Decimal System

Most libraries use a popular system called the Dewey Decimal System to organize books. A library assistant named Melvil Dewey came up with the idea in 1876. His numbers represent different categories of learning.

Melvil Dewey

Here are the 10 basic Dewey categories:

000	Reference works—encyclopedias, newspapers, magazines
100	Philosophy and psychology
200	Religion
300	Social sciences—law, education, customs, everyday life
400	Languages
500	Basic sciences—mathematics, chemistry, botany
600	Applied sciences—technology, medicine, engineering, animals
700	The arts—architecture, painting, music, games, sports
800	Literature—poetry, novels, plays
900	Geography, biography, history

Suppose you are writing a report about butterflies. The call number for the book you want is 595.72 DEN. This shows the Dewey number and the first three letters of the author's last name. All you do is find the shelves numbered 500 and browse until you find the book you want.

ACTIVITY B **Tell what Dewey number you would look for to find these books in the library.**

1. a biography about Abraham Lincoln
2. *World Book Encyclopedia*
3. a book about the French language
4. a book of poetry
5. a book about the Supreme Court
6. a newspaper
7. a book about soccer
8. a book about the geography of Italy

ACTIVITY C **Tell which of these subjects would be found on each numbered shelf in the library.**

1. 600   the human body or children's plays
2. 400   planets or sign language
3. 300   careers or dinosaurs
4. 500   drawing or plants
5. 900   Native Americans or puppets

WRITER'S CORNER

Use the Dewey categories to find a nonfiction book in the library. Look up the book in a library catalog and read the summary of your book.

News Reports

Have you ever watched the news on TV? When you do, you are watching an oral news report. News reports are much like expository articles. News reports tell the audience about a topic, offering important information that focuses on the topic. In this lesson you will present your own news report as part of a class news show.

Choose a Topic

For your news report, think of a topic that will interest your classmates, who will be your audience. You might report on an interesting person at school, an activity students enjoy, or some other topic related to school.

Gather Information

When you have chosen your topic, list several sources you could use in your news report. Then write questions your report should answer, such as *who, what, when, where, why,* and *how.* Interview the people who are sources for your report. Use the library or the Internet to find information. Take notes and write the name of your source below each note.

Organize Your Notes

When you have finished your notes, arrange them in order of importance. Begin your news report with an introduction that includes a topic sentence stating the most important facts about the topic. End with a conclusion that sums up your report.

This is big news!

Tone of Voice

Reporters who deliver news reports usually use a serious tone of voice. They speak clearly and slowly, stating the facts without showing their feelings. If the story is about a lighthearted topic, they might use a cheerful, lively voice.

ACTIVITY A Choose one topic below. Write three questions that a news report about the topic should answer.

A. an author who will be visiting the school

B. the problem of messy desks

C. the new fad of wearing suspenders to school

D. students who find a lost dog

E. the new computer lab planned for the school

F. a fun fest that is set to raise money for the school

G. a summer storm that caused damage in the community

H. the school's girls' soccer team winning the state championship

I. the town's first five-mile run

ACTIVITY B Use the information gathered below to write an introduction for a news report about the topic. Write at least two sentences. Practice delivering the introduction.

- The music teacher is leading a school musical.
- Mr. Ramirez is the music teacher.
- Fourth graders and fifth graders will be in the musical.
- The musical will be *Peter Pan*.
- The musical will take place April 29 in the auditorium.
- Students are excited about being in the musical.

SPEAKER'S CORNER

Interview a partner about a topic that he or she is familiar with. It might be a hobby or a sport your partner plays. Take notes. Get answers to the questions *who, what, when, where, why,* and *how.* Ask any other questions that would help make a complete news report. Organize your notes.

Create Your News Show

In the news you see on TV, a team of reporters works together to present a news show. The reporters take turns delivering their reports. They use visual aids such as photos, film clips, or maps. Sometimes the reporters interview people. The show takes place in a newsroom, with a news desk, microphones, and a sign with the name of the show.

You can create a news show in your classroom. Begin by meeting with a group of four classmates. Work together to decide the order of the reports.

Next, turn your class into a newsroom. Set up a news desk. You could use a toy microphone. You could make a sign that displays the name of your news show.

Finally, make any visual aids that go with your report. You might show an object or a photo that relates to the report. You might even interview a classmate during the show.

Practice

Before presenting your news show, you need to practice. It will be helpful to practice a few times so you can give a good presentation.

Use a clear, serious voice. Speak directly to your audience instead of reading from your notes. You might make cue cards by writing your notes in large print on poster board. Ask a classmate to sit in front of the audience with the cue cards and flip them as you speak.

Practice presenting any visual aids that go with your report. If you plan to interview someone from class, introduce the person before the interview. Go over the questions you will ask and practice the interview a few times.

The first speaker should introduce the name of the show, saying something like "Welcome to Grade 4 Action News. Here is our top story of the day."

When each speaker finishes, he or she should introduce the next speaker. A speaker might say, "And now here's Paul Lewis, who will tell us about our school's new holiday food drive." End your news show by thanking the audience.

Listening to News Reports

When you watch another group present its news show, listen to the reports carefully. Think of any questions you have that were not answered in the report. Give feedback to the group, saying what you liked and asking any questions you have.

ACTIVITY C Work in a group of four to create a news show. Prepare the report you began in the Speaker's Corner on page 461. Prepare any visuals for the report. If you plan to use cue cards, write them on poster board.

ACTIVITY D Set up your newsroom, using the tips from this lesson. Decide the order of the reports. Then practice presenting your news show. Practice speaking in a clear voice. If you use cue cards, ask another student to hold them during your report.

SPEAKER'S CORNER

Present your news show to the class. Set up everything carefully before the show. Speak loudly and clearly, talking directly to the audience. Use your notes or cue cards to help you remember what to say. When you watch your classmates' news shows, listen carefully and give feedback at the end.

Tech Tip Use a video camera to record your news show.

Prewriting and Drafting

What interesting people do you know? What new things are happening in your town or school? Are your friends enjoying any new games, hobbies, or fads? Any of these topics can be fun to explore in an expository article.

Prewriting

André's fourth-grade class was making a class newspaper, and the students were the reporters. Each student was asked to think of a topic for an article. André began by brainstorming ideas for articles. Next, he thought of questions he wanted to ask and gathered information for his article.

Choosing a Topic

André's teacher, Miss Mangus, suggested that each student write a feature article. A feature article is a fun article about a topic that is not too serious. She gave her students these topic suggestions.

- an interesting teacher or someone who has done something unusual
- some part of school life, such as a new club or a favorite class
- a special event at school or in the community
- a new trend, such as a clothing style or kind of music
- a favorite game or activity that many students enjoy

Miss Mangus encouraged students to choose a topic for which they could interview at least a few students.

André used his teacher's ideas to help him think of a topic. He made a list of  topics that fit each suggestion. Then he chose his favorite topic.

André decided to write an article about the touch football games that the fourth and fifth graders played before school. He could describe the games and interview some of the students who played.

Your Turn

Use Miss Mangus's suggestions to help you choose a topic for your article. Write at least one idea for each suggestion. Then choose the idea you think will be the most interesting for your audience.

Gathering Information

After choosing his topic, André thought about the sources he could use to gather his information. He knew he could use his own personal experience because he played in the games himself.

He could interview other people who played in the games. He could also interview Mr. Nelson, the school gym teacher, since he was an expert on football and exercise. André

━━━━━━━━━━━━━━━━━━━━━━
👓 Organization
━━━━━━━━━━━━━━━━━━━━━━

could look on the Internet for articles about touch football. Next, André wrote questions he wanted to answer in his article. Using these answers will help him organize his writing in order of importance. He wrote these questions:

> Who plays in the games?
> What happens when they play?
> Where and when do they play?
> Why did they start playing?
> How do the kids like playing?
> Is it a good game for kids our age?
> Is playing touch football good for you?

André wrote everything he knew about the topic. Then he interviewed some students who played and Mr. Nelson. He asked them some of the questions he had written. André also looked on the Internet for facts about touch football.

Your Turn

Think about sources you could use for your article. Try to think of at least two different sources other than yourself.

- Can you use your own experience?
- Are there students or adults you could interview?
- Are there any books, magazines, or Web sites you could use?

Make a list of questions you would like to answer in your article. Then gather your information, using the sources you thought of. Write anything you know about the topic, but leave out your own opinion. Interview the people on your list and use any other sources.

Drafting

André used the information he had gathered to write his article. He stated the topic of the article in the introduction. He organized the article in order of importance and ended his article with a quotation.

Football in the Morning

Have you seen the kids playing football every morning in the back field of Twin Meadows Elementary School? They're the fourth and fifth graders. They have been playing this fun game before school since the beginning of the year.

It started when fifth graders Joey Padrone and Sanjay Kumar started playing catch after the bus dropped them off before school. They come on the first bus, so they have extra time before the bell rings. Soon other fourth and fifth graders started playing. When they had enough players, they decided to play a real game.

Touch football is a good game for kids. Mr. Nelson, the gym teacher, thinks that it's also good exercise.

"Any time kids are being active and playing together. I'm happy," Mr. Nelson said.

The games are'nt as long as real football games, and usually about 10 kids play. So far, the teams have been the fifth graders against the fourth graders.

"They usually win, because they're better," said Peter Cardillo. "But we won the last game. John Walsh got this great touchdown at the last minute."

Sanjay Kumar said "he started playing just because he was bored, but now he's always excited to play," and other students said playing football before school is much more fun than just standing around and talking.

Your Turn

Use the information you gathered to write your article.

1. Start with an interesting introduction that tells what the article is about. Include a topic sentence that states the most important facts about the article.

2. Write the body of the article, using information that supports the topic sentence. Begin with the most important facts. Answer the questions *who, what, when, where, why,* and *how* in your article.

3. End your article with a conclusion that sums up your information. You might end with a quotation that leaves your readers thinking about the topic.

Using Sources

There are many ways to use your sources in an article. Here are some suggestions.

Personal knowledge: You do not need to name the source if the fact is something you saw or already knew. Just state what you know as fact.

People: If a fact comes from a person you interviewed, name the person in the sentence. You could use a quotation, which should include the person's exact words.

You could also use your own words to

 Voice

explain what a source said. If you do this, do not use quotation marks. However, be sure to name the source.

Written sources: If you use a written source, such as a book, an article, or a Web site, name the source after you state the fact. You do not need to name the source if the fact is something you could find in lots of places.

Prewriting

Drafting

Content Editing

Revising

Copyediting

Proofreading

Publishing

Editor's Workshop

Content Editing

André's expository article was full of information from different sources, and it gave the most important information about the topic. He knew that he could make it even better, however, by content editing it.

First, he read his draft again to make sure it made sense. He checked his notes to make sure he had the important information connected with the right sources. André also made sure his quotations were right. He used the Content Editor's Checklist below.

After reading his draft, André asked his classmate Lauren to read it. He thought she might notice if anything was unclear or missing.

Content Editor's Checklist

- [ ] Does the introduction state the topic of the article?
- [ ] Does the body give all the important information in order of importance?
- [ ] Does the information include sources when necessary?
- [ ] Have the writer's opinions been left out?
- [ ] Do quotations use the source's exact words?
- [ ] Have unimportant details been left out?

This article is a winner.

Lauren read André's article twice and checked it, using the Content Editor's Checklist. She started by telling him what she liked. She thought the quotations were good and the article's topic was clearly stated. Next, she gave these suggestions.

- In the first paragraph, you call touch football a "fun game." Do you have a source for that, or is it just your opinion?
- Since this article is for the school paper, your audience will know which school you're talking about, so you don't have to say it.
- The sentence about why Joey and Sanjay come early doesn't seem very important.
- Some people might get confused when Peter Cardillo says that "they usually win." Maybe you should say what team he's on.
- The quotation from Mr. Nelson is good, but it doesn't seem as important as the other information. Maybe it would fit better at the end.

André thanked Lauren for her suggestions. He liked her ideas and decided to use all of them when he revised his draft.

Your Turn

Read your draft, using the Content Editor's Checklist.

- Trade your draft with a partner.
- Use the checklist to take notes on your partner's draft.
- Tell your partner what you liked about his or her draft.
- Suggest changes your partner could make.

Thank your partner for his or her comments. Think about making any changes that could improve your draft.

Writer's Tip Be open to your partner's ideas for your draft.

Prewriting

Drafting

Content Editing

Revising

Copyediting

Proofreading

Publishing

Revising

This is how André revised his draft after listening to Lauren's suggestions and using his own ideas.

Football in the Morning

Have you seen the kids playing football every morning in the back field of ~~Twin~~ ~~Meadows Elementary School~~ *the school*? They're the fourth and fifth graders. They have been playing ~~this fun game~~ before school since the beginning of the year.

It started when fifth graders Joey Padrone and Sanjay Kumar started playing catch after the bus dropped them off before school. ~~They come on the first bus, so they have extra time before the bell rings.~~ Soon other fourth and fifth graders started playing. When they had enough players, they decided to play a real game.

Touch football is a good game for kids. Mr. Nelson, the gym teacher, thinks that it's also good exercise.

"Any time kids are being active and playing together. I'm happy," Mr. Nelson said.

The games are'nt as long as real football games, and usually about 10 kids play. So far, the teams have been the fifth graders against the fourth graders.

"They usually win, because they're ~~better~~ *older*," said Peter Cardillo *, a fourth grader*. "But we won the last game. John Walsh got this great touchdown at the last minute."

Sanjay Kumar said "he started playing just because he was bored, but now he's always excited to play," and other students said playing football before school is much more fun than just standing around and talking.

Notice the changes André made to improve his draft.

- Was André able to prove that football was a "fun game"? What did he do?
- Did he think the name of the school was necessary? What did he do?
- What sentence did he take out? Why?
- How did André explain which team Peter Cardillo was on?
- Where did André move the quotation from Mr. Nelson? Why?

André made one other change to his article. When he looked over his notes, he realized he had used the wrong word in his quotation from Peter Cardillo. Peter had said that the fifth graders usually won because they were older, not because they were better.

Look over the changes André made to his draft. Would you have made any other changes?

Prewriting

Drafting

Content Editing

Revising

Copyediting

Proofreading

Publishing

Editor's Workshop

Copyediting and Proofreading

Copyediting

After revising his draft, André needed to copyedit. He wanted to make sure that his sentences all made sense and that he had used the right words. He used this Copyeditor's Checklist.

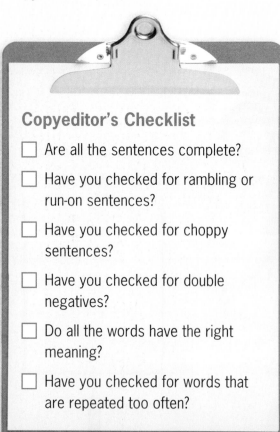

Copyeditor's Checklist

☐ Are all the sentences complete?

☐ Have you checked for rambling or run-on sentences?

☐ Have you checked for choppy sentences?

☐ Have you checked for double negatives?

☐ Do all the words have the right meaning?

☐ Have you checked for words that are repeated too often?

After going over his draft, André decided to make a few changes. The first thing he noticed was a rambling sentence. The sentence that started with "Sanjay Kumar" was too long and had too many ideas. He decided to put Sanjay's reason in one sentence and the other students' reasons in another sentence.

Sentence Fluency

Finally, André realized that calling touch football a "good" game for kids did not use the best word. He was trying to say that lots of kids liked it, a fact that he had learned from the Internet. He changed the word *good* to *popular*.

Word Choice

Your Turn

Copyedit your draft, using the Copyeditor's Checklist. Make any changes that will improve your draft.

Proofreading

After copyediting, André's draft still needed to be proofread. He asked his classmate Isabel to proofread it. She would check  the article for mistakes in spelling, grammar, and punctuation. She used this Proofreader's Checklist.

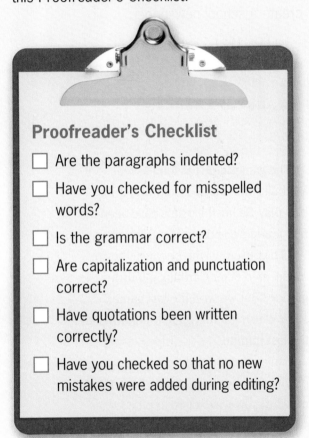

Proofreader's Checklist

☐ Are the paragraphs indented?

☐ Have you checked for misspelled words?

☐ Is the grammar correct?

☐ Are capitalization and punctuation correct?

☐ Have quotations been written correctly?

☐ Have you checked so that no new mistakes were added during editing?

Isabel enjoyed reading André's article. She had wondered how the kids started playing football in the back field. She also pointed out a few mistakes in André's draft.

Isabel found a place where the punctuation for a quotation was written incorrectly. She saw that André had used his own words to write what Sanjay had said. For that reason André did not need quotation marks in the sentence. Next, she noticed that his first paragraph was not indented.

André thanked Isabel for proofreading his draft and made the corrections she suggested.

Grammar in Action

Can you find the contraction in Andre's article that does not use the apostrophe correctly? See Section 7.8 for help.

Your Turn

Read over your article, using the Proofreader's Checklist. Trade drafts with a partner and proofread your partner's draft. Share your suggestions. Make any corrections that will improve your draft.

Prewriting

Drafting

Content Editing

Revising

Copyediting

Proofreading

Publishing

Publishing

André checked over his draft once more, typed it on a computer, and added a photo. He put a title and his name at the top and printed out his article. Then he combined it with other students' expository articles to create a school newspaper.

Football in the Morning

André Andrews

Have you seen the kids playing football every morning in the back field of the school? They're the fourth and fifth graders. They have been playing before school since the beginning of the year.

It started when fifth graders Joey Padrone and Sanjay Kumar started playing catch after the bus dropped them off before school. Soon other fourth and fifth graders started playing. When they had enough players, they decided to play a real game.

The games aren't as long as real football games, and usually about 10 kids play. So far, the teams have been the fifth graders against the fourth graders.

"They usually win, because they're older," said Peter Cardillo, a fourth grader. "But we won the last game. John Walsh got this great touchdown at the last minute."

Sanjay Kumar said he started playing just because he was bored, but now he's always excited to play. Other students said playing football before school is much more fun than just standing around and talking.

Touch football is a popular game for kids. Mr. Nelson, the gym teacher, thinks that it's also good exercise.

"Any time kids are being active and playing together, I'm happy," Mr. Nelson said.

Publishing is the moment when writers

 Presentation share their finished work. There are many ways you can publish your expository article.

 If you have a class newspaper, you might include a few of the articles in each issue. You might print them out in narrow columns, as in a newspaper. Put the name of your newspaper in large type at the top. Make copies of your newspaper so that the school can read all about what is happening in your school and community.

 Videotape classmates' expository pieces in a TV news setting as if they were special feature segments on a daily news show.

 Create a classroom news Web site. Your classmates may have photos or illustrations for their articles. Scan those and include them in your Web site. These are interesting items to attach to the articles.

 Have your class Web site on hand for Parents' Night. You might show it as a PowerPoint presentation.

Your Turn

Read over your draft once more to make sure that everything is correct. Be especially careful that the names of people in your article are spelled correctly and that the quotations are correct.

Once you are ready, print out or neatly handwrite a final copy. Now it is your turn to choose a way to publish your article.

Prewriting

Drafting

Content Editing

Revising

Copyediting

Proofreading

Publishing

Research Reports

LiNK ## Yukon Gold

by Charlotte Foltz Jones

Gold!

The word is electrifying. Even in a world where most of us see gold only in jewelry or as a decoration on our mother's dishes, *gold* still stirs excitement and visions of great wealth.

But a century ago, gold was magical. It could turn a poor person into a millionaire, and there were many poor people.

The economy of the United States fell into a depression in 1893. In the "Panic of 1893," 156 railroads claimed bankruptcy, 15,000 businesses failed, and 642 banks closed, wiping out the savings of thousands of people. One quarter of the country's industries stopped production. Four million people out of a population of 65 million could not get jobs. A man felt lucky if he could get work for a day or two. . . .

> Research reports catch a reader's attention early and show factual information in an organized manner, as shown in *Yukon Gold*.

Become a Healthy Eater

Natalia Tricoci
Room 212B

Did you know that one-quarter of American school-age children do not have healthy eating habits? Some health workers blame TV. Others say parents and children are responsible for what they eat. Experts agree, however, that children should ignore their TV sets and change their eating habits to live healthy lives.

Marlene Most and John Windhauser of Louisiana State University studied how TV commercials affect the children who watch them. On Saturday mornings there are almost as many commercials for fast-food restaurants as there are for breakfast cereals. Children are the main audiences watching these commercials. The fast-food restaurants spend more time talking about the size of the portions than the food itself in these commercials. With most Americans already eating more than they should, Dr. Most warns that making portion sizes larger could be dangerous.

It is important to choose healthy foods and reasonable portion sizes. However, don't expect that just by making the right meal choices, you will be able to keep your weight at a healthy level. You also need to watch the way that you eat. It takes about 15 to 20 minutes for your stomach to tell your brain that you are full. If you gobble down a lot of food quickly, you are more likely to overeat. When your stomach says, "I've had enough," stop eating.

Remember that TV commercials are trying to sell products, not keep you healthy. Ignore them. Follow these healthy eating tips and you will be healthier and happier.

Nutrition Facts
Serving Size 3 oz. (85g)
Amount Per Serving
Calories

What Makes a Good Research Report?

A log cabin in New Salem, Illinois

A research report is a formal paper. There are rules that you must follow. Do not use contractions or abbreviations. Always give credit to the sources of your information. The excerpt on this page uses formal language and avoids using a contraction.

A research report gives information. The writer chooses a topic and finds facts about it in different sources. Then the writer writes this information in a way that gives readers a new understanding of the topic.

Choosing a Topic

When you choose a topic, pick one that interests you and the audience that you are writing for. Choose a topic that is broad enough to find information to write about, but narrow enough to cover in two or three pages.

For example, you might be interested in the Old West. You can find millions of facts about the Old West. You could not write about the Old West in only a few pages. You must think of a narrower topic. You could write about the Pony Express, cattle drives, or train robberies in the Old West.

When you have chosen a topic, think of things that you would like to know about it. Ask questions that you would like to have answered. Use the questions to help you decide what information to look for in your research.

Researching Your Topic

When you look for information about your topic, use more than one source for a variety of ideas. Use different types of sources, such as magazine articles, encyclopedias, nonfiction books, and Web sites. Write each source in which you find information.

Refer to your questions as you research. Don't read an entire book. Use the contents page or the index to find the answers to your questions. If your research brings up new questions, write them and research those questions too.

Be sure to use your own words to rewrite the information you find. Doing that will help you understand what you have read.

ACTIVITY A Read each pair of topics. Tell which one would be better for a research report. Explain your choice.

1. a. Charles Lindbergh   b. the history of flight
2. a. golden retrievers   b. hunting dogs
3. a. the U.S. Space Program   b. the first person on the moon
4. a. electric trains   b. toys
5. a. American railroads   b. the first tracks across America

ACTIVITY B Read each topic. Decide which two sources below it would have good information for a research report about that topic. Then tell why the third source would not have good information.

1. Lion
   a. an encyclopedia, volume L
   b. the movie *The Lion King*
   c. the Web site www.animalfacts.edu

2. St. Louis, Missouri
   a. the magazine *American Cities*
   b. a student's Web site about the Gateway Arch
   c. an encyclopedia, volume M

WRITER'S CORNER

Look through a nonfiction book from the library. Make a list of narrow topics that the book covers. Choose one topic. Write three questions you might want to answer if you researched the topic.

Grammar in Action. → What kind of sentence asks a question, and what end punctuation is used? See Section 7.1.

Settling the Americas

Scientists have never found archaeological evidence of these first Americans, even though they maintained a stable population for a long period. In view of the new findings, that's not surprising. Since Beringia now lies underwater, Mulligan suspects that any remains they left behind are now buried at sea.

Emily Sohn,
Science News for Kids

Children of Beringian heritage

Organizing Your Research Report

When you have finished doing your research, you will have many notes from several sources. You need to organize all this information into writing that flows from one idea to the next.

Introduction

The introduction should tell what the report is about. State the topic in a topic sentence. Try to catch your audience's interest early. Make your readers curious about your topic with an unusual fact or an interesting question.

Body

The body of your research report is where you include the facts that you found in your research. All the information should be important to your topic. Leave out anything that is not important. Give each main idea its own paragraph.

Answer the questions that you asked yourself before you began researching your topic. If some facts raise new questions, find answers to those questions. Your audience will probably wonder about them too.

Organize the information so that similar facts are grouped together. If you are writing about peregrine falcons, finish the section about what they look like before you write about where they live.

Conclusion

The conclusion should sum up your report. The end of your report might repeat the most important information or leave readers with an interesting thought, as shown in the excerpt on this page. Do not introduce new information in the conclusion. A good research report will make readers want to find out more about the topic.

ACTIVITY C Read over page 477 and answer the following questions.

1. What is the topic of this report?
2. Which sentence is the topic sentence?
3. What is the main idea of the second paragraph?
4. What is the main idea of the third paragraph?
5. Does the conclusion fit the guidelines from this lesson? Explain.

ACTIVITY D Read each group of sentences. Tell whether each sentence would belong in the introduction, body, or conclusion.

1. a. Bull riding is the most dangerous event in a rodeo.
   b. Rodeos are hard to beat for bone-jarring excitement.
   c. Do you like to watch contests between people and animals?

2. a. Your parents can probably remember when there were no remote controls.
   b. Garage doors had remote controls before TVs did.
   c. The problem now is remembering where the remote control is.

3. a. Siberian tigers are rare creatures, and we should do our best to save them.
   b. Siberian tigers, the largest living cats in the world, possess both grace and beauty.
   c. This tiger's winter white and yellow top coat protects it in its snowy habitat.

WRITER'S CORNER

Think of a topic that might make a good research report. For the introduction, write a statement that catches the audience's attention. List three details you might include in the body of the research report.

Tech Tip Post your attention-getter on a class blog for feedback.

Researching

A big part of writing a research report is finding information. You can look in books, magazines, and on the Internet. Before you begin your research, look at your questions to help you get started. When you use books to do research, go to the sections that are likely to answer your questions. When you use the Internet, use keywords from your questions in your searches.

Taking Notes

When you take notes, don't just write facts on a sheet of paper. Be organized. One good way is to use note cards. Write one fact on each card, using your own words. This will help you make certain that you understand the ideas.

Look at the bottom of this note card. Whenever you take notes, include where you found the information and who wrote it. That way you can find the information again if you need to.

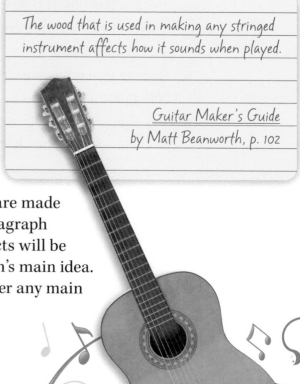

The wood that is used in making any stringed instrument affects how it sounds when played.

Guitar Maker's Guide
by Matt Beanworth, p. 102

After you have taken your notes, arrange them into groups of similar facts. The facts in each group should be about one main idea, such as "what guitars are made of." Each group will become a paragraph in the body of your report. The facts will be details that support the paragraph's main idea. If you have facts that don't fit under any main idea, leave them out.

ACTIVITY A The following groups of facts are on note cards. Find the fact that does not belong in each group.

Group A

1. Koalas have thick, gray coats of fur.
2. They have pouches where they raise their babies.
3. The forests where many koalas live are disappearing.
4. Their paws are adapted for gripping tree branches.
5. Koalas eat only eucalyptus leaves.

Group B

1. Confucius was born in China in 551 BC.
2. Confucius believed in doing what is right and loving others.
3. He thought people should rule by example, not by force.
4. He hoped his ideas would help people rule themselves.
5. Confucius felt that people are responsible for their actions.

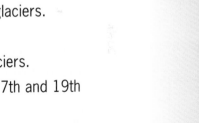

ACTIVITY B The following facts are not organized. Organize them into two groups. Tell what the main idea of each group might be.

1. About 10 percent of the earth is covered with glaciers.
2. Glaciers move slowly over hundreds of years.
3. Most of the world's fresh water is stored in glaciers.
4. Glaciers moved somewhat south between the 17th and 19th centuries because of the cool climate.
5. Glaciers advance to the south and retreat to the north depending on climate change.
6. Almost 90 percent of a glacier is below water.

WRITER'S CORNER

Find five facts from a nonfiction book. Write the facts in your own words.

Listing Sources

At the end of a research report, it is important to tell your audience where you found the information. Listing your sources will also tell them where to look if they want to find out more about the topic. Here are the main ways of listing books, encyclopedia entries, articles, and Web sites.

Galileo experiments with gravity.

Books

When listing a book, write the author first, starting with the last name. Then write the name of the book and underline it.

> **Haywood, Elijah. <u>Galileo's Mystery</u>.**

Encyclopedias

For an encyclopedia entry, write the name of the entry in quotation marks. Then name the encyclopedia and underline it.

> **"Industrial Revolution." <u>The New World Encyclopedia</u>.**

Newspaper and Magazine Articles

For a newspaper or a magazine article, write the author's name, the title of the article, the underlined name of the newspaper or magazine, and the publication date.

> **Previn, Hae Jung. "Whatever Happened to Slide Projectors?" <u>Progress Weekly</u>, December 15, 2010.**

Web Sites

When listing an article from a Web site, write the author's name, the article title, and the Web address in angle brackets (< >). If you cannot find the author's name, begin with the article title.

> **McCarthy, Lauren. "Life of a Ballerina." <www.ballet41.org>.**

ACTIVITY C Read each source. Tell whether it is from a book, an encyclopedia, a magazine article, or a Web site.

1. "Lightning." *World Book.*
2. Lilly, James. "The Morgan Horse."<www.breeds.horses.edu>.
3. Joyce, Emma. "Using a Macro Lens." *Click and Capture.* August 2011.
4. Armstrong, Andrea. *Ocean Wonders.*

ACTIVITY D Use the guidelines on page 484 to list the following sources as they would appear at the end of a research report.

1. The book Bronze Age, which was written by Julio Alvarez.
2. The article "Russia Says Good-bye to a Favorite Son" by Natasha Harding, which appeared in the October 7, 2005, Dallas Morning News.
3. Nancy Cleary's Web page titled "Bats," which can be found at www.pageturner.net/cleary021.htm.
4. The November 2010 issue of Reader's Monthly, where the article "Voyager from the Deep" by Tino Sanchez was found.
5. Carson Peterson's biography of Abraham Lincoln, which is titled Presidential Timber.
6. The Web page titled "Kinds of Mica," which can be found at www.stonecenter.edu/mica.htm. The Web site does not say who wrote the page.
7. The entry for "Meerkat" from Encyclopaedia Britannica.

Meerkat

WRITER'S CORNER

Find two sources for a topic, such as a book, an encyclopedia, an article, or a Web site. Write one fact you learned from each source. Then list the source, using the guidelines on page 484.

Reference Sources

Today people can find information about almost anything in the world. There are so many sources of information that you can do research on just about any topic that you choose. To do thorough research, be sure to use different sources.

The Library

Libraries are an excellent resource when researching information for a report. Most libraries have a section just for reference books, such as encyclopedias, atlases, and almanacs. These books contain information about many different topics. When you use any reference source, write where your information came from.

Always use the most recent reference book that you can find. Check the publication date, which can usually be found on the page right after book's title page.

A good resource in any library is the librarian. If you are unable to find the information that you need, ask a librarian. He or she will help you find the best sources for the information.

Encyclopedias

An encyclopedia is a reference source that contains general information about people, places, things, and events. An encyclopedia may be only one book or it may be a set of many books. Encyclopedia articles are listed in alphabetical order by the topic.

Almanacs

Almanacs are printed every year. They contain very recent facts. They can tell you the population of Brazil, the winner of the 2009 World Series, or last year's total rainfall in South Dakota. Always use the most recent almanac that you can find. Almanacs organize information by type. Use the index to find the information that you need.

Atlases

Atlases are books of maps. They show geographical features such as rivers, lakes, and mountains. Atlases also show political or human-made features, such as roads, cities, and borders. Atlases may also tell the climates and populations of countries. Atlases often organize their maps by region. Look in the index for the locations you are researching.

ACTIVITY A Tell if you would use an encyclopedia, an almanac, or an atlas to find information about these topics. What word would you look under to find the topic in the source?

1. how diamonds are formed
2. the largest lake in Minnesota
3. the discovery of oil in Pennsylvania
4. the coldest location in America last year
5. all the states that border Iowa
6. the population of France
7. the history of the automobile
8. the best highway to take between Phoenix and Tucson, Arizona
9. recent Olympic Games champions

WRITER'S CORNER

Use a reference source in the library to find five facts about a country you would like to visit. Write what you find.

The Internet

The Internet contains more information than any other reference source. This information is often more recent than other sources. It can be posted immediately without waiting for books or magazines to be printed.

Search Engines

Search engines can help you find information on the Internet. To use a search engine, first type a keyword or words into the search box. Use exact words that will help you find only sites about your topic. Leave out the articles *a, an,* or *the.* Then click on the word *Search.* The search engine will look through the Internet for Web sites that contain the keyword and list those sites for you. If you do not know how to use a search engine, ask a librarian for help.

Web Sites

When you use information from the Internet, you must consider the site to decide if the information is reliable.

To decide whether a Web site is reliable, check the letters at the end of the address. Here is what a few of them mean.

.com	commercial sites
.org	sites created by organizations
.edu	sites created by schools
.gov	government sites

Sites developed by organizations or the government are usually reliable. Be careful, however, when using a .com site. People who create these sites are sometimes more interested in selling a product than in giving correct information. A site ending in .edu might be a good source if created by professors or a university. If created by a student, however, the information might not be reliable.

Always try to find out about the author of a Web site. An expert on the subject is more reliable than someone who is not an expert. Also check when the site was last updated. If it was updated recently, the information might be more current.

ACTIVITY B Write the keywords that would be most useful for an Internet search on each of the following topics.

1. the early life of Harry Truman, the 33rd president of the United States
2. how to make chocolate truffles
3. the number of women in the U.S. Senate
4. how Beatrix Potter got the idea to write *Peter Rabbit*
5. the last flight of Amelia Earhart
6. the Civil War battle of Gettysburg

ACTIVITY C Use the Internet to answer the following questions.

1. How did the town of Truth or Consequences get its name?
2. When did the last dodo bird die?
3. What is Virginia Dare's claim to fame in American history?
4. What name do the French give to the English Channel?
5. Who made the first nonstop flight across the Atlantic?
6. What operation was first performed by Dr. Christiaan Barnard?
7. What is the name of a baby koala?
8. What is the speed of light?

Amelia Earhart

WRITER'S CORNER

With an adult, search the Internet for facts about a famous historical person who interests you. Write five facts that you learned.

 Tech Tip Use two search engines and see which you prefer.

Compound Words

Compound words are single words that are made by joining two or more words together. Often the new word makes sense as soon as you read it. For example, a fireplace is a place for fire, and the backyard is the yard in back of a house. Sometimes the two words don't seem to add up to the longer word. The word *understand* doesn't mean to stand under something. A holdup is either a robbery or a delay, not a support. Make certain that you know what a compound word means before you use it in your writing. If you are not sure, check a dictionary.

What two words make up each of these compound words? Can you use each compound word in a sentence?

sidekick	**background**	**faraway**
daydream	**anybody**	**troublemaker**

ACTIVITY A Match each word in Column A with a word in Column B to make a compound word.

Column A	Column B
1. hand	a. cut
2. some	b. plane
3. hair	c. weight
4. air	d. where
5. light	e. made
6. blue	f. berry

That horse was in my daydream.

ACTIVITY B Complete the compound words in these sentences.

1. I wear _____ glasses to protect my eyes in bright light.
2. We packed our winter clothes in card_____ boxes.
3. I hate when it rains on the week_____.
4. Nicky looked for _____ shells along the beach.
5. The farmer used a pitch_____ to toss hay to his horses.
6. The company's _____ quarters are in Dallas, Texas.
7. I do my _____ work on the desk in my bed_____.
8. Does _____ body want to play _____ ball?
9. The car's _____ lights lit up the high_____.
10. Pinecones come from _____ green trees.
11. I put my invitations in the _____ box.
12. This is perfect snow to build a _____ man.

ACTIVITY C Tell what compound words these clues are describing.

1. A jacket that is not very heavy is _____.
2. When you want to walk quietly, you walk on _____.
3. If you wake up before dawn, you might see the _____.
4. The room where your teacher teaches is a _____.
5. If you are climbing up steps, you are going _____.
6. Saturday and Sunday are called the _____.
7. A robin might get wet in a _____.
8. Someone is at your door when you hear the _____.

WRITER'S CORNER

The words *out*, *under*, *sun*, and *up* are often used in compound words. Write as many compound words as you can containing these words. Then write a short poem using some of the words you wrote.

Post your poems on the class blog or wiki.

Spelling Compound Words

Most compound words are easy to spell. You simply write two words as one word. However, some compound words are not as easy to spell.

Some compound words need a hyphen between the two words.

bull's-eye **chin-up** **hand-me-down**

Some compound words need a space between the two words.

leap year **Stone Age** **blue jay**

There is no rule that tells when you should use a hyphen or a space. If you are not sure how to spell a compound word, look it up in a dictionary.

ACTIVITY D Use a dictionary to see how to join the words that are used to make these compound words. Write the words.

1. When my sister got married, I became a (brother + in + law).
2. It seems as if everyone has a (cell + phone).
3. I ate the last (grape + fruit) for breakfast.
4. Dad and I both wanted the (left + over) pizza.
5. Barb is sick, but (never + the + less) she mowed the lawn.
6. Since my (hair + cut) it's easier to (blow + dry) my hair.
7. Franklin forgot to dial the (area + code) and got a wrong number.
8. The (jack + in + the + box) scared my baby sister.
9. Mandy did 25 (sit + ups) in gym class.
10. What is the (list + price) of your (lap + top) computer?

ACTIVITY E Rewrite each of the following sentences, using a compound word to replace two or more words.

1. The knob on the door was sticky.
2. I put on a coat over my clothes.
3. The light of the moon was bright enough for us to play.
4. I have a lot of work to do around the house.
5. Sometimes during the day I just like to sit and dream.
6. The case of books collapsed under the weight.
7. Our teacher often gives us work to do at home.
8. Everyone huddled around the fire in camp.
9. Let's hide in the barn's loft that has hay.
10. Todd took us for a ride on his boat with a sail.

ACTIVITY F Rewrite each of the following sentences, using four or more words to replace a compound word.

1. I like applesauce.
2. We rested on the hillside.
3. Our baseball team got caught in the thunderstorm.
4. A few raindrops won't stop us.
5. Mom likes to shop in bookstores.
6. The kids made a snowman.
7. The shovel hit an underground pipe.
8. The purple bedspread was my favorite at the store.
9. Dad leaned back and rested in the armchair.
10. The skyrocket exploded above us.

WRITER'S CORNER

Look in a dictionary and find three compound words that you have never used before. Read the definitions and write a sentence using each word.

Tech Tip With an adult, use an online dictionary.

Outlines

When you have gathered your facts for a research report, it is important to organize them in a logical order. One way to do this is to create an outline.

To begin an outline, write your topic at the top of a sheet of paper. Then list the main ideas about your topic. Each main idea will sum up the facts in one of your groups of note cards. Put a Roman numeral (I, II, III) and a period in front of each main idea.

Under each main idea, list the facts from that group of note cards. These are the details that support your main idea. Put a capital letter and a period before each detail.

Here is an outline that Patrick, a fourth grader, made for a report about the inside of the earth.

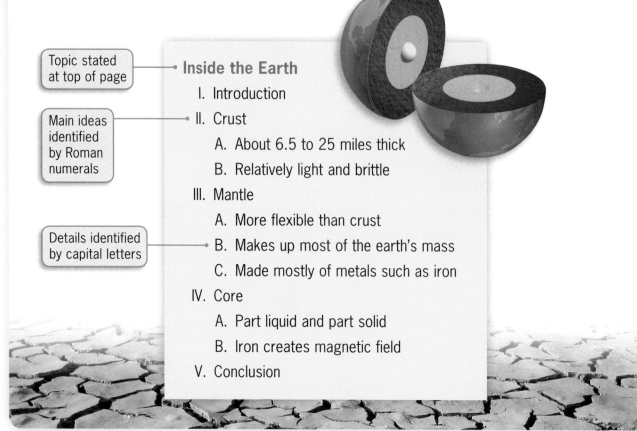

Topic stated at top of page →

Main ideas identified by Roman numerals

Details identified by capital letters →

Inside the Earth
I. Introduction
II. Crust
    A. About 6.5 to 25 miles thick
    B. Relatively light and brittle
III. Mantle
    A. More flexible than crust
    B. Makes up most of the earth's mass
    C. Made mostly of metals such as iron
IV. Core
    A. Part liquid and part solid
    B. Iron creates magnetic field
V. Conclusion

Look at Patrick's outline. He capitalized the main ideas and details in the same way. He lined up the main ideas along the left side. He lined up the details under the main ideas. Be sure to set up your outline in the same way.

Patrick's first main idea had no details. His second main idea had two details, while his third main idea had three details. It is not necessary to have the same number of details for every main idea. Just be sure that if a main idea has details, it has more than one.

All of Patrick's details were written as words and phrases. You should be consistent with your details too. You might use words and phrases, or you might use sentences.

ACTIVITY A **Read the following mixed-up main ideas and details. Organize them and use them to make an outline. The topic is "Dogs That Help People."**

- Sheepdogs help herd livestock.
- Pointers locate birds for hunters.
- Dog guides help people who are blind.
- How dogs help people work
- Sled dogs pull sleds in races.
- How dogs help people play
- Watchdogs help protect property.
- Many dogs catch tennis balls.

WRITER'S CORNER

Create an outline about a part of your school day. Make the different subjects your main ideas. Make the things you learn in each subject your details.

Writing from Outlines

Once you have created your outline, you can begin to write. First, check over your outline. If you find a detail that does not belong with the main idea it is written under, leave it out of the main idea. See if it fits under any other main ideas. If not, leave it out of your outline.

Next, begin to write from your outline. If you wrote your outline in words and phrases, expand them into sentences. Write a paragraph about each main idea. State the main idea in the first sentence of the paragraph.

ACTIVITY B Look at the following outline for a research report about the invention of chewing gum. Move any details that belong under a different main idea. Take out any details that do not fit under any main ideas. Write a revised outline.

The Invention of Chewing Gum

I. Chicle comes to America.

    A. General Santa Anna brought chicle from Mexico.

    B. Santa Anna fought at the Alamo.

    C. He gave it to New York inventor Thomas Adams.

    D. Adams's gum went on sale in 1871.

II. Adams creates chewing gum.

    A. Adams tried and failed to create rubber from chicle.

    B. He remembered that Santa Anna used to chew chicle.

    C. The Aztecs called chicle "chicti."

    D. He tried chewing it himself and liked it.

    E. He decided to sell it as chewing gum.

III. Chewing gum hits the market.

    A. Adams's gumballs were tasteless.

    B. Adams added licorice flavoring, and sales shot up.

    C. Chicle came from the sapodilla, a tree from Mexico.

General Santa Anna

Leaves of the chicle tree

ACTIVITY C Choose one outline section below and write the ideas in paragraph form. State the main idea in your first sentence.

1. **Animals at War**

   II. Pigeons were used for many things.

      A. They carried messages from the front lines.

      B. They carried news about airplanes that crashed at sea.

      C. They carried photos of enemy positions.

2. **Rock 'n' Roll**

   I. Rock 'n' roll is born.

      A. It grew from a 1950s music style called rockabilly that combined country music with rhythm and blues.

      B. The term *rock 'n' roll* was first used in 1951 by Alan Freed, a Cleveland disk jockey.

      C. It was made popular by Elvis Presley.

3. **Animation**

   II. There are many types of animation.

      A. For much of the 20th century, most animation was a series of hand-drawn pictures.

      B. Clay animation is as old as hand-drawn animation, but for a long time, it wasn't popular.

      C. Today most animation is done by computers.

Elvis Presley, 1955

Grammar in Action. To add variety to your sentences, refer to Section 1.10. Avoid run-ons by checking Section 1.11.

Oral History Report

Have you ever wondered how gold was first discovered in California? Would you like to find out how the Panama Canal changed the world? In an oral history report, you can research interesting events and share them with your class.

Think of a topic that is interesting to you. Ask questions that you would like answered about the topic. Keep these questions in mind as you prepare your oral history report.

Research

Researching for an oral report is like researching for a written report. Remember to write questions that can help guide your research.

Search for answers to your questions. If your research raises new questions, write them and look for answers to them too. Use note cards to record and organize your information. Write in your own words the information from the sources. Keep track of which facts came from which source.

As you research, look for pictures, maps, or any other visual aids that might be useful when you speak. Make sure that they are big enough for your audience to see.

Organize

Grab your audience's attention in the introduction of your report. Try to start with an interesting fact or question to make listeners want to pay attention. Be sure to state the topic in the introduction.

Use time order to organize the body of a report about a historical event. First, tell what happened right before the event you are talking about. Then describe the event itself. Finally, tell what happened as a result of the event. Keep in mind the questions you had when you chose your topic. Answer them in the body of your report. Arrange your note cards so that you can present your ideas smoothly.

The conclusion should sum up your report. It should also leave your audience with the feeling that they have learned something interesting or important.

ACTIVITY A **Imagine you are writing oral history reports for the topics below. Write two questions that you think should be answered in a report on each topic.**

Gold miner

1. the California gold rush
2. Lindbergh's solo flight across the Atlantic Ocean
3. the assassination of President James Garfield
4. the Louisiana Purchase
5. the making of Mount Rushmore
6. Neil Armstrong's first walk on the moon
7. the Underground Railroad
8. the great Chicago fire
9. the production of the Ford Model T automobile
10. the Pony Express

ACTIVITY B **Choose an event for an oral history report. You may use a topic from Activity A or you may choose any other topic that interests you. Write additional questions to help guide your research.**

SPEAKER'S CORNER

Gather information about your topic from three different sources. Use note cards to write and organize your facts.

Prepare and Practice

After you have organized your facts, prepare your report. Begin by writing your facts on new note cards. Write a few notes on each card, using keywords and phrases to remind you of what to say. If you plan to use quotations or statistics, write them exactly. Prepare your visual aid and think of the best way to display it.

Practice presenting your report several times. Try giving the information in your own words without looking down at your notes too often. Remember to speak in a clear voice that shows your interest in the topic.

Speaking Tips

Keep these things in mind when you give your report.

- Speak loudly and clearly so that listeners in the back can understand what you are saying.
- Don't stare straight ahead. Look at people in different parts of the room as you talk.
- Stand naturally and don't be afraid to gesture as you speak. Raising your hand or pointing your finger at the proper moment can hold your audience's attention.
- Make your listeners believe that you are an expert about your topic. Try to make them as interested in your topic as you are.

When you have finished your presentation, ask if there are any questions. If your classmates ask questions that you cannot answer, don't make up answers. Instead, provide the resources that you used and suggest that your classmates try to find the answers for themselves.

Listening Tips

Show each speaker the same courtesy that you want when you present your speech. Use these tips to help you be a good listener.

- Look at the speaker while he or she is talking. Don't glance around the room or read books or papers at your desk.
- If the topic interests you, take notes about facts that you would like to research on your own.
- Write any questions that you have as you listen to the report. Wait for the speaker to finish the presentation. Then raise your hand to ask your questions.

ACTIVITY C Work with a partner. Look through any sources you have for visual aids. Talk about ways to display them. Think of other places you could find visual aids for your presentations, such as in an atlas or on the Internet.

ACTIVITY D Practice presenting your report to a partner. Give your notes to your partner so that he or she can tell if you forgot any important ideas. Practice your report at least three times so that you feel comfortable as you speak.

I hope I'm loud enough.

SPEAKER'S CORNER

Present your history report to the class. Remember to make eye contact with your audience and to speak in a clear voice. When you have finished, invite your audience to ask questions. Answer them if you can. Share a list of your sources with classmates who wants to learn more about your topic.

Prewriting and Drafting

Are you interested in a graceful animal or a strange plant? Would you like to know more about an important person or event in history? You can learn all about an interesting topic and share what you learned in a research report.

Prewriting

Maren, a fourth grader, was assigned to write a science report. Before she could write it, however, she would have to choose a topic. Then she would research her topic and organize her information.

Choosing a Topic

Maren had lots of ideas for science topics. She collected insects and enjoyed learning  about them. She also thought volcanoes were interesting. Finally, she decided to write about her favorite animal, the frog.

Maren soon realized that her topic was too broad. She could write books on the general topic of frogs. She tried to choose one interesting thing about frogs. She decided to focus on the way frogs grow from tadpoles, which she thought was amazing.

Researching

Maren thought about what she wanted to find out about her topic. Here are a few questions she hoped to answer.

- What happens to a frog egg?
- What does a tadpole look like?
- How long does it stay a tadpole?

Next, Maren started her research. She looked in an encyclopedia under "Frog." She did a subject search in her library computer catalog, using "frogs" as a subject, and found two books. Finally, she did a Web search, using keywords such as "frog," "life cycle," and "tadpole," and found many Web sites.

As Maren researched, she took notes on note cards. She wrote one fact on each card and listed the source of each fact. Here are a few notes she took.

> Clumps of eggs are laid in the water.
> Sometimes there are more than a thousand.
>   Life Cycle of a Frog,
>   <www.kidslearntoo.org/frogcycle>

> The eggs hatch after one to three weeks.
>   Frogs, Kim Golparvar, p. 29

Your Turn

Gather your facts for your topic.

1. Make a list of questions you would like to answer in your research.
2. Search for books, articles, Web sites, and other sources.
3. Take notes on note cards, writing one fact on each card. Remember to use your own words and write the source on the card.

Organizing Information

Maren began to organize her information. She looked at all her notes and put them into piles. She wanted each pile of notes to be about one main idea. If a note did not fit into any pile, she left it out.

Next, Maren created an outline. She lined up all her main ideas along the left side.

👀 Organization Under each main idea, she wrote the details from that pile of notes. Here is the first part of the outline Maren made.

> Life Cycle of a Frog
>
> I. Introduction
> II. Eggs
>   A. Clumps of eggs laid
>   B. Not many hatch
>   C. Divides into many sections
> III. Tadpole
>   A. Egg hatches after 1-3 weeks
>   B. Feeds on the egg yolk
>   C. Has a tail for swimming

Your Turn

Organize your note cards into piles. Make sure that the notes in each pile are about one main idea.

Write an outline from your notes. Refer to pages 494 and 495 if you need help creating your outline.

Prewriting
Drafting
Content Editing
Revising
Copyediting
Proofreading
Publishing

Drafting

Maren used her notes and her outline to write her first draft. She double-spaced her draft so that she would have room to make changes later. Maren made sure to answer each question she had asked about her topic. She wrote one paragraph for each main idea. She included an introduction that stated the topic and a conclusion that summed up the topic.

The Life Cycle of a Frog

A frog is an interesting animal. I love to look for them in the stream near my house. It starts out as an egg and begins to grow. The egg hatches into a tadpole that swims and grows for weeks. finally, the tadpole turns into a frog. The many changes a frog goes through are kind of amazing.

A frog starts out as an egg. The egg starts out in a big clump, sometimes with thousands of other eggs. Most eggs are laid in calm water to keep them from being moved around. Only a few survive. First, the yolk in the egg splits in two. It then splits into more and more parts. It looks almost like a raspberry at this stage. As it grows inside the egg, it starts to look more like a tadpole.

After it hatches, the animal begins its life as a tadpole. The egg hatches after about one to three weeks. It still feeds on its yolk. It lives in the water. It has a long tail for swimming. When it first hatches, a tadpole sometimes attaches itself to floating grass. After about a week, it starts to swim and eat algae.

Then it slowly starts to turn into a frog. Skin starts to grow over the gills. Tiny legs sprout out, and the tail starts to shrink. It starts living on land instead of under-water. When it grows up, an adult frog may lay eggs and start the cycle all over again.

A frog goes through many changes as it grows up. It starts as an egg and then turns into a tadpole. Then it turns into a frog. This is why the frog is one of nature's coolest creations.

Your Turn

Use your notes and outline to write your draft.

- Your introduction should state the topic in a topic sentence. It should also get the audience's attention.

- Begin each body paragraph with a sentence that states the main idea of the paragraph. Make sure that each fact in the paragraph is related to the main idea. If you find a fact that does not fit, move it to a paragraph where it fits better or take it out. Write with  Voice a confident voice. Make your readers think you are an expert on the topic.

- Your conclusion should sum up the information. End with an interesting statement that leaves your readers thinking about the topic.

Setting Expectations

A good introduction gives readers an idea of what to expect in the rest of the report. The introduction can be like a guide to the report, previewing all the main ideas that will be discussed in more detail later on.

Look at Maren's introduction. She wrote a sentence about each main idea of the report. Then she wrote a topic sentence that summed up all the main ideas. By doing this, she let her readers know what would be coming in each paragraph of her report.

Writer's Tip When writing a research report, write with confidence. You have done your research. Now you are an expert on your topic.

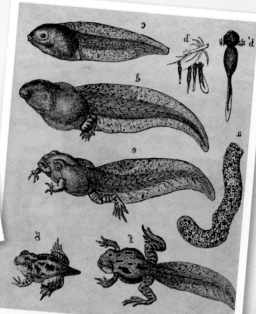

Frog with eggs; illustration of a frog's life cycle

Editor's Workshop

Content Editing

Maren thought she had done a good job of explaining the life cycle of a frog. Her draft was full of facts from different sources. She knew that by content editing, however, she could make it better.

Maren read over her draft to make sure that it made sense. She checked her facts to make sure they were correct. She looked for any facts that did not fit.

Next, Maren asked her friend Evan to content edit her draft. He looked it over to make sure that all the ideas were in the right places and that everything was included. He used this Content Editor's Checklist.

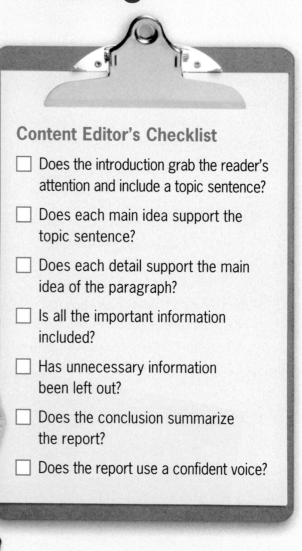

Content Editor's Checklist

☐ Does the introduction grab the reader's attention and include a topic sentence?

☐ Does each main idea support the topic sentence?

☐ Does each detail support the main idea of the paragraph?

☐ Is all the important information included?

☐ Has unnecessary information been left out?

☐ Does the conclusion summarize the report?

☐ Does the report use a confident voice?

Evan read through Maren's draft once to get an idea of what it was about. Then he read it more carefully, checking each item on the checklist as he read.

Evan told Maren that he had enjoyed her report. He found that the introduction stated the topic and that the main ideas all supported the topic sentence. He thought the conclusion summed up the report nicely and that the whole report was written with confidence. Then he made these suggestions.

- Maybe you could change your introduction so it grabs the reader's attention more.
- The sentence about looking for frogs behind your house seems unnecessary. Also, you shouldn't talk about yourself in a formal report.
- I think the sentence about the egg hatching fits better in the section about the egg.
- How does the tadpole feed on the yolk? Does the tadpole eat it?
- When does the frog have gills? You say that skin grows over them, but you never say how they got there.

Grammar in Action

Find the subject and the subject complement in the first sentence of Maren's draft.

Maren thanked Evan for content editing her draft. He had found many ways to improve her draft. Maren decided to use all of them when she revised.

Your Turn

1. Read over your draft and content edit it, using the Content Editor's Checklist. Look for any ideas that should be added, taken out, or moved. Mark on your draft any changes you plan to make.
2. Trade drafts with a partner. Read your partner's draft with the help of the Content Editor's Checklist. Make suggestions that you think would improve your partner's draft. Be positive and supportive with your comments.

Writer's Tip Listen to your partner's suggestions with an open mind. Use only the suggestions that you think will improve your draft.

Prewriting
Drafting
Content Editing
Revising
Copyediting
Proofreading
Publishing

Revising

This is how Maren revised her draft after listening to Evan's suggestions.

Amazing
The ^Life Cycle of a Frog

One of the strangest animals in nature a frog.
^ ~~A frog is an interesting animal. I love to look for them in the stream near my house.~~ It starts out as an egg and begins to grow. The egg hatches into a tadpole that swims and grows for weeks. finally, the tadpole turns into a frog. The many changes a frog goes through are kind of amazing.

A frog starts out as an egg. The egg starts out in a big clump, sometimes with thousands of other eggs. Most eggs are laid in calm water to keep them from being moved around. Only a few survive. First, the yolk in the egg splits in two. It then splits into more and more parts. It looks almost like a raspberry at this stage. As it grows inside the egg, it starts to look more like a tadpole.

After it hatches, the animal begins its life as a tadpole. The egg hatches after about one to three weeks. It still feeds on its yolk, which is inside its belly. It lives in the water and breathes through gills. It has a long tail for swimming. When it first hatches, a tadpole sometimes attaches itself to floating grass. After about a week, it starts to swim and eat algae.

Then it slowly starts to turn into a frog. Skin starts to grow over the gills. Tiny legs sprout out, and the tail starts to shrink. It starts living on land instead of under-water. This whole process is called metamorphosis.
^ When it grows up, an adult frog may lay eggs and start the cycle all over again.

A frog goes through many changes as it grows up. It starts as an egg and then turns into a tadpole. Then it turns into a frog. This is why the frog is one of nature's coolest creations.

Notice the changes Maren made to improve her draft.

- How did Maren change her first sentence?
- Why do you think she took out the sentence about looking for frogs?
- Where did she move the sentence about eggs hatching? Why?
- What information did Maren add about how the tadpole feeds on the yolk?
- What additional information did she add about a frog's gills?

Maren made a few other changes to her draft. She wanted to make her title more interesting, so she added the word *amazing* to grab the reader's attention. She also

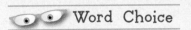 Word Choice

wanted to add another cool new word she had learned in her research. She explained in the fourth paragraph that the process of a frog's development is called *metamorphosis*.

Your Turn

Use your partner's suggestions and your own ideas to revise your draft. When you have finished, go over the Content Editor's Checklist again to make sure that you can answer yes to all the questions.

Prewriting
Drafting
Content Editing
Revising
Copyediting
Proofreading
Publishing

Copyediting and Proofreading

Copyediting

After she had revised her draft, Maren was ready to begin copyediting. By copyediting, she would make certain that her sentences were clear and logical. She would also check that she had used the best words. She used this Copyeditor's Checklist to copyedit her draft.

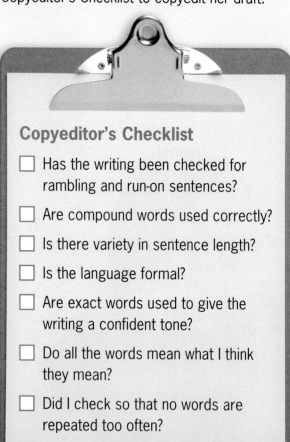

Copyeditor's Checklist

☐ Has the writing been checked for rambling and run-on sentences?

☐ Are compound words used correctly?

☐ Is there variety in sentence length?

☐ Is the language formal?

☐ Are exact words used to give the writing a confident tone?

☐ Do all the words mean what I think they mean?

☐ Did I check so that no words are repeated too often?

Maren found a few ways to improve her draft. First, she changed the words *kind of* in the first paragraph because they didn't seem confident enough. Using the word *truly* gave her report a more confident tone.

Next, she saw that she had used the phrase *starts out* twice in the second paragraph. For variety she changed the phrase to *begins* in the second sentence.

Sentence Fluency

Finally, Maren changed the word *coolest* in her last sentence. She knew that slang words did not belong in a formal report. She changed the word to *greatest*.

Your Turn

Copyedit your research report, using the Copyeditor's Checklist. Look for only one kind of mistake at a time. Make sure that each sentence is clear and correct. Check that your words mean what you think they mean, especially compound words.

Proofreading

Maren wanted someone to proofread her draft to make sure that there were no 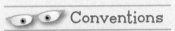 mistakes. She knew that she had read her draft so many times that her eyes might just skip over an obvious mistake. She asked her friend Eric to proofread because she knew Eric was a good speller. Here is the checklist that Eric used.

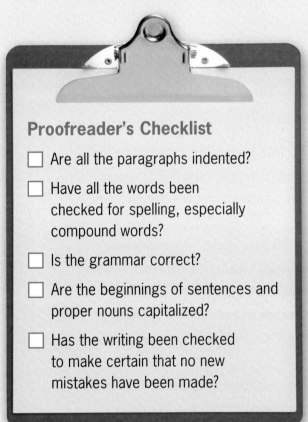

Proofreader's Checklist

☐ Are all the paragraphs indented?

☐ Have all the words been checked for spelling, especially compound words?

☐ Is the grammar correct?

☐ Are the beginnings of sentences and proper nouns capitalized?

☐ Has the writing been checked to make certain that no new mistakes have been made?

Eric read Maren's draft once for fun. He told Maren that he really enjoyed reading it. Then Eric read it more carefully, checking each item on the checklist.

First, Eric noticed that the word *finally* needed to be capitalized in the first paragraph.

Then he found a misspelled word. He saw that Maren had misspelled the compound word *underwater*. The word did not need a hyphen.

Finally, Eric saw that the opening sentence Maren added was not a complete sentence. It needed the word *is* to make it complete.

Maren thanked Eric for finding those mistakes. Maren would make all the corrections Eric suggested before publishing her finished report.

Your Turn

Read through your draft again, using the Proofreader's Checklist.

Exchange your draft with a partner. Read your partner's draft carefully with the help of the Proofreader's Checklist. Look for any mistakes that your partner may have missed. Then return your partner's draft and explain what you found.

Prewriting

Drafting

Content Editing

Revising

Copyediting

Proofreading

Publishing

Publishing

After making her corrections, Maren was almost ready to share her research report with her audience. At the end of her report, Maren listed her sources. This would tell her readers where she got her facts and where they could look for more information.

Maren looked over her report one more time and printed it out. She created a title page with a picture of a frog she had made in art class. She pinned her report on the class bulletin board where other students could read it.

The Amazing Life Cycle of a Frog

By Maren Ediza

One of the strangest animals in nature is a frog. It starts out as an egg and begins to grow. The egg hatches into a tadpole that swims and grows for weeks. Finally, the tadpole turns into a frog. The many changes a frog goes through are truly amazing.

A frog starts out as an egg. The egg begins in a big clump, sometimes with thousands of other eggs. Most eggs are laid in calm water to keep them from being moved around. Only a few survive. First, the yolk in the egg splits in two. It then splits into more and more parts. It looks almost like a raspberry at this stage. As it grows inside the egg, it starts to look more like a tadpole. The egg hatches after about one to three weeks.

After it hatches, the animal begins its life as a tadpole. It still feeds on its yolk, which is inside its belly. It lives in the water and breathes through gills. It has a long tail for swimming. When it first hatches, a tadpole sometimes attaches itself to floating grass. After about a week, it starts to swim and eat algae.

Then it slowly starts to turn into a frog. Skin starts to grow over the gills. Tiny legs sprout out, and the tail starts to shrink. It starts living on land instead of underwater. This whole process is called metamorphosis. When it grows up, an adult frog may lay eggs and start the cycle all over again.

A frog goes through many changes as it grows up. It starts as an egg and then turns into a tadpole. Then it turns into a frog. This is why the frog is one of nature's greatest creations.

Sources:

"Frogs," Jaye's Science Encyclopedia for Children.

Golparvar, Kim. Frogs.

"Life Cycle of a Frog." <www.kidslearntoo.org/frogcycle>.

Vrabel, Monica. Nature's Wonders.

There are many ways you can publish your research report.

 Post your research reports on a class bulletin board. Make an eye-catching title page that includes the title of your report, your name, and a picture or photo of your topic.

 Create a class journal. Include visuals, such as charts, graphs, and photos of your research topic. Arrange the reports in alphabetical order and create a contents page.

 Display your class journal at Parents' Night. You might wish to show it as a PowerPoint presentation.

 Post the reports on your classroom's wiki, blog, or Web site. You can receive comments about your report and review others' work.

 Film it. Make your own documentary. Narrate the report with a backdrop of photos, music, and illustrations. Interview someone who can add information.

Prewriting · Drafting · Content Editing · Revising · Copyediting · Proofreading · Publishing

Common Proofreading Marks

Use these proofreading marks to mark changes when you proofread. Remember to use a colored pencil to make your changes.

Symbol	Meaning	Example
¶	begin new paragraph	over. ¶Begin a new
⌒	close up space	close u p space
∧	insert	students think *should*
℘	delete, omit	that the the book
/	make lowercase	Mathematics
∿	reverse letters	reverse letters
≡	capitalize	washington
∨∨	add quotation marks	I am, I said.
⊙	add period	Marta drank tea

Backyard
My Bird Sanctuary

Watching birds in the wild can be fun, but why not make the birds come to you?
This summer my mom and I made a bird sanctuary in our backyard. First, we went to the garden center. We picked out a nice birdbath. We bought two bird feeders too. We looked at a lot of plants and flowers, but we didn't buy any food, so e got home, we put the birdbath under a tree by th
Different kinds of birds eat food, so
feeders in the tree. I put seeds, nuts, and water.

Grammar and Mechanics Handbook

Grammar

Adjectives

An adjective points out or describes a noun.

Adjectives That Compare

Adjectives can be used to make comparisons. To compare two people, places, or things, *-er* is often added to an adjective. To compare three or more people, places, or things, *-est* is often added to an adjective.

> A moose is **bigger** than a horse.
> An elephant is the **largest** land animal.

Some adjectives that compare have special forms.

> These grapes are **good**.
> These blueberries are **better** than those grapes.
> These raspberries are the **best** fruit in the salad.
>
> The girl had a **bad** cold on Sunday.
> The cold was **worse** on Monday.
> It was the **worst** cold she'd ever had.

Some adjectives that compare use *more* and *most. More* and *most* are used with adjectives of three or more syllables and with some adjectives of two syllables.

> Carla is a **more careful** worker than Luis.
> Marta is the **most intelligent** student in class.

The comparative adjectives *fewer* and *fewest* are used with plural nouns that you can see, touch, and count. The comparative adjectives *less* and *least* are used with nouns that cannot be seen, touched, and counted.

> I have **fewer** pencils than Hannah does.
> Mark has the **fewest** pens.
> I have **less** experience.
> Bo has the **least** curiosity.

Adjectives That Tell How Many

Some adjectives tell how many or about how many.

Only **six** members came to the meeting.

A **few** members were sick.

Some adjectives tell numerical order.

I finished reading the **sixth** chapter.

Articles

Articles point out nouns. *The, a,* and *an* are articles. *The* is the definite article. It points out a specific person, place, or thing. *A* and *an* are indefinite articles. They point out any one of a group of people, places, or things. Use *a* before a consonant sound and *an* before a vowel sound.

The man ate **a** peach and **an** apple.

Demonstrative Adjectives

Demonstrative adjectives point out or tell about a specific person, place, or thing. The demonstrative adjectives are *this, that, these,* and *those.*

Singular	Plural
this flower	**these** bushes
that flower	**those** bushes

This and *these* point out things or people that are near. *That* and *those* point out things or people that are farther away.

This flower is red. (singular and near)

Those bushes are tall. (plural and far)

Descriptive Adjectives

A descriptive adjective tells more about a noun. It can tell how something looks, tastes, sounds, feels, or smells. It can tell about size, number, color, shape, or weight.

A descriptive adjective often comes before the noun it describes.

A **tall** tree stood near the **red** barn.

A descriptive adjective can follow a linking verb as a subject complement. It describes the subject of the sentence.

The tree near the red barn was **tall**.

Possessive Adjectives

A possessive adjective shows who or what owns something. A possessive adjective is used before a noun. The possessive adjectives are *my, your, his, her, its, our,* and *their*.

I have **my** camera, and Lucy has **her** cell phone.

Proper Adjectives

Proper adjectives are formed from proper nouns. A proper adjective always begins with a capital letter.

When we went to China, I ate **Chinese** food.

Adverbs

An adverb tells more about a verb. Many adverbs end in *ly*.

An adverb of time tells when or how often an action takes place.

I went to the mall **yesterday**.
I **sometimes** go to the toy store.

An adverb of place tells where an action takes place.

I went **outside** after dinner.
I played **there** until it was dark.

An adverb of manner tells how an action takes place.

My new skateboard goes **fast**.
I ride it **gracefully**.

Adverbs That Compare

An adverb can compare the actions of two or more people or things. To compare the actions of two people or things, *-er* is often added to an adverb. To compare the actions of three or more people or things, *-est* is often added to an adverb.

Sam went to bed **later** than Henry.

Luke went to bed **latest** of us all.

Some adverbs that compare use *more* and *most.* Use *more* and *most* with adverbs ending in *ly* and with adverbs of three or more syllables.

Sam answered *more* **sleepily** than Henry.

Luke answered *most* **sleepily** of us all.

Negative Words

Some adverbs form negative ideas. Use *not, n't* for *not* in a contraction, or *never* to express a negative idea. Do not use more than one negative word in a sentence.

He will **not** be ready on time.

He **can't** find his sneakers.

He **never** remembers where he left them.

Antecedents

The noun to which a pronoun refers is its antecedent. A pronoun must agree with its antecedent in person and number. The pronouns *he, him,* and *his* refer to male antecedents. The pronouns *she, her,* and *hers* refer to female antecedents. The pronouns *it* and *its* refer to animals or things.

Contractions

A contraction is a short way to write some words. An apostrophe (') is used to show where one or more letters have been left out of a word.

Many contractions are formed with the word *not.*

do not = don't
cannot = can't
was not = wasn't
will not = won't

Many contractions are formed with personal pronouns.

I am = I'm
you are = you're
he is = he's
we have = we've

Coordinating Conjunctions

A coordinating conjunction joins two words or groups of words that are similar. The words *and, but,* and *or* are coordinating conjunctions.

My dad **and** I went to the pool.
I can swim **but** not dive.
The pool is never too hot **or** crowded.

Direct Objects

The direct object in a sentence is the noun or pronoun that receives the action of the verb. To find the direct object, ask *whom* or *what* after the verb. Two or more direct objects joined by *and* or *or* form a compound direct object.

My mom made **pasta** and **salad**.
I helped **her**.

Nouns

A noun is a word that names a person, a place, or a thing.
See NUMBER.

Collective Nouns

A collective noun names a group of people or things.

My **class** saw a **herd** of buffalo.

Common Nouns

A common noun names any one member of a group of people,
places, or things.

My **cousin** saw a **dog** run down the **street**.

Plural Nouns

A plural noun names more than one person, place, or thing.
Most plurals are formed by adding -s or -es to the singular
form. Some nouns have irregular plural forms. Some nouns
have the same form in the singular and plural.

The **children** have some **turtles** and some **fish**.

Possessive Nouns

The possessive form of a noun shows possession or ownership.

A singular possessive noun shows that one person owns
something. To form the singular possessive, add an apostrophe
(') and the letter s to a singular noun.

friend	friend**'s** book report
baby	baby**'s** bottle
Tess	Tess**'s** soccer ball
woman	woman**'s** purse

A plural possessive noun shows that more than one person
owns something. To form the regular plural possessive, add an
apostrophe (') after the plural form of the noun.

friends	friends' book reports
babies	babies' bottles
the Smiths	the Smiths' house

To form the plural possessive of an irregular noun, add an apostrophe and *s* (*'s*) after the plural form.

women   women**'s** purses

mice   mice**'s** cheese

Proper Nouns

A proper noun begins with a capital letter and names a particular person, place, or thing.

Mia saw **Shadow** run down **Pine Street**.

Singular Nouns

A singular noun names one person, place, or thing.

The **girl** has a **kite** and a **skateboard**.

Number

The number of a noun or pronoun indicates whether it refers to one person, place, or thing (singular) or more than one person, place, or thing (plural).

Person

Personal pronouns and possessive adjectives change form according to person—whether they refer to the person speaking (first person), the person spoken to (second person), or the person, place, or thing spoken about (third person).

Predicates

The predicate of a sentence tells what the subject is or does.

Complete Predicates

The complete predicate of a sentence is the simple predicate and any words that go with it.

Tom **rode his new bike**.

Compound Predicates

Two predicates joined by *and, but,* or *or* form a compound predicate.

Jenna **got a glass** and **poured some milk**.

Simple Predicates

The simple predicate of a sentence is a verb, a word or words that express an action or a state of being.

The boys **ran** noisily down the street.
They **were** happy.

Pronouns

A pronoun is a word that takes the place of a noun. See NUMBER, PERSON.

Personal Pronouns

A personal pronoun refers to the person speaking or to the person or thing that is spoken to or about. In this sentence, *I* is the person speaking, *you* is the person spoken to, and *them* are the people spoken about.

I heard **you** calling **them**.

Object Pronouns

An object pronoun can be the direct object of a sentence. The object pronouns are *me, you, him, her, it, us,* and *them.* Two or more object pronouns can be joined by *and* or *or* to form a compound direct object.

Natalie will help **them**.
Chris will help **her** and **me**.

Plural Pronouns

A plural pronoun refers to more than one person, place, or thing.

They are helping **us**.

Possessive Pronouns

A possessive pronoun shows ownership or possession. A possessive pronoun takes the place of a noun. It takes the place of the owner and the thing that is owned. The possessive pronouns are *mine, yours, his, hers, its, ours,* and *theirs.*

My cap is here, and your cap is over there.
Mine is here, and **yours** is over there.

Singular Pronouns

A singular pronoun refers to one person, place, or thing.

I gave **it** to **her**.

Subject Pronouns

A subject pronoun can be used as the subject of a sentence. The subject pronouns are *I, you, he, she, it, we,* and *they.* Two or more subject pronouns can be joined by *and* or *or* to form a compound subject.

She is a great tennis player.
She and **I** play tennis often.
She and Tom like to play video games.

Sentences

A sentence is a group of words that expresses a complete thought. Every sentence has a subject and a predicate. Every sentence begins with a capital letter.

Compound Sentences

Two sentences joined by a comma and *and, but,* or *or* form a compound sentence.

Ming is eating, but Lili is sleeping.

Declarative Sentences

A declarative sentence makes a statement. It tells something. A declarative sentence ends with a period (.).

Your jacket is in the closet.

Exclamatory Sentences

An exclamatory sentence expresses strong or sudden emotion. An exclamatory sentence ends with an exclamation point (!).

How cold it is today!

Imperative Sentences

An imperative sentence gives a command or makes a request. The subject of an imperative sentence is generally *you,* which is often not stated. An imperative sentence ends with a period (.).

Please wear your jacket.

Interrogative Sentences

An interrogative sentence asks a question. An interrogative sentence ends with a question mark (?).

Are you ready?
Where is your jacket?

Subject Complements

A subject complement follows a linking verb in a sentence. A subject complement is a noun or a pronoun that renames the subject or an adjective that describes the subject. Two or more subject complements joined by *and, but,* or *or* form a compound subject complement.

That police officer is a **hero**.
His actions were **brave** and **skillful**.
The officer with the medal for bravery was **he**.

Subjects

The subject of a sentence is who or what the sentence is about. The subject can be a noun or a pronoun.

Complete Subjects

The complete subject is the simple subject and the words that describe it or give more information about it.

The little gray kitten is playing.

Compound Subjects

Two or more subjects joined by *and* or *or* form a compound subject.

> **Gerald** and **Cathy** went to the movies.
> **Henry** or **I** will sweep the floor.

Simple Subject

The simple subject is the noun or pronoun that a sentence tells about.

> His little **dog** likes to chase balls.
> **It** runs very fast.

Subject-Verb Agreement

A subject and verb must agree, whether the verb is a main verb or a helping verb.

> I **like** chicken soup.
> My brother **likes** split pea soup.
> Our parents **like** lentil soup.
>
> I **am building** a birdhouse.
> He **is building** a shed.
> They **are building** a garage.

A collective noun is generally considered a singular noun though it means more than one person or thing; therefore, the verb agrees with the singular form.

> Our **class is entering** the contest.

When a sentence starts with *there is, there are, there was,* or *there were,* the subject follows the verb. The verb must agree with the subject.

> There **is** a **book** on the desk.
> There **were** some **pencils** in the drawer.

Tense

The tense of a verb shows when the action takes place.

Future Tense

The future tense tells about something that will happen in the future.

One way to form the future tense is with a form of the helping verb *be* plus *going to* plus the present form of a verb.

I **am going to make** toast.
Dad **is going to butter** it.
They **are going to eat** it.

Another way to form the future tense is with the helping verb *will* and the present form of a verb.

Our class **will go** to the museum.
The guide **will explain** the exhibits.

Future Perfect Tense

The future perfect tense tells about an action that will have been completed by some time in the future. The future perfect tense is formed with *will* plus *have* plus the past participle of a verb.

I **will have finished** my homework by dinnertime.
I **will have made** a salad by that time too.

Past Perfect Tense

The past perfect tense tells about an action that was finished before another action in the past. The past perfect tense is formed with *had* and the past participle of a verb.

She **had come** straight home after school.
She **had finished** her homework before dinner.

Past Progressive Tense

The past progressive tense tells what was happening in the past. The past progressive tense is formed with *was* or *were* and the present participle of a verb.

I **was feeding** the cat.
My parents **were reading**.

Present Perfect Tense

The present perfect tense tells about an action that happened at some indefinite time in the past or about an action that started in the past and continues into the present. The present perfect tense is formed with a form of *have* and the past participle of a verb.

He **has finished** his homework.
They **have lived** in that house for three years.

Present Progressive Tense

The present progressive tense tells what is happening now. The present progressive tense is formed with *am, is,* or *are* and the present participle of a verb.

We **are watching** TV.
I **am eating** popcorn.
My sister **is drinking** juice.

Simple Past Tense

The simple past tense tells about something that happened in the past. The simple past tense of regular verbs is formed by adding *-d* or *-ed* to the present form of a verb.

We **cooked** breakfast this morning.
Mom **fried** the eggs.

Simple Present Tense

The simple present tense tells about something that is always true or something that happens again and again. The present part of a verb is used for the present tense. If the subject is a singular noun or *he, she,* or *it, -s* or *-es* must be added to the verb.

> Prairie dogs **live** where it's dry.
> A prairie dog **digs** a burrow to live in.

Verbs

A verb shows action or state of being. See TENSE.

Action Verbs

An action verb tells what someone or something does.

> The girl **is singing**.
> Dogs **bark**.

Being Verbs

A being verb shows what someone or something is. Being verbs do not express action.

> The girl **is** happy.
> The dog **was** hungry.

Helping Verbs

A verb can have more than one word. A helping verb is a verb added before the main verb that helps make the meaning clear.

> We **will** go to the movie.
> We **might** buy some popcorn.

Irregular Verbs

The past and the past participle of irregular verbs are not formed by adding *-d* or *-ed.*

Present	Past	Past Participle
sing	sang	sung
send	sent	sent
write	wrote	written

Linking Verbs

A linking verb joins the subject of a sentence to a subject complement. Being verbs can be linking verbs.

> My aunt **is** a professional writer.
> Her stories **are** excellent.
> The winner of the writing award **was** she.

Principal Parts

A verb has four principal parts: present, present participle, past, and past participle. The present participle is formed by adding *-ing* to the present. The past and the past participle of regular verbs are formed by adding *-d* or *-ed* to the present.

Present	Present Participle	Past	Past Participle
walk	walking	walked	walked
wave	waving	waved	waved

The past and the past participle of irregular verbs are not formed by adding *-d* or *-ed* to the present.

Present	Present Participle	Past	Past Participle
do	doing	did	done
fly	flying	flew	flown
put	putting	put	put

The present participle is often used with forms of the helping verb *be*.

> We **are walking** to school.
> I **was doing** my homework.

The past participle is often used with forms of the helping verb *have*.

> We **have walked** this way before.
> He **has done** his homework.

Regular Verbs

The past and the past participle of regular verbs are formed by adding *-d* or *-ed* to the present.

Present	Past	Past Participle
jump	jumped	jumped
listen	listened	listened

Verb Phrases

A verb phrase is made up of one or more helping verbs and a main verb.

I ***should have shown*** you my drawings.

I ***am entering*** them in the art contest.

You ***can see*** them there.

Mechanics

Capital Letters

Use a capital letter to begin the first word in a sentence.

Tomorrow is my birthday.

Use a capital letter to begin the names of people and pets.

Aunt **P**eg let me play with her ferret, **N**ibbles.

Use a capital letter to begin the names of streets, cities, states, and countries.

I live on **R**oscoe **S**treet.
My cousin lives in **G**uadalajara, **M**exico.

Use a capital letter to begin the names of days, months, and holidays.

This year **T**hanksgiving is on **T**hursday, **N**ovember 25.

Use a capital letter to begin a proper adjective.

I like to eat **C**hinese food.

Use a capital letter to begin people's titles.

Mrs. Novak
Dr. Ramirez
Governor Ferdinand Marcic

Use a capital letter to begin the important words in the title of a book or poem. The first and last words of a title are always capitalized. Short words such as *of, to, for, a, an,* and *the* are not capitalized unless they are the first or last word of the title.

The Secret Garden
"**S**ing a **S**ong of **C**ities"

The personal pronoun *I* is always a capital letter.

Punctuation

Apostrophes

Use an apostrophe to form possessive nouns.

> Keisha's skateboard
> the children's lunches
> the horses' stalls

Use an apostrophe to replace the letters left out in a contraction.

> didn't   can't   wasn't

Commas

Use a comma to separate the words in a series.

> Mark, Anton, and Cara made the scenery.
> They hammered, sawed, and nailed.

Use a comma or commas to separate a name in direct address.

> Carl, will you help me?
> Do you think, Keshawn, that we will finish today?

Use a comma before the coordinating conjunction when two short sentences are combined in a compound sentence.

> Dad will heat the soup, and I will make the salad.
> Dad likes noodle soup, but I like bean soup.

Use a comma to separate the names of a city and state.

> She comes from Philadelphia, Pennsylvania.

Use a comma or commas to separate a direct quotation from the rest of the sentence.

> "Hey," called Anthony, "where are you going?"
> "I'm going to the movies," Helen answered.

Use a comma after the word *yes* or *no* that introduces a sentence.

> No, I can't go to the movies tonight.

Exclamation Points

Use an exclamation point after an exclamatory sentence.

We won the game!

Italics

Titles of books and magazines are italicized when they are typed and underlined when they are handwritten.

Charlotte's Web

<u>Mr. Popper's Penguins</u>

Periods

Use a period after a declarative or an imperative sentence.

The cat is hungry.
Please feed it.

Use a period after most abbreviations.

Sun.	Sept.	ft.	yd.
Ave.	St.	gal.	oz.

Periods are not used after abbreviations for metric measures.

km   cm

Use a period after a personal title.

Mr. Frank Cummings
Mrs. Joanna Clark
Dr. Hilda Doolittle
Sgt. Barry Lindon

Use a period after an initial.

John F. Kennedy	U.S.A.
J. K. Rowling	B.S.A.

Question Marks

Use a question mark after an interrogative sentence.

Where are you going?

Quotation Marks

Use quotation marks to show the exact words a person says in a direct quotation.

Carly said, "I can't find my markers."

"Where," asked her mother, "did you leave them?"

Use quotation marks around the title of a poem, story, or magazine article.

"Paul Revere's Ride"

"Kids to the Rescue"

Index

A

Abbreviations, 166, 168, 176, 263, 534
Accent marks, in dictionary respelling, 378
Action verbs, 106, 108, 529
Addresses. *See also* Direct address
  abbreviations in, 166
  on envelopes, 262, 264
  inside, in formal letters, 250
  punctuation and capitalization of, 176
  of Web sites, 488
Adjectives, 152. *See also* Articles
  adding to expand sentences, 414
  colorful, 226
  comparison with, 92, 94, 96, 516
  defined, 80, 516
  demonstrative, 86, 517
  descriptive, 80, 517–18
  diagramming, 188, 200
  irregular, 94
  position of, 100
  possessive, 68, 74, 518
  proper, 82, 518, 532
  as subject complements, 90, 100, 190, 200
  that tell how many, 88, 517
Adverbs
  adding to expand sentences, 416
  comparison with, 148, 150, 519
  defined, 144, 192, 518
  diagramming, 192
  of manner, 146, 518
  negative words as, 152, 448, 450, 519
  of place, 144, 518
  of time, 144, 518
Aesop's Fable, 404
Agreement, subject-verb, 136, 138, 526
Almanacs, 486
Alphabetical order, in dictionaries, 338
Antecedents, 70, 519
Antonyms, 266
Apostrophes
  in contractions, 74, 174, 520, 533
  possessive nouns and, 36, 38, 174, 521, 522, 533
Articles, definite and indefinite, 84, 517
Atlases, 486
Audience
  descriptions, 289
  fables, 422
  how-to articles, 353
  personal narratives, 212
  persuasive writing, 366
Authors, of Web sites, 489

B

Base word, 334
"Bee Mystery" (National Geographic Kids), 444
Beginnings. *See* Introductions
Being verbs, 108, 380, 529
Body
  expository articles, 440
  fables, 406, 422
  formal letters, 250, 251
  how-to articles, 326
  how-to talks, 347
  oral history reports, 498–99
  oral personal narratives, 232
  oral persuasion, 385
  personal narratives, 216
  persuasive writing, 364
  research reports, 480
Books
  in libraries, 458–59
  listing as sources, 484
  titles of, 164, 532, 534-35
Brainstorming, 236, 426
Bridges, Ruby, 210, 212, 216, 222, 226
Business letters. *See* Formal letters; Letters, business

C

Capitalization
  addresses, 176
  I (personal pronoun), 162, 532
  names, 162, 532
  proper adjectives, 82, 532
  sentences, 162, 532
  titles of people, 168, 532
  titles of works, 164, 532
Catalogs, library, 456–57
Characters, in fables, 402, 406, 407, 422
Charts. *See also* Graphic organizers
  for fables, 423
  five-senses, 304
Checklists
  content editor's, 240, 278, 316, 354, 392, 430, 468, 506
  copyeditor's, 244, 282, 320, 358, 396, 434, 472, 510
  proofreader's, 245, 283, 321, 359, 397, 435, 473, 511
Chronological order. *See* Time order
Cities, capital letters for, 532
Closing, in formal letter, 250
Collective nouns, 40, 521, 526
Colorful adjectives, 226
Combining sentences. *See* Compound sentences

Commas
  with addresses, 176, 533
  in compound sentences, 20, 170, 258, 524, 533
  in direct address, 172, 533
  with direct quotations, 178, 533
  in a series, 170, 533
  after *yes* or *no* introducing sentences, 172, 533
Common nouns, 30, 82, 521. *See also* Nouns
Comparisons
  adjectives used to make, 92, 94, 96, 516
  adverbs used to make, 148, 150, 519
Complaints and conflicts, oral, 270–72
Complements. *See* Subject complements
Complete predicate, 8, 522
Complete subject, 8, 525
Compound direct objects, 16, 64, 196
Compound predicates, 14, 194, 382, 523
Compound sentences
  commas in, 20, 170, 258, 533
  conjunctions in, 258, 260
  defined, 20, 200, 258, 524
  diagramming, 200
  punctuation of, 20, 170, 258, 260, 533
Compound subject complements, 18, 198, 200, 525
Compound subjects, 380
  defined, 10, 526
  diagramming, 194
  pronouns in, 62, 524
Compound words, 490, 492
Computers. *See also* Internet
  preparing envelopes on, 264
  using in libraries, 456–57
Conclusions
  expository articles, 441
  fables, 406–7, 423
  how-to articles, 326
  how-to talks, 347
  oral history reports, 499
  oral personal narratives, 232
  oral persuasion, 385
  personal narratives, 216
  persuasive writing, 365
  research reports, 480
Conflict-resolution team, 272
Conjunctions
  in compound sentences, 258, 260, 380, 382
  coordinating, 154, 170, 520
  in rambling sentences, 452
Content editing
  descriptions, 316–17
  expository articles, 468–69

fables, 430–31
formal letters, 278–79
how-to articles, 354–55
personal narratives, 240–41
persuasive writing, 392–93
research reports, 506–7
Contractions
apostrophes with, 74, 174, 520, 533
avoiding in formal English, 252
formal writing and, 230
with *not,* 448, 520
with pronouns, 74, 228, 520
Conventions. *See* Proofreading
Coordinating conjunctions, 154, 170, 520, 533
Copyediting
descriptions, 320
expository articles, 472
fables, 434
formal letters, 282
how-to articles, 358
personal narratives, 244
persuasive writing, 396
research reports, 510
Countries
abbreviation of, 168
capital letters for, 532
Creative writing. *See* Fables

D

Days
abbreviation of, 166
capital letters for, 532
Declarative sentences, 4, 160, 524, 534
Definite articles, 84, 517
Demonstrative adjectives, 86, 517
Descriptions, 286–87. *See also* Sensory language
audience, 289
content editing, 316–17
copyediting, 320
drafting, 314–15
oral, 308–10
organization of, 290
prewriting, 312–13
proofreading, 321
publishing, 322–23
revising, 318–19
sensory language in, 292
topics, 288, 312
Writer's Workshop, 312–23
Descriptive adjectives, 80, 517–18
Details
in formal letters, 277
in how-to articles, 330, 332
in personal narratives, 218

Dewey Decimal System, 458–59
Diagramming
adjectives, 188
adverbs, 192
compound direct objects, 196
compound predicates, 194
compound sentences, 202
compound subject complements, 198, 200
compound subjects, 194
defined, 184
direct objects, 186
possessive nouns, 188
predicates, 184
subject complements, 190
subjects, 184
verbs, 184
Dialogue, in fables, 429
Dictionaries, 252
accent marks in, 378
alphabetical order in, 338
defined, 338
guide words in, 338
pronunciation key in, 377
respellings in, 377
syllables in, 376
word meanings in, 340
Direct address, 172, 533
Direct objects
compound, 16, 64, 196
defined, 16, 44, 186, 520
diagramming, 186, 196
nouns as, 44
pronouns as, 64, 523
Direct quotations, 178, 533, 535
Divided quotations, 178
Double negatives, 450
Drafting
descriptions, 314–15
expository articles, 466–67
fables, 428–29
formal letters, 276–77
how-to articles, 352–53
personal narratives, 238–39
persuasive writing, 390–91
research reports, 504–5

E

Editing. *See* Content editing; Copyediting
Electronic catalogs, 456–57
Encyclopedias, 484, 486
End punctuation, 2, 4, 6, 160, 525, 534
See also Exclamation points; Periods; Question marks
English language, formal, in letters, 252

Envelopes
addressing, 262
preparing on computer, 264
Exact words, 224, 226
Exclamation points, 6, 160, 525, 534
Exclamatory sentences, 6, 160, 525, 534
Expository articles, 438–39
body, 440
conclusion, 441
content editing, 468–69
copyediting, 472
drafting, 466–67
information for, 444, 446, 465
introduction, 440
news articles, 440, 442, 446
news reports, 460–63
order of importance in, 442
prewriting, 464–65
proofreading, 473
publishing, 474–75
revising, 470–71
topics, 464
Writer's Workshop, 464–75

F

Fables, 402–03
audience, 422
characters in, 402, 406, 407, 422
content editing, 430–31
copyediting, 434
defined, 402
dialogue in, 429
drafting, 428–29
moral in, 404, 423
prewriting, 426–27
problems in, 402, 404, 406, 422
proofreading, 435
publishing, 436–37
revising, 432–33
setting, 402, 406, 422
telling, 422–25
Writer's Workshop, 426–37
Facts
checking, 370
defined, 368
Fewer/fewest, 98, 516
Fiction books, 458
First person pronouns, 56, 72
Five-senses chart, 304
Five Ws, the, 446
Formal English, in letters, 252

Formal letters, 248–49
  body, 250, 251
  closing, 250
  content editing, 278–79
  copyediting, 282
  details in, 277
  drafting, 276–77
  folding, 264
  greeting, 250
  heading, 250
  inside addresses, 250
  language in, 252, 254
  letters of complaint, 254, 274–85
  letters of request, 256
  mailing of, 262–65
  prewriting, 274–75
  proofreading, 283
  publishing, 284–85
  revising, 280–81
  signature, 250
  topics, 274
  Writer's Workshop, 274–85
Freewriting, personal narratives, 237
Future tenses, 126, 527
  perfect, 134, 527

G

"Going for the Gold" (Schaak), 438
Good/well, 152
Grammar. *See* Adjectives; Adverbs;
    Capitalization; Conjunctions;
    Diagramming; Nouns; Pronouns;
    Punctuation; Sentences; Verbs
Grammar and Mechanics Handbook,
    515–35
Graphic organizers
  chart for fables, 423
  five-senses chart, 304, 313
  idea web, 306, 389
  outline, 494–96, 503
  T-chart, 274
  timeline, 220–22, 237
Greeting, in formal letter, 250
Guide words, in dictionaries, 338

H

Haiku, 418, 420
Headings, in formal letter, 250
Helping verbs, 112, 116, 126, 527, 529
History reports, oral, 498–501
Holidays, capital letters for, 532
Homophones, 410, 412
How many, adjectives telling, 88
How-to articles, 324–25. *See also*
    How-to talks

  body, 326
  conclusion, 326
  content editing, 354–55
  copyediting, 358
  details in, 330, 332
  drafting, 352–53
  introduction, 326
  prewriting, 350–51
  proofreading, 359
  publishing, 360–61
  revising, 356–57
  time order in, 326, 328
  topics, 350
  Writer's Workshop, 350–61
How-to talks, 346–49
Hyphenation, of compound words, 492

I

Ideas. *See* Topics
Idea webs, 306
I/me, 72
"I messages," 271
Imperative sentences, 6, 160, 326,
    525, 534
Indefinite articles, 84, 517
Information
    gathering for expository article,
      444, 446, 465
    gathering for news report, 460
Initials
    capitalization of, 168
    periods after, 168, 534
Inside address, in formal letter, 250
Internet. *See also* Web sites
    reference sources on, 488–89
    search engines on, 488
    Web sites, 488–89
Interrogative sentences, 4, 160, 525, 534
Interviewing
    for expository article, 444
    for news report, 444, 460
Introductions
    expository articles, 440
    fables, 406, 422
    how-to articles, 326
    how-to talks, 346
    oral history reports, 498
    oral personal narratives, 232
    oral persuasion, 384
    personal narratives, 216
    persuasive writing, 364
    research reports, 480, 505
Irregular adjectives, 94
Irregular plural nouns, 34, 521, 522
Irregular verbs, 118, 120, 529
Italics, 164, 534

J

Jones, Charlotte Foltz, 476

K

Konigsburg, E. L., 286, 290, 293, 301

L

Language
    in descriptions, 289
    in formal letters, 252, 254
    formal vs. informal, 230
    sensory, 292
"Lead" sentence, 440
Less/least, 98, 516
Letters, business. *See* Formal letters
Letters, formal. *See* Formal letters
Letters of complaint, 254, 274–85
Letters of request, 256
Libraries, 486–87
    Dewey Decimal System of, 458–59
    electronic catalogs in, 456–57
    finding information in, 458
    Internet sources and, 488
    reference sources in, 486–87
Linking verbs, 18, 46, 90, 100, 110, 190,
    525, 530
Lion and the Mouse, The
    (Aesop's Fable), 404
Listening tips
    how-to talks, 349
    news reports, 463
    oral descriptions, 310
    oral history reports, 501
    oral personal narratives, 234
    oral persuasion, 386
    telling fables, 425
"Lunar Lander Inventors Win Big"
    (Scholastic News Online), 443

M

Magazines
    listing as sources, 484
    titles of, 164, 535
Mailing, letters, 262–64
Mailing address, on envelope, 262
Me/I, 72
Metaphors, 302, 315
More/most, 96, 150, 516, 519
Muth, Jon J., 400

N

Negative words, 152, 448, 519
    double, 450
News articles. *See also* Expository
       articles
    "five Ws" in, 446
    "lead" in, 440
    order of importance in, 442
Newspapers, 484
News reports, 460–63
Nonfiction books, 458
***Not,* in contractions,** 448, 520
Note cards
    for how-to-talks, 348
    for oral history report, 498, 500
    for oral personal narrative, 234
    for research report, 482
Note taking, 444, 460, 482
Nouns. *See also* Plural nouns;
       Singular nouns
    as antecedent, 519
    collective, 40, 521, 526
    common, 30, 82, 521
    defined, 28, 521
    diagramming, 184, 188
    as direct objects, 44
    irregular plural, 34, 38
    number and, 522
    plural, 32, 34, 98, 521–22
    plural possessive, 38
    possessive, 36, 38, 174, 188, 521,
       522, 533
    proper, 30, 82, 522
    singular, 32, 522
    singular possessive, 38
    as subject complements, 18, 46,
       190, 525
    as subjects, 10, 42, 525
    words used as verbs and, 48
Number, agreement and, 70, 519, 522
Numbers (numerals), as adjectives, 88

O

Object pronouns, 62, 523
Objects. *See* Direct objects
Opinions, defined, 368
Oral complaints and conflicts, 270–72
Oral descriptions, 308–10
Oral history reports, 498–501
Oral personal narratives, 232–34.
    See also Personal narratives
Oral persuasion, 384–86
Order
    of importance, 442
    space, 290

    step-by-step, 326, 328
    time, 214, 220, 290, 326, 328
Organizations, abbreviation of, 168
Organizing
    descriptions, 290, 313
    expository articles, 465
    fables, 427
    formal letters, 274
    how-to articles, 351
    news reports, 460
    oral descriptions, 308–10
    oral history reports, 498–99
    personal narratives, 237
    persuasive writing, 388–89
    research reports, 480, 503
Outlines, for research reports, 494–96

P

Participles. *See* specific types
Past participle, 116, 130, 132, 134, 530
    irregular verbs, 118, 120, 529, 530
    regular verbs, 116, 530, 531
Past tenses
    irregular verbs, 118, 120, 529, 530
    perfect, 132, 527
    progressive, 128, 528
    regular verbs, 116, 530, 531
    simple, 124, 528
    of verbs, 116, 118, 120, 530, 531
Perfect tenses, 130, 132, 134, 527, 528
Periods
    in abbreviations, 166, 534
    as end punctuation, 2, 4, 6, 160,
       524–25, 534
    initials with, 168, 534
    in personal titles, 168, 534
Person
    adjectives and, 68, 522
    agreement and, 70
    pronouns and, 56, 66, 72, 519, 523–24
Personal narratives, 210–11
    audience, 212
    body, 216
    conclusions, 216
    content editing, 240–41
    copyediting, 244
    details in, 216
    drafting, 238–39
    introductions, 216
    oral, 232–34
    point of view, 213
    prewriting, 236–37
    proofreading, 244–45
    publishing, 246–47
    revising, 242–43
    time lines for, 220–22, 237

    time order, 214, 220
    topics, 212, 236
    Writer's Workshop, 236–47
Personal pronouns. *See also* Pronouns
    antecedents and, 70, 519
    capitalization of, 162
    contractions and, 74, 520
    defined, 54, 56, 523
    as objects, 64, 523
    person and, 522
    singular and plural, 58
    as subjects, 60, 62, 524
Personal titles. *See* Titles (personal)
Persuasive writing, 362–63
    audience, 366
    body, 364
    conclusion, 365
    content editing, 392–93
    copyediting, 396
    drafting, 390–91
    facts and opinions in, 368, 370
    introduction, 364
    point of view in, 368
    prewriting, 388–89
    proofreading, 397
    publishing, 398–99
    revising, 394–95
    topics, 364, 388
    Writer's Workshop, 388–99
Phrases. *See* Verb phrases
Planning. *See also* Organizing
    fables, 427
    formal letters, 275
    oral persuasion, 385
Plural nouns
    defined, 32, 521
    irregular, 34, 521
    possessive, 38, 521
Plural pronouns, 56, 58, 523
Poetry
    haiku, 418, 420
    titles of, 164, 534–35
Point of view, 213, 271, 368
Possessive adjectives, 68, 74, 518
Possessive nouns
    apostrophes with, 36, 38, 174, 188,
       521, 522, 533
    defined, 36, 188, 521
    diagramming, 188
    irregular plural, 38, 522
    plural, 38, 521
    singular, 36, 521
Possessive pronouns, 66, 524
Postal abbreviations, for states, 166,
    176, 263
Practicing
    how-to talks, 348

news reports, 462–63
oral descriptions, 308–10
oral history reports, 500
oral personal narratives, 234
oral persuasion, 386
telling fables, 424
Predicates
complete, 8, 522
compound, 14, 194, 382, 523
defined, 2, 8, 10, 14
diagramming, 184, 194
simple, 10, 14, 184, 523
Prefixes, 334
Preparing
how-to talks, 348
oral history reports, 500
Presenting
descriptions, 323
expository articles, 475
fables, 437
how-to articles, 361
oral history reports, 500
personal narratives, 247
persuasive writing, 399
research reports, 513
Present part, of verbs, 116, 118, 120, 530
Present participle, 116, 530
irregular verbs, 118, 120
regular verbs, 116
Present tenses
irregular verbs, 118, 120
perfect, 130, 528
progressive, 128, 528
regular verbs, 116, 531
simple, 122, 529
Prewriting
descriptions, 312–13
expository articles, 464–65
fables, 426–27
formal letters, 274–75
how-to articles, 350–51
personal narratives, 236–37
persuasive writing, 388–89
research reports, 502–3
Principal parts of verbs, 116, 530
Problems
in fables, 402, 404, 406, 422
in oral complaints and conflicts, 271
Progressive tenses, 128, 528
Pronouns. *See also* Personal pronouns
antecedents and, 70, 519
in compound subjects, 62

contractions with, 74, 228, 520
defined, 54, 56, 523
number and, 70, 522
object, 62, 523
personal, 54, 56, 162, 523
person and, 56, 66
plural, 58, 523
possessive, 66, 524
singular, 58, 524
subject, 60, 62, 524
as subject complement, 525
Proofreading
descriptions, 321
expository articles, 473
fables, 435
formal letters, 283
how-to articles, 359
personal narratives, 244–45
persuasive writing, 397
research reports, 511
Proofreading marks, 245, 514
Proper adjectives, 82, 518
capital letters for, 82, 532
Proper nouns, 30, 82, 522. *See also* Nouns
Publishing
descriptions, 322–23
expository articles, 474–75
fables, 436–37
formal letters, 284–85
how-to articles, 360–61
personal narratives, 246–47
persuasive writing, 398–99
research reports, 512–13
Punctuation. *See also* specific marks;
specific marks
of addresses, 176
of compound sentences, 20, 170, 258,
260, 524, 533
of direct quotations, 178, 533, 535
end, 2, 4, 6, 160, 524–25, 534
run-on sentences and, 22
of titles of works, 164, 532, 534–35

Q

Question marks, 160, 525, 534
Questions
compound predicates in, 382
compound subjects in, 380
for research reports, 478, 479, 480, 498
Quotation marks, 164, 178, 535
Quotations
direct, 178, 533, 535
divided, 178

R

Rambling sentences, 452
revising, 454
References, 467, 484, 486–89
almanacs, 487
atlases, 487
encyclopedias, 486
search engines, 488
Web sites, 488–89
Regular nouns, 38
Regular verbs, 530, 531
Reports. *See* Research reports
Researching, 479, 502–3
listing sources, 484
note taking, 482
oral history report, 498
Research reports, 476–77
body, 480
conclusion, 480
content editing, 506–7
copyediting, 510
drafting, 504–5
introduction, 480, 505
note taking, 482
oral, 498–501
organizing, 480
outlines, 494–96
prewriting, 502–3
proofreading, 511
publishing, 512–13
revising, 508–9
sources for, 484, 486–89
topics, 478, 502
Writer's Workshop, 502–13
Return address, on envelope, 262
Revising
descriptions, 318–19
expository articles, 470–71
fables, 432–33
formal letters, 280–81
how-to articles, 356–57
personal narratives, 242–43
persuasive writing, 394–95
rambling sentences, 454
research reports, 508–9
time lines, 222
Run-on sentences, 22

S

Schaak, Chandler, 438
Search engines, 488
Second person pronouns, 56
Sensory language, 292
Sentences. *See also* Compound
sentences; Diagramming;

Predicates; Punctuation; Subjects;
    specific kinds
capital letters in, 162, 532
declarative, 4, 160, 524
defined, 2, 524
exclamatory, 6, 160, 525
expanding, 414, 416
imperative, 6, 160, 525
interrogative, 4, 160, 525
punctuation of, 2, 4, 6, 160, 524, 525
rambling, 452, 454
run-on, 22
Series, commas in, 170, 533
Settings, in fables, 402, 406, 422
"Settling the Americas" (Sohn), 480
Short stories, titles of, 164
Signatures, in letters, 250
Similes, 300, 315
Simple direct objects, 16
Simple predicates, 10, 14, 184, 523
Simple subjects, 10, 12, 42, 184, 526
Simple tenses
    past, 124
    present, 122
Singular nouns
    defined, 32, 522
    possessive, 36, 521
Singular pronouns, 56, 524
Slang, 252
Sohn, Emily, 480
**Solutions, in oral complaints and
    conflicts,** 272
Sources
    for expository articles, 467
    listing, 484
    reference, 486–89
Spatial order, in descriptions, 290
Speeches
    fable telling, 422–25
    how-to talks, 346–49
    news reports, 460–63
    oral complaints and conflicts, 270–73
    oral descriptions, 308–10
    oral history reports, 498–501
    oral personal narratives, 232–34
    oral persuasion, 384–86
Step-by-step order, 326, 328
Study skills. *See* Dictionaries; Libraries
Subject complements
    adjectives as, 90, 100, 200
    compound, 18, 198, 200, 525
    defined, 18, 42, 46, 110, 525
    diagramming, 184, 190, 198
    nouns as, 18, 46, 190, 525
    pronouns as, 525
Subject pronouns, 60, 62, 524

Subjects
    complete, 8, 525
    compound, 12, 194, 380, 526
    defined, 2, 525
    diagramming, 184, 194
    nouns as, 8, 42, 525
    pronouns as, 60, 525
    simple, 10, 42, 184, 526
Subject-verb agreement, 136, 138, 526
Suffixes, 296, 298
Syllables, 96, 376
    in haikus, 418
Synonyms, 372, 374

T

Taking notes. *See* Note taking
Talks. *See* How-to talks
Tenses, verb, 122, 527–29. *See also*
    Future tenses; Past tenses; Perfect
    tenses; Present tenses; Progressive
    tenses; Simple tenses
There is/there are, 138
Third person pronouns, 56
Three Questions, The **(Muth),** 400
Through My Eyes **(Bridges),** 210, 212,
    216, 222, 226
Time lines, for personal narratives,
    220–22, 237
Time order
    descriptions, 290
    how-to articles, 326, 328
    personal narratives, 214, 220
Time words, 144, 342, 518
Titles (personal), 168, 176, 532, 534–35
    abbreviation of, 168
    in addresses, 176
    capital letters for, 168, 532
    periods with, 168, 534
Titles (works), 164, 532, 534–35
    personal narratives, 239
Tone of Voice *See also* Voice
    news reports, 461
    oral personal narratives, 233
    telling fables, 424
Topics
    descriptions, 288, 312
    expository articles, 464
    formal letters, 274
    how-to articles, 350
    how-to talks, 346
    news articles, 440
    news reports, 460
    oral descriptions, 308

oral persuasion, 384
    personal narratives, 212, 236
    persuasive writing, 364, 388
    research reports, 478–79, 502
Topic sentences, 440

U

Underlining, of titles, 164, 534
Units of measure, abbreviation of,
    166, 534
Us/we, 72

V

Velveteen Rabbit, The **(Williams),** 406
Verb phrases, 114, 531
Verbs. *See also* Adverbs; Direct objects;
    Past participle; Past tenses;
    Present participle; Present tenses;
    Suffixes; Verb phrases
    action, 106, 108, 529
    agreement with subjects, 136, 138, 526
    being, 108, 380, 529
    defined, 529
    diagramming, 184
    helping, 112, 116, 527, 529
    irregular, 118, 120, 529, 530
    linking, 18, 90, 100, 110, 190, 525, 530
    as predicates, 8, 10, 12, 523
    principal parts of, 116, 530
    regular, 116, 530, 531
    strong, 224
    words used as nouns and, 48
Verb tenses. *See* Future tenses; Past
    tenses; Perfect tenses; Present
    tenses; Progressive tenses;
    Simple tenses
Verse. *See* Poetry
View from Saturday, The
    (Konigsburg), 286, 290, 293, 301
Visual aids, for news reports, 462
Vocabulary. *See* Language
Voice. *See also* Tone
    descriptions, 315
    expository articles, 467
    fables, 429
    formal letters, 281
    how-to articles, 350
    personal narratives, 238
    persuasive writing, 395
    research reports, 505
    tone of (*See* Tone of Voice), 461

W

Web sites, 488–89
    listing as sources, 484
Well/good, 152
We/us, 72
Williams, Margery, 406
Win/Win guidelines, for oral
    complaints and conflicts, 271
Words
    antonyms, 266
    compound, 490, 492
    exact, using in writing, 224, 226
    homophones, 410, 412
    meanings in dictionaries, 340
    negative, 152, 448, 450, 519
    prefixes, 334
    sensory, 292
    suffixes, 296, 298
    synonyms, 372, 374
    time, 144, 342
    used as nouns and verbs, 48

World Book of America's Heritage,
    The, 478
Writer's Workshop
    descriptions, 312–23
    expository articles, 464–75
    fables, 426–37
    formal letters, 274–85
    how-to articles, 350–61
    personal narratives, 236–47
    persuasive writing, 388–99
    research reports, 502–13
Writing, formal and informal, 230

Y

Yukon Gold **(Jones),** 476

Acknowledgments

Art and Photography

When there is more than one picture on a page, credits are supplied in sequence, left to right, top to bottom. Page positions are abbreviated as follows: (t) top, (c) center, (b) bottom, (l) left, (r) right.

Photos and illustrations not acknowledged are either owned by Loyola Press or from royalty-free sources including but not limited to Alamy, Art Resource, Big Stock, Bridgeman, Corbis/ Veer, Dreamstime, Fotosearch, Getty Images, Northwind Images, Photoedit, Smithsonian, Wikipedia. Loyola Press has made every effort to locate the copyright holders for the cited works used in this publication and to make full acknowledgment for their use. In the case of any omissions, the Publisher will be pleased to make suitable acknowledgments in future editions.

Frontmatter: iii(bl) LC McClure.

iStockphoto, Frontmatter: iii, v–viii **Section 1:** 2, 12, 15, 18 **Section 2:** 29, 31, 32, 34–40, 44, 46–48 **Section 3:** 55, 57, 58, 62, 64–67, 74 **Section 4:** 80–84, 86, 88, 90, 94–97, 101 **Section 5:** 110, 115, 117, 118, 120–124, 126–129, 134, 136, 138, 142 **Section 6:** 145–147, 150, 151, 154, 155 **Section 7:** 160, 163–177 **Section 8:** 186–193, 195, 201–203 **Chapter 1:** 210, 211, 213–215, 218, 220, 223, 225, 227, 229, 232–235, 237–242, 245–247 **Chapter 2:** 248, 249, 257–260, 262, 263, 265, 269, 270, 271, 274, 276–279, 277, 279–281 **Chapter 3:** 286–291, 293, 299, 300, 302–304, 312–323, 313, 314, 316–322 **Chapter 4:** 324–326, 328, 330, 331, 333, 335, 336, 338–343, 346, 347, 350, 352, 354, 355, 356, 361 **Chapter 5:** 362–365, 367, 368, 370, 371, 378–379, 381–385, 388, 389, 390, 391, 392, 394–399 **Chapter 6:** 400, 401, 403, 409, 411, 413–415, 417, 418, 420–423, 426, 428–434, 436, 437 **Chapter 7:** 438–442, 444, 446, 448, 449, 453, 459, 461, 463–469, 471–475 **Chapter 8:** 476–478, 481–483, 491, 493, 494, 502–513

Jupiterimages Unlimited, Frontmatter: iii–viii **Section 1:** 12–15, 17–23 **Section 2:** 28, 30, 33, 36–38, 40–42, 44, 45, 47, 49, 52 **Section 3:** 54–56, 59, 60, 63, 69, 71, 73, 74 **Section 4:** 81, 86, 88, 89, 90, 104 **Section 5:** 106, 107, 109, 113, 116–120, 127, 129, 131, 134–137 **Section 6:** 144, 146, 148, 150, 152, 153, 155 **Section 7:** 178–179 **Section 8:** 184, 189, 190, 194, 197, 198, 200, 204, 205, 208 **Chapter 1:** 210, 211, 214, 220, 224, 228, 230, 231 **Chapter 2:** 248–256, 259, 260, 266, 268, 272, 273, 276 **Chapter 3:** 286, 287, 289–291, 294, 296, 298, 300, 301, 308–312, 314, 315, 319, 321 **Chapter 4:** 324, 325, 327, 330, 334, 337–339, 344, 345, 346, 348, 351–353, 357, 361 **Chapter 5:** 362, 363, 369, 372, 374, 375–378, 380–382, 391–393 **Chapter 6:** 400–408, 411, 417–419, 422, 424, 425 **Chapter 7:** 438, 439, 441, 444, 445, 447, 455, 456, 458, 459, 462, 467 **Chapter 8:** 476, 477, 486, 488, 492, 493, 498, 500, 501, 512

Section 1: 11 Blue Lantern Studio/Corbis. **17** Look and Learn/The Bridgeman Art Library.

Section 2: 31(t) Bettmann/Corbis. **41(t)** Ellen Denuto/Veer. **43** Pictorial Press Ltd/Alamy.

Section 3: 60(b) Dantheman9758/Wikipedia. **70** Italian School/ The Bridgeman Art Library/Getty Images. **71(t)** Keren Su/Getty Images. **75** Peter Arnold, Inc./Alamy. **78** DaTo Images/The Bridgeman Art Library.

Section 4: 87 Bettmann/Corbis. **91** Bettmann/Corbis. **92(br)** North Wind Picture Archives/Alamy. **93(t)** Trinity Mirror/ Mirrorpix/Alamy. **100** Arco Images GmbH/Alamy.

Section 5: 107 Historical Picture Archive/Corbis. **114(b)** Photos 12/Alamy. **115(b)** Bureau L.A. Collection/Corbis. **130** Chief 'Crazy Horse' (1838–77) (oil on canvas), Lindneux, Robert Ottokar (1871–1970)/Private Collection/Peter Newark American Pictures/The Bridgeman Art Library. **135(b)** Sean Justice/Riser/Getty Images. **139** Synthetic Alan King/Alamy.

Section 6: 149 Phil Martin Photography. **158** Swim Ink 2, LLC/Corbis.

Section 7: 165 Melissa Donald Productions, Inc. **168(b)** Getty Images/Staff/Getty Images News/Getty Images.

Section 8: 185 Blue Lantern Studio/Corbis. **195(b)** Danita Delimont/Alamy.

Chapter 1: 210(bl) Associated Press. **212** Jeff Greenberg/Alamy. **216(t)** David J. & Janice L. Frent Collection/Corbis. **222** Bettmann/ Corbis. **226** Bettmann/Corbis. **236** Phil Martin Photography. **241(t)** Phil Martin Photography. **247(r)** Phil Martin Photography.

Chapter 2: 264(t) Phil Martin Photography. **264(c)** Phil Martin Photography. **264(b)** Phil Martin Photography. **274(b)** Russell Tate. **275** Phil Martin Photography. **277(b)** Phil Martin Photography. **279(r)** Phil Martin Photography. **281, 284–285(bl)** Russell Tate. **281(br)** Phil Martin Photography. **285(br)** Phil Martin Photography.

Chapter 3: 299(t) PoodlesRock/Corbis.

Chapter 4: 329 Paul Bricknell © Dorling Kindersley. **333** Nina Shannon. **336(b)** James W. Porter/Corbis. **338(br)** Phil Martin Photography. **348(br)** Phil Martin Photography. **349(c)** Phil Martin Photography. **351(br)** Phil Martin Photography. **353(c)** Phil Martin Photography. **354(br)** Phil Martin Photography. **355(c)** Phil Martin Photography. **357(c)** Phil Martin Photography. **361(br)** Phil Martin Photography.

Chapter 5: 370(tl) Time & Life Pictures/Getty Images. **373** PhotoStock-Israel/Alamy. **376(l)** Mathew B. Brady Studio/ Bettmann/Corbis. **379(t)** Steven Georges/Press-Telegram/Corbis. **385(t)** Zia Soleil/Iconica/Getty Images.

Chapter 6: 420(bl) Asian Art & Archaeology, Inc./Corbis. **422(bc)** Phil Martin Photography.

Chapter 7: 438(c) Rob Stapleton/Associated Press. **458** Bettmann/Corbis. **460** Phil Martin Photography.

Chapter 8: 480 Courtesy of the U.S. NPS, Alaska Region, Shared Beringian Heritage Program. Photo by Vic Knox. **484** Look and Learn/The Bridgeman Art Library. **487(t)** Doug Pensinger/Staff/ Getty Images Sport/Getty Images. **496(b)** The Natural History Museum/Alamy. **497(t)** Michael Ochs Archives/Stringer/Getty Images. **497(b)** Michael Ochs Archives/Stringer/Getty Images.

Literature

Common Proofreading Marks

Use these proofreading marks to mark changes when you proofread.
Remember to use a colored pencil to make your changes.

Symbol	Meaning	Example
¶	begin new paragraph	over. ¶Begin a new
⌒	close up space	close u p space
∧	insert	students think (should)
ℛ	delete, omit	that the the book
/	lowercase letter	Mathematics
∼	letters are reversed	letters are reversred
≡	capitalize	washington
∨∨	quotation	I am, I said.
⊙	add period	Marta drank tea